D0220479

Community Media
People, Places, and Communication Technologies

While transnational conglomerates consolidate their control of the global mediascape, local communities struggle to create democratic media systems. This groundbreaking study of community media combines original research with comparative and theoretical analysis in an engaging and accessible style. Kevin Howley explores the different ways in which local communities come to make use of various technologies such as radio, television, print, and computer networks for purposes of community communication and considers the ways these technologies shape, and are shaped by, the everyday lived experience of local populations. He also addresses broader theoretical and philosophical issues surrounding the relationship between communication and community, media systems, and the public sphere. Case studies illustrate the pivotal role community media play in promoting cultural production and communicative democracy within and between local communities. This book will make a significant contribution to existing scholarship in media and cultural studies on alternative, participatory, and community-based media.

KEVIN HOWLEY is Assistant Professor of Media Studies at DePauw University. He has published in a number of journals including *International Journal of Cultural Studies, Journal of Film and Video, Journal of Radio Studies,* and *Ecumene.*

Community Media
People, Places, and Communication Technologies

Kevin Howley

Assistant Professor

Department of Communication and Theatre

DePauw University

PUBLISHED BY THE PRESS SYNDICATE OF THE UNIVERSITY OF CAMBRIDGE
The Pitt Building, Trumpington Street, Cambridge CB2 1RP, United Kingdom

CAMBRIDGE UNIVERSITY PRESS
The Edinburgh Building, Cambridge, CB2 2RU, UK
40 West 20th Street, New York, NY 10011-4211, USA
477 Williamstown Road, Port Melbourne, VIC 3207, Australia
Ruiz de Alarcón 13, 28014 Madrid, Spain
Dock House, The Waterfront, Cape Town 8001, South Africa

http://www.cambridge.org

First published 2005

Printed in the United Kingdom at the University Press, Cambridge

Typeface Plantin 10/12 pt.   *System* LaTeX 2_ε [TB]

A catalogue record for this book is available from the British Library

ISBN 0 521 79228 2 hardback
ISBN 0 521 79668 7 paperback

For my parents, Robert and Jean Howley

Contents

Figures

Acknowledgments

To those educators, activists, and collaborators – among them Shirley Ann Bruno, Hal Himmelstein, George Dessart, and the late Loomis C. Irish – who sparked my initial interest in community media, I offer my sincere gratitude. Thanks also to dozens of community media workers around the world who encouraged me to not only examine, but also to value media making as a social practice. In your dedication and by your example, you vividly demonstrate the cultural significance and political relevance of community media. I hope my words do justice to your efforts.

Various institutions and agencies supported this work. The Graduate School of Indiana University, Bloomington, provided important seed money during this project's initial stages as a doctoral dissertation. The National Endowment for the Humanities, and the Marion and Jasper Whiting Foundation supported additional fieldwork in New York City and Halifax, Nova Scotia respectively. Research support and course release time at Northeastern University and DePauw University allowed me to spend considerable time and effort conducting research, refining the project, and completing this manuscript.

Material from Chapter 3 has previously been published in the *Journal of Radio Studies* and the *Historical Journal of Radio, Film and Television*. Portions of this revised manuscript have also appeared in the online publications *The Qualitative Report* and *Transformations*. Finally, an earlier draft of Chapter 6 appeared in the conference proceedings for the Communication Law Centre's meeting entitled "Cultural Crossroads: Ownership, Access and Identity."

Over the course of the past ten years, I received invaluable support from mentors, colleagues, and friends who, at various times, contributed to this project throughout its protracted development. While working on my doctorate at Indiana University, Michael Curtin, Chris Anderson, Harmeet Sawhney, and Andrew Dillon helped forge this project's design and inform its intellectual foundation. Special thanks also to my "long lost" friend and colleague Alex Leidholdt of James Madison University for all of his support and encouragement.

At Northeastern University, P. David Marshall, Murray Forman, Joanne Morreale, Michael Woodnick, and Alison Hearn were all generous with their time and in their fellowship. Special thanks to Alan Zaremba, a superb colleague, a gifted teacher, and a valued friend, whose sage advice and good company helped make this a much better manuscript. Thanks especially to my research assistant, Ed Grady, and the members of my seminar courses on Communication and Community for their stimulating questions and hard work.

At DePauw University, faculty colleagues, administrators, and staff likewise provided enormous support. Thanks especially to Jonathan Nichols-Pethick and Dennis Trinkle for their thoughtful comments and good conversation. And for all her logistical support, I thank Joyce Christiansen of the Department of Communication and Theatre, who demonstrated her dedication, resourcefulness, and good humor at every turn.

For her patience and unfailing support, I extend sincere thanks to Sarah Caro, my editor at Cambridge University Press. In the wake of formidable obstacles, Sarah encouraged my efforts and granted me additional time to deliver the completed manuscript. Thanks also to her assistants Jackie Warren, Elizabeth Davey, and Laura Hemming for their attention to this manuscript as well as to the anonymous reviewers whose insights and suggestions likewise contributed to this project's realization.

Of course, this study would not be possible without the insights, assistance, and access afforded me at each of the organizations described in these pages. For their wit, wisdom, and companionship, I thank some of my friends at WFHB, especially Brian Kearney, Jim Manion, Jeffrey Morris, Richard Fish, John Westhues, Mike Kelsey, "Tall Steve" Volan, Jason "Sideways," and Daniel Grundmann.

Thanks also to Jon Alpert and Keiko Tsuno at Downtown Community Television, who graciously allowed me to work alongside their staff, students, and interns during the summer of 2000. The entire DCTV crew, especially Tatiana Loureiro, Catherine Martinez, John Kaplan, Orlando Richards, Renata Gangemi, and Craig Renaud, made me feel right at home in the firehouse studio.

In Halifax, Nova Scotia, the staff and volunteers at *Street Feat*, in particular Juan Carlos Canales-Leyton, Michael Burke, and Peter McGuigan, were equally welcoming. I am especially indebted to them and their colleagues at CKDU, campus/community radio from Dalhousie University, for their compassion for this visiting American academic in the hours and days following the horrific events of 11 September 2001.

Special thanks to Adrian Bates, Stuart Hall, and Garry Hardy for your assistance in coordinating online data collection efforts at Victoria's Network. Without your help, I would never have made it Down Under by desktop; cheers to you and all those who help make VICNET a vibrant community. One day I hope to make my way to Melbourne and look you up off-line.

Likewise, I extend my deepest appreciation to all those community media activists and enthusiasts, far too numerous to mention by name, who contributed to the global overview of community media in Chapter 2. Your passion for media making is palpable and your commitment to community communication, contagious. Those insights I have gleaned from your efforts make this a compelling account of media activism and social justice. Any errors, oversights, or omissions are, of course, my sole responsibility.

To my wife and my love, Debora Frazier, I can scarcely begin to thank you for all you have given me. Your generosity inspires me, your kindness shelters me, your love nourishes me, and your presence is a blessing to me and to our families. Now for some time "well spent" together.

Finally, I dedicate this book to my parents with love and gratitude. An academic book may be a curious way to thank you for a lifetime of unconditional physical, emotional, and spiritual support, but it's a start. My admiration for both of you is boundless. And your love is with me, always.

Introduction

I was having this discussion in a taxi headed downtown.
Paul Simon, *Gumboots*

My first night in Bloomington, Indiana – the small mid-western city I would call home for the next four years – I took a taxi downtown. When I visit a city I'm not familiar with, I'll take a long walk or maybe hop in a cab to get a sense of the place. Perhaps I'll ask the driver for a restaurant recommendation, or inquire about the local sports team, or absent-mindedly comment on the weather. But on that balmy June evening I had to find out what station my driver had tuned in; the music coming from the dashboard radio was a rather obscure country blues number. "Oh," he said with a distinct sense of pride, "that's our community radio station, WFHB." He went on to give me an abridged version of the station's turbulent history: the early fundraising and organizing difficulties; the fierce competition for available frequencies; the protracted licensing procedure; and the search for a permanent downtown location.

As luck or fate would have it, my destination – a newly opened restaurant called Positively Fourth Street – was located directly across the street from the radio station's future home: the old city firehouse. As I emerged from the cab, the driver, perhaps sensing my growing curiosity, encouraged me to join the station once I'd completed my move from New York City. In early September, I took up the driver's advice and introduced myself to the station's program director. Within a matter of months, I landed an air-shift during WFHB's Monday afternoon music mix.

Over the course of the next three and a half years, I became involved in a variety of the station's daily operations. In addition to attending monthly general membership meetings, I participated in various station functions, including a number of street festivals and other fundraising activities, served as a member of the program selection and development committee, and played left field for the station's softball team, the WFHB Junkyard Dogs. Like others whose work or studies have taken them to Bloomington in recent years, WFHB became a home away from home.

Equally important, I had serendipitously stumbled upon an intriguing site of analysis for my doctoral studies in the Department of Telecommunications at Indiana University. All thanks to a tip I got from a local cab driver.

That cabby's name is John Westhues, and on Friday nights in Bloomington, he doesn't drive fares around town. He produces a show on WFHB featuring the music of Finland, Sweden, and the North Countries: a program he calls "Scenes from the Northern Lights." Although John Westhues' show is unique in many respects – after all, there are few (if any) programs on US commercial, public, or community radio, for that matter, that feature such a lively mix of jazz, pop, rock, and traditional folk music from northern Europe – the energy, commitment, and passion John brings to his program is not uncommon. Once a week John and a cadre of long-time residents, and not a few transients, bring Bloomington a vibrant, and decidedly eclectic, noncommercial alternative to the commercial and public service radio stations that serve south central Indiana.

This book is about community media. By community media, I refer to grassroots or locally oriented media access initiatives predicated on a profound sense of dissatisfaction with mainstream media form and content, dedicated to the principles of free expression and participatory democracy, and committed to enhancing community relations and promoting community solidarity. Specifically, the book examines the motivations behind and the ways in which local populations come to make use of various technologies – radio, television, print, and computer networks – for purposes of community communication.

In the pages that follow, I argue that community media are popular and strategic interventions into contemporary media culture committed to the democratization of media structures, forms, and practices. Popular in that these initiatives are responses to the *felt need* of local populations to create media systems that are relevant to their everyday lives; strategic in that these efforts are purposeful assertions of collective identity and local autonomy in the era marked by the unprecedented concentration of media ownership on the local and national levels and by the attendant proliferation of transnational media flows. All of which is to suggest that community media are part of a wider movement encompassing direct action campaigns, trade union and media work reform efforts, culture jamming, and communication scholarship, among other *critical interventions*, committed to the struggle for "communicative democracy" (Hackett 2000).

Significantly, this book appears at a time when the centrality of communication to the health and well being of democratic society has received considerable attention in both the academic and popular press. Among the many concerns voiced in recent years has been a persistent unease over the consequences of media privatization and consolidation on democratic processes. Critics contend that participatory democracy is undermined by inequitable access to communication channels and by the narrow range of voices and interests presented through the mass media. If, as communication scholar Robert McChesney (1999) suggests, the level of public participation in communication policy-making processes is indicative of any given society's level of participatory democracy, then the current state of democracy in the United States is poor. When this same formula is applied globally, McChesney's critique takes on even greater urgency in light of an "information revolution" that arguably has been left to the devices of a handful of nation-states and transnational corporations. And yet, despite the proliferation of academic tomes that denounce the threat to democratic societies posed by deregulation – or what Ken Robins (1995) more accurately describes as a process of re-regulation – and the subsequent spate of industry mergers and acquisitions, relatively few political economists have offered sustained analyses of locally oriented, participatory media of the sort discussed in these pages.

And despite their keen appreciation for local cultural production and their affirmation of popular forms of resistance, cultural studies scholars likewise and inexplicably overlook community media. Indeed, much has been made of audiences' ability to produce meaning and (re)produce culture through the artifacts of the media industries. Useful as these insights are, however, there has been a tendency to overstate audience autonomy. As media scholar Ien Ang notes: "It would be utterly out of perspective to cheerfully equate 'active' with 'powerful', in the sense of taking control at an enduring, structural or institutional level" (1990: 247). Influential as Ang's analysis has been, cultural scholars consistently overlook community media: a site that not only indicates considerable audience activity but vividly demonstrates tangible audience power. That is to say, by collapsing the distinction between media producers and media consumers – a convenient fiction manufactured by the culture industries and legitimated over time by administrative and critical communication scholars alike – community media provide empirical evidence that local populations do indeed exercise considerable power at precisely the lasting and organizational levels Ang describes. Indeed, community media underscore the creativity, pragmatism, and resourcefulness of local populations in their struggle to control media production and distribution.

Furthermore, given concerns surrounding the role communication technologies play in articulating a "sense of place," it is not only surprising, but somewhat alarming, that communication and cultural studies scholarship has consistently overlooked and undervalued community media as a site of analysis. The growing body of literature devoted to the use of media in diasporic cultures is testament to the centrality of communication to the construction of individual, ethnic, and cultural identities across time and space (King and Wood 2001; Morley 2000; Sakr 2002). And yet, locally oriented, participatory media's role in facilitating this process of collective identity construction in geographically defined communities has not received the same attention. An important subtext of this book, therefore, is the contention that community media represents a significant, but largely untapped site of analysis into the dynamics of media culture.

All too often, academics and other observers tend to conflate community media with public service broadcasting as well as so-called "alternative media." Here, I am thinking of Lewis and Booth's (1990) analysis of public service, commercial radio, and community radio; Ralph Engelman's (1996) concise yet incisive discussion of public access television in the context of US public service broadcasting; several case studies from John Dowling's (1984) seminal volume on what he describes as "self-managed" media systems; and Chris Atton's (2002) recent work on alternative media. In the last instance, the phrase "alternative media," which all too often serves as a "catch-all" that embraces a variety of media forms and practices – some participatory in nature, others not, that may or may not have very much relevance to geographically situated communities – confounds the study of participatory communication models like those associated with community media (Protz 1991). To my mind, these varied and influential works nonetheless constitute an ill-defined sub-set of media studies devoted to community-based media.

Scholar and activist Dorothy Kidd (1999) comes closest to explicating a relationship between alternative and community media, which captures the dynamics of locally oriented, participatory media organizations that are my focus in this study. Kidd's elegantly simple definition parses out the phrase "alternative" in a fashion that crystallizes our understanding of community-based media. From Kidd's perspective, alternative media are predicated on altering or changing prevailing media systems and the broader socio-cultural environment. The emphasis on critical intervention and social change is paramount here. Equally important, in Kidd's formulation alternative media is "of, by, and for" people living in a specific place. Kidd concludes,

Alternative media grow, like native plants, in the communities that they serve, allowing spaces to generate historical memories and analyses, nurture visions for their future, and weed out the representations of dominant media. They do this through a wide combination of genres, from news, storytelling, conversation and debate to music in local vernaculars.

(116)

All of which is not to suggest, however, that communication and cultural studies scholars have failed to produce vivid and insightful scholarship on community media. In recent years, a number of scholars have written very excellent case studies of community media organizations. Here I am thinking of Alan O'Connor's (1990) discussion of community radio in Bolivia; Norma Fay Green's (1998) work on Chicago's *Street Wise* publication; and more recently Clemencia Rodriguez's (2001) collection of case studies dedicated to what she describes as "citizens' media." Conversely, other analysts have examined the history and development of a particular technology used for purposes of community communication. Douglas Kellner's (1991) and Kim Goldberg's (1990) work on public access and community television come to mind, as does Howard Rheingold's (1993) popular text on community networks, as well as Jo Tacchi and Eryl-Price Davies' (2001) global overview of community radio.

The result is an impressive body of literature, which nonetheless suffers from theoretical underdevelopment (Jankowski 2003). That is to say, these engaging and richly detailed case studies often fail to situate community media in the context of contemporary cultural theory, or within the wider contours of our rapidly changing communication environment for that matter. Not one to argue theory for theory's sake, I am nonetheless convinced that in the absence of a more theoretically informed approach to community media, one that can guide further investigation and analysis of locally oriented, participatory media organizations and practices, we fail to fully appreciate one of the more dynamic aspects of contemporary media culture. This project seeks to rectify this situation inasmuch as I attempt to provide a theoretical framework that might inform a more fully sustained cultural analysis of community media.

No doubt, the difficulties associated with adequately defining the term "community" have confounded the study of community media. I disappeared down that particular rabbit hole while writing my doctoral dissertation and have no desire to repeat that academic exercise here. Suffice it to say that I base my analysis upon literature from diverse sources in political science, sociology, anthropology, and cultural studies concerned with what might best be summarized as "the symbolic construction of community." For instance, political scientist Benedict Anderson's (1991) influential text, *Imagined Communities*, explicates the decisive role print-capitalism played in the construction of the modern nation-state. Anderson draws our attention to the symbolic space and simultaneity of experience created by the production and ritual consumption of the daily newspaper. Incorporating the novel and other aspects of print culture, including record keeping and other governmental and bureaucratic uses of print and related technologies, Anderson's analysis foregrounds the role that communication technologies play in creating and sustaining the "deep, horizontal comradeship" that is the imagined community of nationalism (Anderson: 7).

Working along similar lines, anthropologist Anthony Cohen contends that the borders or boundaries that both "contain" and "differentiate" communities are, in large part, symbolically constructed. Through an array of symbolic practices – language, dress, custom, and ritual – communities come to identify themselves. By participating in these symbolic practices and investing meaning in them, individuals define themselves as members of a particular community. In turn, these symbolic practices help differentiate communities from one another. This, according to Cohen, is "the triumph of community" (1985: 20). That is, communities are *expressions of commonality as well as difference*. All of which underscores the fundamental, yet enigmatic relationship between communication and community. Following on from John Dewey's oft-cited remark (e.g. Carey 1975; Hardt 1975): "There is more than a verbal tie between the words 'communication' and 'community'"; this book foregrounds the role communication plays in *articulating* community.

Here, I am using the phrase articulation in the double sense of the word employed by Stuart Hall (1986). Articulation refers at once to "speaking" or "uttering" as well as to a "connection" or "linkage" between disparate elements, such as the connection between a truck and a trailer that is pulled from behind. In Hall's formulation, the alliance between different social actors or groups, as in political coalitions, is an example of articulation. Significantly, for Hall, this connection is neither necessary nor inevitable; rather these linkages or articulations are contingent and volatile. Under the rubric of cultural studies, the concept of articulation helps to explain the "complex totality" of social formations and provides a method of analysis for examining how unities are forged out of distinct elements that have no inherent sense of "belongingness." Used in both senses, then, articulation offers a way to conceptualize community as a unity of differences; a unity forged through symbol, ritual, language, and discursive practices.

This insight has significant political implications inasmuch as it highlights the role of human agency in shaping or rearticulating social formations. From this perspective, then, articulation serves not only as an analytical tool for theorizing and examining social formations, but also an organizing strategy for progressive social change. As Jennifer Daryl Slack suggests, articulation "is crucial for understanding how cultural theorists conceptualize the world, analyze it and participate in shaping it" (1996: 112). With this in mind, articulation provides insights into the ways in which local populations come to acquire and make use of communication technologies for community communication. Equally important, articulation offers cultural analysts a range of methodological approaches, most notably participant observation, from which not only to consider but also to work in tandem with these popular interventions into contemporary media culture.[1]

This book, therefore, examines the complex and dynamic relationship between people, places, and communication technologies. It explores the arrangements between various players and interests – community organizers, NGOs, philanthropic organizations, government agencies, technology manufacturers, artists and other cultural workers, and geographically situated populations – in creating and sustaining locally oriented, participatory media organizations. Furthermore, it investigates the remarkable and multifaceted uses and applications of communication technologies in communicating a sense of place, belonging, fellowship, and solidarity.

Specifically, the book considers four institutions: WFHB, community radio in Bloomington, Indiana; Downtown Community Television in New York City; *Street Feat*, a "street newspaper" in Halifax, Nova Scotia; and VICNET, a community computer network sponsored by the state library of Victoria, Australia. Taken in turn, each of these four cases highlight the complex, contested, and contradictory process of building and sustaining a community media organization in an increasingly privatized global media environment; together, they suggest an implicit, cross-cultural, and timeless understanding of the profound linkages between community cohesion, social integration, and communicative forms and practices.

Each site was selected for its unique setting and characteristics. Thus, the case studies are properly seen as purposive samples of community media initiatives. For example, WFHB is notable for several reasons, not least of which because WFHB's experience is a telling illustration of community media's significance in correcting dramatic imbalances in the political economy of the media industries. On the other hand, Downtown Community Television (DCTV) illuminates community media's role in promoting and facilitating local cultural production, especially among those groups and individuals who have been economically or culturally marginalized by mainstream media. DCTV's long history of community outreach illuminates the relationship between cultural politics and technological form.

For its part, *Street Feat* represents an extraordinary new trend in newspaper publication. Like other so-called "street newspapers," *Street Feat* constitutes an alternative public sphere (Fraser 1992) among Halifax's homeless, unemployed, and working poor by publishing the opinions, perspectives, and experience of the city's growing indigent population. In the hopes of fostering a critical consciousness of economic and social justice issues, *Street Feat* attempts to communicate the experience of impoverished peoples to wider publics through the sale of a monthly newspaper. Lastly, VICNET uses the latest in communication and information technology (CIT) to promote the state government's new vision of Victoria as a sophisticated, multicultural player in the emerging post-industrial economy of the Pacific Rim. As cultural historian Carolyn Marvin (1988) reminds us, the introduction of new technologies challenges, upsets and alters the character and conduct of social intercourse within and between communities. Viewed in this light, then, VICNET demonstrates community media's role in (re) imagining community.

The book is organized as follows. Chapter 1 attempts to "locate" community media in a broader social, cultural, and political context. To that end, this discussion examines the consequences associated with media consolidation and the proliferation of transnational media flows. In the first section of this chapter, I examine the threat media privatization represents to participatory democracy on local, national, regional, and international levels. The discussion situates the study of community media in relation to media studies scholarship informed by political economy and cultural studies, among other theoretical orientations. Next, I revisit debates over cultural imperialism with particular attention to the impact of transnational media flows on local cultural autonomy. Throughout, I lay out insights and perspectives that help to situate community media in relation to contemporary critical and cultural theory.

Chapter 2 provides a global perspective on local uses of specific technologies. What is distinctive and unique about each of the book's substantive case studies becomes more apparent against the backdrop of historical developments in community communication and a contemporary overview of the present state of community media. This concise, but by no means comprehensive look at community media around the world provides this context. By incorporating an overview of community media initiatives around the world, the book is designed not only to underscore that which is distinctive about the four case studies, but also to highlight the patterns, trends, and tendencies that are common to community media initiatives generally.

Significantly, this chapter draws upon the work of a number of national and international NGOs interested in community communication.

Organizations such as the World Association of Community Broadcasters (AMARC); the European Alliance for Community Networking (EACN); the North American Street Newspaper Association (NASNA); and the Alliance for Community Media (ACM), to name a few, provide technical, legal, and logistical support for community media initiatives around the world. Incorporating information and insights gleaned from these organizations provides this study with a broader, global perspective on community media that the discrete case studies cannot provide in isolation.

Chapter 3 presents the first of four in-depth case studies. It relates the long struggle to establish community radio in Bloomington, Indiana, from its origins at the National Alternative Radio Konference (NARK) in 1975 to the present day. Through the recollections of WFHB's founding members, popular press accounts, and participant observation, this discussion examines the legal, technical, and economic obstacles that faced Bloomington's community radio movement. It links WFHB's institutional philosophy and programming style to various alternative radio practices that proliferated in Bloomington throughout the 1970s and 1980s, as well as to the broader tradition of community radio in the United States. Throughout, I discuss WFHB's attempts to negotiate the tensions between noncommercial, locally oriented radio and the economic realities of broadcasting, especially as they relate to the arena of news and public affairs programming.

Downtown Community Television is the subject of Chapter 4. Operating for well over a quarter century, Downtown Community Television has had a dramatic impact on the lives of people who live and work in Lower Manhattan. This chapter relates DCTV's extraordinary history with special emphasis on the role community outreach has played in creating a viable community television organization. Participant observation, historical research, and in-depth interviews with DCTV staff and producers illuminate community television's role in identity politics, community organizing, and cultural expression. Throughout, I emphasize DCTV's commitment to media education, cross-cultural communication, and independent journalism.

Chapter 5 turns to a consideration of Halifax, Nova Scotia's street paper, *Street Feat*. Founded in 1997, in response to the growing problem of homelessness throughout Atlantic Canada, *Street Feat* has struggled to become a "voice of the poor" as well as a viable business concern. Written and distributed by people who are homeless or otherwise economically disadvantaged, *Street Feat* is committed to empowering marginalized people, effectively communicating their plight to the wider community, and ultimately ending homelessness. Text-based analysis of the newspaper in addition to in-depth interviews with the paper's staff and readership provide insight into *Street Feat*'s efficacy as a tool for progressive social change and as the locus for the construction of "an alternative public sphere" for the poor and those who work on their behalf.

The last of the case studies, Chapter 6, explores the use of computer-mediated communication in building and maintaining a sense of community in the state of Victoria, Australia throughout the late 1990s – the dawn of the information age. Here, I examine the varied motivations behind the Victorian state government's large-scale capital investment in computer-based and information technologies. In describing the network's disparate services, this discussion illuminates Victoria's transition from an industrial to an information-based economy. It also discusses how VICNET's design philosophy may confound popular participation in community networking and probes the contradictory impulses behind this information age community development scheme.

Mindful of the similarities between all of these efforts to reclaim the media, the final chapter surveys the particular and distinctive articulations of community media in each of the communities profiled throughout. Conversely, I hope to illuminate the more universal and general impulses that fuel community media initiatives across the globe. In doing so, I underscore community media's role in promoting civic participation, enhancing community relations, and supporting local cultural autonomy. Finally, I suggest the study of community media provides a useful site of analysis, and an equally fruitful site of intervention for scholars of communication, political economy, and cultural studies. Throughout, I argue that interrogating the social, cultural, and political dynamics of community media provides a convenient, but curiously overlooked lens to examine the fundamental but paradoxical relationship between communicative forms and practices and popular conceptions and articulations of community.

Much has been made of the potentially liberating effect of communication and information technologies (CIT). The proliferation of small format video cameras, for instance, is hailed as a boon for individual self-expression. Likewise, the diffusion of relatively inexpensive radio transmission gear, computers, high-quality printers, and web-related technologies is viewed by some as the beginning of a great reawakening of the democratic spirit. The emergence of Independent Media Centers (IMCs) helps fuel these notions. Cropping up in tandem with organized protests surrounding international trade meetings, global economic summits, environmental debates, and, more recently, anti-war protests, IMCs make shrewd and rather sophisticated use of digital production and distribution equipment to circumvent the gatekeeping function of corporate controlled media (Tarleton 2000). Acting as a foil to the largely uncritical press coverage of popular protests, and as a corrective to the misinformation surrounding these public demonstrations, the IMCs produce news and information that challenges the hegemony of mainstream media coverage. In the process, the IMCs vividly demonstrate the centrality of communication technologies to preserving and sustaining democracy movements around the world.

Yet, it would be a mistake to succumb to blind optimism in the wake of technological development (Sussman 1997). If the history of communication technologies teaches us anything, it is this: the emancipatory potential of technology is greatly overstated. Although technological development does afford a measure of decentralization in the production and distribution of communicative forms and practices, there is a related tendency for these emerging systems to become reconstituted into ever more centralized production and distribution systems (Abu-Leghold 1992). Likewise, the diffusion of technology is not nearly as rapid, nor as widespread as it may at first appear. Amid the glut of news, political rhetoric, and advertising copy that celebrates the "information revolution," the specter of an emerging and growing digital divide looms large in most advanced industrial societies. This divide is evident and perhaps most stark on the global level (Murdock and Golding 1998).

Furthermore, many of the uses and applications of affordable and so-called "user-friendly" technologies are, in turn, either trivialized or commercialized. For instance, when the work of "amateur" videographers does reach a national audience, it is relegated to the status of innocuous, often self-deprecating, home movies. Programs like *America's Funniest Home Videos* – and its counterparts around the world – suggest, in none too subtle ways, that non-professional media makers are best left to recording life's little embarrassments, foibles, and peculiarities. Implicit in such programs is the notion that media production and distribution is serious business indeed and that the work of "non-professionals" is technically inferior and socially irrelevant when measured against that of corporate sponsored media professionals.

This book, therefore, is not about the diffusion of technological innovation per se. Nor does it uncritically accept the utopian rhetoric of equality and prosperity common to technocrats. Rather, this volume interrogates the challenges and opportunities presented by rapid technological innovation as it celebrates the ingenuity and creativity of local populations as they make sense of this new environment. In doing so, it highlights the persistent significance of place to a sense of individual and collective identity and well being in an increasingly interdependent and interconnected world: a world made smaller, yet, paradoxically more complex, by communication and information technologies. Furthermore, by shunning a fetishistic attitude toward these instruments, this book underscores the varied and ingenious ways in which people actively and consciously shape technology to meet their needs and desires. Rather than marvel at technological innovation, this book is testament to human agency. In short, the mediators are the message.

1 Locating community media

> Unless there is organized public intervention, the mass media of the twenty-first century will not represent a parliament of the people but the organizing of masses of children and adults everywhere, including the Third World, into an electronic shopping mall devoted to the culture of wasteful and ultimately fatal use of the planet's natural resources and a diminishing of the human spirit.
>
> Ben Bagdikian, *Brave New World Minus 400*

In the days leading up to the April 2000 International Monetary Fund (IMF) meeting in Washington, DC, three reporters from WORT-FM, community radio in Madison, Wisconsin, were denied press credentials to cover the proceedings. Like their colleagues from commercial and public service media outlets, the reporters faxed their applications, complete with photo IDs, to the IMF press office well before the application deadline. And yet, WORT's reporters were denied press accreditation without explanation. Following repeated requests for clarification on accreditation procedures, William Murray, Senior Press Officer for the IMF, informed WORT's news director, Elizabeth DiNovella, that the reporters' press credentials were denied because they worked for a "community radio station" (WORT 2000). It soon became apparent that community radio was not singled out in this regard; journalists from other community-based and independent media organizations, such as *The Boulder Weekly* and the CorporateWatch website, were similarly denied access to the IMF meeting (AMARC/IFEX 2000a).

In an e-mail message to Craig Hymson of the Seattle Independent Media Center (IMC), Murray succinctly described the IMF's position: "We do not provide press accreditation to public access TV, community radio, nor student or academic publications to attend our meetings" (WORT). Word of the IMF's press restrictions spread quickly among community and independent media outlets. Within days, official statements by several US-based organizations, including the National Federation of Community Broadcasters (NFCB), Fairness and Accuracy in Reporting (FAIR), the Media Alliance, and Project Censored, condemned the IMF's actions

and called on the international body to explain its policy. These senti-
ments were echoed in a joint statement issued by two international organizations, the World Association of Community Radio Broadcasters
(AMARC) and the International Freedom of Expression Exchange.

Voicing their support of community journalists, these groups made
several salient points. For instance, the NFCB noted that community
radio in the United States has a long tradition of providing local, regional,
and national news to thousands of listeners across the country. In a similar
vein, AMARC observed: "Community media, in particular community
radio, are essential to developing nations around the world, where they are
sometimes the primary means of communicating news and information."
The IMF decision, therefore, effectively prevented whole populations
from learning about, let alone commenting on, decisions that have a
direct effect on their lives and their communities.

Other objections focused on the question of professionalism, a slip-
pery distinction to be sure, but one that was central to the IMF's outright
dismissal of community and independent journalists. Community radio
journalists, the NFCB argued, abide by the same journalistic standards
as do their counterparts from commercial and public service media outlets. Moreover, the NFCB was quick to point out, community reporters
are consistently recognized for excellence by their peers; community and
independent journalists routinely receive DuPont, Peabody, Associated
Press, and Polk awards for their work. Still, the IMF's press policy im-
plied that community journalists are somehow less prominent, if not less
qualified, than their colleagues in the mainstream press.

What was most alarming about the IMF's decision, especially for foreign observers, was the IMF's wholesale violation of international decla-
rations which affirm the right to communicate as a fundamental human
right (Universal Declaration of Human Rights 1948). The irony that such
flagrant disregard for the principle of freedom of speech took place in the
capital of the United States – a country that vociferously defends press
freedoms and champions human rights – was not lost on the twenty-five
signatories of the IFEX's resolution on community media and the IMF.
Among other things, the resolution called upon the IMF to "encourage
freedom of expression and opinion by adopting principles of openness
and transparency in its own dealings with the media" (AMARC/IFEX
2000b).

If the IMF's policy toward community media was far from open,
its motivation for denying community journalists press credentials was
rather transparent; the IMF was determined to limit press access to those
media organizations that were sympathetic to its agenda. Four months

earlier, demonstrators successfully stalled talks during the World Trade Organization (WTO) meetings in Seattle. One of the defining features of the Seattle demonstrations was the establishment of an Independent Media Center: a loose affiliation of activists, community media producers, and independent journalists who provided pool coverage of the meetings and the surrounding protests. Unlike their counterparts in the commercial and public media sector, whose reports were barely distinguishable from WTO press releases, community and independent journalists provided substantive analysis of the impact this latest round of trade agreements would have on the environment, job security, economic equality, third world debt relief, the rights of indigenous peoples, and other issues related to economic globalization (Hazen 1999). By any measure of journalistic performance, the volume, breadth, and depth of the Seattle IMC's output was impressive. Over the course of the five-day world trade meeting, the IMC posted first-person accounts of the demonstrations online; produced *Blindspot*, a daily newsletter; aired a daily radio program, *World Trade Watch Radio*; and transmitted video feeds to public access television outlets nationwide.[1]

The unprecedented success of the Seattle IMC sparked worldwide interest in the establishment of locally based news and information outlets that provide an alternative to corporate-owned media. By the end of 2000, as many as thirty-seven independent media centers were operating in cities and countries around the world. Based on the Seattle model, these IMCs occupy two spaces: one physical, the other virtual. During a major political event or protest, such as the March 2000 Bio Devastation gathering in Boston or the following September's World Economic Forum (WEF) meeting in Sydney, community producers and independent journalists act as a news-gathering and distribution collective. Within days of a major event, the IMCs erect hi-tech newsrooms complete with video and audio equipment, computers and laser printers, fax machines, cell phones, and even satellite transmission gear (Paton 1999). Long after the protest is complete, and the makeshift newsrooms have been dismantled, the IMCs continue to operate online.

The eruption of independent media centers underscores two significant features of community media at the threshold of the twenty-first century. First, as suggested by the range of issues and concerns addressed by the IMCs, and as dramatically illustrated by the IMF's suppression of basic press freedoms, community media inhabit a highly contested field of social, economic, and political relations. The hegemony of dominant media institutions in shaping public opinion, championing neo-liberal economics, cultivating a consumer culture, and fashioning domestic and international communication policy undermine the legitimacy, let alone the viability, of community media initiatives (Bowen 1996; Carpentier, Lie and Servaes 2003). Second, in light of the growing influence of transnational media corporations in the production and distribution of news, information, and culture, community media have enormous relevance within the emerging global political and cultural economy. In the absence of a plurality of voices, opinions, and perspectives available in the mainstream media, people across the globe have taken it upon themselves to appropriate communication technologies in an effort to enlarge the terms of public discourse, secure a space for local cultural expression, and enhance participatory democracy on local, national, regional, and international levels (Hamelink 1994: 132–149). As we shall see, community media initiatives are one of the more effective strategies in the global struggle to democratize communication and ensure local autonomy in the wake of rampant media privatization and consolidation.

In many respects, then, the IMC movement shares many of the same concerns as earlier forms of community media. Operating as an alternative to profit-motivated and corporate-sponsored media, the IMCs are "dedicated to building media democracy by providing progressive, in-depth, and accurate coverage of issues which affect all communities and by increasing community access to available technologies and information for the production and distribution of news and analysis." The motto: "Everyone is a witness. Everyone is a journalist" is a common refrain within the emerging indymedia movement. Independent journalists, community activists, and others are invited to contribute news stories and analysis, opinion pieces, still images, and audio and video files that are then uploaded to the IMC's website. Like other forms of community media, then, IMCs are models of participatory communication (Kelly and Gibson 2000). Furthermore, by making communication technologies accessible to those whose voices and perspectives are either marginalized by or misrepresented in mainstream media, the IMCs decentralize and diversify cultural production. Finally, by recording and preserving local cultural histories, such as political demonstrations and popular uprisings like those in Seattle, the IMCs offset the historical amnesia engendered by nationalist, state-run, and commercially supported media industries. In so doing, the IMCs advance the cause of social and economic justice locally as well as globally, and help promote a sense of belonging and solidarity within and between geographic communities. Thus, the IMC's efforts to create and sustain a democratic media culture correspond to the philosophical origins and socio-cultural aims of community media.

Media and democracy

Mainstream press accounts of the WTO meetings in Seattle provide important insight into the ways that corporate media undermine democratic processes. A brief examination of these reports reveals a number of distinct, but related news frames at work (Ackerman 2000). In the first, protesters were stereotyped as odd-looking and misinformed students living out fantasies of 1960s-era youthful protest. Stories in this vein took a dismissive, often condescending attitude toward the protesters. A second news frame indicates an overwhelming reliance on and deference to "official sources" for information and opinion: opinion that reflects many of the same attitudes and assumptions of corporate sponsored media. In this mode, observers scarcely contained their disbelief that such protests could take place in an era of unparalleled peace and prosperity. A third news frame, and one that colored subsequent press coverage of similar direct action campaigns, focused on the destruction of private property and violence in the streets.

The contemptuous tone and alarmist quality of these stories represent a willful and purposeful distortion of the conduct of the demonstration, the legitimacy of the protesters, and the validity of their concerns. The lead paragraph from an article appearing in *Newsweek* magazine – a US-based general interest publication with a nationwide circulation of over three million that also publishes several international editions – typifies mainstream press accounts of the WTO protests:

The nose-ringed woman in the thick knit poncho looked admiringly at the twisted letters on the marquee of the Nike Store. Man, she said, they f----d that up good! Nearby, two young men stood chest to chest, screaming in each other's faces, both tear-stained from the pepper gas wafting along Sixth Avenue in downtown Seattle. One wanted to smash the Nike window, the other to stop him. How do you think they stopped Vietnam? demanded the one with the rock. It was the opening day of the World Trade Organization meeting in Seattle and all hell was breaking loose.

(Klee 1999: 32)

Significantly, stories like these – while critical of a small minority of demonstrators who did in fact vandalize property in downtown Seattle – supported and ultimately sanctioned the state-sponsored use of excessive force. Despite the dangerous implications this episode represents for the viability of future civil disobedience campaigns, the mainstream media remained remarkably silent in this regard. On the other hand, press reports consistently portrayed this latest round of trade agreements as "inevitable": the dominant view proffered in these accounts was that advances in communication and transportation technologies unavoidably lead to the dissolution of antiquated and irrelevant trade restrictions. Furthermore, these reports suggest that despite the objections of a few malcontents, there is a growing consensus in favor of economic globalization in the United States and abroad. On the whole, then, dominant news frames of the Seattle protests either trivialized or demonized demonstrators while simultaneously providing near unanimous and unqualified support for the WTO agenda.

Missing from these reports was anything resembling an accurate account of the showdown in Seattle. Let alone a substantive analysis of the issues raised by well over 50,000 protesters – environmentalists, native peoples, students, migrant workers, trade unionists, and others – exercising their constitutional rights of freedom of assembly and expression (Solomon 1999). In the process, the mainstream media ceded its responsibility to inform and engage the public in a debate over questions of so-called "free trade." Viewed in this light, the press coverage of the WTO meetings, and the surrounding protests, is one more indication that a handful of powerful economic and political elites have come to dominate both the terms and conditions of public discourse in the United States. Indeed, critical analyses of journalistic practices suggest that there was nothing either new or anomalous about the press performance during the Seattle protests (e.g., Chomsky 1989; Downing 1989). Rather, corporate-owned media – the dominant form of news, information, and culture in the United States, and, increasingly, around the world – exhibit a tendency to reinforce and reflect the narrowly defined interests of transnational capitalism (Chomsky and Herman 1988; Croteau 1994; McChesney, Wood, and Foster 1998).

This is not to suggest, however, that transnational capitalism is neither monolithic nor univocal. To be sure, governmental and corporate elites do not always share the same concerns; indeed their interests are often contradictory and almost always competitive (see, for example, Willis 1990: 156). However, because the interests of transnational capitalism are, more often than not, consistent if not coterminous with those of corporate-owned and operated media, and since these same industries dominate the media landscape, news, information, and culture tend to reflect those same interests. Consequently, the public's capacity to participate in decision-making processes in an informed and deliberative fashion is severely compromised. Herein lies the great threat to democratic societies posed by corporate-controlled and commercially sponsored media (McChesney 1997).

In the decade following the collapse of the Soviet Union and the "opening up" of once closed societies in Central and Eastern Europe, China, and to a lesser extent, North Korea, much has been made of the triumph of capitalism and the flourishing of democracy across the globe (Friedman 1999; Fukuyama 1992). According to this perspective, the establishment of a global market economy is a necessary condition for the worldwide expansion of liberal democracy. However, with the realization that the concept, let alone the practice, of democracy is exceedingly ambiguous and often contradictory, these claims are highly suspect. As Ingunn Hagen (1992) observes, democracy is a "God-word": a phrase that encompasses a range of meanings, including governmental procedures, terms of citizenship, political and social systems, and even whole societies. One need only recall the calamity surrounding the 2000 US presidential election to appreciate the problems associated with democratic praxis. Still, despite the vague usage of the term and the difficulties associated with putting democratic theory into action, an effective system of political communication is deemed essential to democratic processes, institutions, and values. To be effective, however, democratic communication demands active and engaged civic participation.

The concept of the public sphere, as described by Jürgen Habermas, provides a robust theoretical framework to examine the crucial link between democratic self-governance and communication. Habermas (1993) argues that the public sphere is the foundation for civil society; it is a forum for the citizenry to reach consensus on the issues and policy decisions that affect public life. In Habermas' formulation, the public sphere is a realm, insulated from the deleterious influence of state and commercial interests, in which citizens openly and rationally discuss, debate, and deliberate upon matters of mutual and general concern to a self-governing community. Isolated or "bracketed" from both state and market forces, this public sphere is the space in which a public comes to understand and define itself, articulate its needs and common concerns, and act in the collective self-interest. In short, it is a space in which a social aggregate becomes a public.

According to Habermas, an effective and robust public sphere depends on two conditions: the quality of discursive practices and the quantity of participation within this discourse. The first requirement calls for rational-critical debate based not on the speaker's identity or social standing, but upon the reasoned and logical merits of an argument. The second requirement entails opening up the debate to the widest public possible and encouraging the inclusion of competing opinions and perspectives. The threat to the public sphere, as Habermas sees it, is the encroachment of the state and commercial interests into this realm. Habermas observes that as the public sphere shrinks, there is a marked increase in political apathy, a relentless pursuit of economic and material self-interest, and a rising tide of cynicism and social alienation. The collapse of the public sphere is therefore a danger to the very core of civil society. In Habermas' historical account, the public sphere has eroded since its inception in the late seventeenth and early eighteenth centuries, due in large part to the detrimental effects of commercial media, state intervention into family life, and the corporatization of public and private life.

Notwithstanding criticisms of the exclusivity, historical accuracy, and idealized quality of Habermas' construct, the concept of the public sphere has enormous relevance for the ongoing project of building and sustaining a more democratic media culture (Garnham 1993). In an era marked by the increased interrelatedness and interdependence of local populations in the realms of politics, economics, culture, and the environment, deliberative democracy takes on global significance and urgency (Axtmann 1997). Put another way, as the nature of citizenship changes in an increasingly integrated world, the question of who deliberates has enormous implications. And yet, in the wake of fundamental questions over matters such as resource allocation and distribution, the privatization of public goods and services, and the need to encourage and ensure sustainable development, there is relatively scant popular participation in this deliberative process.

The irony in all of this is easy to see. In the so-called "information age" deliberative democracy is by no means assured, even in so-called information-rich societies like the United States (Schiller 1996). In an era that is heralded by some – most notably equipment manufacturers, content providers, advertisers, and political leaders – as a new age of information, enlightenment, and democracy, economic and material barriers of access to information production and distribution persist. Moreover, the public's ability to make sense of and take action upon this information – what might usefully be described as "communicative competence" – is undermined by a flood of information devoid of context (i.e., historical specificity and structural analysis) and in the absence of alternative information sources. As a result, the formation of public opinion in the United States is largely dependent upon the way in which government and corporate elites frame an issue and set the terms of a debate, if it could even be described as such (Chomsky 1989; Entman 1993). This same dynamic has been observed in other national and discursive contexts as well (Cohen and Wolfsfeld 1993; Hall, et al. 1978; Semetko and Valkenburg 2000). Notwithstanding the existence of so-called "sunshine laws" and other variants of freedom of information legislation around the world, there is a marked increase in secrecy on the part of government officials, state bureaucracies, and private enterprise (Curry 1988; Roberts 2000). The Bush Administration's response to the terrorist attacks of 11 September 2001 serve to heighten fears over the dismantling of civil liberties, the erosion of press freedoms, and the attendant media subservience to official sources. In short, without equitable access to information, and in the absence of accurate representation of disparate social groups and political positions within the media, the prospects for democratic communication are not promising.

This condition is further exacerbated by dramatic changes in the composition and orientation of systems of political communication, broadly conceived (Golding 1990). In the United States, the twin forces of deregulation and technological convergence have accelerated a process of media consolidation that has historical antecedents in the last half of the nineteenth century (Bagdikian 1997). Most recently, the Telecommunications Act of 1996 – a specious piece of "reform" legislation crafted largely by the very industries it was meant to regulate – fueled the latest round of high-stakes media acquisitions and mergers. Not surprisingly, a deregulatory move ostensibly designed to open up competition in media ownership and control has instead created even greater barriers of entry into the media industry, especially among women and minority owners (Labaton 2000). As a result, the media landscape in the United States is dominated by a handful of conglomerates with control over and financial interests in print, radio, television (broadcast, cable, and satellite) telephony, and computer-related technologies.

For instance, equipment manufacturer General Electric owns NBC, program syndicator Viacom owns CBS, Rupert Murdoch's media empire, News Corporation, owns Fox, and Disney, one of the world's largest media conglomerates with holdings in radio, film production and distribution, and cable sports channels, owns ABC. Similar ownership patterns are evident in the film and music industries, newspaper and magazine publishing, radio broadcasting, cable and satellite television, and telecommunications. Increasingly, media consolidation is a global phenomenon. Presently, the global media marketplace is dominated by five transnational corporations – Disney (US), NewsCorp (AU), Time-Warner (US), Viacom (US), and Bertelsmann (GDR) – all with substantial holdings in print, audio-visual, and "new media" (Levi 1999; McChesney 2000). As one indication of the enormous resources at their disposal and the incredible wealth generated by these media giants, the merger between Time-Warner and Internet service provider AOL was estimated at more than US$183 billion. Among other things, this deal epitomizes the global dimensions of media consolidation: regulatory approval for the merger was needed in Europe as well as the United States.

A related development is the push in recent years toward privatization that has undermined the once vibrant public service sector common to many industrialized nations (Atkinson and Raboy 2003; Tracey 1998; Traquina 1998). Beset by competition from commercial media outlets, and faced with the prospect of dwindling audiences and significant reductions in government financing, public broadcasters have reoriented themselves in an ever more competitive media environment. As a result, public service broadcasting increasingly resembles both the form and content typically associated with commercial media (Achille and Miege 1994; Collins, *et al.* 2001). Even Britain's vaunted BBC has succumbed to financial pressures and entered into lucrative marketing agreements for its programming in order to generate much needed income (Brech 2000). In many respects, the BBC's strategy is not at all dissimilar to that of the American public service broadcasting system. It remains to be seen, however, if the BBC and other public service media outlets will suffer the same consequences as have their US counterparts.

Over the past twenty years, public radio and television in the United States has consistently watered down its news and public affairs programming in order to appease federal legislators and retain its modest government subsidy. Furthermore, faced with shrinking federal appropriations, public broadcasters have in recent years looked more favorably on corporate underwriting to support program production costs. News, public affairs, and cultural programming is therefore increasingly designed to reach decidedly upscale audiences in an attempt to curry favor with a growing list of corporate sponsors (Hoynes 1994, 1999; Ledbetter 1997). As a result, public broadcasting's mandate to reflect America's political and cultural diversity goes largely unmet.

Equally striking are the changes taking place in state-run media systems. Increasingly, government-operated media in China, across Central and Eastern Europe, and throughout the developing world have relaxed their control on information flows and begun to embrace, with mixed, often contradictory results, media privatization (Splichal 1994; Zaffiro 1993). Clearly, technology has played a prominent role in this process. For instance, generations of Europeans living under communism listened fervently to broadcasts from the BBC and Voice of America (VOA) for news, information, and entertainment. These broadcasts offered a range of alternative perspectives and cultural forms (such as rock and roll music) that contradicted Soviet-run media and helped undermine communist authority. Likewise, technology played a decisive role in opening up China, most dramatically during the 1989 student-led protests in Tiananmen Square (Calhoun 1989). However, technology alone did not produce these changes, nor has technology necessarily liberated these societies. More often than not, policy decisions have encouraged the development and expansion of privatized media systems. As a result, the monopoly on information once held by the state has simply been replaced by a corporate oligopoly: hardly a recipe for democratic communication.

Indeed, for many post-Communist and post-colonial societies, a tension arises between the desire to democratize communication systems for purposes of education, development, and national sovereignty and the pressure to embrace privatized media as mechanisms of modernization and as a vehicle to gain access to regional and international markets. For instance, the liberalization of media policy in India has bolstered the position of the national broadcaster, Doordarsah, by allowing the state service to enhance its dealings with private media companies. However, the nationalist and increasingly commercial orientation of India's media environment threatens the viability of traditional public service or community-oriented broadcasting (McDowell 1997). In many respects, then, the "triumph" of liberal-democracy around the globe has not delivered on its promise to provide a robust, nor even a necessarily competitive, marketplace of ideas. Instead, a small and highly profitable cartel of corporate media giants has emerged in recent years, threatening to further erode an already weakened public sphere.

The detrimental effects of a highly commercialized media system on political life in the United States represent a rather gloomy case study in this regard (Bagdikian 1996). Despite federal legislation that requires broadcasters to serve "the public interest, convenience or necessity" commercial broadcasters have consistently, even brazenly, flaunted these requirements. As the broadcast industry grew rich on their profits, its influence on politics in general, and communication policy making in particular, increased as well (McChesney 1993; 1999). A report in the *Columbia Journalism Review* indicates the severity of the problem. Corporate influence – in the form of lobbying, campaign contributions, and so-called political "junkets" – has undermined public policy making on a host of issues including campaign finance reform, intellectual property rights, television violence, and, not surprisingly, media ownership (Lewis 2000). Over the past sixty years, American-elected officials have learned all too well the political expediency of acquiescing to the desires of corporate-controlled media. Politicians whose views and policy recommendations challenge corporate interests are rarely seen or heard in the mainstream media. Conversely, those who are sympathetic to and support corporate policy tend to receive favorable coverage in the press. As a result, alternative positions on public policy and oppositional views on corporate culture are rarely publicized, let alone opened up for broad popular debate.

Commercialization's negative effects are by no means limited to the realm of electoral politics. The profit motive that drives corporate media diminishes the wider political culture as well. Treating the public primarily as consumers – rather than as citizens with a stake in social, economic, and cultural policy decisions – corporate media depoliticizes both the public and private spheres. In their efforts to deliver audiences to advertisers, commercial media socialize people to believe that health, happiness, and the good life are to be found in the implacable, competitive pursuit of consumer goods. This is not to suggest that advertising is entirely successful in its efforts to mold buying habits and manipulate consumer behaviors; advertising campaigns routinely fail and persuasive pitches often miss their mark. Rather, it is to assert that commercial media are deeply implicated in and constitutive of the development of a consumer culture: a whole way of life based upon spurious promises of better living through conspicuous consumption (Schudson 1986). Furthermore, as a number of critics have observed, advertising was instrumental in engineering a shift from a producer ethic to a consumer ethic (Ewen 1976; Williams 1982). In so doing, advertising and consumer culture divert the public's attention, energy, and resources away from society's fundamental needs like public education, health care, the environment, economic justice, and racial, ethnic, and gender equality that are essential to the health and well being of any community. Put another way, those social institutions, needs, and values that are not based on capital accumulation or profit generation are all but ignored by commercial media.

A related tendency that likewise compromises the quality of information citizens receive is the rising influence of the public relations industry in news production. Newsgathering and dissemination are inherently expensive and time-consuming endeavors. The imperative to minimize costs and maximize profits has led the corporate media to a two-fold strategy. First, news divisions have been, to use the appropriate euphemism, "downsized" in terms of both staffing and resources. Second, these "more efficient" and "cost-effective" operations are then expected to turn a profit. As a result, news organizations are required to do more with less. Aside from alienating reporters and editors who take seriously their charge to inform the citizenry in a moral, ethical, and socially responsible manner, this market-based approach to journalism places enormous pressure on journalists (Schudson 2003; Rieder 1996). In their struggle to fill an increasingly competitive 24-hour news hole, journalists have become increasingly dependent on other "news" sources. For a great many media outlets, the solution has been to turn to "pre-packaged" news items like press releases and video news releases (VNRs) produced by public relations agencies in the service of corporate clients (Drobis 1992).

The corporatization of news has serious implications for the quality of information the public receives (Stauber and Rampton 1995). This is especially relevant in terms of policy debates over trade agreements, health care, and, as a study of public relations efforts leading up to the Gulf War suggests, even the commitment of troops in times of war (Rowse 1991). Leveraging their vast resources on public relations campaigns designed to influence and shape public opinion, corporate interests preclude community groups, civic associations, and non-governmental organizations (NGOs) from entering into substantive policy debates. The result is a dangerous level of misinformation that threatens to undermine deliberative democracy by promoting one particular view on issues of public concern to the virtual exclusion of alternative or oppositional perspectives (Kuklinski, *et al.* 2000). And, like media consolidation, this rather disturbing trend that has matured in the United States over the past twenty years has emerged elsewhere (McGregor 2000; Zhang and Cameron 2003).

Amid all this media consolidation and corporate influence, an equally troubling condition further threatens to undermine democratic communication. Rather than improve access to information services and enhance competition between content providers, the privatization of media outlets, and the attendant commodification of news, information, and culture has exacerbated inequities based on income and education levels. The proliferation of "new and improved" communication technologies and services from cable and satellite television, to cellular phones, computers, and Internet-based services – has divided the public into information haves and have nots. Indeed, constant investment in technology and assorted peripherals amount to high-risk acts of consumption that only financially secure households can afford to take. The net result is a technological divide – based on *existing* social divisions – that threatens to intensify rather than alleviate, as some technophiles suggest, class differences (Golding and Murdock 1989). The advent of digital broadcasting likewise brings with it related costs that many consumers may be unable to pay.

This disparity between the information-rich and the information-poor is further heightened in light of fee-based access to goods and services that were formerly available free of charge either through commercial and public service broadcasting or by public institutions like schools and libraries. The proliferation of fee-based services creates formidable barriers of access to news, information, and culture. The implications of the 1998 Digital Millennium Copyright Act (DMCA) are particularly disturbing in this regard. Ostensibly designed to extend intellectual property rights in the digital realm, this legislation represents a dangerous legal precedent in the privatization of digital materials. In particular, the lack of so-called "first sale" provisions seriously compromises existing fair use policies: policies that encourage the public dissemination and use of scientific, educational, and cultural materials.[2] Moreover, this legislation makes provision for pay-for-use schemes that seriously compromise consumers' ability to make use of, let alone share, information or creative content. Dotcom hyperbole to the contrary, the digital divide grows deep and wide. And, in a global media environment, this development has implications far beyond the borders of the United States. All told, then, the commodification of public communication belies claims that the information age will free the minds and liberate the spirits of the world's people.

Cultural globalization

Accompanying the instantaneous, worldwide flow of market data, financial information, and business transactions that are the hallmarks of economic globalization is the global traffic in music and movies, radio and television programs, advertisements, entertainment spectaculars, sporting events, and all manner of cultural fare. Although the historical antecedents for this condition extend at least as far back as the late nineteenth century with the laying of transoceanic telegraph lines, the advent of satellite telecommunications heralded a new epoch in human history: the emergence of what communication theorist Marshall McLuhan cheerfully described as a "global village" (McLuhan 1964). The ability to see and hear events in real time and across vast expanses of space, McLuhan argued, extends human sensory perception, thereby enlarging our awareness of, and, more important, awakening our responsibility to, one another and to the planet. Put another way, the satellite's ability to annihilate time and space inevitably fosters the emergence of a global consciousness.

McLuhan's vision of an all-encompassing global conversation that would eradicate political, linguistic, and cultural differences and unite the world's people captured the collective imagination of a generation. As Deirdre Boyle (1997) notes, the video underground of the late 1960s was interested in exploring McLuhan's theories of media – particularly those related to television's retribalizing influence on modern experience and consciousness – through a radicalized and decentralized mode of video production. Not surprisingly, McLuhan's vision also appealed to American business leaders: most notably, durable goods manufacturers, Hollywood production studios, and the three national television networks. Despite his lasting influence on the 1960s counterculture and subsequent community and alternative media movements, however, McLuhan's uncritical acceptance of dominant media institutions and practices made him little more than an apologist for the colonizing impulses behind corporate America's enthusiasm for global communication (Williams 1992: 120–122).

Indeed, the revolution in satellite communication that made McLuhan's vision plausible was fueled, in large measure, by the Kennedy Administration's expansionist and increasingly interventionist foreign policy; a foreign policy committed not only to containing a communist threat but also expanding US business interests in overseas markets (Curtin 1995). On 25 May 1961, in a speech before the US Congress made memorable by the president's challenge to put a man on the moon by the decade's end, John F. Kennedy requested a budget appropriation of $50 million to "make the most of our present leadership, by accelerating the use of space satellites for world-wide communications" (Kennedy 1961). Thus, US control over satellite communication would not only yield a strategic military and ideological advantage over the Soviets but, equally important, provide US businesses with a distinct economic advantage over the rest of the industrialized and developing world.

With the successful launch of the Telstar communication satellite in 1962, the United States began to pursue its objective of establishing dominance over the emerging telecommunications industry. Two years later, agencies from eighteen Western nations formed the International Telecommunications Satellite Consortium (INTELSAT), to coordinate the development of an international satellite telecommunications network. Significantly, the US space agency, NASA, was contracted to launch the consortium's satellites, giving the United States enormous influence over the shape the nascent global communication network would take. This in turn gave the industrialized nations in general, and the United States in particular, a significant advantage over developing nations in setting the terms and conditions of an emerging world information order. It also heightened the developing world's dependency upon Western news agencies, cultural exports, production and distribution technologies, and, through training and aid agencies, ideologically charged notions of expertise and professionalism (Golding 1977; Mattelart 1980). Finally, and perhaps most ominously, increased cooperation between the military and commercial interests – especially in the area of research and development – led to the formation of interlocking industries with interests in telecommunications, surveillance technologies, entertainment, and most recently, warfare modeling and simulation programs (Hamelink 1983: 47–53; Herz 1997: 197–213). All told, these developments concentrated enormous power in a handful of communication corporations that promoted Western ideologies and effectively stifled competition in the emerging field of telecommunications.

The dramatic global imbalance in access to communication and information infrastructures heightened tensions between the industrialized democracies of the North and the developing nations of the South. Throughout the late 1970s and 1980s, calls for a New World Information and Communication Order (NWICO) that would restructure the existing telecommunication infrastructure and ensure greater access to this system were met with equal measures of condescension and resistance by several industrialized nations, most notably Great Britain and the United States (Roach 1997). Moreover, the discrepancies between the high-minded but non-binding recommendations of the United Nations-sponsored commission on international communication, summarized in the McBride Report (UNESCO 1980), and the political realities they were meant to address seriously compromised the realization of a more just and equitable global communication policy (Hamelink 1997).

In the early 1980s, at about the same time that UNESCO articulated fears that the developing world's struggle for self-determination was threatened by the encroachment of Western cultural forms and practices, the media industries began to expand their global reach as never before. Technological developments, most notably in the realm of digital production, transmission, and storage, coupled with the implementation of neo-liberal economic and regulatory policies fundamentally altered the manner in which cultural forms circulate around the world. The convergence of once discrete media industries, technologies, and texts not only facilitated the production and distribution of new and disparate cultural forms but also afforded synergies between equipment manufacturers and content providers. That is to say, formerly distinct, but related media industries could now combine their operations in the production, distribution, transmission, and marketing of texts (books, magazines, films, music, and video) and technologies (CD players, VCRs, radio and television receivers, camcorders, and personal computers).

For example, in 1989, the equipment manufacturer Sony purchased Columbia Studios and CBS Records. As a result, Sony could leverage its relationship with both the film studio and the music producer to diversify, enhance, and multiply revenue streams based on a constellation of related texts and technologies.[3] Sensing the enormous possibilities of such a strategy, the Disney Company quickly followed suit. With its takeover of Capital Cities/ABC, Disney was uniquely positioned to engineer global marketing campaigns for any number of its productions: feature films, videotapes, musical recordings, theatrical shows, and television programming. Moreover, with its theme parks in the United States, Europe, and Japan, and through lucrative licensing agreements with other transnationals (clothing manufacturers, toy makers, software developers, and fast food franchises), Disney markets a range of products throughout the world. Synergies like this make it possible even for a box office failure like the animated feature *The Hunchback of Notre Dame* to recoup its losses and turn a tidy profit in ancillary markets like cable television, home video, and product merchandising. A worldwide success like *The Lion King* yields enormous profits for relatively minimal investment.

A major consequence of cultural globalization, therefore, is a marked increase in the application of instrumental rationalization to the realm of cultural production. New imperatives, most notably risk avoidance and the relentless pursuit of economies of scale, rather than an openness toward aesthetic innovation or concerns with the social or artistic value of cultural expression, have a profound influence on media form and content. The implications of this development were famously, if rather pessimistically, laid out in a theory of cultural production first enunciated by Theodor Adorno and Max Horkheimer. Writing as political refugees from Nazi Germany living in the United States, Adorno and Horkheimer warned against the detrimental effects of what they called "the culture industry" on social values, civic participation, and moral and aesthetic sensibilities (Adorno and Horkheimer 1993).

Significantly, the social and historical context in which this theory developed reflected concerns over the use of media in the realms of politics and culture. In Germany, print, film, radio, and even the new medium of television were all used to considerable effect in propaganda campaigns that facilitated the rise of Fascism. By contrast, many of the same techniques used for purposes of political persuasion under the Nazi regime were decisive in crystallizing a consumer culture that was emerging in the United States.[4] Indeed, the mid to late 1940s was a pivotal period in the development of highly centralized, commercially supported, profit-oriented media systems. At that time, the American print, film, and broadcasting industries began to coalesce around a set of assumptions and practices that reflected their economic orientation and determined their organizational structure. Thus, despite the different properties and characteristics of each medium, these industries quickly developed a remarkably similar *mode of production* – one biased toward the standardization and homogenization of cultural forms and the centralization of cultural production.

Today, the proclivity for media mergers and acquisitions serves to encourage and promote market-oriented approaches to cultural production around the world. No longer constrained by public service obligations or technical limitations that once concentrated efforts on the development of national audiences, newly partnered media producers and technology manufacturers aggressively pursue global markets based on taste, lifestyle, and economic status rather than regional, national, or cultural identities. Dissolving racial, ethnic, and national differences in this manner engenders the growth and development of a global culture of sorts. However, it is a culture based primarily on acquisitiveness and capital accumulation rather than social value and community development. Furthermore, in creating new markets and forging new media spaces that traverse national borders, the culture industries destabilize established modes of affiliation and identity formation. The result is the deterritorialization of culture: the erosion of established settings, institutions, and practices associated with cultural production and dissemination. This loss of cultural space undermines local cultural autonomy and diminishes the prospects of self-determination.

For these reasons, then, McLuhan's dream of a global village is met with great trepidation. According to some critics, the prospect of a monolithic global culture – one that unequivocally reflects Western, most notably Anglo-Saxon cultural forms, values, and beliefs – amounts to an insidious form of domination: cultural imperialism (Mattelart 1979; Schiller 1976; Tunstall 1977). Variably described as the "Cocacolonization," "Disneyfication," or "McDonaldization" of the world, cultural imperialism is defined as "the systematic penetration and domination of the cultural life of the popular classes by the ruling classes of the West in order to reorder the values, behavior, institutions, and identity of oppressed peoples to conform to the interest of the imperial classes" (Petras 1993: 140). Communication theorists are not alone in these concerns; nor is this solely a problem for developing countries. Policy makers and elected officials in Canada and France, for example, are among the most vocal proponents of quotas that limit foreign imports, generally American films and television programming. Concerns that an endless stream of American popular culture systematically erodes national and cultural identities provoke intense anxieties the world over.

In recent years, the economic and technological determinism of the cultural imperialism thesis has met with some much needed criticism (Garofalo 1993; Tomlinson 1997). To begin with, the emphasis on mass media in this formulation invariably leads to the rather simplistic, and by now indefensible assumption that media have direct, uniform, and powerful effects on otherwise passive and unsuspecting victims of ideological conditioning. This so-called magic bullet theory of media effects fails to account for the mediating influence personal experience, educational background, ethnicity, locality, and a host of socio-cultural factors have on individual and collective responses to the mass media (e.g., Morley 1980). Conversely, the cultural imperialism thesis fails to recognize the contradictory messages produced by the media industries, not to mention the pleasures audiences derive from media texts and technologies (Fiske 1989; Newcomb and Hirsch 1994). In doing so, this perspective over-looks evidence which suggests that media institutions and technologies do not inevitably serve the interests of those who own and operate them. Indeed, because they are first and foremost social institutions, the media industries themselves are open to internal, as well as external, contest, challenge, and change (Lull 1991: 92–126; Negus 1992). Equally im-portant, audience studies indicate that people make use of media texts and technologies in creative, surprising, and sometimes subversive ways that undermine the intention of media producers and industries (Ang 1990; Fiske 1993; Katz and Liebe 1984). All told, then, cultural imperi-alism's reliance on a strictly causal model of media effects diminishes its explanatory potential.

More critically, however, focusing as it does on the relatively recent de-velopment of transnational media flows, cultural imperialism elides the historical legacy of colonialism and dependency on the everyday lived experience of peoples throughout the developing world. Taking a far more anthropological approach to culture than text-centered perspec-tives typically afford, Annabelle Sreberny-Mohammadi (1997) helps us to understand imperialism, in all its guises, as a form of *cultural contact* replete with ambiguities and contradictions for both the colonized and the colonizer. In doing so, Sreberny-Mohammadi usefully calls our at-tention to the "many faces of imperialism," including missionary work, educational systems, language instruction, government administration, and travel and tourism that amount to discrete, but related forms of in-teraction and interpenetration within and between disparate cultures. All of which have had and continue to have an enormous influence on the lives, experiences, and cultures of post-colonial societies. In short, media flows are not the only, nor necessarily the most enduring form of cultural contact between the West and its former colonies.

Finally, but perhaps most importantly, there is a tendency among some proponents of cultural imperialism to essentialize culture, especially so-called "third world" cultures. This rather paternalistic attitude suggests that pure, authentic, and egalitarian cultures are "contaminated" by the destructive force and modernizing influence of Western culture. There are compelling arguments supported by a growing body of empirical evi-dence to dispute such assumptions. Consider, for example, the introduc-tion of television in a rural village in India. In her ethnographic analysis of television's impact on family relations, Neena Behl (1988) observes strik-ing changes in the domestic political economy of households long bound by traditions of inequality based on gender and generational hierarchies and distinctions. By reorganizing work and leisure-time activities and routines, and by altering the character and conduct of familiar relations within and between households, television works to equalize status among family members.

In such instances, the values, institutions, and practices associated with globalization open up new realms of possibility for individuals and social groups long dominated by repressive relations of power in local cultures. The principles of individual rights and personal freedom associated with Western culture challenge oppressive and authoritarian regimes both ancient and modern (Giddens 1991). Moreover, evidence suggests that the global diffusion of communication texts and technologies does help to promote literacy skills and to open up educational and employment opportunities for people around the world (UNESCO 1982). From this perspective, then, communication texts and technologies are but one site of cultural contact, which allow individuals to construct identities, based upon values, norms, and practices that challenge and sometimes subvert extant power relations and structures.

Taking a nostalgic or romanticized perspective to local cultures, therefore, fails to appreciate two fundamental aspects of culture. First, culture is neither static nor rigidly determined. Rather, culture is mobile, adaptive, and dynamic. There is no such thing as a pure or authentic cultural form or practice. Second, all cultures are embedded with and operate in accordance to relations of power and authority. This is not to suggest, however, that some cultures are not more equitable and responsive than others. Rather, it is to indicate that so-called "traditional cultures" are not always already egalitarian, nor are so-called "modern" cultures either wholly or inevitably oppressive. Understanding the cultural dynamics of globalization therefore calls for a rejection of the normative baggage associated with both "the local" and "the global" (Cvetkovich and Kellner 1997).

With that said, it would be a grave mistake to underestimate the potentially debilitating effects of transnational media flows – especially in terms of their *scope, intensity, and direction* – on local sovereignty and cultural autonomy. Doing so greatly overstates resistance to cultural oppression at the risk not only of undermining oppositional movements based on collective action but also legitimating systems of political domination and economic subordination. As Peter Golding and Phil Harris caution: "Whatever the form and character of the new international [communication] order, it remains deeply and starkly inegalitarian, in ways which mark the lives of the privileged minority as much as the impoverished majority" (1997: 7). Only with these caveats in mind can we move, as

Golding and Harris would have it, "beyond cultural imperialism" and critically evaluate this latest stage in global communication, international relations, and social organization locally as well as globally.

Community media as socio-cultural mediation

Community-oriented media provide an exceptional vehicle to move beyond cultural imperialism without losing sight of the asymmetrical relationship between transnational media corporations and local populations, and to interrogate the contradictory tendencies and countervailing trajectories associated with globalization. The growing popular interest in community media across the globe indicates profound dissatisfaction with media industries preoccupied with increasing market share and profitability at the expense of public accountability and social value. Community media likewise manifest an intense desire to reassert local autonomy and defend particularistic identities in the wake of transnational media flows and the attendant homogenization of cultural forms. As such, community media represent a dynamic response to the forces of globalization, not unlike other more frequently discussed phenomena, such as the rise of ethnic nationalism, religious fundamentalism, terrorism, or popular demonstrations surrounding WTO and G8 meetings in Seattle, Genoa, Cancun, and elsewhere (Barber 1995; Buchanan 2002; Norberg-Hodge 2002; Smith 1991). Like other socio-cultural formations, then, community media vividly demonstrate that the logics of economic and cultural globalization are not nearly as universal as some adherents suggest nor as totalizing as other critics fear. Rather, community media are a site of interpenetration between local and global actors, forces, and conditions: one of the many "heterogeneous dialogues" associated with globalization (Appadurai 1993).

In this light, community media are properly viewed as a complex form of resistance and accommodation to transnational media flows. Here, Jesus Martin-Barbero's (1993) insights into what he describes as "mediation" are most helpful. Martin-Barbero recommends a fundamental reorientation in communication studies away from industry critiques and textual analyses to the social, political, and cultural mediations that take place within and through communicative forms and practices. Prompted by the inadequacy of imported research traditions from Europe and North America and the specificity of the Latin American media environment, this move not only acknowledges media reception as a site of cultural production, but also highlights the complex and dynamic role communication plays in cultural change.

The problems of communication have become part of the debate not simply from a quantitative and topical view – the enormous economic strength of the communication industries – but in a qualitative sense, namely, that the processes of redefining a culture are the key to comprehending the communicative nature of culture.

(Martin-Barbero 1993: 211)

This perspective provides enormous insight into the ongoing struggle – processes Martin-Barbero characterizes variously as "confrontation and exchange" or "conflict and dialogue" – over the meanings communicated within and through media technologies and texts. Throughout his discussion, Martin-Barbero demonstrates how mass media are embedded in the everyday lived experience of local populations and illuminates the distinct role various cultural forms (e.g., theater, cinema, radio dramas, and telenovelas) play in the construction of national and cultural identities. In this way, the concept of mediation encourages the examination of both micro and macro level processes of cultural production from a socio-historical perspective. As such, mediation provides a valuable analytical perspective from which to consider community media.[5]

For instance, at one level community media can be viewed as a tactical response to the commodification of culture and the attendant homogenization of media form and content. Akin to the practice of appropriation so often celebrated by cultural analysts, community media form and content is a bricolage of artifacts and routines generally associated with the culture industries. Like textual poachers (e.g. Jenkins 1992), community media producers glean bits and pieces of media culture and invest this material with their own social experience in attempts to make sense of their lives. And, like the fan culture commonly associated with textual poaching, community media represent distinctive cultural practices that create and nourish affective relations. For example, producers at Boston Neighborhood Network, a community access television service in Massachusetts, appropriate familiar forms, such as the innocuous television cooking show, to promote healthy eating habits for people who are HIV-positive. In doing so, community television producers leverage modest resources to build community and meet their particular needs; needs that go unmet, and largely ignored, by commercial and public service media alike.

Significantly, community media also represent strategic alliances between social, cultural, and political groups mounting and organizing resistance to the hegemony of dominant media institutions and practices. As a resource for local social service agencies, political activists, and others whose missions, methods, and objectives are antithetical to existing power structures, community media publicize oppositional messages that are either distorted by or altogether omitted from mainstream media coverage. Here, the independent media movement is an especially forceful illustration of the efficacy of cooperative and collaborative efforts between various interest groups. The IMC's ability to record, publicize, and preserve popular demonstrations helps support social and political agendas that question the wisdom, let alone the inevitability, of economic globalization. These initiatives diminish the debilitating effects of political-economic systems that cater to well-heeled special interests by enhancing the capacity of local communities to organize themselves and participate in political processes.

Similarly, as a forum for local arts and cultural organizations, community media support and encourage local cultural production. In the face of the homogenizing influence of national media industries and the encroachment of cultural forms produced and distributed by transnational corporations, community media provide a measure of local cultural autonomy in an increasingly privatized, global media environment. Furthermore, as a physical as well as a virtual space (i.e., electronic commons), community media organizations are one of the few remaining public spaces where community members can gather to debate political issues, to celebrate local cultural heritage, and to join together as a community. In this respect, then, community media are strategic initiatives to counteract a climate of political apathy and social alienation that confounds a sense of belonging in local communities.

These tactical responses and strategic interventions constitute but several facets of what critic Ien Ang describes as the "broad range of creative and contradictory practices which peoples in different parts of the world are inventing today in their everyday dealings with the changing media environment that surrounds them" (Ang 1990: 257). In Martin-Barbero's formulation, then, community media are important sites of confrontation and exchange between the culture industries and local audiences. In saying this, I want to underscore not only the glaring power differentials at work here but also the inherent contradictions of this process. As Martin-Barbero observes: "Not every assumption of hegemonic power by the underclass is a sign of submission and not every rejection is resistance. Not everything that comes from above represents the values of the dominant class. Some aspects of popular culture respond to logics other than the logic of domination" (1990: 76). Indeed, community media provide a unique site to illuminate hegemonic processes: community media demonstrate not only signs of resistance and subversion but evidence of complicity and submission as well.

Perhaps the most forceful illustration of this contradictory process is the appropriation of leisure-time and work-related technologies such as audio cassette players, video cameras, and personal computers for purposes of community communication. Manufactured and marketed as consumer goods, these products enable local populations to subvert the dominance of the culture industries and resist the seduction of consumer ideology. In the hands of community media producers, these consumer goods are, in the words of Ithiel De Sola Pool (1983), "technologies of freedom": instruments to mobilize political resistance, articulate cultural identities, preserve popular memory, and sustain democratic movements.

Yet, the logic of the culture industries persists in these oppositional forms and practices. The reluctance on the part of some community media producers to deviate from established norms of production and distribution – as suggested by an overriding concern with Hollywood production values, a preoccupation with audience numbers, an emphasis on individual achievement versus collaborative effort, and the uncritical mimicry of familiar styles and genres – indicates how difficult it is for community media producers and audiences alike to move beyond expectations forged by daily interactions with mainstream media form and content (e.g., Higgins 1991).

Furthermore, the culture industry's dismissive attitude toward the technical abilities of "non-professionals" and the social value of their work underscores the adversarial relationship between dominant and community media. All too often, the work of "amateurs" is marked as esoteric, frivolous, and apolitical. Rarely do commercial or public service broadcasters even acknowledge the existence of community media organizations.[6] More often than not, when community media is acknowledged, it is invariably depicted as a refuge for outsider artists, hatemongers, pornographers, and the radical fringe: a perception some community media producers enthusiastically embrace. As a result, producers and audiences alike are complicit in accepting and circulating the notion that community media are aesthetically inferior to mainstream media form and content, and socially and politically irrelevant for popular audiences. Perhaps the prevalence of these biases and misconceptions accounts for the reluctance of communication scholars to engage more thoroughly with the phenomenon of community media.

Despite the antagonistic relationship between mainstream and community media, however, there are multifaceted levels of exchange. Indeed, one can detect a symbiotic relationship between these two modes of communication that illuminates the dynamics of cultural change in subtle but profound ways. Take, for example, the case of community access television in the United States. During the cable industry's formative years, community television advocates and cable television representatives enjoyed a congenial relationship and successfully lobbied federal, state, and local governments to award cable companies lucrative franchise agree-ments (Engelman 1990). Once their operations were secured, however, the cable industry quickly and ruthlessly discarded community television advocates and reneged on most of their promises for long-term finan-cial, technical, and logistical support of participatory television for local communities. Despite the enormity of this setback for the prospects of in-vigorating community communication, community television advocates were instrumental in legitimating the cable television industry. Without this support, the explosive growth of cable television in the United States would surely have been constrained by protracted regulatory processes and the objections of a powerful broadcast industry. As has been well documented, cable television significantly altered America's electronic environment and produced considerable cultural change (Dizard 2002: 109–129).

Less well known and rarely acknowledged is the influence community video has had on mainstream television form and content. Champions of lightweight portable video recording systems, community producers reveled in their ability to document everyday life with a force and clarity heretofore unknown on commercial television. The verité sensibility that was once the sole purview of the avant-garde and community video mak-ers is now commonplace in electronic news gathering, hour-long episodic television like *ER* and *NYPD Blue*, and most recently, in so-called "real-ity" programs like *Cops* and *Survivor*. A more infamous example of this symbiotic relationship is the television skit and subsequent feature film *Wayne's World* – a self-serving caricature of community access television's most excessive, base, and demeaning tendencies. *Wayne's World* went on to become an enormous financial success and something of a global cultural phenomenon – largely at the expense of community access television.

While these instances vividly demonstrate the (uneven) exchange be-tween community media and transnational media corporations, commu-nity media also serve as an important, but largely overlooked form of cultural mediation within and between disparate social groups. Nowhere is this tendency more evident than in multifaceted uses of media in pre-serving and maintaining cultural identities across space and over time (e.g., Gillespie 1989; Lee and Heup Cho 1995). Indeed, the creation of new cultural territories and the preservation of existing cultural spaces takes on enormous significance in light of the ease with which people, sounds, imagery, and cultural practices circulate about the globe. Com-munity media therefore contribute to the reterritorialization of culture by establishing new structures and creating new spaces for local cultural production. In this light, community media can be viewed as a dramatic expression of the felt need of local populations to exploit as well as contain these forces in their efforts to make sense of the dramatic, and at times traumatic, upheavals associated with globalization.

None of which is to suggest, however, that community media provide an unproblematic solution to the deep-seated anxieties and very real antagonisms associated with increasingly pluralistic societies. To the contrary, community media are often used to disseminate hurtful and at times inflammatory messages that promote intolerance, injustice, and violence (e.g., Harmon 1991; Zoglin 1993). In their commitment to the principles of free speech and deliberative democracy, community media organizations are sometimes obliged to distribute material that exacerbates tensions within the community. As unsettling and repugnant as this first appears, there is some value in this, not least of which is an unequivocal repudiation of any notions of happy pluralism. With an intensity, depth, and clarity far superior to anything found in their commercial or public service counterparts, community media illuminate the process of conflict and dialogue that is fundamental to community building and maintenance. In this way, community media underscore the enormous challenge confronting democratic societies struggling to reconcile the high-minded ideals of civil rights and equal opportunity with the harsh realities of structural inequalities, institutionalized racism, gender inequity, and ethnocentrism.

That is to say, by giving voice to varied and competing groups, community media graphically illustrate profound differences throughout the community. Moreover, community media undermine essentialist notions of race, gender, and ethnicity by illuminating differences within such monolithic categories as Black, Hispanic, Asian, Gay, and Lesbian. Therefore, unlike either commercial or public service media – which rarely allow people to speak for themselves – community media underscore the constructed and contested quality of individual and collective identity. As such, community media represent a unique site to interrogate the process of identity formation through communication technologies, and to examine the dramatic impact of social and technological change on the everyday lived experience of disparate groups within a geographically based community. Put another way, attending to the institutions, forms, and practices associated with community media provides enormous insight into the relationship between people, places, and communication technologies. We begin our examination of this profound yet enigmatic relationship with an overview of community media initiatives around the world.

2 Tracing the global through the local: perspectives on community media

> Globalisation can thus be defined as the intensification of worldwide social relations which link distant localities in such a way that local happenings are shaped by events occurring many miles away and vice versa. This is a dialectical process because such local happenings may move in an obverse direction from the very distanciated relations that shape them.
>
> Anthony Giddens, *The Consequences of Modernity*

Drawing on scholarship aimed at theorizing globalization from a cultural perspective, this chapter employs community media in an effort to trace the global through the local (see Ang 1990; Cvetkovich and Kellner 1997). Specifically, I use community media as a lens to examine the dialectical (if uneven) process between global forces and conditions and the everyday lived experience of local communities. Throughout, I take up the argument laid out in Chapter 1 related to issues of cultural imperialism. That is, I want to challenge the notion that local populations are simply subject to, or dominated by, national, regional, and increasingly transnational political and economic arrangements, structures, policies, and prerogatives.

That said, I am keenly aware of the dangers associated with overstating popular resistance to global incursions on local economies, social relations, and cultural sensibilities. Media scholar David Morley sums up this quandary as "a question of steering between the dangers of an improper romanticism of 'consumer freedom' on the one hand, and a paranoiac fantasy of 'global control' on the other" (1991: 1). What I want to suggest is that community media provide an empirical setting in which to interrogate the play of local and translocal forces associated with "globalization."

For my purposes here, this discussion focuses on several aspects of globalization particularly relevant to the study of community media. They are: the role regulatory policies and philosophies play in shaping local, national, and transnational media systems; the interaction between social movements and so-called "identity" or "cultural politics" and community media initiatives; and finally, the significance of distinct, but related developments in transportation and communication technologies in facilitating transnational flows of people, cultures, capital, goods, and services. Throughout, I hope to demonstrate that community media represent an important although undervalued site to examine the dynamics of globalization *from the perspective of local communities*.

Put differently, I want to underscore what I see as a defining feature of community media. That is: locally oriented, participatory media organizations are at once a *response* to the encroachment of the global upon the local as well as an *assertion* of local cultural identities and socio-political autonomy in the light of these global forces. This perspective owes a great deal to recent thinking in cultural theory, most notably Appadurai's (1993) notion of disjunctive moments, forces, and conditions within the global cultural economy. In short, I suggest that community media serve as a fertile site to consider the consequences of globalization in various locations, for disparate populations and under very different circumstances.

This chapter is organized into four sections. Each section describes how local communities make use of a particular technology: radio, television, print, and computer networking. Rather than attempt to present an exhaustive or comprehensive overview of community media initiatives around the world, however, I explore the impulses and motivations behind various efforts to restructure media systems to meet the needs and interests of local populations. In doing so, I sketch out the historical development of each technology as it has been appropriated for purposes of community communication.

My intention here is not to provide a techno-centric chronicle of community media, however. Instead, I place particular emphasis on the interplay between community media initiatives and broader social, economic, and political forces and conditions. As we shall see, community media are inextricably bound up in cultural politics operating at the local, national, and international level. Thus, community media's intervention into contemporary media culture depends not simply on the appropriation of communication technologies, but on the rearticulation of these technologies in the service of local populations. Throughout this discussion, then, I make note of the various players and institutions that fund, organize, and otherwise support these local efforts to reclaim the media.

Wireless world

A number of scholars trace the development of community radio as it is commonly understood and currently practiced to the pioneering efforts of KPFA, Pacifica Radio in Berkeley, California (Barlow 1988; Lewis and

Booth 1990). A contentious and internally divisive organization, Pacifica nonetheless represents a triumph in the ongoing struggle for communicative democracy. Pacifica Radio did so by forging a new model of radio broadcasting in the post-World War II period. The Pacifica Network continues to do so today – providing listeners with news, information, and cultural programming of the sort rarely carried by US commercial or public service outlets. Through its innovations in listener sponsorship, investigative reporting, audio documentary, and free form music presentation, Pacifica Radio has been at the social, cultural, and political vanguard of American broadcasting for well over a half century (Land 1999).

Appalled by commercial broadcasting's unrelenting commercialization and the industry's attendant silence on the militarization of everyday life, Pacifica's founders sought to remake radio for purposes of promoting dialogue, understanding, and peaceful coexistence among all the peoples of the world. To that end, Pacifica Radio pledged to "engage in any activity that shall contribute to a lasting understanding between nations, races, creeds, and colors; to gather and disseminate information on the causes of conflict between any and all such groups" (Pacifica Foundation 1946). Working alongside a cadre of dedicated volunteers, Lewis Hill, KPFA's visionary founder, sought to realize broadcasting's untapped potential to educate listeners, to challenge them, and to promote all manner of creative self-expression.

This nexus of political, philosophical, and cultural programming would, in Hill's estimation, resonate with listeners whose interests, passions, and tastes were unmet by commercial broadcasting. Moreover, this alternative broadcast service would encourage listeners' voluntary financial support. To that end, Hill championed "listener sponsorship" as the station's primary funding mechanism. In doing so, Pacifica would insulate itself from commercial pressures – those institutional constraints and economic prerogatives that demand that broadcasters meticulously avoid controversial issues and treat audiences as consumer aggregates – which undermine radio broadcasting's communicative potential. This model of community broadcasting, based upon an abiding respect for listeners and supported through "subscription fees," served as the cornerstone for what came to be known as "community radio" in the United States and throughout much of the industrialized world.

Taking its name from an international movement dedicated to world peace, Pacifica's local initiative was, from its inception, informed by a global political consciousness. Pacifica's "brash experiment" emerged at a time when Cold War politics undermined civil liberties at home and threatened peace and security abroad. Broadcasting lively, freewheeling discussions on a variety of "hot topics" – nuclear arms, conscription, foreign aid, the redistribution of wealth, and civil rights – Hill and his colleagues sought to counter the rhetoric of the national security state and challenge the emergence of the military-industrial complex. As radio historian Jeff Land argues, KPFA embraced what might be called "radical pacifism" of the sort practiced by Mahatma Gandhi's Quit India Movement (2000: 32–34). That is to say, Pacifica's founders were committed to active nonviolent resistance to militarism and other forms of social, economic, and political repression. As we shall see in Chapter 3, Pacifica's illustrious history of dissident expression, coupled with an insistence on promoting dialogue and negotiation rather than conflict and militarism, has exerted considerable influence on the US community radio movement. We can detect these same impulses to challenge authority, celebrate local culture, and nurture community relations in less well-known, but equally impressive efforts around the world.

Consider, for example, Radio Suara Persaudaraan Matraman (RSPM) in East Jakarta. Founded by M. Satiri, a local radio technician, RSPM grew in response to the uneasy and often hostile relations between two squatter communities in the Matraman district (Senevirante 2003). Dubbed the "peace music station" by Satiri, the station features so-called "dangdut" music, an indigenous variant of Indian popular music that appeals to young people from both warring factions. Over the course of the past three years, Satiri's home studio served as a meeting ground for young people to encounter one another without fear of violence. Instead, young people produce their own music programming and learn valuable production skills.

RSPM's resemblance to Pacifica Radio goes beyond this commitment to promoting tolerance and understanding, however. RSPM's funding mechanism is reminiscent of KPFA's model of listener sponsorship; albeit on a more modest, but no less effective scale. Charging listeners 1,000 rupiah (12 US cents) per request, Satiri not only supports his efforts but also attracts listeners as well as volunteers to the station. RSPM's journalistic endeavors have likewise yielded impressive results. Rather than simply report on hostilities, RSPM uses radio to resolve conflicts. Here again, RSPM operates along the same lines envisioned by KPFA, the flagship station of the Pacifica Radio Network. That is to say, by opening up its doors and the airwaves to discussion, negotiation, and conflict mediation, Indonesia's "peace music station" gives local residents a nonviolent alternative to thirty years of feuding and bloodshed.

In the years since Suharto's regime ended, Indonesian broadcast policy has undergone significant if incremental changes. A media landscape that was once tightly controlled by Suharto supporters has opened up considerably. Predictably, commercial interests have rushed to the air-waves, but so too have more community-minded broadcasters. Impatient for regulatory authorities to officially sanction community radio, RSPM, like hundreds of other community stations across the country, began broadcasting without a license. In certain respects, then, the emergent Indonesian community radio sector resembles the informal network of micro-broadcasters that took to the airwaves in Japan throughout the 1980s (Kogawa 1993) and more recently in the free radio movement in the United States (Sakolsky and Dunifer 1998).

Like radio enthusiasts across the Indonesian archipelago, so-called microwatt broadcasters took advantage of legislative loopholes, improved technical capabilities, and fissures in spectrum management schemes to "seize the airwaves" for purposes of community communication. What links these distinctive community radio initiatives together, despite the disparate national contexts and local circumstances in which they oper-ate, is that these efforts to democratize the airwaves are often articulated within and through broader socio-political agendas and movements.

For example, throughout the 1970s, feminist groups across Western Europe were especially active in establishing free radio stations commit-ted to promoting women's rights and extending women's presence into social and political arenas traditionally reserved for men. Stations like the Parisian-based Les Nanas Radioteuses or Radio Donna in Rome aired programs that dealt with controversial issues like abortion and reproductive rights at a time when mainstream media outlets rarely, if ever, broached such subjects (Jallov 1992). In doing so, these unlicensed stations anticipated the philosophical orientations, organizational struc-tures, and institutional practices that exist today throughout Western Europe's dynamic and multifaceted community radio sector.

Germany's radio st. paula illustrates this last point. Since 1991 radio st. paula has produced more than 600 programs related to women's is-sues, lesbian culture, local politics, sports, and music (radio st. paula n.d.). Listeners and local residents are invited to radio st. paula's weekly meeting to pitch program ideas, learn technical skills, assist with adminis-trative functions, coordinate community outreach efforts, and otherwise socialize with a close-knit group of likeminded individuals.

A collective of approximately twenty women, radio st. paula is one of the founding members of Freise Sender Kombinat (FSK): a "free" com-munity radio station based in Hamburg, Germany. FSK encourages com-munity participation in every aspect of the station. Moreover, FSK serves as the parent organization of a network of local radio projects includ-ing, Radio Loretta, Forum Radio, Stadtterilradio, UniRadio/Academic Hardcore, and, of course, radio st. paula. Like many free radio stations across Europe, FSK is non-commercial, listener-supported radio that produces independent news and cultural programming largely through volunteer efforts. In this way, FSK and other "free radio" stations across Europe create what Caroline Mitchell (1998) describes as a "feminist public sphere."

Community radio, therefore, occupies a significant but often-overlooked site of "identity politics" on the local, national, and, increasingly, international levels. Nowhere is this more evident than in so-called indigenous or native peoples' broadcasting. Community radio in Bolivia provides a case in point. Unlike much of Latin America – whose long tradition of alternative, grassroots, and guerrilla radio is threatened these days, not by repressive governments, but by the enormous influence commercial broadcasters yield in the policy making arena – the Bolivian community radio sector is thriving, thanks in large part to the World Association of Christian Communicators' (WACC) long-time support of development communication schemes and, in particular, indigenous peoples' radio.

For instance, in Cochambamba, Radio Esperanza (Hope Radio) broadcasts daily in the local dialects of the Quechua people. Like other indigenous peoples' stations, Radio Esperanza's emphasis on participatory communication takes full advantage of the medium's social, technical, and cultural biases. That is, in light of the high rates of illiteracy throughout Cochambamba, Radio Esperanza capitalizes on the Quechua's formidable social networks, their rich oral traditions, and radio's popularity throughout the region. Educational programs draw on local women's indigenous knowledge of time-honored healing techniques and natural medicines. Broadcasting this information not only promotes better health care, but has also helped elevate women's status within the community. Likewise, cultural programs celebrate local traditions and histories. One such program has been praised for reviving as many as 150 ancient riddles and 30 traditional folk tales that might otherwise have been lost to future generations (WACC 1994).

Indigenous peoples' radio has made its mark in industrialized societies as well. In Australia, for example, Aboriginal broadcasters have made good use of radio and satellite delivery systems to create a nationwide network of Aboriginal community radio. With technical and financial support from the Australian government, Aboriginal community radio reaches millions of listeners in urban centers and rural villages alike. Aboriginal stations are remarkable instances of the global meeting the local, of the past merging with the present. This condition is not without its complexities and contradictions, however. As Donald Browne (1990) observes, non-Western cultural values and practices are often at odds with the institutional arrangements, aesthetic and professional standards, and cultural forms associated with mainstream Australian broadcasting.

> The Aborigines who broadcast over those stations had to learn a good deal by trial and error, including what form 'Aboriginal radio' might take. Although they distrusted 'European' radio, which has almost totally neglected them from the time of its creation, it was the only kind they knew.
>
> (1990: 113)

In this respect, then, aboriginal radio reveals the tensions between assimilation and accommodation that mark the everyday lived experience of indigenous people throughout the world. Conversely, Aboriginal radio has greatly influenced and enhanced the wider Australian culture and society.

For instance, using the occasion of the bicentennial of European settlement in Australia, aboriginal radio publicized the detrimental consequences of this encounter for the indigenous population. As a result, European settlement is viewed in far less benign fashion than it had previously been. In the realm of popular culture, Aboriginal broadcasting introduced non-Aboriginals to music, poetry, and folk tales that have likewise entered into mainstream Australian culture. Through an ongoing process of accommodation, then, aboriginal broadcasting preserves ancient cultural forms and practices through modern communication technologies (Molnar and Meadows 2002). In this way, Aboriginal radio manifests the wider struggle to maintain a sense of cultural identity while simultaneously engaging with an increasingly multicultural society.

So-called native or indigenous radio has also played a decisive role in challenging existing regulatory schemes, thereby promoting the emergence of a nascent community radio sector. For example, historical studies of Canadian community broadcasting highlight the decisive role played by native people in pioneering the form (Salter 1981). Some of Canada's earliest experiences with what would later become community radio were the experimental efforts to use radio communication in isolated aboriginal communities of the north. Radio studies scholar Chris Fairchild describes one such experiment, a mobile radio station called Radio Kenomadiwin that visited indigenous communities to offer radio production training to aboriginal peoples and promote local program production.

While the effort ultimately took a form somewhat contrary to its original motivations, Radio Kenomadiwin marked an important precedent for others to follow; one of the staff involved in the project was later involved in the creation of Co-op Radio in Vancouver in 1973, one of the first urban community radio stations in the country. The most important result of these developments was the necessary practical and policy precedents, which allowed the development of future community-based radio experiments in southern cities and towns.

(Fairchild 1998: 50)

Today, Canada enjoys a "mixed" broadcast system featuring national and regional public service broadcasting, US as well as Canadian commercial stations, and a vibrant campus-community sector that encourages partnerships in locally oriented, participatory broadcasting between colleges and universities and the surrounding communities. Thus, not only have indigenous populations made effective use of community-based radio to preserve their culture, publicize their concerns, and secure some semblance of self-determination, in some instances, indigenous stations have provided invaluable insights that would help shape and inform subsequent community radio efforts.

And yet, while locally oriented, participatory radio practices have helped "free the airwaves" throughout much of the world, the struggle for communicative democracy is ongoing and volatile. As alluded to earlier, this is perhaps most evident in Latin America – once a rich site of clandestine, guerrilla, and grassroots radio (e.g., Crabtree 1996). For example, in Peru, recent regulatory "reforms" have virtually barred non-profit stations from generating income through advertising. Likeminded regulatory changes in Chile, Brazil, and Argentina weaken community radio's legal status and encourage private ownership and consolidation. As sociologist Rafael Roncagliolo (1999) observes, "Until recently, Latin America's local radio stations coexisted with commercial stations without too much trouble. But the concentration of the media over the past few years has tended to push non-profit radio and small stations in general out of the picture. This has inevitably led to few voices being heard on the air" (43).

On the other hand, however, deregulation has created some, albeit limited, opportunities for community-oriented radio to gain a foothold in media environments heretofore dominated either by the state-run, public service, or commercial interests. In Africa, for example, local groups have taken advantage of ambiguous or ill-defined broadcast regulations and established unlicensed community radio stations. These "illegal" stations forced the issue of community broadcasting onto the legislative agenda. Such is the case of Bush Radio in South Africa. Sometimes referred to as the Mother of Community Radio in Africa, Bush Radio began as an unlicensed broadcaster on 25 April 1993 (Ibrahim 2000). Within days, South African authorities seized the station's equipment and arrested two staff members. Following intense lobbying efforts, however, the case was dismissed and Bush Radio was granted a broadcast license on 1 August 1995.

Since that time, Bush Radio has served the communities throughout the Cape Flats region of Cape Town in myriad ways. In addition to training the next generation of radio journalists and music presenters, Bush Radio has been active in mediating conflicts between vigilante groups, drug dealers, and local reporters; distributing condoms in the fight against AIDS; rallying opposition against child sexual exploitation; and lobbying for tighter gun control measures. What's more, Bush Radio has generated considerable interest overseas and has proven itself rather influential in international circles. At the time of his visit to Bush Radio, former Federal Communications Commissioner William Kennard was considering a proposal to create a new, community-based radio service in the United States. Bush Radio's managing director, Zane Ibrahim, encouraged the FCC chairman to support so-called "low power FM" (LPFM) broadcasting (pers. comm., 22 November 1999).[1]

In short, the effects of media deregulation around the world have been complex and contradictory, in some instances enabling the development of community radio while in other contexts further constraining the development of the sector. Nowhere have these contradictions played out with greater frequency and variation than in Western Europe.

Discussing dramatic reversal of fortunes of community radio (*radio libres*) in France, James Miller observes that despite its long tradition of state-run broadcasting, France "has been, since the 1980s, at the forefront in redefining the relationship between electronic cultural media and the European state" (1992: 261). Miller's analysis highlights the contradictions of the Socialist government's 1981 decision to legalize *radio locales* – unlicensed broadcasters (sometimes referred to as "pirate" broadcasters) serving the interests of young people, cultural minorities, and others whose interests were unmet by the rather staid programming offered by state-run radio.

In legalizing these local stations, the Mitterrand government put an end to the labor-intensive, time-consuming, and costly jamming and enforcement efforts that frustrated grassroots efforts to produce lively, relevant radio for local populations. As a result, deregulation opened up the broadcasting landscape to scores of community-minded broadcasters, what would become known as *radio libres*. However, this same legislation prompted a similar explosion of commercially driven stations, commonly referred to as *radio privée*. Shortsighted and ill-advised restrictions on the operation of *radio libres* coupled with inadequate funding mechanisms undermined the development of France's nascent community radio sector. In short order, the *radio libres* were unable to compete with private concerns that quickly consolidated their holdings and began to form regional and national commercial networks. As James concludes, "Through liberalization French radio has quickly and nearly completely become dominated by North American-style commercial networks" (272).

With the recent passage of the Communication Bill into law – thanks in large measure to the persistent lobbying efforts and policy analyses conducted by the Community Media Association (CMA) – the situation in the United Kingdom is more promising. Following years of incremental measures – including a number of cable radio experiments, the introduction of local BBC outlets and Independent Local Radio (ILR), and the establishment of restricted service licenses (RSLs) – the government's latest Communication White Paper (UK 2000) encouraged regulators and community media activists to develop a framework for promoting and supporting community broadcasting.[2]

Over the past several years, RSLs and other "experiments" have had good results. The success of operations such as Wear FM, Tynesound Radio, and more recently, Smethwick Sound is encouraging inasmuch as they demonstrate a keen and broad-based interest in community radio. Equally important, the so-called "access radio" pilot program has demonstrated the vital role community radio can play in the lives of immigrant and diasporic communities throughout the United Kingdom. For example, Me FM, which bills itself as Aberdeen's "first and only" multi-ethnic community radio station, provided a unique opportunity for African and Caribbean groups to use radio for purposes of community communication in an area beset with racial tension and ethnic rivalries.

Similarly, Radio Fiza serves the growing South Asian community of Nottingham. Under the terms of its one-year experimental license, Radio Fiza operates as a frequency-sharing arrangement between two local concerns: the Asian Women's Project Ltd and the Karimia Institute. Both groups feature local and community news, current affairs, phone-in discussions, as well as a variety of cultural programs, including music, poetry, and spoken word in Urdu, Hindi, Mirpuri, Gujarati, as well as English. According to the CMA website, Radio Fiza is the first of three Access Radio licensees providing services specifically for Asian ethnic groups in the UK. It remains to be seen, however, if these new regulatory provisions and funding mechanisms can ensure the long-term viability of community broadcasting in the UK.

The development of community radio in Ireland may offer a note of encouragement in this regard. Not unlike the English experience, pirate stations were commonplace throughout Ireland in the 1960s and 1970s.[3] Following years of organizing efforts, community radio enthusiasts managed to persuade the Independent Radio and Television Commission (IRTC) to use the guidelines set forth by the World Association of

Community Radio Broadcasters (AMARC) as a reference for defining, establishing, and regulating an Irish community radio sector.[4] This development promises to ensure community radio's long-term viability in Ireland.

In other parts of the world, however, deregulation has done little more than weaken already fragile state-run monopoly broadcasters. India, the world's most populous democracy, provides a dramatic case in point. Ever since the government "liberalized" its communication policy in 1999, the once dominant All India Radio (AIR) must now share the airwaves with commercial broadcasters. On one hand, these commercial broadcasters provide much needed relief from a highly centralized broadcast service that had grown increasingly irrelevant to listeners. Indeed, in its capacity as a state-run monopoly, AIR seldom exercised editorial independence, effectively serving as a mouthpiece for the national government. On the other hand, under the terms of license agreements private broadcasters are prohibited from operating news channels. In this way, government regulations encourage commercial stations to broadcast a steady diet of music and entertainment programming augmented by little more than traffic reports and weather forecasts. In sum, India's regulatory framework fails to leverage the medium's capacity to provide useful and relevant news and information for an ethnically and linguistically diverse population.

Observing this uneven development, journalist Fredrick Noronha writes, "India has only so far developed its commercial-urban broadcast facilities, while ignoring its public service, community, educational and development broadcast networks" (1999). Indeed, India's initial broadcast reform measures failed to even mention community radio. Moreover, by demanding exorbitant license fees, the new regulatory scheme favors entrenched media interests, most notably India's successful newspaper publishers, and international investors, effectively shutting out non-profit groups and small business owners alike.

Despite the Indian government's staunch refusal to surrender its control over news and information programming or to promote locally relevant development communication, a handful of community-oriented projects have taken shape. The Bangalore-based VOICES, a not-for-profit development organization, lobbies on behalf of community and development radio initiatives. These efforts have had moderate success insofar as community groups, such as Radio Ujjas in western India, can now purchase airtime over the state-run service to broadcast programming produced by, for, and about the people of Kutch, an isolated region not far from the Pakistani border (Kennedy 2003). Organized under the auspices of Kutch Mahila Vikas Sangathan (KMVS), a rural women's group, and working alongside media professionals, Radio Ujjas trains local women how to conduct interviews, create news reports, and produce radio programs using minidisk recorders and computer-based editing tools.

Over the past three years, Radio Ujjas has expanded its programming considerably. What began as a soap opera, a form that allowed producers to slyly circumvent AIR's content restrictions, has evolved into a magazine program featuring investigative reports, travelogues, folk music, and, of course, the much beloved soap. All told, then, the results have been impressive. Indeed, despite its grassroots sensibility, by transmitting via AIR local facilities, Radio Ujjas reaches nearly a million listeners – an enviable audience for any community broadcaster. Equally important, the broadcast has had a palpable effect on the quality of life of workers, farmers, and fishermen throughout the region. For example, investigative reports, known as "Parda Faash" (literally "lifting the veil"), have helped villagers win significant concessions from local landowners and other elites.

Despite the success of these rural initiatives, however, community radio remains a cipher among Indian politicians and media regulators. At the level of policy making, then, we can detect the global in the local. As long-time community media advocate Peter Lewis observed some years ago, the struggle for communicative democracy at the local level reflects the realities of a global political economy increasingly dominated by transnational media corporations:

> The complaint of Third World countries about the unjust effects of allowing information to be at the mercy of the 'free play' of market forces – in other words serving the interests of rich and powerful nations and transnational conglomerates – is exactly mirrored at the level at which community radio operates in places where, in Western societies, marginalized groups have an inadequate share of resources. There is more than a likeness between the arguments of community media proponents and those supporting the New World Information Order. Both need each other's perspectives. The battle line against the corrupting power of multinational commercial interests is a continuous one, and if the battle is lost on the local level, it will have been in vain for regulatory authorities to impose quotas in national channels or attempt to create cultural 'tariff barriers' across regions.
>
> (Lewis 1984: 148)

Sponsoring the McBride Report and endorsing calls for the New World Information and Communication Order (NWICO), UNESCO sought to influence global communication policy at precisely the moment when Western governments embarked upon a new deregulatory regime. Although UNESCO's efficacy on this score is debatable, the international development organization and other NGOs nonetheless recognize community radio's value for preserving local cultural autonomy, encouraging sustainable development, and promoting participatory democracy.

Planet television

While many scholars identify participatory film and television production with the Canadian *Challenge for Change* program, Shelia James (1990a, 1990b) makes a convincing argument that this approach has its origins in the work of the iconoclastic Soviet filmmaker Dziga Vertov. James traces the innovative practices associated with various "subject-centered" documentary traditions – John Grierson's British Documentary School, Jean Rouch's anthropological films, the direct cinema of Robert Drew, D. A. Pennebaker, and Richard Leacock, and the participatory film and video making of Colin Low, Bonnie Klein, Dorothy Hénaut, and others associated with the National Film Board of Canada's *Challenge for Change* – directly to Vertov's theory and practice.

Specifically, Vertov's notion of Kino Pravda, literally "film truth," rested on an iterative process of film making in which the subjects of a film project contribute to its production. To that end, Vertov's agit prop film train brought the production and exhibition apparatus directly to the people in a concerted effort to first, demystify the medium, and then to deploy it as an occasion for discussion, deliberation, and, ultimately, action.

> Films, lectures, skits and shows with accompanying discussions occurred in every conceivable place where a community could gather and films be seen by day and night: in city movie theaters, large store windows, from rooftops, on sheets hung in the street, at railway stations, on river banks, in docks and fields, in mobile cinemas and in *agitpunkti* (purpose-built community centres).
>
> (James 1990a: 112–113)

These insights provide a fruitful vantage point from which to examine the impulses behind community television and participatory video initiatives across the globe. Indeed, the successful deployment of participatory video production practices and techniques for development purposes across Latin America, Africa, and Asia bears more than a striking resemblance to Vertov's methods and practices (FTP 1999/2000). And, as we shall see in Chapter 4, this tradition of participatory video making and community-based media training is likewise evident in Downtown Community Television's ongoing efforts to bring television production and exhibition directly to the people.

All of which is to underscore Vertov's keen appreciation for the moving picture's facility in mobilizing people, organizing collective action, and building community. Viewed from this longer historical perspective, then, the contemporary community television movement shares with various documentary traditions – agit prop, cinema verité, and the social issues documentary – the impetus to use film and other visual media for purposes of social animation and community development. We can detect these influences in the celebrated community-action film and television projects championed by the National Film Board (NFB) of Canada, especially in what has become known in the participatory and development communication literature as "the Fogo Process" (Williamson 1991).

In 1967, the NFB undertook one of the earliest and best-known efforts to democratize television production. As part of the experimental broadcast television series *Challenge for Change*, The Fogo Island project brought the subjects of a television documentary into a new, collaborative relationship with the filmmakers. Embracing and elaborating upon the tradition of the issue-oriented, advocacy filmmaking championed by John Grierson, *Challenge for Change* undertook the ambitious, if not entirely unprecedented task of systematically involving the subjects of their films throughout the production process. To that end, *Challenge for Change* senior producer Colin Low and his crews invited Fogo Island residents to contribute story ideas, screen and comment on rushes, and collaborate on editorial decisions. Thus, the producers of *Challenge for Change* sought to use film not merely to document the everyday, lived experience of island residents, but also as a catalyst for social change.

Like other depressed, rural communities throughout Canada, Fogo Island inhabitants faced formidable social and economic hardships. Located some ten miles off the coast of Newfoundland, Fogo Island, "like Newfoundland itself, was isolated from without. Again, like Newfoundland, as a whole, Fogo was isolated within itself. Fewer than five thousand people lived on the Island, but they lived sealed off from one another by religion and background in ten tiny settlements" (Engelman 1990: 8). Throughout the 1950s and 1960s, large-scale commercial fishing interests threatened the traditional way of life Fogo Islanders had known for well over 300 years.

The rapid decline of the local fishing industry in and around Fogo Island had a devastating impact on the lives of island residents: over half of the island's population was receiving some form of government assistance and many long time residents fled the island in search of economic opportunity on the Canadian mainland. The Fogo community was no longer considered economically viable and the provincial central planning authority decided to abandon the island. Government plans included the relocation of the remaining island inhabitants. The economic depression suffered by island residents soon turned to collective despondency.

Not surprisingly, then, the filmmaking process uncovered deep resentment toward the government's decision. In doing so, the process fostered a dialogue between the islanders that resulted in definitive plans to revitalize the local economy. Thus, the Fogo Process gave island residents a vehicle to articulate their concerns and formulate solutions. Moreover, the Fogo Island films served as an occasion for local residents to exhort the provincial government to reconsider its plans: "The Fogo films had a direct impact on the island's negotiations with government officials on the mainland. For example, past efforts to convince authorities to establish a cooperative fish-processing plant had failed. Now the Fogo films were sent to the provincial government to make the case for the cooperative. Through film, fishermen were talking to cabinet ministers" (Engelman 1996: 226–227). As a result, the planned relocation efforts were scrapped in favor of economic restructuring.

Initially conceived in terms of a traditional broadcast documentary, the Fogo Island project evolved into the production of twenty-eight short films, focusing on discrete events, specific issues, or particular members of the Fogo Island community. For instance, some of these "modules," as they came to be known, featured islanders' views and perspectives on the fishing industry, their relationship with local, provincial, and federal government, the location of the local high school, and gender issues; others portrayed the island's rich cultural traditions: house parties, step dancing, storytelling, and the like. "What emerged in the totality of the modules was a holistic view of life on Fogo Island as perceived by the people themselves" (Williamson 1991: 272). In essence, the films were less about the people of Fogo Island per se, than a resource for community communication within and between Fogo Islanders. As Ralph Engelman (1996: 226) notes, "The process by which the films were made and screened was central to their impact on the lives of the islanders. Group viewings organized all over the island fostered dialogue within an isolated, divided population. The films and discussions heightened the awareness of the people that they shared common problems and strengthened their collective identity as Fogo Islanders."

Perhaps to put too fine a point on it, as finished products the films themselves were secondary to the process of communication the films engendered among the local population and with government officials. The emphasis on process rather than product would become a hallmark of the *Challenge for Change* program's subsequent work. In particular, the participatory video techniques employed by Bonnie Klein and Dorothy Hénaut helped usher in an era of community-action video that continues

to exert considerable influence on the effort to democratize television production, exhibition, and distribution across North America – and indeed
around the world (Gillespie 1975).

The *Challenge for Change* program's innovation practices migrated to
the United States in the person of George Stoney, often referred to as
the "father of public access television." Stoney began his career working in the rural South as part of the New Deal. Through his training as
a journalist and educational filmmaker, Stoney came to appreciate media's role in facilitating a critical dialogue between government officials
and local communities. His use of still photographs, film, and radio at
public meetings helped him publicize and gain local acceptance of federal programs that were often met with suspicion and stiff resistance.
Equally important, Stoney understood the value of letting people speak
for themselves through the media. The use of media to address local
issues and concerns and to promote the exchange of perspectives and
ideas pervades Stoney's work as filmmaker and public access advocate
(Boyle 1999; Jackson 1999). Today, George Stoney sits on the board of
directors of Manhattan Neighborhood Network (MNN) – the borough of
Manhattan's public access organization – and his philosophy is reflected
in MNN's outreach and neighborhood organizing efforts. His influence
on the history and character of public access television in Manhattan is
inestimable.

Shortly upon his return to the United States in 1970, following a
successful term as guest executive producer of the *Challenge for Change*
program, Stoney and his colleague, Canadian documentary filmmaker
Red Burns, established the Alternative Media Center (AMC) in New
York City. Stoney's community organizing skills complemented Burns's
fund-raising prowess. In short order, Burns secured a three-year grant of
$250,000 from the John and Mary R. Markle Foundation to support their
efforts. Housed on Bleeker Street in Greenwich Village, the Alternative
Media Center at New York University began its efforts "to inform and
educate people who are becoming increasingly confused by the integration of new technologies into their lives; to provide a basis upon which
people can control these vital information resources . . . and to increase
communication among diverse groups of people" (Engelman 1996: 248).
Thus, the AMC's goals were twofold: to educate the public about the significance of these technologies; and to promote the use of the new media
to facilitate intercultural communication.

The Alternative Media Center's legacy rests upon its successful adaptation of the *Challenge for Change* model of participatory media from
Canada's public service broadcasting milieu into the privatized communications environment of the United States. Like the Canadian project,

the Alternative Media Center gave people the means to produce their own videotapes. Through the Center, individual citizens and local community groups became active participants in the production and dissemination of television programming by, for, and about themselves. Moreover, the Center sought to end the isolation of individuated television viewing at home through public screenings at the AMC and around the city. In so doing, the AMC sought to raise the consciousness of local individuals and groups and promote social action by fostering a critical dialogue within and between community members.

Crucially, the Alternative Media Center provided a meeting ground where access enthusiasts, independent film and video makers, and non-profit groups could share their experiences, network with likeminded individuals and groups, and develop strategies to support their goals. The AMC produced demonstration tapes highlighting portable video production potential to facilitate communication within the local community. In addition, the Center provided the technical resources and logistical support for the production and dissemination of community programming on a local, regional, and national level. To that end, one of the AMC's primary strategies was to train facilitators who would then fan out across the country and help organize community access centers. Over the next five years, the Alternative Media Center became "the focal point of the community television movement in the United States by channeling the efforts of the disparate constituencies interested in public access on cable television" (Engelman 1996: 235). In this respect, the AMC helped mediate the rather profound differences within the early access movement in order to shape a new means of public communication.

As media activists in the so-called industrial democracies looked for models of locally oriented, participatory television, they began to emulate, refine, and particularize the so-called "public access model" common to North America. Among the more innovative access television services in Europe, for instance, is local television in Amsterdam. Like the pirate radio operators that helped promote community radio in the Netherlands and across much of Western Europe, public access television in Amsterdam owes its existence in no small measure to so-called "hackers" who, throughout the late 1970s, made use of empty channels on the country's emerging cable television service.

Constructed ostensibly to improve the reception of national television signals, visual artists, punks, pornographers, and others brought an avant-garde aesthetic to cable television which, despite its illegal status, nonetheless proved enormously popular with cable television viewers. As cable companies developed technological solutions for dealing with video hackers, demand for community access channels and services grew more vocal. These efforts helped influence policy decisions, ultimately leading to regulations with explicit public access provisions.

Amsterdam's "open channel" – the appellation used across Europe for public or community access television – remains quite distinctive, due in large part to the spirited, anarchic, and aesthetically adventurous fare first propagated by local hackers. For instance, Hokesteen Live, a weekly, 16-hour live television event, features an assortment of interviews, video art, performance pieces, and late night/early morning viewer phone-ins (Smits and Marroquin 2000). Salto, the organization charged with facilitating the open channel, retains the spirit of the early hackers by accommodating and supporting new producers and especially cutting-edge and experimental television of a sort quite uncommon even by public access television standards.

What is common among Europe's Open Channel services is the popular interest in locally oriented, participatory television among diverse publics: migrants, artists, independent video makers, students, workers, and even televangelists. Despite an explosion of interest in community television – fueled in part by the diffusion of small format video production equipment and cable television's "channels of abundance" – the Open Channel or Public Access model faces considerable obstacles, primarily in the form of privatization and the attendant diminution of public funds to support these community-oriented institutions and services.

In a move designed to legitimate and justify continued public financing for community access television, Offenen Kanal (Open Channel) in Hamburg, Germany, for instance, has shifted its emphasis in recent years. Once operating from the "first come, first serve" philosophy of access television associated with North America, Open Channel has adopted a practice of thematic programming in an effort to make its resources, facilities, and programming more relevant to what Leonhard Hansen (2000) describes as an "unaffiliated public." These outreach efforts help to enlarge as well as diversify the ranks of community television producers, thereby yielding television programs that vividly reflect Western Europe's multicultural dynamics.

Access advocates across North America have likewise begun to re-examine the philosophical underpinning of public access that places a premium on individual free speech rights in favor of a strategy predicated on community building. No longer satisfied with providing a "content neutral" approach to the provision of television production equipment and distribution services, several influential access television advocates across the United States promote a new vision of the access center as a resource for nurturing the civic, social, and cultural life of local communities.

Community television pioneers such as George Stoney (2001) champion access television's ability to create a politically engaged public, set the local agenda, analyze community issues and problems, and actively pursue community-based solutions. Long-time community television proponent Bob Devine (2000), puts it this way: "Our community-building efforts at MATA (Milwaukee Access Telecommunications Authority) were aimed at moving beyond the simple facilitation of first-come/first-served access by initiating and facilitating a set of "animations" aimed at bringing various constituents together in addressing the most pressing issues in our community." Thus, access centers across the United States are reevaluating the long cherished "first come, first served" philosophy that characterized access television in North America for the better part of a quarter century.

Changes in the Canadian community television sector are likewise underway. However, as community television advocate Cathy Edwards observes, the impetus behind this stems not so much from thoughtful reconsideration of access television's philosophical foundation as from the steady erosion of regulatory policies that once supported community television initiatives, as well as the attendant privatization and consolidation of local, national, and international media systems. These changes threaten the very survival of Canada's once vibrant community access television sector.

For example, in response to the Canadian Radio-Television and Telecommunications Commission's (CRTC) decision to lift longstanding license requirements that cable operators provide funding and resources to support a community television channel, Rogers Cable of Vancouver closed three of its four neighborhood production facilities. In 2001, Shaw Cable, who purchased the cable system from Rogers, eliminated all community-produced programming from its access channel and replaced it with staff-produced material. As long-time cable advocate Kim Goldberg notes, Shaw's plan effectively precludes substantive community involvement in television production and neutralizes the social, political, and cultural relevance of community access channels across Canada. "It's a format Shaw is implementing nationally – a mind-numbing cross between community TV and McDonalds's, barfing out a nightly box of televised tidbits" (Goldberg 2001: 9).

Working with the various constituencies in the city's community media sector, most notably the Community Media Education Society (CMES), the Indigenous Media Arts Group, and United Native Nations, community television advocates established the Independent Community Television Cooperative (ICTV). Modeled in some fashion after Vancouver's exceptional community broadcaster, Co-op Radio, the ICTV plans to construct and operate a low-power, community-run broadcast television outlet. In doing so, ICTV hopes to launch a community television service for Vancouver that rivals other likeminded grassroots television initiatives making use of low-power terrestrial transmissions.

For example, located on the outskirts of Paris, Telebocal operates what might best be described as a full-service neighborhood media arts center. A focus of community activity, Telebocal operates as a low-power TV station and media training facility in a shared space with a theater company and photo gallery. Established in the mid-1990s by local film and video enthusiasts, Telebocal routinely screens its work throughout the neighborhood – at local bars and cafes, the celebrated Goumen Bis, an abandoned building that serves as the neighborhood cultural center, and, on some occasions, via low-power terrestrial broadcasts.

One of several "telelocals" operating in France during the 1990s, Telebocal is part of Media Libre, a national coalition of noncommercial media artists and producers who have had a measure of success lobbying local authorities and national regulators regarding the establishment of a community television sector, something akin to the Open Channel system described above. Sadly, factionalism within the Media Libre threatens to undermine the group's efficacy and its influence with policy makers and regulatory agencies.

On one hand, some members of Media Libre advocate a national public access service, while others, most notably and vocally, perhaps, Telebocal, seek to retain their local orientation and autonomy. As Jeff Hansell (2000) observes, despite the infighting within France's community television movement, Telebocal enjoys a unique position within the global community media sector: a grassroots arts and cultural organization, Telebocal is a "player" in local as well as national communication policy making.

Due to the slow and uneven development of cable television, community television advocates in the United Kingdom and Australia have likewise taken to the airwaves. As Nick Hunt (n.d.) reminds us, television in the UK developed in the context of a well-established national structure. As a result, "the question of local television and its role in the community is therefore relatively new. Not that the democratic concerns of community for self-representation have been ignored; the demands for community access have been focused on national television." The introduction of cable television offered the potential to build a local television sector to complement the existing national broadcasting services.

Operating under the direction of the Home Office,[5] the UK's early experiments with community access television were confounded by content restrictions that called for "neutrality" and "impartiality" – effectively depoliticizing community access cable television (Bibby, Denford, and Cross 1979). Echoing the objections of community television workers and access television advocates, a report issued by the Sheffield TV Group argued that the structural constraints regarding licensing, facilities, and financing would likewise inhibit the growth and development of community television in the UK. As Nick Hunt concludes, given the impartiality requirements noted above "this would be especially the case for 'committed material' that challenged local authorities, promoted collective action or agitated for social change" (Hunt n.d.).

As we shall see, this tension between "neutrality" on one hand and "advocacy" and "committed" media on the other informs the day-to-day operation and program production philosophy of each of the case studies to follow. Whilst WFHB (Chapter 3) adheres to the notion of neutrality, both Downtown Community Television (Chapter 4) and *Street Feat* (Chapter 5) embrace their roles as advocates for disenfranchised individuals and groups and enthusiastically cultivate the production, distribution, and exhibition of "committed material." For its part, by publishing material from government sources, business and commercial interests, as well as community groups, activists, and ethnic communities, VICNET (Chapter 6) achieves a rather enviable balance to this central problematic of community media.

Not surprisingly, then, given the content restrictions and structural constraints facing the UK's cable community access experiments of the 1970s, most of these operations, including Milton Keyne's Channel 40 and the Bristol Channel, ended their community access television operations by the end of the decade. Only Swindon Viewpoint, one of the subjects of Bibby, Denford, and Cross's critique of community television in Britain, remains operational. In the intervening years, both BBC and ITV introduced various community access schemes, some of which have been quite successful in leveraging the advent of small-format equipment and growing interest in participatory video (Dovey 1995).

As media activist and producer Tony Dowmunt (2001) notes, innovative and participatory program production schemes such as the BBC's Community Programme Unit and the Independent Film and Video Department at Channel 4 have made significant contributions to the development of the so-called "video diary" genre of subjective television, thereby providing what he describes as a "new tone of voice" in television. Regardless of the critical and popular success of these participatory production schemes, however, the aforementioned CMA continues to lobby and advocate for the establishment of a robust community broadcasting sector across the UK.

Community television advocates in Australia have likewise taken to the airwaves, albeit under somewhat dissimilar circumstances and with different results. Anxious to make use of television for purposes of community communication, advocates lobbied state and federal regulators to support locally oriented, participatory television in a fashion not unlike provisions for community radio. Until quite recently, then, the Australian community media sector was curiously out of balance. That is to say, Australia boasts one of the most vibrant and well-organized community radio sectors in the world (Meadows and Molnar 2002). By contrast, however, community television in Australia suffers dramatic underdevelopment. In 1993, after years of lobbying, agitation, legal action, and "test transmissions" on restricted licenses, the Australian government made provisions for full-time permanent community television licenses. Communities across the country are now eligible to apply for community television licenses over UHF-31.

The Australian focus on terrestrial broadcasting coupled with provisions that allow non-profit community broadcasters to raise revenue through various sources, including program sponsorship and advertisements, suggests that the emerging sector may soon be a viable concern. That said, the long-term future of Australian community television remains somewhat uncertain, in light of uncertainties surrounding the specifics for community television's transition from analog to digital terrestrial broadcasting (Davey 2001).

In contrast to the Australian solution and most other low-power community television initiatives, Community Tele Vision (CTV) Fiji claims to be the only community broadcaster operating on the VHF band. Financial support for the project comes from a variety of sources; some close to home, others from a world away. Although CTV's license prohibits commercial sponsorship, local residents and business owners are generous supporters. Conversely, international aid organizations including World Association of Christian Communication (WACC), the Canada Fund, and UNESCO provide additional support. Following several successful years of broadcasting and youth education programs, the Japanese Embassy awarded CTV a sorely needed equipment grant.

With transmission facilities in the capital city, Suva, and repeaters on the island's north end, CTV reaches well over 90,000 viewers with locally produced news, information, and cultural fare. Phone-in programs are among the most popular of CTV offerings. Volunteers produce the bulk of CTV's programs. In stark contrast, then, to the imported programming from New Zealand and the United States aired on Fiji's commercial service, Fiji One, and any number of Western satellite television channels available throughout the Pacific Rim, CTV's work emphasizes local cultural traditions and values. Like Jon Alpert and Keiko Tsuno, whose community media center Downtown Community Television is the subject of Chapter 4, John Yates and his wife Regina work closely with at-risk youth by providing them with job training, employment opportunities, and a unique opportunity to create television that is meaningful and relevant to their everyday lives.

An analogous global dynamic is at work in the Russian hinterlands. Located in the city of Tomsk, what locals refer to as the "Siberian Athens," Tomsk TV2 operates "to surmount the history of official misinformation [and] fashion a new model of independent, critical reporting" in the post-Soviet era (Park 2000: 20). In partial fulfillment of this mission, the station established the Tomsk Community TV School, to provide young people with technical training and to give them an opportunity to participate in program production and information dissemination. Unlike the other five broadcasters serving the West-Siberian Plain, the community TV school is the only television service featuring locally produced, non-commercial programming.

Tomsk Community Television School receives substantial financial support from a number of international sources, most notably the United States Agency for International Development (USAID) and Internews Network, an international non-profit organization that supports independent journalism in so-called "emerging democracies." A collaborative effort between TV2's Arkardy Mayofis and independent journalist Jon Alpert, Tomsk Community TV School is modeled after Alpert's Downtown Community Television (DCTV), the subject of Chapter 4.

In late 1996, two seasoned instructors from DCTV, Martin Lucas and Duncan Cameron, traveled to Tomsk and conducted a series of video production and post-production workshops for the fledgling media arts center. As part of DCTV's Global Exchange Program, a short time later three student producers from New York City traveled to Siberia to work alongside their Russian counterparts. Meanwhile, six Russian students made the long journey to DCTV's firehouse studios on Manhattan's Lower East Side to likewise collaborate on news stories and feature reports.

Over the years, these collaborative efforts have grown in size and scope, thanks in large part to the support of SPAN (Sustaining Partnerships in the Next Century), a collaborative effort of the aforementioned USAID and the International Research and Exchanges Board (IREX). Like other youth media initiatives, then, Tomsk Community TV School gives young people the opportunity to express themselves through television pictures and sound. Not only do these students gain valuable professional skills, equally important, they come to appreciate the dynamic role television plays in shaping individual and collective experience, identity, and consciousness.

This crucial, yet commonly under-appreciated aspect of community television is perhaps most forcefully articulated in Latin America's grassroots and popular video movements (Rodriguez 2001). Across the region, disparate groups including organized labor, indigenous peoples, social workers, political activists, religious leaders, and educators have embraced participatory video as a means to promote solidarity, agitate for social, economic, and political justice, preserve local cultural traditions, and otherwise create community.

In her overview of Latin American video initiatives, media critic Patricia Aufderheide notes that television has "played neither the liberating nor demonic role often assigned to new media technologies. It has, instead, often been used as a strategic tool, both on and off air, when used in conjunction with social organizing" (2000: 257). With considerable alacrity and ingenuity, then, disparate peoples throughout Latin America, from the slums of São Paulo, to the remote mountain tops of Bolivia, to the tribal villages along the Amazon, have articulated television with other social institutions, settings, and practices to better reflect their needs, protect their interests, and defend their way of life.

Despite new threats to communicative democracy across Latin America, this time not in the guise of repressive military dictatorships, but in the form of a regime of private ownership and corporate consolidation of communication systems, community-oriented television continues to be a dynamic site of political resistance, cultural renewal, and community organizing.

Word on the street

Likening contemporary street papers to earlier forms of dissident, underground, and alternative publications, Norma Fay Green (1998) calls our attention to the Salvation Army's *War Cry*. Providing food and shelter to the poor and needy of London's East End, the Salvation Army supported its charitable and reformist efforts in part through sales of the *War Cry*. First published in 1879, the *War Cry* proved an effective means of publicizing the corps' relief efforts, exposing deplorable conditions at factories and workhouses, and promoting its evangelical message.

In this last instance, the presence of Salvation Army "officers" and recent converts hawking copies of the *War Cry* on city streets was a particularly effective strategy. "Through street sales, the buying public came in deliberate contact with the disenfranchised who moved from the periphery and into the limelight, if only momentarily" (Green 1998: 35).

Unlike conventional transactions between news sellers and the reading public, then, sales of the *War Cry* were explicitly designed to call attention to the plight of the poor and needy. By employing the homeless and working poor to distribute their publications, street papers use this same strategy – what the editors of *Street Feat* (Chapter 5) describe as "a little stone in your shoe" – to force into consciousness the problems of unemployment, hunger, and homelessness.

The *Hobo News* represents yet another important precursor of the street newspaper. Despite what historian Lynne Adrian (1998) describes as the paper's "curious and uneven" publication record, the parallels between the *Hobo News* and street papers are striking as well as instructive. Sponsored by James Eads How, whose inherited wealth served to motivate as well as enable his philanthropic efforts, including the founding of the International Brotherhood Welfare Association (IBWA), the *Hobo News* (1915–1930) was a publication of, by, and for migratory workers, so-called "hoboes."

Although the *Hobo News* featured writing from any number of well-known labor organizers, anarchists, socialists, and members of the Industrial Workers of the World (IWW), the paper's commitment to reader participation encouraged hoboes to contribute work of their own, including oral histories, travelogues, illustrations, poetry, and fiction. Street newspapers likewise encourage contributions from the homeless and the working poor, as well as activists, policy analysts, and others whose lives and experiences are informed by social, economic, and political marginalization.

Moreover, just as the *Hobo News* tapped into existing networks of migratory workers, union organizers, and others, so too street papers rely upon and expand the formal and informal relationships that exist between the homeless, the unemployed, and the working poor, and the shelter managers, health care workers, community activists, and others who work on their behalf. In this light, both the *Hobo News* and contemporary street papers share a commitment to organizing various constituencies and mobilizing their readership while simultaneously seeking to publicize their efforts, and their plight, to wider publics. Whilst this emphasis on "consciousness raising" is common to community media in general, articulating the correspondence between symbolic and material relations of power in such a forceful and provocative fashion is unique to the street paper.

Shortly after the death of its principal benefactor, James Eads How, the original *Hobo News* stopped publication in 1930. Four years later, however, a likeminded publication, operating under the same name, emerged in New York City under the direction of Pat Mulkern (Pager

1949). Although the relationship between the two publications is uncertain, Mulkern's effort is clearly part of the tradition of self-publication evident in today's street papers.

Monthly editions of Mulkern's *Hobo News*, sold for ten cents on New York City street corners, featured cartoons, poems, news items, and commentary written by freelancers, would-be artists and writers, and not a few prison inmates. In contrast, then, to the vast majority of "competing" publications that appealed primarily to middle class sensibilities, the *Hobo News* described, examined, and celebrated the working class and hobo lifestyles prevalent in America during the first half of the twentieth century. This focus on the everyday lived experience of hoboes – including tips on traveling cross country via freight trains or broadsides against the police and penal system – is remarkably similar to the journalistic approach taken by the contemporary street paper inasmuch as these publications feature the views, perspectives, and opinions of community members whose lives are paradoxically quite public, yet largely unknown and often misunderstood.

Mulkern, himself a hobo, demonstrated considerable editorial acumen, counseling his contributors to write material that would appeal to a reader's appreciation for a simple, direct prose style. This same approach is the hallmark of the contemporary street newspaper. As we shall see, street papers speak with a native eloquence to the conditions of unemployment, poverty, and economic injustice increasingly common in post-industrialized societies, so-called emerging democracies, and across the developing world (Garafola 1999; van Lier 1999).

Thus, as an example of a self-published monthly periodical committed to documenting the lives and experience of a marginalized class, the *Hobo News*, in all its guises, provides important insight into the role newspaper publication plays in creating a forum in which the disenfranchised can articulate their concerns, coordinate their efforts, and forge a coherent, collective identity.

Furthermore, the *Hobo News* not only gives us a window into the everyday lived experience of migratory workers, but also provides unique perspective into "the complex relationship between migratory workers, their organizations, and general working-class organizations" (Adrian 1998: 114). In a similar vein, close readings of street newspapers illuminate the relations within and among disenfranchised people and the social service, humanitarian organizations, and governmental bureaucracies they deal with on a regular basis. These perspectives likewise bring into sharp relief tensions within the street paper movement, especially the competing logics of charity, activism, and entrepreneurialism, which inform disparate street paper initiatives.

The prototype of contemporary street publications found across North America and throughout much of Europe, New York City's *Street News*, provides important clues for appreciating the growth and development of the street paper movement. Billing itself as "America's motivational non-profit newspaper," *Street News* offered vendors a modest but nonetheless viable alternative to panhandling. In doing so, *Street News* sought to provide a measure of self-sufficiency for the city's homeless and unemployed.

Hawking the paper on street corners and in subway stations throughout the city, vendors would keep 50 cents for every 75-cent paper they sold. The remaining money was split between covering the costs associated with the paper's operational expenses and a general "apartment fund." This money was used to help vendors save towards a deposit on accommodation. Early reports indicated that as many as seventy-five vendors used their savings to get off the streets or out of the city's notoriously grim shelters, and into their own apartments (Jacobs 1990). With a growing number of success stories to its credit *Street News* soon became a hit with readers and the local business community (McAuley 1990).

Initially published twice a month, *Street News* ran news stories and commentary on the city's lack of affordable housing, rising unemployment, substance abuse, and a growing intolerance for homeless people among policy makers, police officers, and the general public. This material publicized, in stark, dramatic, and often-unsettling terms, the living conditions of the city's homeless. In doing so, *Street News* explored issues like the deterioration of social service programs or the affordable housing crisis that other local media outlets persistently overlooked or ignored.

In addition, early editions of *Street News* featured job listings, some prose and poetry written by homeless people, and opinion pieces by local celebrities. Although celebrity-penned pieces on topics like balancing work and family helped to attract middle class readers, as well as considerable media attention, to the new publication, over time news and commentary written by and about homeless people became the paper's principal focus.

Despite auspicious beginnings, *Street News* soon fell on hard times. Street Aid, the non-profit organization that published *Street News*, was the subject of complaints to the Better Business Bureau regarding its financing and bookkeeping procedures (Hemphill 1990; Teltsch 1990). Soon thereafter, the paper's founder, street musician Hutchinson Persons, became the target of an investigation by the state attorney general. Allegations of mismanagement and subsequent drops in sales and advertising revenue were compounded by the departure of key staff and editorial board members. These events dealt *Street News* a series of blows from which the fledgling publication never fully recovered.[6]

Street News' mercurial relationship with vendors, contributors, readers, and city law enforcement officials is not unique. Chicago's *StreetWise* is a case in point. Founded by Judd Lofchie, a local lawyer and social activist whose non-profit organization, People Fighting Hunger, provided an institutional base for the fledgling publication, *StreetWise* quickly established itself as one of the nation's premier street publications, boasting a monthly circulation of well over 120,000 (Tyson 1999: 3).

When it began publishing in 1992, *StreetWise* operated as an advocacy newspaper for the homeless and working poor. To that end, *StreetWise* provided vendors, many of whom were unemployed or living on the street, with a modest living. In addition, *StreetWise* offered extensive job training as well as referral services that place vendors in drug and alcohol rehabilitation programs, high school equivalency classes, and job placement centers. Following the July 1995 shooting death of one of its vendors at the hands of a Chicago police officer, *StreetWise*'s advocacy took on a decidedly more radical tone. Over the next several months, *StreetWise* led direct action campaigns that pressured city politicians and local law enforcement to suspend the officer in question. The incident also sparked a series of investigative reports detailing changes in the city's legal system that effectively criminalized the homeless.

In recent years, however, the paper's critique of social injustice and economic disparities has been diluted in favor of advertiser-friendly content (Kharkar 2001). The change in the paper's philosophy and its deviation from advocacy journalism led to in-fighting between management, staff, and the vendors. According to some former staff members, editorial control now rests with the board of directors, who are more interested in profit making than with assisting the homeless. Indeed, the departure of a number of the paper's long-time staff and contributors indicates that the paper's progressive content is likely to evaporate. Increasingly, *StreetWise*'s content reflects the editorial board's interest in "toning down" its coverage of homelessness and providing greater coverage of arts and cultural news.

Whilst *StreetWise*'s emphasis has changed over time and its advocacy efforts have diminished, other street papers retain their brash, outspoken, and decidedly oppositional politics. Take San Francisco's *Street Sheet*, for example. Since 1989, *Street Sheet* has been the voice of the Coalition on Homelessness (COH) a grassroots advocacy group dedicated to finding community-based solutions to poverty and homelessness (COH n.d.). *Street Sheet*'s organizational culture reflects the perspectives of long-time Bay Area activists who recognized the strategic importance of communication to community organizing. That is to say, COH founders realized that no matter how thoughtful or persuasive a single advocate might be, without the backing of community service agencies and the people they serve, lone voices are rarely heard and seldom respected. On the other hand, when aid agencies or community service organizations operate without the input, counsel, and participation of their clients, they lose legitimacy with funding agencies, community leaders, and other support mechanisms. Thus, community outreach and participatory decision-making are the core principles guiding COH's efforts and the editorial approach taken by the volunteers and staff of *Street Sheet*.

Within months of its first publication, *Street Sheet* outgrew its original newsletter design and adopted a tabloid format to accommodate additional material. Like other street papers, *Street Sheet* provides a forum for homeless people to express themselves through essays, news reports, poems, and illustrations. In addition, *Street Sheet* does an enviable job of updating readers on a host of social, cultural, and political activities and features regular updates on legislative initiatives and policy deliberations that have a direct and immediate effect on the poor and disenfranchised. Unlike other street papers, *Street Sheet* staunchly defends its editorial independence by refusing advertising or government support. These prohibitions no doubt help explain the persistence of *Street Sheet*'s self-proclaimed "shit stirring editorial tone."

Street Sheet further distinguishes itself from other street publications in its relationship with vendors. While most street papers require vendors to purchase the papers they sell, *Street Sheet* is available to vendors at no charge. What's more, vendors keep all the proceeds from their labor, rather than a percentage of their total sales, as is common for most street publications. Finally, like few other street papers, *Street Sheet* does not require vendors to undergo training, wear badges, or enroll in social service programs in order to sell the paper. The results have been quite impressive. In 1993, *Street Sheet* recorded its one-millionth sale; in 1995, *Street Sheet* received an award from the Society of Professional Journalists, and *Street Sheet*'s investigative reports helped remove a corrupt administrator from a local service agency.

In the absence of consistent, let alone sympathetic press coverage of COH's advocacy and community organizing efforts, *Street Sheet* publicizes and lends credibility to community-based solutions to systemic and seemingly intractable societal problems. Equally important, *Street Sheet* reinvests currency into the long tradition of muckraking and advocacy journalism that, according to Paul Boden of the COH, corporate media "shun like the plague" (quoted in Messman 1999).

Corporate media figure prominently in the dramatic interest in a street paper movement that has taken on global dimensions (Harris 1999). As discussed in Chapter 1, media deregulation and the attendant privatization of communication systems have seriously undermined the character, conduct, and content of socio-political discourse. By narrowing the range of opinion and debate on public policy issues and uncritically accepting the supremacy of market-based solutions to social problems, corporate-controlled media are complicit in demonizing the poor while promoting a neo-liberal agenda that puts profits before people.

By contrast, then, street papers open up discursive space for the poor, homeless advocates, and others interested in promoting social and economic justice. Vancouver's *The Long Haul* publication is a case in point. Published by End Legislative Poverty (ELP), a coalition of local anti-poverty activists, *The Long Haul* helps put issues of economic justice on the political agenda. Several years ago, *The Long Haul* was instrumental in mobilizing public opinion in favor of increasing the minimum wage: a modest but nevertheless critical step toward reducing poverty. By bringing disparate constituencies together and providing a forum for activists, social service providers, the homeless, and the working poor to communicate with each other and with wider publics, *The Long Haul* helps articulate the anti-poverty movement throughout British Colombia.

This same dynamic is evident at the national and international level. In August 1996, representatives from twenty-six street papers across the United States and Canada met in Chicago to meet and discuss common strategies and concerns. There, conference participants from *La Quete* (Quebec), *Spare Change* (Boston), and *Real Change* (Seattle), among other street papers and affiliated organizations, including the US-based National Coalition on Homelessness, established the North American Street Newspaper Association (NASNA). Every summer since then, street paper publishers, editors, writers, and vendors gather to network, share resources, and learn about the particular conditions facing the homeless and working poor in various host cities.

These yearly meetings serve a number of important functions. First, they allow participating members to coordinate their efforts, formulate policy, and develop strategic plans while creating a sense of solidarity among participating members. Second, annual meetings feature workshops on the theory and practice of street publications. That is to say, while some workshops cover the "nuts and bolts" of newspaper production – writing, editing, layout, and the like – other sessions deal with the social practice of newspaper publication and address topics such as fostering a collaborative work environment, creating participatory governance structures, and placing the homeless in leadership positions throughout the community.

Finally, NASNA conferences give program participants an opportunity to draw local media attention to their efforts. For instance, at the 1998 meeting in Montreal, NASNA participants and representatives from Montreal's *L'Itineraire* held a press conference that received considerable media attention, culminating in an hour-long television interview featuring NASNA representatives. According to Eric Cimon of *L'Itineraire*, the Montreal street paper's participation in NASNA has given the local paper greater legitimacy throughout the city and especially with local media outlets. "Now when there's something happening related to homelessness, we're called" (NASNA 2000). Predictably, perhaps, not every encounter between NASNA and local media has been quite so cordial or as fruitful.

At the 2001 meeting in San Francisco, for example, NASNA helped organize a direct action campaign against two local newspapers, the *Chronicle* and the *Examiner*, in opposition to their coverage of homelessness in the Bay Area. Protesters claimed that both daily papers failed to provide adequate coverage of policy issues that directly affect the city's poor and homeless. Working with local community groups, homeless advocates, and members of San Francisco's own *Street Sheet*, NASNA drafted a series of demands calling for fair, accurate, and substantive coverage of homelessness and so-called economic redevelopment schemes. In addition, demonstrators demanded that both news organizations include the voice of the homeless and community organizers who challenge the city's forced relocation program, question downtown gentrification, and oppose city ordinances that criminalize homelessness.[7]

NASNA's inspiration comes from earlier, likeminded organizing efforts among Europe's emerging street paper sector. Established in 1994, under the auspices of the European General Assembly, the International Network of Street Newspapers (INSP) currently boasts participants from across Europe, including the Netherlands, Spain, Sweden, Austria, Germany, the Czech Republic, Greece, Russia, as well as members in South Africa, Australia, and South America. In 1997, the European Commission's temporary financial support for the INSP ended. Since that time, funding for the network's activities, including support for the organization's secretariat and newsletter, has been provided by the UK-based, *The Big Issue*, arguably the world's most successful and, as we shall see, somewhat controversial street paper.

Like its North American counterpart, the INSP coordinates collaborative efforts between participating members, including the design and distribution of a common cover used in observation of World Poverty Day (17 October), co-sponsoring journalism courses, conducted in association with Reuters News service, and providing technical, logistic, and financial support for new or struggling street papers. In this last instance, the INSP encourages member publications to work with NGOs around the world to help build an international street paper sector. For instance, in 1999, the Non-Profit Foundation partnered with *The Big Issue* in Scotland to embark upon an ambitious program to establish street papers across Central and Eastern Europe. Street paper workers in the United Kingdom and Hungary coordinated this regional effort known as No Borders.

One of the INSP's perennial concerns is to ensure the continued operation and long-term viability of the Russian street paper *The Depths*, based in St. Petersburg.[8] In addition to facing the usual constraints – inadequate facilities, lack of stable financial support, public indifference, and a fluid and volatile workforce – *The Depths* has made enemies in high places. According to *The Depths'* editor, Valeriy Sokolov, the paper brought the Russian government up on human rights violations before the United Nations (Harris 1999). Drawing upon the long history of dissident publications in the former Soviet Union, *The Depths'* unflinching and outspoken criticism of human rights violations has raised the ire of the authorities. The INSP provided financial support, on the order of £20,000, to keep *The Depths* from folding. Equally important, however, the moral support and political legitimacy attached to the INSP may have ensured the paper's survival.

Conversely, the prominence human rights issues received in *The Depths* and other street papers has politicized the INSP, particularly in terms of the organization's approach to overt political intervention in various national contexts. That is to say, when the INSP was established, its principal focus was on developing street papers as a "social business." The organization's emphasis was on jobs creation, capacity building, and networking. Increasingly, however, the INSP confronts a host of human rights issues related to the global traffic in migrant labor, guest workers, asylum seekers, war refugees, and others.

The vast movements of people across Europe and indeed throughout much of the world taxes local housing stock, places considerable strain on health care and other social services, and enflames animosities between disparate national, racial, ethnic, and religious groups. Moreover, national governments and local authorities have grown increasingly intolerant of immigrants. Unless or until they find more gainful employment, many recent immigrants come to work for street papers in their adopted homes, thereby generating some hostility between local populations and street newspapers. In defending its participating membership and their employees, the INSP asserts its commitment to the Universal Declaration of Human Rights. In doing so, the INSP plays an increasingly prominent role in articulating a global movement aimed at reducing poverty and promoting economic justice.

None of which is to suggest, however, that the street paper movement is monolithic, let alone harmonious. Since its inception in 1991, the afore-mentioned *The Big Issue* (TBI) has been the center of controversy within the street paper movement (Charlton 1998). Taking a page from New York City's *Street News*, Jon Bird and Gordon Roddick founded TBI with a grant from the Anita Roddick's Body Shop Foundation. Despite mod-est beginnings, London-based TBI soon took off and over the course of the next decade it was at the center of an "empire" of street papers across the globe.

From the outset, TBI's approach – glossy covers, a paid, professional writing staff, general interest features, celebrity news, advertisements for upscale products, and a modest, but regular column featuring work by homeless people – alienated street paper workers whose vision was more activist oriented, less entrepreneurial. The clash between these two posi-tions came to a head in 1998, when TBI launched a regional edition in Los Angeles (Boukhari 1999). Fearful that her far more modest *Making Change* newspaper in Santa Monica could never compete with the likes of TBI-Los Angeles, Jennifer Waggoner appealed to the NASNA for help. Despite good faith efforts to accommodate both the local street paper and the regional edition of TBI, neither party was completely content with a compromise solution reached between TBI and NASNA. Moreover, the agreement caused a rift between various factions within NASNA that remains a sore point for participating members.

Herein lies the fundamental tension within the street paper movement. For some, like Jon Bird, publisher of TBI, street papers are a business whereby the homeless and unemployed can earn a "respectable living" selling periodicals in streets, train stations, and other public spaces. This orientation is closest to the model Hutchinson Persons established with *Street News* in New York City. In retrospect, Persons' entrepreneurial fervor obscured the rather disingenuous notion that selling newspapers could eliminate poverty and that the problem of homelessness and un-employment was the fault of the individual, not a structural problem or a systemic failure.

For others, such as Timothy Harris, founder of Boston's *Spare Change* and, a few years later, *Real Change* in Seattle, street papers are politically progressive publications of news, information, and opinion that promote grassroots activism and are committed to altering the material and sym-bolic relations of power within their respective communities. All too often, however, dissident publications find themselves ghettoized by their own slavish adherence to ideological purity. That, or the writing is either too esoteric or too incomprehensible to be of much interest to the average reader. Carol Lloyd succinctly captures the ambivalence many people feel when reading street papers with a decidedly more radical approach to journalism: "It isn't the best place to find well-oiled prose or even logical arguments, but it is the only place where I can hear the voices – enraged, sad, incoherent and sometimes wise – of people who have nothing" (1998).

For these reasons, then, street papers attempt to strike a balance between what Harris describes as "readability" on one hand and progressive community activism on the other. As we have seen thus far, and will consider at greater length in the case studies to follow, local communities articulate communication technologies and communicative forms and practices to meet their particular and distinctive needs. *Hencho en Buenos Aires* (Made in Buenos Aires) Argentina's first street paper, is a case in point. Based on TBI, but responsive to local conditions, editor Patricia Merkin sees TBI in the same light as other forms of globalization (Moss 2000). Like McDonalds and Coca-Cola, these global institutions, practices, and artifacts are always already subject to local appropriation and interpretation.

With this caveat in mind, we conclude this whirlwind tour of community media around the world with a concise discussion of local articulations of computers and related technologies for purposes of community communication.

Community IRL

Howard Rheingold's *The Virtual Community* (1993) brought the phrase "cyberspace" out of the realm of science fiction and into the popular vernacular.[9] Rheingold's account of the growth and development of the WELL (Whole Earth 'Lectronic Link), an "online community" established over a commercial computer conferencing system, introduced readers to an array of esoteric concepts and curious acronyms – Computer-Mediated Communication (CMC), Bulletin-Board Systems (BBS), Multi-User Dungeons (MUDs), Internet Relay Channels (IRC), and the like. In doing so, Rheingold succinctly captured the ambivalence many people harbored about an emerging form of social interaction: networked computer communication.

On one hand, these technologies facilitate the establishment of community without propinquity – geographically separated people who nevertheless form "webs of personal relationships" through social intercourse conducted by means of telephone lines, modems, keyboards, and computer terminals (Rheingold 1993: 5). Likening these so-called virtual communities to ancient Athens, Rheingold suggests that electronic democracy would encourage a renaissance of reasoned, civic discourse, facilitate cooperative efforts and collective action, and help to keep government and elected officials accountable to their constituencies.

On the other hand, Rheingold notes how these same technologies exacerbate anxieties that already fragmented communities will become even more fractured and divisive. For some, the move toward virtual community signaled a retreat from physical, place-based communities – what some computer users blithely refer to as community "in real life" (IRL) – further alienating individuals from one another and the social, political, and cultural institutions of local communities. Moreover, computer-mediated communication threatens to widen the gap between information "haves and have-nots" and inspires a host of Orwellian fears about electronic surveillance and the loss of individual privacy.

The hopes and fears, anxieties and desires Rheingold articulates are manifest in an array of local initiatives with different names such as free-nets, civic networks, community networks, telecottages, public access networks, and community informatics. Despite variation in labeling these efforts, the impulse remains constant: the provision of computer and networked information resources and services to local populations (Morino 1994). As community network advocate Doug Schuler (1995: 38) points out, community networks

are not designed to be on-ramps to the internet, however, as this metaphor implies that the purpose of the system is to help people escape from their local community. While virtually all community network systems do offer access to at least some internet services (e-mail at a minimum) the focus of a community network is on the local community.

Like other forms of community media described in these pages, community networks are articulated through strategic alliances between various institutions, groups, and individuals who leverage available resources in order to accommodate local interests and concerns. A brief review of some of these efforts reveals the particular and distinctive motivations behind, support mechanisms for, and emphases of community networking initiatives around the world.

In the 1970s, Berkeley, California was the home of one of the first community computing systems, the so-called Community Memory project. With terminals housed in the Berkeley Public Library and other public spaces, such as community centers and neighborhood laundromats, Community Memory provided free access to messages posted on an electronic bulletin board. For the nominal charge of 25 cents, users could add their comments to an ongoing discussion. For one dollar, they could start a new discussion or "thread" as it is known today. Organized and coordinated by Lee Felsenstein, Community Memory encouraged community residents to join an electronic conversation, read and place classified ads, or even publish poetry and short fiction (Cisler 1994a). This emphasis on local content remains a defining feature of community networking.

A particularly telling illustration of the sort of local material produced, stored, and distributed through Community Memory was the Alameda County War Memorial, organized by musician and anti-war activist Country Joe McDonald (Schuler 1995). An electronic memorial dedicated to local residents who died fighting America's wars of the twentieth century – World Wars I and II, Korea, and the ongoing conflict in Vietnam – Community Memory provided a searchable database of fallen soldiers that also allowed users to add their own comments and reflections.

Herein we can detect the correspondence between the mission and social function of community networks and public libraries. As the Community Memory project's name implies, community networks constitute a dynamic repository of local cultural history, not unlike a library. Indeed, public libraries have long been involved in community networking initiatives. Leveraging the library's function as a local resource for information, the community network piggybacks on the skills, tools, and services traditionally associated with the public library. Conversely, libraries take advantage of community networks' outreach efforts.

This symbiotic relationship brings patrons and publicity to both organizations, while providing a mutually beneficial integrative function. As librarian and information specialist Karen G. Schneider observes, "community networks are often created in collaboration with other local agencies and advocacy groups, weaving libraries more tightly into the community organism" (1996: 96). As we shall see in Chapter 6, the state library provides a particularly appropriate setting for VICNET's statewide mandate to provide computer networking skills and resources to residents across Victoria, Australia.

This is but one noteworthy dimension of community networking. An even more fundamental impulse behind community networking initiatives is the provision of computer-related technologies, resources, and skills to local populations, especially disenfranchised members of the community. For instance, one of the first efforts to provide computers for low-income and minority populations was the Playing2Win project in Harlem, New York.

Founded in 1980 by Antonia Stone, Playing2Win began operating out of the basement of a neighborhood housing project. Initially conceived as part of a prison rehabilitation program, Playing2Win worked with prison inmates and ex-convicts on basic computing and literacy skills. Stone's vision was to harness the educational and career development potential of desktop computing for those with limited academic and economic opportunities. Beginning in 1983, Playing2Win extended its program to the wider community, making it the first inner-city public access computing center in the country. Over time, Playing2Win would become a neighborhood resource center, serving local residents of all ages, from toddlers to seniors.

Equally important, Playing2Win became a model that communities across the United States, and indeed, around the world, would emulate. With grant support from the National Science Foundation, Stone and her organization launched the Community Technology Center Network (CTC Net), a national affiliation of community technology initiatives aimed at providing computer and information technology training and resources in America's inner city. More recently, Play2Win's approach to public access computing has taken root in South Africa, Poland, and Northern Ireland. For instance, the Bytes for Belfast program, modeled on Playing2Win's community education program, provides job training for unemployed youth ages 16–25. Not only has the Bytes program encouraged young people with little or no academic opportunity to develop technical skills and aptitudes but it has also helped reintegrate them into the local community's social, civic, and cultural life.

Thus, community networking initiatives help alleviate social exclusion associated with the "digital divide" – a concept which, in its fullest sense, does not simply refer to technology access, but makes explicit the fundamental relationship between the political economy of communication systems and broader questions of democratic self-governance and basic human rights (Carvin 2000). Viewed in this light, then, community networking, like street papers and other community media initiatives described above, represents conscious efforts to create a more just and equitable society by altering the symbolic as well as the material relations of power within and between geographic communities.

The "telecottage movement" of the 1980s serves to illustrate this last point. Telecottages grew out of Scandinavian experiments with distance learning. "The goal of each is to reach learners that are distant from the source of knowledge through online courses, satellite television broadcasts, and interactive telecommunications courses" (Cisler 1994b). Akin to the public access model described above, the telecottage houses an assortment of telecommunication equipment, including computers, printers, fax, and telex machines. People in remote communities are encouraged to visit these regional telecommunication facilities and make use of the equipment at little or no cost. From modest beginnings in the mid-1980s, the telecottage movement gained momentum across Europe, Australia, and in the so-called developing world (Cisler 1994b). Like

Community Memory and Playing2Win, then, telecottages are precursors of contemporary articulations of community-based computing systems.

Throughout the late 1980s and early 1990s, the so-called "Free-Net" model was the most visible, influential, and, arguably, the most successful expression of the emergent community networking movement. Although Free-Net is often used as a generic term to describe a community network, as Ann Beamish (1995) points out, Free-Net refers to a very specific network design and organization affiliated with the National Public Telecomputing Network (NPTN).

The Free-Net model was based on an experimental program called "St. Silicon's Hospital and Information Dispensary" coordinated by Dr. Tom Grundner. An electronic bulletin board that enabled computer users to post medical questions online and later receive a response from health care professionals, the computer service attracted the attention of Ohio Bell, the local telephone service provider, telecom giant AT&T, as well as the University Hospitals of Cleveland (Nolan 1994). Together, these organizations provided start-up funds and institutional support to expand and elaborate Grundner's experimental design.

Housed at Case Western University, the Cleveland Free-Net went online in 1989. That same year, Grundner established the NPTN, a non-profit organization that provides technical and logistical support to groups and organizations interested in sponsoring a Free-Net in their own communities. Over time, the NPTN became a leading advocate for community networking initiatives in telecommunication policy deliberations. In addition to supporting community networking initiatives across the United States, the NPTN was a leading proponent of the Free-Net model around the world (Commings 1995). Indeed, Grundner's Free-Net model was adapted across North America and throughout Europe and the Pacific Rim. For instance, in 1992, Singapore launched the first of several community computer systems based on the Cleveland Free-Net (Ong 1992).

By 1997, however, the NPTN folded. Despite the organization's initial success, the NPTN faced mounting opposition from commercial service providers, while the Free-Net model attracted fewer adherents. Commercial interests charged that by virtue of their free e-mail and Internet access policies, Free-Nets represented unfair competition in an emerging information services market (Beamish). As the Free-Net model grew more popular with local communities in big cities and rural areas alike, commercial service providers threatened legal action. Vowing to stave off potential legal challenges, the NPTN gradually lost sight of its principal objectives: to promote a public access model of networked communication and to link these local systems into a national network.

For their part, community network enthusiasts grew increasingly frustrated with FreePort, Free-Net's text-based interface. In light of rapid advances in graphical user interface (GUI), the text-only interface NPTN offered its affiliates was outmoded and local community networking enthusiasts looked to develop alternative solutions that would allow them to offer their users a more dynamic user interface. Moreover, NPTN's ambitious plan to create a national "cybercast" network – modeled on National Public Radio (NPR) and the Public Broadcasting Service (PBS) – was proving to be a formidable challenge (Abernathy 1995). Indeed, given US public broadcasting's rather poor track record for supporting local production, it seems likely that community network enthusiasts thought better of an affiliation with NPTN. The planned Corporation for Public Cybercasting (CPC) never materialized, due in part to fears that such a service might undermine the grassroots and local orientation of the Free-Net model that community network enthusiasts found most appealing.

Having said all this, the Free-Net model nevertheless helped shape and inform any number of notable community networking initiatives. For instance, the National Capital Free-Net (NCF) in Ottawa, Canada went online in November 1991. Thanks in large measure to the NCF's efforts, today Ottawa is a digital hub and one of the nation's most wired cities.

Like its predecessor in Cleveland, Ottawa's NCF grew from an existing public information service based at a local university (Weston 1997). Drawing on the "electronic city" metaphor used by the Cleveland Free-Net and common to most Free-Net initiatives, the NCF mimics urban geography to orient users to community information, events, and services. Using text-based designations for "social services," "community associations," and "government centre," the NCF encourages users to "visit" these spaces and retrieve information that has been generated by various institutions. Public access computer terminals and kiosks throughout the city allow local residents and visitors alike to use the system free of charge.

NCF's primary goal, therefore, is to provide community members and public agencies with networked information services and resources. In doing so, the NCF aims to "prepare the community for full and broad participation in rapidly changing communication environments" (quoted in Das 1996). This sentiment underscores the NCF's political orientation. As communication scholar Jay Weston puts it:

The National Capital Free-Net was an imagined public space, a dumb platform where all individuals, groups and organizations could represent themselves, where conflict and controversy could occur as the manifestation of conflict and controversy already occurring within the community. As a public space, no one, and certainly no group or institution, would be held responsible for one another's ideology, moral standards, expectations, or motivations. On the other hand, each person or organization would be accountable for themselves. Such a space could be constructed only by the community acting as a community, and not by any public or private organization acting on behalf of the community. At least that was the idea in 1991.

(Weston 1997: 199)

Whilst government and public institutions train their existing workforce or hire "information specialists" to maintain and keep online information current, Free-Nets and the community organizations that supply content to these community information services depend upon staff and volunteers to make certain information is timely and accurate. Thus, the participatory dimension of community networking is radically decentralized and potentially more democratic than conventional modes of production associated with broadcasting or newspaper production.

This emphasis on participation, local content, and especially the impulse to revitalize the civic life of place-based communities is the motivation behind yet another strain of the community networking movement, so-called civic networking. Like Free-Nets, civic networks are characterized by their emphasis on the local community. That is to say, in their efforts to bring computer and information technologies (CIT) to local populations, civic networking encourages broad-based community participation in the planning, design, construction, and maintenance of information resources: technology and training provided to community residents and organizations at little or no cost.

Equally important, civic networks are explicitly designed to encourage and facilitate discussion within and between local residents, thereby promoting participatory democracy at the community level. A cursory examination of the *UK Citizens Online Democracy* website demonstrates that civic networking has particular resonance for cities and towns throughout England and Ireland. For instance, the Community Information Network of Northern Ireland, the Inner City Community Network of Dublin, and the Manchester Community Information Network, to name but a few, are devoted to the provision of access and services designed to promote engaged citizenship and deliberative democracy through online discussions of local issues and concerns.

Today, Free-Nets, civic networks, and other likeminded efforts aimed at promoting democratic communication are quite common across Europe. The Agora Telematica in Rome, Italy is perhaps one of the more striking manifestations of the impulse to deploy networked communication for purposes of democratic deliberation and passionate political debate. A multilingual system, Agora Telematica is closely affiliated with the Radical Party (Parrella 1994). Beginning in the 1960s, the Radical Party engaged in any number of popular struggles – abortion rights, drug legalization efforts, and the anti-war and student movements. Employing the principles of non-violence and direct action campaigns, the Radical Party drew considerable media attention to their efforts and eventually made some, albeit limited inroads into mainstream politics. In the 1980s, the Radical Party used a government grant to organize its own radio station and by the end of the decade, had set up Agora as a tool for political organizing and public communication.

One of the principal concerns of the Agora Telematica is to engage in the struggle for human rights and cultural autonomy in an increasingly transnational media system. Far from being isolationist, however, the Agora's multilingual design is central to its mission of facilitating communication within and between disparate national, linguistic, and cultural groups. Like Free-Nets, the Agora provides its services to individuals free of charge. The Agora receives financial support from various national and international businesses and NGOs, including Amnesty International and Federazione dei Verdi (the Italian Green Party), who make use of its services. Moreover, like civic networks, the Agora provides users with electronic mail services as well as access to discussion fora, national and international databases, news services, and other resources in an effort to create an informed and engaged user community that transcends national borders and linguistic differences.

This same internationalist spirit manifests itself in the Russian CIVNET initiative: a collaborative effort between Russia and American civic networking enthusiasts (Russian Communities Online 2004). The program's initial goal was the establishment of civic networks in six Russian communities. Research and analysis of each of these sites would then be disseminated throughout the emerging civic networking sector with the idea of developing models that might be replicable in other locations.

What makes the CIVNET initiative unique is the scale, scope, and sheer diversity of its financial, technical, and logistical support. The US-based Ford Foundation provides considerable financial support for the CIVNET effort, as does the equally prestigious Eurasia Foundation. In contrast to these impressive international donors, the decidedly grassroots Friends and Partners, an Internet-based project that seeks to foster mutual understanding and cooperation between the Russian and American people, has taken the lead on the CIVNET project. Because of this unique and multi-faceted Russian-US partnership, CIVNET has emerged as an important planning and demonstration project for civic networking initiatives across Russia.

Civic networking in the United States owes a great deal of its strength and popularity to the organizing campaigns, lobbying efforts, and policy analyses conducted by the Center for Civic Networking (CCN). A non-profit organization dedicated to "putting the information infrastructure to work within local communities," the CCN articulated the relationship between networked information systems, civic engagement, and economic and community development that informs any number of public/private partnerships involved in community networking (see Civille 1993).

One of the premier examples of this approach is the Blacksburg Electronic Village (BEV) in southwestern Virginia. A collaborative effort between the local university, Virginia Tech, the town of Blacksburg, and local civic groups and businesses, BEV has helped provide local residents with Information Technology (IT) training, brought high-speed Internet access to local schools, attracted outside investment from dozens of IT firms, and otherwise transformed Blacksburg and the surrounding Montgomery County into one of the most technologically rich regions in the United States (Cohill and Kavanaugh 2000). Recognized as a leader in community networking, BEV's digital library collects technical reports, planning documents, and policy primers for groups and organizations interested in starting their own community network.

For many localities, then, community networks have come to be seen as strategic initiatives to support economic and community development efforts (Pigg 1999). Technology manufacturers, local and national governments, and international aid agencies are among the most visible players in community networking schemes designed, in large part, to promote sustainable development in the information age. In post-industrial societies, community networks play an important role in economic regeneration efforts. For example, the principal aim of the South Bristol Learning Network in England was to end structural unemployment associated with the erosion of Bristol's manufacturing base during the last half of the twentieth century. By providing local residents and schools with access to information technology and training, the government-funded scheme sought to create a labor force that might attract investment and support the establishment of a local IT sector (Davitt 1995). The impulse to deploy community computing as an engine of economic and community development is a motivating force behind the state government's enthusiastic support for VICNET, Victoria, Australia's community network, discussed in Chapter 6.

In the so-called developing world "telecentres," not unlike the aforementioned telecottages, serve as community communication centers providing a host of services, including satellite television, video recording, desktop computers and printers, as well as Internet access. Akin to community networks in industrialized societies, local populations, national governments, NGOs, and international aid organizations alike view telecentres as tools for community and economic development. Indeed, like all of the local initiatives described above, telecentres are local manifestations of the information age. Conversely, these local efforts help to articulate an emerging global information infrastructure. As with the other forms of community media discussed above, these telecentres provide yet one more opportunity to trace the global through the local.

Consider for example an e-mail message that I read on my desktop in Bloomington, Indiana. Forwarded over the Digital Divide list serve maintained by the US-based Benton Foundation[10] with the subject heading "UNESCO Supports Creation of Free Community Telecentere in Brazil," the post begins:

It was on November 19, 2003 at 11:30AM, when visitors of the first of five pilot telecentres of the NGO "Gems of the Earth Rural Telecentere Network" sent out their first e-mails from Sao Goncalo do Rio das Pedras, a community of about 1,500 people in the Jequitinhonha Valley in Brazil.

(UNESCO 2003)

The post goes on to describe the NGO, Gems of the Earth, and its partnership with UNESCO's "Free Community Telecentre Network," which has plans to establish additional telecentres in Paraguay and Argentina.

Spearheaded by former NASA engineer Marco Figueiredo, the Brazilian initiative seeks to construct telecentres in four other villages with less than 2,500 inhabitants. Like Figueiredo's adopted home of Sao Goncalo, the other sites are rather remote, economically depressed villages that were mobilized by Gems of the Earth to develop a plan of sustainable development for the telecentres. In addition to UNESCO support, the Brazilian Ministry of Communications donated equipment and resources, including hardware, to provide broadband Internet access via satellite, high-end computer servers, and multimedia terminals for each of the five communities involved in the pilot program. Local community associations and volunteers will run the telecentres until each of the five villages can establish a permanent, local non-governmental organization to supervise the centre. In the meantime, Gems of the Earth is working on developing web-based distance learning materials to support job training and other capacity-building initiatives within each of the local communities.

Community communication efforts designed to promote media literacy and spur economic development are generally associated with so-called "underdeveloped" countries. It is rather telling, then, that community networking vividly reveals the relationship between communication and development in the "first world" as well as the "third world." From this perspective it becomes clear that development is never completely achieved; that community building and maintenance is contingent and volatile: an ongoing process. All of which underscores the notion that communities are not naturally occurring phenomena, nor are they static or fixed entities. Rather, communities are dynamic, evolving, and contested social constructions. As the preceding discussion suggests, and as the following case studies demonstrate, communities are articulated within and through a constellation of social agents, practices, and institutions. With this in mind, we turn to the first of our case studies in an effort to examine how locally oriented, participatory media reflect and embody this process of articulation. And, how, in turn, these manifestations of collective action articulate community.

3   Finding a spot on the dial: Firehouse
Broadcasting from Bloomington, Indiana

> Community radio is characterized by access, public participation in
> production and decision making and, predominantly, by listener-
> financing. The intention is that management of the station is in the
> hands of those who use and listen to it. Though the workings of such
> stations are never easy, the structure does offer the possibility of
> accountability to the audience/user in a way state and commercial
> stations do not.
>
> Jon Bekken, Community Radio at the Crossroads

An editorial appearing in the 11 January 1996 edition of the *Bloomington
Voice*, a free weekly newspaper serving south central Indiana, criticized recent programming decisions by Bloomington's community radio station,
WFHB. According to the editorial, WFHB fails to live up to its promise
of providing alternative news and information to the greater Bloomington community. The opinion piece suggests that WFHB's reluctance to
air "controversial" programming stems from fears that such programs
might offend some listeners and underwriters, possibly leading them to
withdraw their financial support for the station. The editorial concludes
that while WFHB provides a diverse and welcome mix of music and entertainment features, the station is reluctant to air politically progressive
programming in order to accommodate conservative listeners and local
business interests.

   Published within days of the station's third anniversary, the editorial
signaled a shift in popular attitudes toward WFHB. Prior to the editorial's
publication, press coverage WFHB received in the *Bloomington Voice*, as
well as the *Herald-Times*, Bloomington's only daily newspaper, was nothing short of unqualified praise. When WFHB commenced broadcasting
three years earlier, a cross-section of the community – artists, musicians
and writers, local merchants, elected officials, business leaders, and university students, faculty, and staff – embraced the station and hailed its
efforts to bring Bloomington a "sound alternative" to the commercial
and public broadcasting services operating in and around south central
Indiana.[1]

Now, it seemed, certain segments of the community were troubled by station management's decision to indefinitely postpone airing *Counter Spin* and *Making Contact*, two syndicated programs commonly associated with community radio in the United States.[2] In the weeks and months following the editorial's publication, a rather heated debate ensued – in print, over the airwaves of WFHB, and on "spot-online," the station's internal electronic distribution list – surrounding Bloomington community radio's mission, its operating principles, and ultimately, its responsibility to the community.

These concerns are best summed up this way: in what ways does Bloomington community radio reflect and embody dissatisfaction with dominant media form and content? How does WFHB encourage access and participation in the operation, management, and governance of a community-based radio station? Moreover, how does WFHB accommodate varied interests within the city of Bloomington? In short, as a case study in community radio, what can WFHB's experience tell us about the political economy of US broadcasting? For that matter, what does WFHB tell us about community radio's potential to promote and enhance communicative democracy?

To answer these questions, I draw upon my experience as a participant observer at WFHB between 1993–1997. As noted in the Introduction, while pursuing my doctoral studies at Indiana University, I was a WFHB volunteer. In addition to working as a music programmer, I was a member of the program selection committee and volunteered at numerous station benefits. My participation afforded me considerable insight into the station's philosophical orientation, organizational structure, and day-to-day operations. During that time, I conducted a series of formal and informal interviews with station management, staff, and volunteers. Used in tandem with local press accounts these interviews inform my analysis of the station's growth and development.

When I moved away from Bloomington to take a teaching position in Boston, I kept abreast of station developments through various channels of communication, principally by way of my subscription to the "Spotlight," the station's monthly program guide and, in a far more dynamic fashion, via the station's electronic mailing list. I continued to do so until my return to Bloomington in July 2002. Since then, my participation in the station has been confounded by my teaching schedule and, more critically, by programmatic and philosophical differences between station management and myself regarding WFHB's latest news and public affairs initiative. These differences are not unique to WFHB, however. Rather, they are indicative of the more general problematics of participatory governance associated with what John Dowling (1984) describes as "self-managed" media systems.

In saying this, I want to underscore two related points. First, despite our differences, I have tremendous admiration for those individuals who spent the better part of two decades making community radio in Bloomington a reality. Moreover, I deeply appreciate the ongoing efforts of station management, staff, and volunteers to make Bloomington community radio a vibrant and vital local resource. Put differently, these people are not simply "research subjects"; they are my colleagues, friends, and neighbors. All of which suggests another point: that is, the personal investment afforded by participatory media, and participatory research for that matter, is at times a mixed blessing. That is to say, the passionate commitment community media staff and volunteers bring to their work often leads to sharp differences of opinion and can be a source of tension, even among likeminded media activists and friends. I conclude this chapter with some thoughts on this methodological quandary.

To begin with, however, I offer a brief description of Bloomington, Indiana. Here, I draw attention to the city's distinctive cultural geography with special emphasis placed on the role Indiana University plays in shaping and informing Bloomington's surprisingly cosmopolitan sensibility. Following this, I recount WFHB's long and rather convoluted history, as those who have dedicated a significant portion of their lives to the establishment and maintenance of community radio for the people of Bloomington related it to me. Throughout, I reveal how various players, interests, institutions, and socio-cultural movements within and far beyond south central Indiana articulate community broadcasting in Bloomington.

My analysis then turns to a consideration of the debate over news and public affairs programming on WFHB described above and to the implications of all this on what media scholar John Hochheimer (1993) describes as "democratic radio praxis." Here, I contrast WFHB's "theory and practice" to the tradition of US community radio associated with Lewis Hill and his associates at KPFA, the flagship station of the Pacifica Radio Network. Throughout, I draw upon a number of scholarly sources to inform my analysis. For instance, in his discussion of US community radio, William Barlow (1988) examines the ideological orientation that has guided the community radio movement in the United States and identifies the social, economic, and political constraints that likewise shape and inform community radio practice. Barlow's insights help situate WFHB in relation to broader trends and tendencies within the US community radio sector.

Conversely, Jeffery Land's (1999) comprehensive account of the rise of the Pacifica Radio Network provides invaluable insight into the philosophical foundations and practical realities of Pacifica's "brash experiment" with artistically adventurous, politically dissident radio. As noted in Chapter 2, Pacifica's legacy has exerted considerable influence on community radio worldwide. WFHB's experience illustrates the continuities and change associated with the model of listener-supported radio first championed by KPFA. As we shall see, this tradition, and WFHB's relationship to Pacifica's legacy, was a major source of tension during the aforementioned debate over news and public affairs programming. As WFHB commences its second decade of community broadcasting, this tension continues to inform the station's philosophy, practice, and programming. Throughout this discussion, I hope to demonstrate the strengths as well as the limitations of participatory media as they struggle to create viable organizations that are at once relevant and accountable to the local communities in which they operate.

Small town city

Nestled in the rolling hills of southern Indiana, Bloomington is succinctly described by local singer-songwriter Michael White as a "small town city."[3] Indeed, Bloomington's bucolic atmosphere stands in stark contrast to the cosmopolitan character of its inhabitants and environs. Established in 1818 as the seat of Monroe County government, Bloomington's fate was irrevocably tied to that of the State Seminary, the modest schoolhouse that would eventually become known as Indiana University, founded in 1824.[4] In large measure, then, the presence of Indiana University accounts for Bloomington's ambiguous, somewhat enigmatic character.

According to one local history, the state seminary "was the pride of the town and the means of rapidly and greatly increasing its population, enterprise and material wealth" (Blanchard 1993: 458). By the middle of the 1830s, students attending Indiana College, the recently renamed seminary, began exerting considerable influence on the town's character.[5] Primarily a mill town and trading center for dry and wet goods (liquor), leather and tailored merchandise, as well as domestic and farming implements, the town's educational resources gave Bloomington a "literary and social caste probably possessed by no other town in the State" (Blanchard: 459).

Bloomington's formidable educational opportunities are not solely responsible for the community's distinctive character, however. The town's geography likewise made it a focal point of human migration from across the nation and around the world. Immigrants from Ireland and Germany settled in Bloomington as they helped build the nation's railroads. Quakers, Covenanters, and other abolitionists established Bloomington as a "station" on the Underground Railroad: the network of clandestine transportation routes used by blacks to escape slavery. And in the years prior to the American Civil War, opposition to slavery brought thousands of white migrants from Slave States to south central Indiana, many of whom established residence in Bloomington, the region's emerging transportation hub.

As early as 1836, local businessmen, the Orchard Brothers, appreciated Bloomington's strategic geographic location. Exploiting the town's proximity to new and established transportation routes, the Orchards saw economic and community development opportunities and went about establishing long distance stagecoach lines connecting Bloomington with major population centers and trade routes in the west and south. Based out of their Temperance Hotel in downtown Bloomington, the Orchard Brothers' stagecoach served passengers traveling between Leavenworth, Kansas and Indianapolis, Indiana, as well as those making their way to Louisville, Kentucky and on to New Orleans, Louisiana. Over the years, Bloomington would emerge as an important crossroads between east and west, north and south. No doubt, this contributes to the "transitory" nature of the town's population and helps to explain the community's cultural eclecticism.

The Orchards likewise anticipated community development opportunities presented by the railroad. As plans were made to extend the New Albany and Salem line – what would later be known as the Monon Route that connected Louisville, Indianapolis, and Chicago with stops in Bedford, Bloomington, Greencastle, Crawfordsville, and Lafayette, Indiana[6] – the Orchards set about building a new hotel, described in local histories as "the best between Indianapolis and Louisville" (Savage 1988: 3). In short, the railroad facilitated Bloomington's regional and national integration, created considerable employment opportunities, and otherwise stimulated the town's social, economic, and cultural development.

For instance, the railroad was instrumental in building Bloomington's manufacturing base. The railroad brought raw materials from across the nation to Bloomington and subsequently carried all manner of manufactured goods away to national markets. Throughout the late nineteenth and early twentieth centuries, manufacturing was crucial to the area's economic development and, with the lure of good paying factory work, helped stimulate growth of the town's population. One of the most successful businesses at this time was Showers Brothers Furniture. At the height of their success, the Showers Brothers factory was the largest of its kind in the world. Today the site is the home of Bloomington's city government. Moreover, much of the housing stock in Bloomington's historic near west side was built to accommodate Showers Brothers' employees, predominantly blacks who settled in and around the new facilities in the mid-1880s.

In addition to moving people and manufactured goods in and out of Bloomington, the railroad played a pivotal role in resource extraction from south central Indiana. The region's principal export was limestone, valued among builders and architects for its beauty, strength, and durability. When Richard Gilbert opened the region's first quarry in 1820, limestone quickly became a staple of local building and design. The costs associated with moving the stone limited its export value, however. The railroad changed all that and by the middle of the nineteenth century, Bloomington's growth was inextricably linked to the stone industry.

As contemporary writer Scott Russell Sanders points out, limestone from southern Indiana was used as so-called "dimensional" or structural stone in the construction of New York City's Empire State Building, San Francisco's City Hall, the Pentagon, Chicago's Tribune Tower, and the Dallas Museum of Fine Arts among many other well and less well-known buildings across the country and around the world. Sanders concludes, "Over the past century, the destinations for this stone read like a graph of America's growth: first the great international cities, Chicago and Boston and New York; then the muscle cities of the Midwest, Pittsburgh and Cleveland, St. Louis and Indianapolis; now the glittering cities of the sunbelt" (1985: 6).

For the better part of a century, then, Bloomington's "big three" employers had been the railroads, the furniture industry, and the limestone quarries (Travis 2003: 6). In the middle of the twentieth century, however, Bloomington's manufacturing base underwent dramatic transformation. The Showers Brothers factory closed down and changes in architectural style and building design led to a steep decline in the limestone industry. And with the development of the interstate highway system, the railroads found it increasingly difficult to compete for passenger travel and commercial transportation revenue.

Only those heavy industries that began to emerge in Bloomington throughout the 1940s and 1950s, Otis Elevator, Hotpoint, Radio Corporation of America (RCA), Westinghouse, and General Electric, continued to make use of Bloomington's impressive rail infrastructure. Throughout the 1980s and 1990s, however, these industries relocated, due in large part to the economic "efficiencies" and "opportunities" afforded them by post-Fordist production techniques and neo-liberal trade policies, such as the North American Free Trade Agreement (NAFTA). In their wake, these industries left environmental hazards, widespread economic displacement, and land use issues that the city continues to wrestle with.

While Bloomington's manufacturing base rose and fell with changing economic conditions, Indiana University (IU) flourished. By most accounts, Indiana University's extraordinary growth and rapid transformation into an internationally recognized center for teaching, research, and scholarship were the result of one man's vision: Herman B Wells.[7] Born in Jamestown, Indiana, Herman Wells served as an assistant professor of economics until 1935, when he assumed the position of dean of the School of Business. Two years later, Wells was named the university's "acting president," a post he was eventually named to permanently and continued to hold until 1962. He then served as the university chancellor for the next thirty-seven years.

Throughout most of his ninety-seven years, Wells' name was synonymous with Indiana University. Under his leadership, the university quadrupled in physical size and student enrollment skyrocketed from 3,000 in the 1930s to well over 25,000 students by the 1970s. Wells vividly demonstrated his lifelong commitment to academic freedom when he supported Dr. Alfred Kinsey's work in the midst of the controversy that erupted over the 1948 publication of Kinsey's report on human sexuality (Capshew n.d.). Formidable as his commitment to research and scholarship was, Wells was also an enthusiastic patron of the arts. This is perhaps most evident in his unflinching support for the IU School of Music. Aside from recruiting a first-class professoriate and overseeing construction of impressive performance venues, such as Recital Hall and the Music and Art Center (aka "The MAC"), Wells helped secure a noncommercial educational broadcast license for WFIU, now a local National Public Radio (NPR) affiliate. To this day, the School of Music exerts considerable influence over WFIU's format and program schedule.[8] Under Wells' guidance, then, Indiana University's School of Music became one of the premier programs of study in the world.

Finally, Wells' many and varied public service commitments, most notably perhaps his involvement with the United Nations Educational and Scientific and Cultural Organization (UNESCO), helped secure Indiana University's international reputation. With his keen wit and gregarious nature, Wells cultivated influential contacts throughout the state, across the nation, and around the globe (Griff 1988) – contacts who would help support Wells' initiatives at home and abroad.

Wells' frequent overseas missions instilled in him the desire to make Indiana University a world-class teaching and research institution. His success in this regard manifests itself across campus and all over the city; quite unlike other college towns in America, Bloomington is famous for its cultural diversity and vitality. In short, Bloomington's cosmopolitan ambiance owes a great debt to the global vision of Herman B Wells.

Today, students and scholars from across the country and around the world come to the Bloomington campus of Indiana University. Beyond the campus Sample Gates lies downtown Bloomington, a bustling little metropolis that is home to an eclectic assortment of academics, students, bohemians, and town folk. Bloomington's reputation as a welcoming, desirable, and dynamic community attracts a diverse population. The impressive number of students who remain in Bloomington long after their schooling is finished not only offsets the transitory character of the student population but also testifies to the community's lasting charms.

A major draw for the city is the aforementioned School of Music, which attracts gifted musicians from around the world and helps make Bloomington a vibrant, if somewhat unexpectedly dynamic site of cultural production. Ironically, the Law School lays claim to Bloomington's most famous musician: Hoagy Carmichael. One of the icons of American popular song, Howard Hoagland ("Hoagy") Carmichael, was born and raised in Bloomington, Indiana. Hoagy came of age when ragtime music, stimulated by the recording industry and the new medium of radio, swept the nation. Apart from sound recordings and radio broadcasting, the young jazz enthusiast took inspiration from his home and community. From his mother, who played piano at campus fraternity parties and local movie theaters, Hoagy learned to emulate ragtime's jaunty, free-wheeling style. And from the black families and churches in his neighborhood, Hoagy came to appreciate African-American spirituals and the blues. Carmichael's popularity and enduring influence rests in part on his unique synthesis of disparate American musical traditions.

While attending Indiana University in the late 1920s, Hoagy established a reputation as a superb instrumentalist and songwriter. One of his frequent hangouts, the historic Book Nook on Indiana Avenue, was a focal point for artists, writers, and intellectuals.[9] There, he frequently performed with Carmichael's Collegians, a popular dance band on campus. It was also at Indiana University that Hoagy Carmichael first met the legendary cornetist Leon "Bix" Beiderbecke. Through his association with Bix, Hoagy's compositions received national exposure and ultimately led to his first recording date, with Gennett Records of Richmond, Indiana, in 1926.

All of which underscores the fact that throughout the first two decades of the twentieth century, jazz bands crisscrossed the Midwest and helped stimulate the development of a regional recording industry. Specializing in jazz, blues, and the region's traditional music – a hybrid of gospel, dance, and so-called "mountain music" – recording studios and record labels sprang up all across Indiana. Bloomington was a focal point for much of this activity. Today, the city continues to enjoy a reputation as a regional hub for musical expression and innovation.

Bloomington is, therefore, very much an artist's community, enticing musicians, as well as writers, poets, painters, and others drawn by the area's scenic beauty and cultural vitality. The curious mixture of small town charm and big city attractions also attracts tourists and residents alike to Bloomington and surrounding Monroe and Brown Counties.[10] However, the contradictory impulses behind Bloomington's desire to maintain its rustic character and simultaneously forge an urban identity exacerbate tensions between the university and the local community.

These tensions are the subtext of former Bloomington resident Steve Tesich's Oscar-winning screenplay for the 1979 film *Breaking Away*. Ostensibly a quirky "coming of age" film, *Breaking Away* portrays the anxieties local residents feel when outsiders threaten their way of life and their community. By most accounts, the film is an accurate and often poignant depiction of the inflammatory relationship between working class town residents and the more well off college students who attend Indiana University.[11] In a related vein, another Bloomington resident, rock star John Mellencamp, captures the contradictions of Bloomington's identity in his words and music. Mellencamp's "working-class heroes" bemoan the loss of economic self-sufficiency and the profound sense of belonging associated with small town community.

The loss of community and class antagonisms reflected in these popular culture forms belies the city's prosperous and harmonious image. Prior to my departure from Bloomington, I witnessed first hand such disruptions to the community when, in 1997, the French-owned Thomson electronics corporation announced plans to relocate its operations from Bloomington to Juarez, Mexico. Around 1,100 workers lost their jobs as a result of that single plant closing. Since that time, "downsizing" at Otis Elevator, General Electric, and CSX, the railroad line, likewise eliminated hundreds of jobs. More recently, downtown development, in the form of upscale housing, ongoing concerns over PCB contamination of local groundwater, and the incendiary debate over plans to construct a major highway, I-69, on the outskirts of town, have further contributed to the animosity between economic elites and commercial interests, and environmentalists, historical preservationists, and other local residents who favor sustainable development.

Described by residents and visitors alike as an "oasis" from the rest of the state's political and cultural conservatism, Bloomington's character is at once cohesive and fragmented, rural and urban, traditional and postmodern, local and global. These competing, yet oddly complementary qualities have forged a rather dynamic local culture – a culture that is reflected, celebrated, shaped, and shared over the airwaves of community radio for Bloomington, Indiana, WFHB.

1. Promotional banner for WFHB featuring Spot, official mascot of Firehouse Broadcasting. (Photo by the author)

Finding a spot on the dial

In the summer of 1975, Jim Manion and Mark Hood returned to Bloomington after attending the National Alternative Radio Konference (NARK) with visions of establishing a community radio station in Bloomington, Indiana.[12] Theirs was a vision shared by a number of local musicians, sound technicians, and radio enthusiasts. In September of that year, a coalition of local advocates founded a non-profit corporation dedicated to bringing community radio to Bloomington, Indiana: The Community Radio Project, Inc.

Among the first to be captivated by the idea of community radio in Bloomington was Jeffrey Morris, Hood's roommate and audio engineering colleague. Over the course of the next eighteen years, Morris' persistence and determination proved crucial for realizing their heady notion. Morris kept the project alive while the enthusiasm for community radio in Bloomington waned in the wake of numerous frequency searches, several failed licensing requests, protracted legal battles, and sporadic organizing and fund-raising efforts.

Hailing from Gary, Indiana, Morris was exposed to radio emanating from one of the nation's premier broadcasting centers, Chicago, Illinois. Morris' appreciation for the eclectic radio programming from the greater Chicagoland area soon turned to rabid enthusiasm for radio electronics. Morris recalls how the idea of a community radio station resonated with his life-long interest in what he describes as "nonprofessional" radio:

I was into amateur radio as a kid. I remember seeing an article when I was in junior high school about some kid who had put – a Class D it was called then – a ten-watt FM station on in his high school. This was the fifties . . . this was like 57 or 58 or so. So, I had it in my head. I was ripe for it. I wanted to do it. I was involved in the local music scene, I could see the talent that was here, and so the concept was there. When Mark and Jim came back from the [NARK] conference, they were enthusiastic about the idea of a community station. When they told me about it, I of course jumped right in.

In the early and mid-1970s, Bloomington, Indiana was a breeding ground of musical entrepreneurism and experimentation. The regional music scene was flourishing and musicians and production personnel alike were anxious to be a part of it.

Both Jeffrey Morris and Mark Hood lived in a converted garage next door to the Gilfoy studios, southern Indiana's first 16-track, two-inch recording studio. Studio owner and local jazz musician Jack Gilfoy cut a deal with Hood and his friend, music producer Mark Bingham, that during studio down time, they could use Gilfoy's facilities to produce their own work. Provided, of course, that Gilfoy received a percentage should any of the projects generate profit.

Using Gilfoy's studio, Hood and Bingham recorded a number of local bands – the Screamin' Gypsy Bandits, singer/songwriters Bob Lucas and Bill Wilson, the Al Cobine Big Band, and the legendary MX-80 – for Bar-B-Q records. A local label, Bar-B-Q records was financed in part by Kathy Canada, an aspiring musician and granddaughter of Eli Lilly, of Lilly Pharmaceuticals, a great benefactor of the local art scene in Bloomington.[13] Sensing a groundswell in musical activity in and around Bloomington and beginning to appreciate community radio's potential to promote the local music industry, Gilfoy gave the Community Radio Project (CRP) a commitment to locate a broadcast tower outside of his studios on West 17th Street in Bloomington.

According to FCC regulations, in addition to finding an available frequency, noncommercial broadcasters must also demonstrate they have a site to erect a broadcast tower. Gilfoy's promise provided the CRP with an essential component for their license application. Morris, Manion, and Hood then began the tedious process of putting together a construction permit for the tower and began a frequency search. Within a year, however, Gilfoy's operations went bankrupt and with that, CRP lost its tower site. Without a location for the broadcast tower, CRP never filed an application with the Federal Communications Commission

(FCC). The CRP suffered a major blow to its efforts. As it turns out, this was the first of several defeats for Bloomington's community radio movement.

Intrigued by the possibilities of community radio, local engineer and one time apprentice to Mark Hood, Richard Fish, stepped into the breach and offered his assistance to the Community Radio Project. In a letter of intent to the CRP, Fish agreed to locate a broadcast tower adjacent to his own Homegrown Studios, south of town. With new life breathed into the project, the corporation changed its name to Clear Creek Sounds in February of 1977 and Jim Manion renewed organizing and fundraising efforts.[14]

By July of 1980, Clear Creek Sounds had identified what it thought to be an open, noncommercial frequency and had generated enough financial support to submit an application for licensing to the FCC for 90.5 FM. Unbeknownst to the Bloomington applicants, sometime earlier the public radio station in Louisville, Kentucky had successfully applied to upgrade their signal from 10,000 to 50,000 watts. Jeffrey Morris notes that with today's computerized databases, the search for an available frequency is much easier. The potential interference problems could have been avoided. Prior to this, frequency searches were conducted using often outdated materials from the *Broadcasting Yearbook* and other publications. When Clear Creek Sounds applied for 90.5 FM, the Louisville station's upgrade was not published.

Within a matter of months, the FCC rejected the Clear Creek Sounds application due to objectionable interference with the Louisville station's signal. Actually, the area of interference lies in the Hoosier National Forest, and yet, broadcast regulations at that time made few allowances for any such interference. The setback was an unmitigated disaster. Financial backing for the project all but dried up and local enthusiasm diminished precipitously. Significantly, the FCC's ruling made no mention of an even greater difficulty facing future applications: what is commonly referred to as a Channel 6 problem.

Briefly stated, the Channel 6 interference problem arises when a noncommercial broadcast signal (88 to 92 MHz) is located close to and is powerful enough to interfere with the audio portion of a TV signal on Channel 6, which operates between 82 and 88 MHz. Antenna booster amplifiers tend to exacerbate the problem and, given the area's topography, the use of these amplifiers is a necessity in and around the city of Bloomington. If Bloomington Community Radio were ever to broadcast from the noncommercial band, engineers would need to "work around" the Channel 6 problem. In the early 1980s, however, the FCC had yet to set out the specifications for such a solution.

Between 1980 and early 1983, the drive for community radio in Bloomington lay dormant. Many of the principals either left town or pursued other personal and professional goals. Jeffrey Morris maintained the corporation's not-for-profit status by filing the necessary corporate reports with local and state officials. Morris recalls those years this way:

I was waiting for some help. I was waiting for things to come back together, for new people. Up until that point there's two whole sets of people who have gone through. The initial half dozen or so, who came and went, 'cause Bloomington's transitory people come, they get enthusiastic about things, they get jobs elsewhere and they go. Or they graduate. . . . So when that last application failed, things really dispersed.

Things did start coming together again, slowly. In 1979, Brian Kearney, newly arrived in Bloomington from Croton, New York, got involved with the Clear Creek Sounds group. Kearney recalls that when he first unpacked his bags to begin his studies at Indiana University and turned on the radio he was "aghast" by the lack of good programming around the dial. Having grown up listening to some of the nation's premier radio stations in New York City, Kearney had a keen appreciation for diverse musical styles: big band jazz, rhythm and blues, and rock and roll. The dearth of energetic and challenging radio in a college town bewildered him.

I remember sitting in my dorm room, you know just tuning the dial. There were these huge gaps. There'd be like, nothing! And then you'd get something and it was terrible. I could not believe it. . . . There's nothing but country and top 40. Oh, it was bad! And I couldn't believe that the university only had this classical station [WFIU]. And I'm thinking to myself, where's the college rock station? You know, what are the students doing?

Kearney soon found his way to two student-run organizations: WIUS and WQAX. Through his contacts at WQAX, Kearney first heard the phrase "community radio" and while the concept of community radio was new to him, his interest was piqued. For a short time, Kearney attended some of the organizational meetings and even performed at one of the now-legendary "Trance Dance Benefits."

These benefits were meant to showcase local talent while supporting the community radio initiative. In March of 1980, 400 people crowded into the former Moose Lodge at College and 4th Street to hear local punk rock bands at the first Trance Dance Benefit. Punk music had effectively been shut out of the local bars and cover bands dominated the music scene. The Trance Dance Benefits played a modest role in supporting the community radio initiative. Equally important, these showcases ushered in a new era in Bloomington, a volatile music scene that vacillates between enthusiastic support for local bands and fierce resistance to anything other than established artists and musical genres. Despite the energy and enthusiasm the Trance Dance Benefits generated, Kearney left town still unsure of what community radio was.

After a year in Madison Wisconsin, where he first heard the eclectic programming and creative potential of community radio on WORT, Kearney returned to Bloomington in 1982 ready to renew the push for community radio. WORT was founded soon after the NARK meeting of 1975. Since its inception, WORT has evolved from a freewheeling collective to an efficiently organized, economically viable station that requires the support of five full-time and four part-time staff. True to its radical roots, WORT features an adventurous music mix, local call-in programs, as well as progressively minded local news and public affairs programs. With WORT as his inspiration, Brian Kearney redoubled his interest in community radio for Bloomington.

A marketing and business major at Indiana University's School of Business, Kearney put his training to the test and began yet another round of fundraising for the newly renamed non-profit organization, Bloomington Community Radio (BCR). More important, Kearney changed tactics. Although Kearney was sympathetic to the idea of community radio, he recognized that the drive for the station was led by a relatively small segment of the Bloomington community, predominantly the bohemian music and artistic types that came to Bloomington for their schooling or to escape the cultural conservatism of their native Indiana. If community radio was to become a reality, Kearney believed, other segments of the community must be involved.

My hunch was that the problem that they had was that they were reaching out to the wrong people. Not so much the wrong people. But in terms of our timing, they were the wrong people. The bohos were not the ones you wanted yet. They were the ones you wanted when the station was on the air. Then you needed them, you needed the people with time on their hands; the one's with energy, and creativity. All that stuff. Then you needed them. But as far as this bureaucratic, engineering, legal shit, everybody's eyes were going to glaze over. Whose eyes will not? Well, who else does this sort of thing? The pillars of the community probably do. They probably deal with lawyers and such. I began to get an inkling that if this was going to work, it would take awhile and that who we needed to see us through were these "other" people. They were the ones we needed. In fact, it probably would be better if we ignored us, the bohos, for a time.

With this strategy in mind, Kearney set out to identify and make contact with, as he puts it, "the pillars of the community." Fortuitously, one of his first contacts was with the most respected man in town, Herman B Wells.

Kearney often refers to Wells, the long-time Indiana University chancellor, as Bloomington community radio's "single greatest ally" (Mills

1995: C1). Certainly, no one involved in the decades-long struggle to establish community radio in Bloomington would challenge the validity of Kearney's claim. Wells' association with the project proved decisive in realizing the dream of community radio in Bloomington. As Kearney suggests, "I'm not sure we'd be here without him" (Mills 1999). However, Wells did not come to the project of his own volition; throughout the 1980s Kearney developed and nurtured Wells' involvement and support.

Curiously, Kearney first came to know of Wells, and realize the need to cultivate a relationship with Bloomington's most prominent citizen, through one of Kearney's bohemian contacts, local graphic illustrator and WFHB music programmer extraordinaire, Mark Beebe. Kearney recalls:

I used to visit Mark on campus every once and a while. We'd talk about music and all. Anyway, he used to work in Owen Hall, which is Herman's building. And umm, and I remember, the first time he told me about Herman Wells. He goes "You know there's this guy," [Laughter] he goes "How many people are there who are alive who have busts of themselves? Herman Wells does. He's got a bust of himself, you know, over by Kirkwood Hall. It's like, that doesn't happen. Everybody loves this guy. He's like this really powerful guy, and everybody loves him. He's alive and there's a bust of him like he's a god."

As noted above, Beebe's assessment was no understatement. Right up until the time of his death in March 2000 Wells wielded considerable influence on local, state, national, and even international levels. Kearney reasoned that Wells' backing would open doors for him throughout the Bloomington business community as well as with local and state government representatives.

Kearney's plan was to get a letter of endorsement from the esteemed Indiana University chancellor. This in turn, would give legitimacy to Kearney's fund-raising efforts in the local business community. Kearney recalls: "The thing to do is to go to him and get a blessing. Have him anoint us. . . . and be blessed by a letter, because you could not have better credibility. You could not have a better piece of paper to walk around with." Kearney was confident that with Wells' endorsement and a dedicated group of volunteers behind him, he could "sell" the concept of community radio to the local business owners who might otherwise support, but not necessarily financially contribute to, a community radio station. And as we shall see, Kearney's financial strategy prefigured Bloomington community radio's departure from the approach and ultimately the mission of community radio first established by Pacifica Radio.

But Wells was not so quick to offer his support. Despite the Indiana University affiliation of most of the principles associated with

Bloomington Community Radio, the chancellor was unmoved by the well intentioned, but lofty goals of a handful of local artists and musicians. Both Kearney and the BCR would have to earn Wells' approval. In 1986, Kearney took a crucial step in securing Wells' respect when he became the IU chancellor's personal assistant. In time, Kearney's sweat equity secured for him the coveted letter of endorsement from Wells.

The concept of sweat equity is important to Kearney, both personally and professionally. In order to gain the respect of local business leaders, Kearney thought it was important to show some initiative and hard work. In the spirit of grassroots fundraising efforts Kearney and Chet Chemeski, one-time host of WFHB's popular Louisiana music program, Crawfish Fiesta, launched the Community Radio Lawn Service. This was but one of several creative, if less than lucrative, fundraising schemes the BCR tried during those lean years. In the final analysis, however, Wells' on-going support for the station came not so much from the BCR's hard work and perseverance but from the close personal relationship that developed between the aging university administrator and the young radio enthusiast.

In the meantime, Kearney's contacts at the National Federation of Community Broadcasters (NFCB) – the national lobbying group for the US community radio sector – alerted him to BCR's considerable Channel 6 difficulties. Located fifty miles south of Indianapolis, Bloomington's use of noncommercial FM frequencies was severely restricted by WRTV, the local ABC affiliate's television signal. These problems were compounded by WRTV's well-deserved reputation for thwarting the license applications of would-be noncommercial broadcasters throughout central Indiana. As Jeffrey Morris explains:

We knew that we were in the fringe of channel 6 TV and that we had this interference problem. But we didn't know that we wouldn't be able to work it out with them. [Laughs] We thought, well this, this shouldn't be that bad, we're just this little station down here. But in fact, WRTV had a record with other stations trying to get on. And the problem with Channel 6 interference was something that was not resolvable at the time. Most Channel 6 stations would just put you on their budgets as a, you know, an item year after year for legal fees to just continue to block it. In fact, they blocked Ball State University's application for nine years.

Ball State University's public radio station, WBST, finally resolved its Channel 6 problems by following an FCC suggestion to request noncommercial status for the first unoccupied commercial frequency in Muncie, 92.1 FM. WBST engineering and administrative staff suggested BCR take the same approach. Citing a similar strategy successfully employed

BLOOMINGTON
COMMUNITY RADIO LAWN SERVICE

BCR is a group of people interested in bringing a community oriented, community access radio station to Bloomington. We are an organization in its infancy and in need of raising money to build our organization. Help make the dream of healthy community radio a reality. . .

GET YOUR LAWN MOWED.
HELP BLOOMINGTON COMMUNITY RADIO
GET OFF THE GROUND.
REASONABLE RATES — GOOD FOLKS
CALL TODAY!!

BRIAN 333-6085
CHET 339-6111

2. BCR's grassroots fundraising efforts included the Community Lawn Service. (Courtesy Brian Kearney)

years earlier by Indiana University's public radio station, WFIU, BCR filed a Petition for Rule Making with the FCC to acquire noncommercial status for an available commercial frequency at 95.1 FM. Confident their request would succeed, the BCR envisioned community radio from Bloomington, Indiana reaching listeners across south central Indiana over a commercial broadcast frequency.

Once again, however, these efforts were thwarted, this time by a rather infamous character in Bloomington's radio history: Bruce Quinn (a.k.a. Jolly Roger). For several years, Quinn and some of his associates ran a clandestine radio operation in Bloomington. A radio enthusiast, and one-time community radio supporter, Quinn's outlandish behavior at times enthralled, but more often than not alienated community radio advocates who were ever mindful to avoid antagonizing the FCC. Around the time BCR came upon its new strategy, Quinn decided to "go legitimate" and submitted applications for licensing with the FCC. The increasingly antagonistic relationship between Bruce Quinn and BCR members came to a head. Jeffrey Morris recalls:

He was going around applying for all kinds of things. And he fought us on this. He applied in Bloomington. We applied as opposing him, actually as competition to him. . . . He immediately switched his application to Nashville, Indiana, which was a gimmick, because that meant he could claim that that was a first service to Nashville, Indiana. . . . Nashville, Indiana, there's about 700 real people in town. They listen to Columbus, Indianapolis, and Bloomington. And, we made arguments to the effect that Nashville doesn't really suppose a first service that they were served in all these different ways. We spent $10,000–$12,000 fighting this battle over three and a half years. We ended up losing that battle. Basically, with Reagan Administration appointees [to the FCC] license applications for commercial stations won out over noncommercial applications. But I think we got taken for a ride a little bit too. In our enthusiasm, we believed more in this than was we really should have. I think this lawyer and engineer could have told us "Look this is not gonna fly. You're chances are very slim." . . . But they didn't. They took our money. . . . So the petition for rule making failed. . . . But in the process of this, Andy Rogers [a local businessman], who is interested in broadcasting became a friend of ours and gave us a couple of sizable donations and a few thousand dollars. Bruce Quinn managed to piss him off, which got us a few more bucks.

Reeling from their defeat, but with some desperately needed seed money, the stalwarts of BCR regrouped and began the process anew. To this day, however, the failure to win the petition for rule making weighs heavily on BCR members. Jeffrey Morris notes, "If we had gotten that frequency [95.1 FM] we'd have 6,000 watts in town. This is part of the reason why we pursued it in the first place. We could have had a much stronger signal. We knew we could wiggle something into the noncommercial band at that point, but we didn't know how much." The strength of the signal, and the location of the broadcast tower were subject to austere FCC regulations.

During the course of the three and a half year long court battle with Quinn, engineering formulas were developed by the FCC, the NFCB, and others to address the Channel 6 interference problem that had plagued educational and other noncommercial broadcasters for years (FCC Docket 29735). For BCR, this meant returning to the noncommercial band in search of a frequency that could reach the greater Bloomington community without interfering with the audio portion of WRTV's television signal. The solution allowed BCR to "squeeze" a signal into the noncommercial portion of the FM band, and according to Morris, it's a tight fit. "They didn't give us much. Basically, they said, here's a formula that defines the interference area, if there are more than 3,000 people in it, you can't do it. So what that means is that you have to move your transmitter ten, twelve miles out of town and try to aim it back into town."

With this information and the help of a new engineer, Ken Devine of Broadcast Technical Inc., and a new lawyer, Harry Cole of the Washington DC-based law firm Bechtel and Cole, BCR conducted yet another frequency search. In April of 1990, BCR submitted its Construction Permit to the FCC for 91.3 FM. With the paperwork into the FCC, BCR entered negotiations with a local land developer for a tower site southwest of town. As a result, WFHB's broadcast tower, then operating at 2,500 watts, is located on an acre of land located some 11 miles south west of downtown Bloomington. WFHB's inaugural broadcast took place from a cinderblock shack that served as the station's on-air studio during that first, jubilant year of community broadcasting.

With a tower site and Herman B Wells' assistance in expediting the station's license application at the FCC – Wells is said to have pulled a few strings at the FCC with a little help from two well-connected Indiana politicians, congressional representative Lee Hamilton and US Vice President Dan Quayle – Kearney redoubled his fundraising efforts. Kearney then took Wells' endorsement to local philanthropist Cecil Waldron. As it turned out, Wells linked Kearney up with the community radio's single most important financial benefactor.

I was working for Herman, looking for money, and had been courting Cecil Waldron for years . . . going out to Meadowood [a local retirement home], sitting down with her, she, telling me stories. You know, like once a month, she'd put me in this big easy chair. I'd kinda lay back. She'd repeat a lot of the same stories. . . . She worked as a clerk in the old city hall. Her husband owned the south side of the square. Her husband's grandfather helped start First National Bank. Herman knew that the geography of her life was good for the Bloomington Area Arts Council, and what the council was trying to pull off, which was trying to get money for that building. Herman's like, "Well, there's this old gal who used to work in that building. And her family is not really recognized in this town. And she could, you know, really go for this idea as a possible naming opportunity in the very place where a good deal of her life took place."

Shortly after being elected to the Board of Directors of the Bloomington Area Arts Council (BAAC), Kearney was approached with the idea of locating the radio station in the city's historic firehouse, adjacent to the old city hall building, the future home of the Waldron Arts Center. BAAC member Frank Young recruited Kearney to the board for strategic purposes. Young and others felt that the Waldron Arts Center might become an elitist institution that would neither sponsor nor support local artists. From Young's perspective, Kearney's relationship with the Bloomington arts community, as well as his growing influence in the local business leaders, might help "balance" the board and ensure that the Waldron functioned as a community-based teaching, exhibition, and performance space for local artists and performers. Young's strategy proved beneficial for both the Bloomington Area Arts Council and the stalwarts of community radio.

Although the BCR enthusiastically supported the idea of locating the community radio station adjacent to the new arts center, the community radio project was confronted with another problem: raising $125,000 to purchase the old firehouse. The city sold the former city hall building to the BAAC for one dollar. Why the firehouse came with such an exorbitant price tag remains unclear. Kearney speculates that some BAAC members hoped the space would be leased to a commercial interest. In any event, Kearney's relationship with Mrs. Waldron was about to pay off in a big way.

I'm on the board of the Waldron. I mean, this is getting better all the time. Cecil likes me. The project is coming along and she loves that I'm on the board. Now I can float this next idea in front of her. 'You know. I've been talking to people, and a lot of people think it would be great, both for the Waldron and Bloomington Community Radio if we could be in the Firehouse. The thought is that we could broadcast from there, do interviews and that, and that it would be a good sort of artistic identity for us to be there too. That this would be like a mecca for arts and artistic activity. Draw people . . . this is the idea that we're cooking up right now. So I asked her, you know, what are you're thoughts?' And the first thing she said was 'You two need each other.'

The BAAC received a gift of $365,000; through Kearney, BCR requested and received $225,000 from the now deceased patron of the downtown Bloomington art scene. The significance of Cecil Waldron's generosity cannot be overstated. The Waldron Arts Center is home to several galleries, music and theatrical stages, and classrooms for arts education. Indeed, the relationship between the Waldron Arts Center and WFHB is, as Cecil Waldron had envisaged it, mutually beneficial. For instance, every month WFHB broadcasts live performances by local musicians from the Rose Firebay on a program called *Saturday's Child*. Since 1994, when the station finally took up permanent residence in the former city firehouse that now serves as WFHB's downtown studios, the Waldron

3. Jeffrey Morris making last-minute preparations for WFHB's inaugural broadcast on 4 January 1993. (Courtesy Jeffrey Morris)

Arts Center has been the site for dozens of station benefits and hundreds of live broadcasts.

For the BCR, the gift gave community radio in Bloomington a permanent, rent-free home and considerable "start-up" capital to purchase a parcel of land for the tower site and begin building the station. As Kearney notes, "We were stabilizing ourselves from day one in ways that most community radio stations rarely do. Most stations pay rent, most stations lease tower space and we were not ... we had capitalized ourselves enough." With the purchase of the firehouse, BCR's deliberations on appropriate call letters for the new station were straightforward enough. Community radio in Bloomington would be known as Firehouse Broadcasting: WFHB. Julie Barnett, a local illustrator, designed the station's logo: the firefighter's best friend, a dalmatian. Of course, the dog was named Spot, and the station's motto succinctly captures the essence of Firehouse Broadcasting: "WFHB – Your Spot on the Dial."

Turn your radio on!

Following a formal station identification nervously recited by Jeffrey Morris, Jim Manion, Richard Fish, and Brian Kearney, the principal

4. Radio Ridge, WFHB's transmitter site and on-air studio during the first jubilant year of community broadcasting. (Courtesy Jeffrey Morris)

architects of community radio in Bloomington, Indiana, the sound of a Chinese gong – on loan for the occasion from Indiana University Chancellor Herman B Wells – radiated over the airwaves of 91.3 FM. The foursome then cued up a scratchy vinyl recording of Roy Acuff's rendition of the old Christian standard, "Turn Your Radio On." And with that modest ceremony, the eighteen-year struggle to establish community radio in Bloomington, Indiana ended on 4 January 1993.[15]

Within a matter of months, WFHB was an unqualified hit with local audiences in Bloomington and throughout south central Indiana. In celebration of its first anniversary, the station moved from its modest cinderblock house out on "Radio Ridge" – the affectionate name given to the station's tower site – to its permanent downtown location in the historic firehouse. Within the year, WFHB expanded its music, cultural, and public affairs offerings and commenced programming twenty-four hours a day, seven days a week. Soon thereafter, the station added a 250-watt translator at 98.1 FM, to improve service in downtown Bloomington.[16] By 1996, WFHB has dozens of local business underwriters, upwards of 150 volunteers, and well over 1,000 contributing members.

In addition to sponsoring concerts and other local cultural events, WFHB began experimenting with new media technologies to bring community radio from south central Indiana to the world. For instance, on 13 November 1995, WFHB's second annual "Live Wire Blues Power" concert featured local musicians performing for a live audience in the Rose Firebay of the Waldron Art Center, to a local radio audience in south central Indiana, and to geographically dispersed listeners in Wisconsin, New Jersey, California, Japan, the Netherlands, Norway, and Switzerland via the Internet. This marked the first of many occasions that WFHB made use of new communication technologies to bring music from down the block, to the planet.[17] Judging by listener feedback from across the country and around the world, WFHB's creativity and eclecticism is a hit with listeners far and wide.

WFHB's "overnight" success is, in fact, the realization of a decades-long collective vision of diverse, non-commercial, community-oriented radio. An approach to radio that not only demonstrates the medium's creative and expressive possibilities, but also resonates with listeners who have grown disillusioned with broadcasting's conventional, formulaic, and often uninspired programming. It would be a mistake, however, to characterize WFHB's achievement solely in terms of surmounting legal, bureaucratic, financial, and technical hurdles. WFHB's success in overcoming the considerable barriers of entry into US broadcasting owes a great deal to the rich tradition of indigenous radio practices that helped shape and continue to inform community radio in Bloomington.

For example, at the height of its clandestine operation, Bruce Quinn's Jolly Roger Radio had a staff of twenty or more people who gave their time, effort, and on occasion their personal living space to bring so-called "pirate radio" to Bloomington, Indiana – and well beyond. In its heyday, Jolly Roger Radio broadcast a rambunctious mix of punk rock, ethnic music, and amusing and provocative banter to twenty-four states and four Canadian provinces over AM, FM, and shortwave frequencies. In keeping with the legacy of unlicensed and clandestine broadcasters operating across the United States during the 1960s and 1970s, Jolly Roger Radio produced imaginative, challenging, innovative, and decidedly unruly radio: without advertising, without offices, without prohibitive capital investment, and, most notably, without all that onerous FCC paperwork.

A PSA for Jolly Roger put it plainly: "We are Jolly Roger Radio home entertainment service. Jolly Roger Radio is not a business, and this radio station has no income. Jolly Roger Radio does not ask for money. We serve one and only one purpose, and that is to share fine music with you, our friends. We hope you enjoy it." Enjoy it they did! Listeners called in requests to public phones around the city, manned by Jolly Roger volunteers, who then relayed the information to disc jockeys operating from any number of "undisclosed locations" throughout Bloomington.

In 1980, following several boisterous years of operation, the FCC finally caught up with Bruce Quinn and Tom Preston, the masterminds behind Jolly Roger Radio. Despite its makeshift, let alone illegal character, Jolly Roger Radio garnered enthusiastic listener and volunteer support. "The half-dozen glowing articles in the Indianapolis and Bloomington newspapers" suggest that Jolly Roger Radio provided a welcome alternative radio service for listeners in Bloomington and south central Indiana (Ganzert 1994: 22). Notwithstanding disparate strategies and tactics, then, the success of both Jolly Roger and, later, WFHB rests in large part on the ability of these grassroots organizations to involve listeners in realizing the creative, expressive, and community-building potential of broadcasting. The demise of Jolly Roger Radio brought a dynamic chapter in Bloomington's radio history to an end. But the desire for lively radio in Bloomington had another, legal if still somewhat "underground," outlet: WQAX.

In 1973, the Indiana University Student Association (IUSA) began a fledgling operation using cable-FM to supplement the carrier current service provided by the "official" Indiana University student-run radio station, WIUS. WIUS had a history of protracted bureaucratic battles between station management, the student organization, and the university administration, all of which contributed to the station's growing insularity from and irrelevance to the student body. Fed up with WIUS's complacency and ineffectiveness, a number of IUSA representatives, including Steve Miller, Jim Burke, and Tom Hirons, secured equipment loans and set up a "renegade" operation in the Indiana Memorial Union: WQAX.

Jim Manion, a young sophomore from Evansville, Indiana, stumbled across an ad in the student newspaper, the *Indiana Daily Student* (IDS), announcing the establishment of WQAX. For Manion, whose father worked in the radio and television business for years, WQAX was a godsend. One of the station's original members, Manion would be involved in various capacities with WQAX from 1973–1988. As it happens, dozens of future WFHB music programmers likewise cut their teeth at WQAX.

Growing up around the broadcasting industry and listening to short-wave radio as a teenager, Jim Manion's enthusiasm for radio is palpable. In large part his passion for, and encyclopedic knowledge of, the world's musics was nourished by radio broadcasting from across the country and around the world. Manion's radio surfing introduced him to what, in the late 1960s and early 1970s, was commonly referred to as *free form* radio: a programming philosophy which abjures play lists and is characterized by its spontaneous and eclectic style.[18]

As William Barlow observes, commercial stations in major markets across the United States were experimenting with so-called progressive formats and adopted this free form sensibility. "They employed disc jockeys with a talent for programming musical selections that explored themes, told stories and conjured up images of the emerging youth-oriented 'counter-culture.' Individual tastes and independent convictions were a vital part of the mix of music and commentary" (1988: 87). In short, free form radio is characterized by a comprehensive knowledge of disparate musical forms and styles as well as by each individual programmer's facility for language and their ability to communicate effectively and engagingly through words and music.

Manion caught bits and pieces of free form radio over his shortwave radio, listening to domestic stations like WCFL in Chicago as well as international broadcasts emanating from over sixty countries. But his immersion in free form radio came from an unlikely source, a local station in his hometown of Evansville. Manion explains:

A lucky thing happened in Evansville. ABC, in 1970, attempted to create a network of free form radio, that they called "Love Radio." [Laughs] They had a station in L.A.; they had a station in San Francisco; and they had a station in New York. And their Midwestern test market was Evansville. And so, what was on the air in Evansville, for over a year, they would get big reel-to-reels of these, these free form shows from different cities and play them in Evansville! So, I got exposed to this whole style of free form mixing and all that, through high school.

This free form sensibility was central to WQAX's on-air sound; a crucial component for building an audience for the renegade operation and distinguishing the station from its more conventional counterparts on campus: the university's public broadcasting affiliate, WFIU, whose schedule was dominated by classical music; and WIUS, the rather staid college radio station.

WQAX's free form programming proved extremely popular with listeners dismayed by the dearth of adventurous radio in Bloomington. More important, for purposes of this discussion, this style of broadcasting continues to inform the programming philosophy Manion takes to his position as Program Director of WFHB. The success of WFHB's morning and afternoon mix programs, in particular, is testament to the appeal of free form radio's eclecticism. That said, WFHB's claims to the mantle of free form radio require some qualification.[19] Like its approach to the tradition of community radio associated with the Pacifica stations, WFHB embraces certain aspects of free form radio while refashioning others.

Specifically, WFHB's broadcast schedule is far more structured by day part than past or even contemporary incarnations of free form radio.[20] For instance, morning programmers are encouraged to feature acoustic music. Throughout the day, the tempo and diversity pick up and listeners can expect to hear everything from punk and bluegrass, to ethnic music and avant-garde jazz, as well as blues, hip-hop, and "alternative" country. On the other hand, evening and weekend programming in particular is the domain of specialty shows that rarely stray from a specific musical genre or ethno-cultural tradition. Thus, while WFHB's broadcast schedule provides a diverse and welcome alternative to the commercial and public service broadcasters serving Bloomington, neither these specialty shows, nor the mix programs approach the free form sensibility, "a collage of live interviews, political commentary, dramatic sketches, poetry, satire, public events and listener call-ins," associated with earlier incarnations of community radio (Barlow 1988: 87).

WFHB's approach to free form radio, therefore, is limited primarily to music, with remarkably little in the way of listener call-in, public events, radio theater, or spoken word material making its way into regularly scheduled music programs.[21] Accordingly, there are no play lists at WFHB. Volunteer programmers have significant creative control over their shows. However, mix programmers are required to play a specific amount of recent and newly released music each hour. And despite the fact that the content of each day part's "music feature" is up to the individual programmer's discretion, the program schedule determines the exact time and duration of these special features. While these stipulations help to keep WFHB's mix programs sounding consistent and contemporary, this and other requirements – most notably an adherence to keeping talk between music sets to a minimum – constrain the individuality, autonomy, and loquaciousness of each programmer: a central tenet of the free form philosophy.

More to the point, programmers are strongly discouraged from adding personal, social, or political commentary to their broadcasts. As we shall see, this prohibition is in keeping with WFHB's institutional commitment to "neutrality," a philosophy that more established community stations and their forerunners – the ethnic broadcasters of the 1920s and 1930s and African-American radio stations of the post-war period – rarely embraced. As Barlow points out, these stations encouraged and cultivated outspoken, provocative, and lively discussion as a means of realizing broadcasting's communicative potential and for rearticulating the medium as a locally relevant resource for news, opinion, creative expression, community organizing, and political mobilization. With these important qualifications in mind, the linkages between the institutional history and programming philosophy of WQAX and WFHB's growth and development are nonetheless significant and merit exploring in some detail.

In the summer of 1982, WQAX lost the support of the IUSA. The equipment upgrade that was earmarked for the cable-FM operation was rather unceremoniously offered to WIUS. In effect, IUSA abandoned WQAX. At this point, WQAX was, in Manion's words, an "orphan on the street." But the membership decided to keep the operation running and over the course of the next ten years, WQAX was housed in the Allen building on Kirkwood Avenue, in offices located on the downtown square, and in other locations throughout the city.

The core of programmers that kept WQAX running learned some valuable lessons during their transient radio days. Despite the sorry state of their modest equipment and the anarchic character of their organization, the WQAX staff gained invaluable experience in producing entertaining and innovative radio. Jim Manion observes WQAX's significance to WFHB's on-air sound this way:

When FHB signed on at least half of our programmers were former QAX programmers with years and years and years of doing really great mix shows that they were really intensely, creatively involved in. That maybe, you know, at the most 100 people at any given time were listening to. So very low audience numbers but very high level of creativity and passionate interest in music and I think that's a crucial element in terms of how we kicked off FHB with a bang. Because, I think potential listeners, and especially people in the local broadcast community like at the other stations were really prepared for FHB to come on and be amateur hour and be real green behind the ears, like we don't know what the fuck we're doing. And we came on like gangbusters. And people are going, 'Wow, Laurie Anderson, blues, you know, jazz, alternative music, international music, whoa! And you know what you're talking about, and you know how to mix it up.' That wouldn't happen without QAX.

Equally important, WQAX gave Manion and others tremendous insight into the dynamics of building a volunteer operation, making it a vital and relevant organization and keeping it together. Manion suggests:

I think what it comes down to is WQAX was totally essential in terms of how successful WFHB has been. Not only our on-the-air experience, but also the experience of keeping a grassroots organization going. . . . I was certainly influenced and inspired by how people could just get an idea about something that they wanted to do, that was missing, that they really liked, and put some juice into it, and get it going.

This same spirit survives and is reflected in the creativity and eclecticism of WFHB's program schedule. Indeed, a handful of WFHB's most popular shows, *The Beat Party*, *WomenSpace*, and *Scenes from the Northern Lights*, among them, all had their start on WQAX.

For all its lively, energetic, and creative potential, however, WQAX was severely constrained from reaching a substantial listening audience. Listeners were not likely to stumble upon WQAX, a cable-FM service, as they might an over the air signal. In order to receive a cable-FM signal, listeners must know how to hook up their cable to their stereo systems. For all but the most avid music enthusiast, this was something of an inconvenience. And for obvious reasons, listeners could not tune in WQAX on their car or portable radios. Furthermore, WQAX's potential reach was defined in terms of the city's cable television penetration rate. In sum, reception of WQAX was extremely limited; broadcasting, on the other hand, offered WQAX programmers the opportunity to reach a much larger portion of the Bloomington community.

Yet, community radio advocates were determined to insulate the community radio project from WQAX. Manion contends that "the community radio project was not an effort to get QAX on the air." This proved to be a pragmatic and rather savvy strategy. In Manion's estimation, there was a downside to WQAX's organizational culture and the innovative radio practices the station's free form philosophy engendered. To begin with, WQAX's reputation was somewhat suspect. Its rather inauspicious beginnings as a renegade student-run organization preceded it. Moreover, the split between the student association and WQAX was far from amicable.

Despite its imaginative use of the medium, then, WQAX had an image problem and the advocates of community radio in Bloomington did not want their efforts to be associated with it. "The official ties, I never wanted to make, because QAX was always such a shaky organization. QAX was always on the verge of falling apart and not being able to pay their bills. And I knew it would not be healthy for this new effort to be tied to the health of QAX. I knew it would be an energy drain and a financial drain and I was adamant about keeping it separate."

For a variety of personal, administrative, logistical, and ultimately very practical reasons, WQAX was never explicitly linked to the community radio project. The irony in all of this is not lost on Jim Manion. In his capacity as WFHB's long-time program director, Manion is the first to admit: "If you look at it now, QAX is on the air!" This means that programming on WFHB is polished and challenging. Volunteer programmers, in some cases with decades of "broadcast" experience, bring their talents to an appreciative and growing listening audience.

Aside from WFHB's popular weekday music mix programs, listeners respond just as enthusiastically to Bloomington community radio's many excellent specialty shows. Significantly, while these programs cater to specific interests, they are meant to be heard by all. A common refrain on *WomenSpace* puts it plainly, "Music by women, for women, and everyone." Offering far more than the work of female singer/songwriters, *WomenSpace* is a conduit for news, arts, and entertainment information related to women's issues. In doing so, *WomenSpace* and other specialty shows create a space on the programming schedule for programming of particular interest to a specific group, while making these interests available to the community at large.

For instance, students from the IU Ethnomusicology Student Association explore traditional and contemporary global sounds on the *World Music Show*. Other programs celebrate a specific ethnic and regional sound. *Reggae Children*, *Hora Latino*, and *The Old Changing Way* feature Jamaican, Latin, and Celtic music respectively. *SonRise* and *Sounds of Inspiration* bring Contemporary Christian sounds to the community. *Rural Routes* and *Old Time Train 45* celebrate southern Indiana's rich traditions of bluegrass and old-time music while *Melody Unasked For* and *Headphone Tourist* feature cutting-edge experimental audio work that appeals to audiophiles of every race, creed, and color.

The diversity of musical styles shared and celebrated over the airwaves of WFHB suggests that the local interest in passionate, innovative, and decidedly unconventional radio broadcasting is, at long last, being met. To be sure, unlike its commercial counterparts – contemporary country music and "progressive" rock stations, or the classical music programming that fills the bulk of the local NPR affiliate, WFIU's broadcast day – WFHB plays music that is not heard anywhere else in or around Bloomington.

Undeniably, then, WFHB provides a vibrant sound alternative to the Bloomington community. But to what extent do community residents determine the character and content of these alternatives? As John Hochheimer (1993) suggests, community radio raises profound questions regarding issues of praxis that complicate and confound the effort to create a locally oriented, participatory medium.

Who speaks for which community interests? Who decides what are the legitimate voices to be heard? . . . What happens when ideas and technical skills are at odds? How are community views solicited, encouraged? In other words, to what degree does/can the station bring its audiences into the process of programme production for themselves?

WFHB's experience with these difficult questions is not unique. Like other community radio stations, WFHB confronts these issues on a daily basis. Upon closer examination WFHB's philosophical orientation and operating practices reveal ruptures as well as continuities between the Bloomington radio project and the tradition of community broadcasting associated with Lewis Hill and Lorenzo Milam, two pivotal figures in the US community radio movement, who not only sought to involve listeners in the daily operations of a community station, but who conceived community radio as a critical intervention into politics and well as culture. The debate over public affairs programming discussed at the outset of this chapter underscores WFHB's reworking of that tradition. As such, it provides important insight into the distinctive fashion Bloomington community radio takes in negotiating the profound and fundamental tensions associated with building and maintaining a viable, responsive, and accountable community media organization.

Negotiating the airwaves

As noted in Chapter 2, the community radio movement in the United States and indeed throughout much of the world owes a great debt to the innovative strategies employed by Pacifica Radio. This tradition can be traced to the vision of Pacifica's founder, Lewis Hill. A journalist and conscientious objector during World War II, Hill lamented what he perceived to be the media's "conspiracy of silence, entertaining and distracting rather than educating the public during and after World War II" (Land 1999: 2). Hill reasoned that the demands of commercial radio – to produce safe, predictable, and inoffensive programming designed to maximize audience numbers and thereby please commercial sponsors – failed to leverage the medium's capacity to educate and enlighten the listening public, to enrich local and national cultures, and to promote peace and justice at home and abroad.

At the heart of Lew Hill's disdain for commercial radio was an astute recognition of the economic realities of broadcasting. Hill understood the pressures associated with commercial broadcasting and the constraints commercial sponsorship places on a station's resources and ultimately, its programming. In a letter to a contributor, Hill observed:

The consequence [of commercial sponsorship] is, as you know if you listen much to the radio, that creative radio programming, programming which is genuinely good not once a week but all the time, is quite rare. Even if the radio industry were full of creative and imaginative people, which I am afraid it is not, the commercial exigencies . . . the sheer physical facts of necessary staff distribution would force a de-emphasis of programming.

(quoted in Stebbins 1969)

According to Hill, radio could realize its creative, expressive, and communicative potential through listener sponsorship.

Central to Hill's vision of listener-supported radio was the belief that such an arrangement would insulate broadcasters from commercial pressures, thereby giving programmers an opportunity to create challenging, thoughtful, informative, and engaging radio; radio that rewarded innovation, engaged controversial social and political issues, questioned established orthodoxies, and was, at the end of the day, accountable to a community of listeners. Through volunteerism and financial contributions, listeners would enter into a productive and mutually beneficial relationship with a local broadcast service (Hill 1958; 1966). To be sure, much that is praiseworthy about community radio – especially its emphasis on providing information and entertainment alternatives to commercial and public service programming – stems from the passionate volunteer involvement and the attendant insulation from commercial interests that listener support fosters.

While Hill's listener-support model went a long way toward securing local enthusiasm and financial support for creative and challenging programming, the listener-support model presented a number of problems as well. As Jeffrey Land observes, "over time his listeners' engagement would lead them to do more than simply sponsor programs or volunteer to answer phones; they would come to feel they had the right to participate in all aspects of station activity, from broadcasting to management policy" (1999: 48). Thus, while this sense of ownership is essential to the success of noncommercial radio, the emphasis upon listener support opens up these organizations to pressure from individuals and interest groups.

Invoking the term community to describe a radio station likewise invites the varied and competing interests within the community to make demands on the station to address the issues and concerns deemed most important to different constituencies. As a result, the scarce resources available to these organizations (e.g., equipment, air-time, finances, personnel) become a site of intense struggle within and between these competing groups, ultimately confounding listener-supported radio's relevancy to the community as a whole. In short, the strength that listener support brings to community radio has the potential to undermine a station's ability to serve the disparate tastes and interests within a community. These problems are at the core of the Pacifica station's perennial difficulties and remain one of the fundamental challenges facing community radio (Land 1999; Lasar 2000).

A veteran of Pacifica's early institutional struggles, Lorenzo Milam recognized the danger factionalism posed to listener-supported, community-oriented radio. And yet, the KRAB Nebula – a loose affiliation of community stations Milam and his colleagues helped organize throughout the 1960s and 1970s – nonetheless championed participatory governance and community involvement in station management, program production, engineering, and operations.[22] Described by William Barlow as the "decentralized, anarchist wing of the growing community radio movement," Milam's KRAB Nebula was characterized not least for its musical diversity and lively socio-political commentary but also for its commitment to community ownership and control. "An anti-bureaucracy ethos prevailed among the leadership of the KRAB Nebula station. They attempted to implement democratic procedures within the stations *with varying amounts of success*" (emphasis added; Barlow: 93).

Committed to the twin ideals of access and participation, then, Milam's passion for community radio lies in his keen appreciation for the medium's potential to enhance civic life through creativity, spontaneity, risk taking, and impassioned political debate. In doing so, Milam sought to provide a lively, engaging, and relevant alternative to what he colorfully describes as the "toads and bores" of commercial radio and public broadcasting respectively (1988: 19). Throughout the late 1960s and early 1970s, Milam's vision sparked tremendous interest in community radio, especially within the anti-war and counter-culture movements. That Milam's vision resonated primarily among white, college-educated students is testament to the progressive sensibilities of the times. Conversely, it is indicative of the model's limited relevance to those uninvolved in either war resistance or the counter-culture.

The lessons learned from this legacy of listener-supported, community broadcasting were not lost on the founders of WFHB. Bloomington Community Radio (BCR) members made conscious decisions to avoid the pitfalls of Lew Hill's listener-support model while playing to the strengths of Hill's vision. Former WFHB General Manager Brian Kearney notes: "If the organization wanted to follow the status quo established by the community stations that preceded it, then WFHB could have developed a culture that would focus on the disenfranchised of the community and give them a voice. This would have been more in keeping with the tradition of the Hill model" (1996: 45). But BCR was determined to avoid repeating the mistakes that began to plague "traditional" community radio stations across the country: namely, community radio's isolation from and irrelevance to whole segments of the community. Over time, it became clear that by providing services to specific under-represented groups and marginalized constituencies within a particular place, community radio has a tendency to define the community in very limited terms.

That is to say, in their efforts to serve the disenfranchised and progressive political constituencies, community radio sometimes excludes significant portions of the community. The case of KOPN in Columbia, Missouri provides a sobering example in this regard. In 1991, the lease agreement for KOPN's office and studio space was up for renewal. Since the station's operating budget could not cover a significant rent increase, KOPN began the search for a new home. A capital campaign designed to raise the funds to finance the move proved an eye-opener for KOPN's management. When they were approached for financial support, the "movers and shakers" of Columbia's business establishment were reluctant to help. Significantly, the reluctance to support the community station was not so much a matter of political orientation, per se; rather it stemmed from a profound sense of alienation from the station's programming.

BCR's adaptation of Hill's listener-sponsored model strategically employed a more inclusive view of community – in an effort to involve a cross-section of the community in building and maintaining Bloomington's community radio station – while serving the diverse interests and needs of the local population. Kearney notes that once the decision was made to adapt the listener-sponsorship model: "The next step was to craft a mission statement that would reflect *a more inclusive and less-politicized view of community* (emphasis added; 45).

This perspective illuminates the cultural values and complex ideological functions embedded in popular conceptions of "community." That is to say, while BCR's "less politicized" strategy is surely less threatening to established social, political, and economic power blocks within the community – thereby enabling the station to secure desperately needed financial backing – it is altogether misleading. Far from highlighting the contested quality of communal relations, a "more inclusive" view of community obscures the inequity of power relations within the city of Bloomington. Adopting this perspective, therefore, serves to reinforce these power differentials under the rubric of inclusion. As a result, depoliticizing community radio in the fashion advocated by the BCR provides a vehicle for the expression of "alternative," but not necessarily *oppositional* forms of expression. Thus, the community WFHB articulates consists primarily of those groups and individuals with the significant economic resources or those with the requisite "cultural capital" (Bourdieu 1984).

For BCR, then, the cost of doing business with "the pillars of the community" is high; many of the voices most often left out of mainstream media – labor, the poor, racial and ethnic minorities, political activists – are once more barred from speaking for themselves and in their own behalf. That is to say, the individuals and groups marginalized by WFHB's adaptation of the community radio tradition are, in large part, the same groups and individuals whose interests, values, and beliefs are most often misrepresented or unheard in dominant media. While not necessarily hollow, BCR's victory is nonetheless incomplete. That is to say, by adopting this strategy WFHB successfully negotiates the economic realities of radio broadcasting and allows Bloomington community radio to bring always passionate, often innovative, and sometimes challenging radio to the local airwaves.

Working with David LePage, representative of the National Federation of Community Broadcasters' (NFCB) Healthy Station Project, WFHB management, staff, and volunteers set out to craft a mission statement that balanced the desire for WFHB to be a forum for diverse information, opinion, and cultural expression while ensuring WFHB's financial health and viability. The result is a succinct mission statement that makes no mention of serving marginalized, disenfranchised, or under-represented groups. It reads: "WFHB exists to celebrate and increase the local cultural diversity and to provide a neutral forum for the discussion and exchange of ideas and issues." For all its "simplicity," however, WFHB's mission statement is somewhat deceptive, and in theory as well as practice, is fraught with contradictions.

That WFHB enhances the Bloomington area's music and cultural scene is undeniable. Through the station's efforts, local talent receives previously unimagined regional, national, and international exposure (Bambarger 1996). Moreover, nationally and internationally renowned performers arrive in town with greater frequency every year, thanks in large part to WFHB's enthusiastic support of local clubs, promoters, and performances. Of special note in this regard are the synergies between Bloomington community radio and the Lotus World Music and Arts Festival. A not-for-profit educational and cultural organization, the Lotus Festival is named in honor of Quinten Lotus Dickey (1911–1989) from nearby Paoli, Indiana. Lotus Dickey was "discovered" by Indiana University folklorists and soon became a much beloved member of the Bloomington old time music scene.

The festival that bears his name celebrates southern Indiana's rich musical heritage and brings world music to local audiences. In the weeks leading up to the Lotus Festival, WFHB's program schedule prominently features visiting artists. In addition to helping promote, organize, and staff the Lotus Festival, WFHB music programmers and volunteers welcome Lotus performers to the Firehouse Studios for on-air interviews and live performances. Among the hundreds of artists who have appeared at the Lotus Festival and performed over the airwaves of WFHB are Diane Jarvi, Pranita Jain, Huun-Huur Tu (throat singers from Tuva), Liz Carrol, Robert Mirabal, Saba, Guang-Zu Li, and the Master Musicians of Jajouka. Without the Lotus Festival, and WFHB's support for this much-anticipated yearly event, it is unlikely that very many international artists of this caliber would ever visit Bloomington, Indiana.

Thus, even if one were to accept the rather suspect notion of "neutrality" that is central to WFHB's philosophy, this fervent and spirited dissemination of music represents a critical intervention into contemporary media culture and as such is properly viewed as a form of cultural politics. That is to say, advocating and promoting cross-cultural communication and fostering relationships within and between disparate geographic and socio-cultural communities in this way undermines the hegemony of media institutions (e.g., commercial and public service broadcasters, as well as "major" recording labels) and challenges the legitimacy of dominant media practices. More to the point, the struggle to establish community radio in Bloomington is, in and of itself, an admirable, even heroic attempt to reassert local cultural autonomy and redress stark inequalities within the political economy of US broadcasting. As such, it is a decidedly political act.

And yet, the philosophical and programmatic emphasis WFHB places on neutrality acts as a bulwark against overtly oppositional discourse, effectively limiting the range of ideas and opinions presented over local airwaves and thereby reinforcing many of the same social, political, and cultural inequities a participatory medium like community radio professes to rectify. WFHB's approach to community broadcasting therefore is quite distinct from the ideological orientation shared by many US community broadcasters, an orientation that "champions progressive politics, alternative cultures and participatory democracy" (Barlow 1988: 83). Put another way, unlike other stations in the US community radio sector, WFHB deliberately avoids any hint of political partisanship or advocacy.

Significantly, this strategy was a conscious decision on the part of the BCR to ensure the station's economic viability. As Brian Kearney recalls: "The people who got together [to write the station's mission statement] in March, 1993 felt that this was the most sensible way to do community radio. A non-judgmental forum could include conservatives as well as liberals, Christians as well as Pagans and so on. The idea was to foster dialogue or debate and then let the audience make up its own mind. *This approach also seemed like a better audience building strategy.* If people with different tastes and perspectives felt that their views were accommodated, then they'd be more likely to listen and support such a station" (emphasis added).

In sum, WFHB's strategy is at once an acknowledgment of the traditions of listener-supported, community radio and a reworking of this tradition in order to accommodate varied interests within the Bloomington community and remain economically viable. Ironically, it is this more *inclusive* notion of community that not only marks a dramatic difference between WFHB and "traditional" community radio stations, but more important, confounds Bloomington community radio's participatory potential.

For a time it seemed WFHB had successfully negotiated the desire for innovative, provocative, and diverse radio programming with the economic prerogatives of radio broadcasting. However, as the debate surrounding public affairs programming illustrates, this process of negotiation is contingent, volatile, and ongoing. In May 1996, approximately five months after the *Bloomington Voice* ran its editorial, WFHB began airing *Counterspin* and *Making Contact*, two public affairs programs produced and distributed by a consortium of community radio stations from across the country. The debate over public affairs programming sparked by the editorial ended.

While the resolution of the debate was important, its significance for understanding the character of Bloomington community radio cannot be overstated. The manner in which the debate was conducted, the contradictions it uncovered, and the process it illustrates emphasize not only the evolution of the listener-support model of community radio, but more importantly, demonstrate the problems as well as the promise of this participatory medium.

For WFHB, the controversy highlighted several relevant issues. First, the debate "made public" the process by which new programming is evaluated for inclusion in WFHB's schedule. The incident served as a primer on how constituencies might approach WFHB management with programming suggestions. Second, it became clear that the station needed a more concerted community outreach effort. In order to fulfill its mission, WFHB's task is to identify the diverse constituencies present within the Bloomington community; elicit the input of these heterogeneous groups; and finally, make the station's resources available for these constituencies.

For the first time in its brief existence, WFHB had to scrupulously examine the logistics involved in evaluating programming requests from the community. If the station was to be a "neutral forum for the discussion and exchange of ideas and issues" then WFHB must be prepared for requests from not only progressives, but conservatives, and potentially, from "extremists" on both the left and right. Not to mention the class, gender, ethnic, racial, and cultural communities WFHB must likewise serve in order to fulfill its mission. Finally, and perhaps most dramatically, the discussion made it clear to WFHB volunteers, staff, and management, that while the decades-long struggle to establish community radio for Bloomington was over, the struggle to keep WFHB on the air is ongoing. This process is complicated by the economic demands of broadcasting, as well as by the station's "more inclusive" approach to community radio.

An editorial appearing in the *Herald-Times* in defense of the station's policies suggests the trouble with WFHB's approach. "It appears that

The Newsletter of WFHB 91.3/98.1 FM   Vol. 4, No. 1 March, 1996

No Left Turn?

Station's role as an
"alternative" community
voice debated on-air

By Jacques DuBois

Should WFHB be a source of "alternative" information and news to its listeners, or would such activities typecast the station as "leftist," and hence cut it off from the majority of the members of its potential listening community? Does the station avoid "bad" politics only because they are bad for fund raising, or must it first establish its own identity before it can stray too far left (or right) of center?

These and other questions were brought out of the corridors of WFHB and into the public spotlight recently when Station Manager Brian Kearney and Program Director Jim Manion crowded into the station's tiny production studio along with *Bloomington Voice* writer Chris Gaal for a spirited exchange

of views on a special edition of "Conversations" with Debra Kent. The impetus for the show was a column Gaal wrote for the *Voice* which was critical of the station for its "failure" to air alternative types of news programs such as "Radio Pacifica" or "Counterspin."

The approval of "Counterspin" to the station's schedule and subsequent delay in its implementation was not the result of a unilateral veto on the part of station management. Rather, after the initial approval by the program review committee, a meeting was convened between the Board of Directors and the committee. At that meeting, a request was made that the shows be put on hold pending broader outreach to the community. An additional request was to have the shows re-considered as soon as the outreach process was complete. The vote was unanimously in favor of both requests.

In a word, Gaal believes that as a community radio station, WFHB has an obligation to provide programming for members of the community who are not

reached by the mainstream media; Kearney believes that the inclusion of this programming could cut the station off from a substantial portion of its potential audience.

A total of twelve calls (a record for a one-hour talk show on WFHB) were re-

(Continued on page 3)

It's Bruce!?

Hey there, Hi there, Ho there, fellow Jazz-a-teers, this week's profile is on Bruce Baker, WFHB's own Grand Old Man of Jazz. See page 7.

5. The debate over public affairs programming featured in WFHB's newsletter, *The Spotlight*. (Courtesy WFHB)

some people feel that WFHB should reflect the concern of the 'left' in order to counter-balance the air-time given to political views of the 'right' that can be heard on other radio stations. To me, WFHB is trying to reflect the community as a whole, not just the opinions of one group, no matter how vocal. This is not the easy road to follow" (Smedberg 1996). Implicit in this comment is the realization that the difficulty inherent in WFHB's approach is two-fold. On one hand, by providing information and entertainment alternatives to the mainstream media outlets serving Bloomington, WFHB goals are consistent with those of "traditional" community radio stations across the United States. On the other hand, in order to fulfill its mission WFHB must also provide a range, if not a balance, of opinion within its own program schedule. The difficult road WFHB follows is a direct result of its reworking of the community radio tradition. Significantly, while the station's decision to "stray" from this tradition prompted the debate, the debate itself made explicit WFHB's departure from that tradition.

Responding to the *Bloomington Voice* editorial, a former WFHB board member observed the distinction between "traditional" community radio and WFHB's approach. "Some people seem to have the mistaken idea that a community radio station means 'progressive left-wing.' That is just one of the many perspectives in our community. One of the goals of WFHB is to provide true community dialogue, not just a preaching to the choir monologue" (Thrasher 1996). The desire to hear the multiplicity of voices within the community, establish a dialogue between constituencies, and avoid preaching to the converted is central to WFHB's strategy for building a large and heterogeneous audience base while serving the diverse needs of the entire Bloomington community. The resultant tensions inherent in such a strategy demand negotiation between the varied interests within the community.

In a graphic demonstration of community radio's potential to encourage such a dialogue, this process of negotiation was conducted over the airwaves of Bloomington community radio, when Chris Gaal, the author of the *Bloomington Voice* editorial, joined WFHB General Manager Brian Kearney and Program Director Jim Manion for a live discussion of the issues.[23] During a special edition of *Conversations*, WFHB's short-lived public affairs program, Chris Gaal noted the frustration some residents felt with WFHB's performance.

When we heard there was going to be a community radio station starting in Bloomington, many people were extremely excited ... this is fantastic, now we'll be able to have access to the shows that we associate with community radio. ... As time went on, there was a growing level of disappointment that the station wasn't moving in that direction or providing those things.

At the heart of this disillusionment with WFHB is the station's rupture with the tradition of US community radio. The expectation Gaal and others held out for community radio in Bloomington was shaped by the lasting influence of Lewis Hill's listener-support model, Lorenzo Milam's KRAB Nebula, and dozens of stations across the country, many of which were established soon after the NARK meeting that inspired Jim Manion and others to establish community radio in Bloomington in the first place. So prevalent is this model, that certain programming, including *Counterspin*, *Pacifica Network News*, and *Alternative Radio*, is "naturally" associated with community radio.

While understandable, these expectations fail to appreciate the complex and diverse nature of community radio in the United States. The heterogeneous character of these stations is indicative of the manner in which local populations articulate community broadcasting based on a particular set of economic, social, and cultural forces and conditions. Moreover, the "rules" of community radio have changed. WFHB Program Director Jim Manion captures the difficulty in defining community radio in terms of a "tradition," or in reference to specific program content this way:

There are approximately 150 community radio stations around the country . . . When I first got involved in the effort to get this station on the air . . . twenty-one years ago, there was only maybe twelve community stations around the country. Back then it would have been much easier to make a generalization about what community radio is, and what all community radio is like, and what type of programming a community radio station does. At this point community radio across the country is a much more diverse range of stations.

In the mid-1970s, when Manion and others began their effort to bring community radio to Bloomington, Lew Hill's model was accepted as "the way to do" community radio. As Manion notes, "Stations tended to establish themselves more in the niche of serving just one constituency. And more often than not . . . left-wing, progressive, alternative communities." During the intervening years however – while applying for a station license and construction permit, filing numerous FCC petitions, doing frequency searches, and fund raising – the proponents of community radio in Bloomington began to recognize the shortcomings of the "traditional" community radio model. That is, by catering to a particular constituency and broadcasting a specific type of programming, community radio was, in fact, failing to serve, and even alienating, large segments of the local community.

It became apparent to Kearney, Manion, and others that to ensure the station's financial stability and create a neutral forum for a range of opinion and cultural expression, WFHB could ill afford to serve but one niche audience. In other words, to remain economically viable, and become relevant to the entire community, the tradition of community radio Gaal points to in his critique of WFHB was adapted, not abandoned. WFHB General Manager Brian Kearney's response to Gaal's criticism illustrates just this.

I think it's [Gaal's editorial] implying that we're not following the tradition. And I agree, we're not. But I think there's a reason why we're not. The tradition, in my opinion, is flawed. And the problem is that you bring on the constituents who often are left leaning, the underserved, people who don't have a voice in the media, you include all those people. And it's a totally legitimate model. But what happens is, then the programming that is reflected then and broadcast out, the people that are listening are also those disenfranchised people . . . they're not reaching the undecided and the people that disagree. And I think that's who you want to reach. That's the kind of station we're trying to build here.

Therefore, the conscious decision to provide a neutral forum was at once an acknowledgment of the diverse range of opinion and cultural expression within the Bloomington community, and an effort to bring these varied interests and concerns into dialogue.

According to Jim Manion, this neutrality allows for greater, community-wide discussion. "Programs of this nature [e.g., *Counterspin*, *Making Contact*], programs of an opposite nature, if we add them to the schedule, are going to have their most effect, in terms of people getting new ideas, people getting into a dialogue, if the broadest range of people are listening." The concern on the part of WFHB management for including *Counterspin* and programs like it was a fear of having the station identified as a left-wing operation. Such a perception would, according to station management, limit the listenership and restrict the community dialogue WFHB was attempting to promote and enhance.

This rationale was questioned on several counts. The idea that the station would be labeled left wing for including one or two programs featuring progressive, or leftist material was suspect. Gaal observes that *Counterspin*, for example, is carried not only by community radio stations across the country but by a significant number of public radio stations as well. The fears that WFHB would be somehow marginalized for including this type of programming are, according to Gaal, exaggerated.

This is not to suggest that Gaal and others do not recognize the need for WFHB to build its audience and avoid alienating potential listener-supporters with programming they may find objectionable. Gaal's concern lies with the request for programming voiced by the station's *current* supporters.

WFHB is still attempting to establish itself more so in the community. I think that what has to be recognized, however, is that we're talking about WFHB's current listenership, its current audience. I doubt that there's been as overwhelming a number of requests for any show that's in the line-up right now. I know there have been lots of letters that have been sent to the station requesting *Counterspin*.

WFHB's decision to postpone airing nationally syndicated public affairs programming was contradictory on two counts. First, the concerns voiced in Gaal's critique of WFHB suggest that an established, loyal, and rather sizable audience was being alienated by the station's programming policy. Longtime supporters of Bloomington community radio felt that their requests for specific programming were unilaterally dismissed. Rather than alienate potential listeners, WFHB's decision caused a rift within its current audience. Second, far from offending potential financial supporters, Gaal notes that the *Bloomington Voice* offered to underwrite *Counterspin*. Rather than lose financial support, the station was positioned to gain an important and influential underwriter.

A more philosophical, but no less pertinent issue exacerbated the tension surrounding WFHB's decision. The notion that the station could somehow remain neutral was challenged repeatedly. As one caller to the show put it: "There is no such thing as neutrality. There's a Christian show, a New Age show, even some people who listen to something that seems neutral like the medical show might think it's too AMA or something like that. The idea of having neutrality, I think, is impossible. I would like to see more plurality."

Over the following weeks and months questions regarding the wording of WFHB's mission statement, particularly the use of the phrase "neutral forum," became a source of heated discussion among WFHB volunteers, staff, and management. So too, the need for "balance" within WFHB's program schedule, and in relation to other media outlets, was hotly debated. In an electronic mail message posted to the station's in-house distribution list, one programmer wondered:

Are we going to cut all this programming [e.g., world music] because it might alienate Pat Robertson fanatics? No, of course not, so why should we resist 'liberal' talk shows on the same grounds. Especially when there are two dozen radio stations in southern Indiana pandering to the conservative Christian listener. Maybe I'm one of those 'elitist liberals' the media is always talking about, but I totally agree with Chris Gaal. The notion of building a listenership among ALL factions of the community is an admirable ideal, but I think a somewhat naive one. It is based upon the same assumptions as the myth of 'journalistic objectivity.' . . . Most WFHB staffers have a left-wing bent; it seems disingenuous to try to disguise this fact in order to appeal to a group that is, let's face it, going to be extremely suspicious of us anyway.

These comments capture the range and complexity of the issues WFHB staff and management faced during the first half of 1996. For this and many other programmers, the notion that WFHB somehow remains neutral was moot. Rather than try to placate conservative interests, the station should openly and unabashedly "take on" mainstream media. This argument suggests that like its bold, eclectic music mix, public affairs programming on WFHB should provide substantive alternatives to mainstream media content. Ever mindful of the risks associated with this strategy, proponents of WFHB's neutrality caution that such an approach might "ghettoize" WFHB and cripple its long-term economic viability and the station's relevance to the greater Bloomington community.

Although the debate over the inclusion of "progressive" public affairs programming subsided for a time, the issues raised by this incident remain relevant. At the time, the debate cast some doubt over the future of community radio in Bloomington. At the risk of alienating some of WFHB's most ardent supporters, the decision to postpone scheduling nationally syndicated public affairs programming might have been extremely detrimental, if not fatal, to the station's continued success. Instead, the debate afforded the station an opportunity to re-evaluate its operating procedures, its role in the community, and to scrutinize the implications of its philosophy in a public forum.

As Chris Gaal mentioned during the on-air discussion, "This can be a very constructive, productive debate that we're having right now. Because WFHB hasn't ever, it seems to me, articulated its vision of what it believes community radio to be as publicly as we are doing here tonight." The cordial, frank, and passionate discussion illustrated not only the volatile nature of community radio, but more important, the participatory and self-reflexive quality unique to community media. To be sure, few commercial or nominally public service broadcasters for that matter would provide significant airtime to critics or detractors.

Equally important, the debate represented a moment for WFHB to revisit the station's mission, re-evaluate its day-to-day practices, and reconsider its role in the community. The implications of WFHB's more inclusive model of community radio were, perhaps for the first time, brought into dramatic relief. Program Director Jim Manion observed that the discussion proved how important it is "for us, at this early stage of our growth, to examine just how do we respond to such requests. If it wouldn't have been the coalition of people who approached us on this matter, it could have very well have been another constituency that wanted a certain range of programming." By postponing the decision, the station had an opportunity to determine how future requests would be handled.

Furthermore, the debate sparked renewed interest in conducting community outreach. Speaking to the need for such efforts, Brian Kearney noted that in order to fulfill its mission, WFHB must take on a more proactive role in determining who the various constituencies are within the community, and addressing the needs and interests of these groups.

Your programming is...ideally a reflection of the community. And so, we're trying to take the unique aspect of Bloomington and this area where our signal is and reflect that back. There are a lot of different constituencies that are here [in town]...but that doesn't mean that they are necessarily aware of other communities within this community. That's Jim's job, that's my job. That's my responsibility...to be aware of what the entire community is. Who are these people? We're still meeting them and in fact, we're still introducing this station to a lot of people.

Perhaps community radio's greatest strength is its ability to foster an awareness of one's own community apart from those people, institutions, and events one encounters on a daily basis. To force into consciousness the complex and dynamic process through which community is articulated, thereby creating, in the words of cultural theorist Raymond Williams (1973), a "knowable community." In doing so, community radio highlights difference within the sameness of community; gives voice to this difference, and cultivates a greater understanding and appreciation of the constructed nature of community and community relations. Certainly, such awareness can intensify the divisions that exist between various segments of a community. So too can difference be the fuel for discussion and the engine for change. Through a local, participatory medium, like community radio, these overlooked or unconscious relations of significance within a community can be articulated into relations of solidarity.

It is unclear, however, whether or not WFHB's "neutral forum" is appropriate in this regard. Without question, WFHB's eclectic music and entertainment programming enlivens Bloomington's cultural milieu. So much so that some local radio stations, including the rather stuffy NPR affiliate, WFIU, have embraced a far more adventurous programming mix. Furthermore, this strategy has endeared the station to local residents and business owners alike, who appreciate all WFHB does to enhance Bloomington's image as a surprisingly cosmopolitan town in the American Midwest.[24] Thus, through its music and cultural programming, WFHB plays an important role in marketing Bloomington at a time when local communities deploy cultural institutions in their efforts to position themselves in an increasingly global marketplace (Haider 1992).

In short, by adopting a mantle of "neutrality" WFHB positions itself not unlike commercial broadcasters, who, under the guise of objectivity and the marketplace of ideas, seek to minimize conflict and controversy in order to appeal to advertisers, or in WFHB's case, underwriters and listener supporters. As a result, WFHB achieves a measure of economic viability that has eluded many other community radio stations. Moreover, this strategy enables WFHB to produce innovative, sometimes challenging cultural programming. What gets left out of the mix, however, is the sort of relevant, critically informed, locally produced news, information, and public affairs programming that has long been the rationale behind, and a centerpiece of, community broadcasting.

Ten years after

Apart from the early efforts of long-time WFHB volunteer Mike Kelsey, whose newscasts were both engaging and informative, WFHB's local news could best be described as being of the "rip and read" variety. For coverage of international and national events, WFHB newscasters usually read or refashioned wire copy from the Associated Press (AP) and other mainstream news services. As for the station's coverage of city, county, or regional stories, WFHB news workers typically "lifted" items from Bloomington's daily newspaper, the *Herald-Times*.

For some listeners, who whimsically refer to the periodical as the "Horrible Terrible," WFHB's local news was something of a disappointment. Rather than make its newscasts distinct from competing media outlets, WFHB local news uncritically mimicked the headline news featured in the daily paper and on local radio stations. In sharp contrast, then, to the "sound alternative" WFHB's music and cultural programming provided for local listeners, Bloomington community radio's local news was indistinguishable from other media outlets.

Over the course of the station's ten-year broadcast history, local public affairs programming has fared better. However, like daily local newscasts, these efforts have been sporadic, under-staffed, and under-resourced. In saying this, I do not want to dismiss some truly remarkable accomplishments that WFHB management, staff, and volunteers rightly take great pride in. For instance, the now-defunct *Branches Radio* addressed some of the area's most pressing environmental issues, including sustained coverage of the on-going fights over the Westinghouse PCB (polychlorinated biphenyls) clean-up and efforts to preserve the region's hardwood forests. Likewise, the short-lived *Conversations* covered a variety of timely and relevant topics, including gender equity in the local workplace, domestic violence in Bloomington and Monroe County, pedestrian safety in and around downtown, and a host of pertinent issues.

Only the Herculean efforts of Brian Hendrickson and his dedicated crew have kept *Interchange*, WFHB's longest-running and arguably its most successful weekly public affairs program, on the air following the departure of its two long-time hosts and producers, Shana Ritter and Daryl Neher.[25] Billing itself as a public affairs program presenting "local issues with a global perspective and global issues with a local perspective," *Interchange* features interviews with area newsmakers, academics, community organizers, political activists, religious leaders, and others. Significantly, *Interchange* is one of but a handful of programs on WFHB that encourage listeners to call in and participate in live on-air discussions.

Herein lies one of the more perplexing aspects of WFHB's approach to news and public affairs programming. Call-in programs are quite common to broadcasting; commercial, public, and community stations across the country and indeed around the world have embraced this relatively inexpensive program format as a way to build audiences, attract sponsors, and enhance listener participation in radio broadcasting. Undeniably, the call-in represents an excellent vehicle for WFHB to fulfill its mission to provide "a neutral forum for the discussion and exchange of ideas and issues"; and yet, call-in programs are all too infrequent on Bloomington community radio.

Several factors may account for WFHB's disinclination to produce call-in programs and, more generally, the intermittent and inconsistent nature of its local news and public affairs programming. First, WFHB bills itself primarily as a music station.[26] Intimately tied to the local music scene, WFHB's founders saw in community broadcasting a way of promoting local artists, studios, labels, and venues. For many of the station's founders and early supporters, Bloomington was, and remains, primarily a music and arts community. Second, local news and public affairs programming are not as "glamorous" or as much "fun" to produce as music programming. Indeed, newsgathering is time and labor intensive, as such news and public affairs programming require considerable financial, technical, and human resources. Unlike a music mix or specialty show, where an individual programmer, working alone and with relative ease, can organize a two or three-hour program, news and public affairs typically require a team of writers, reporters, engineers, and producers to generate story ideas, conduct research, contact news sources, record and edit interviews, and prepare stories for broadcast.

Finally, in the aftermath of the debate over news and public affairs programming described above, WFHB incorporated a number of very fine syndicated programs, including *Alternative Radio*, *New Dimensions*, and, for a short time, *Voices of Pacifica*, into its broadcast schedule. While these nationally syndicated programs help fulfill the station's promise to provide news, information, and public affairs programs, the costs associated with acquiring nationally syndicated programming often leave fewer resources available to support local efforts.[27]

Welcome as these syndicated programs are and helpful as they can be for attracting listener supporters and program underwriters, they nonetheless present other less conspicuous, but nonetheless germane problems. For instance, syndicated shows of this sort do not provide local listeners opportunities to call in or otherwise participate in an on-air discussion, as do locally produced programs. Equally troubling, the emphasis on national and international issues featured on WFHB's syndicated talk shows shrewdly elides particularly troublesome local politics. That is to say, by stacking its news and public affairs offerings with nationally syndicated programs, issues closer to home, such as affordable housing, sustainable development, unemployment, and, most recently, city council hearings on a so-called "living wage" ordinance, don't receive the sort of sustained coverage they demand. In the absence of ongoing and substantive coverage of these issues, WFHB fails to leverage community radio's greatest asset: its ability to engage listeners in discussion, deliberation, and debate over local problems and concerns.

Nonetheless, upon my return to Bloomington in July 2002, I was delighted to see a message from a listener, posted on the station's internal distribution list, requesting the inclusion of *Democracy Now!* on the WFHB program schedule. As station management, staff, and volunteers had just launched a "strategic plan" (see Carrothers 2002) to enhance WFHB's news and public affairs programming, the timing of the listener's request seemed fortuitous. Hosted by award-winning journalists Amy Goodman and Juan Gonzalez, *Democracy Now!* is the nation's premier independently produced daily newscast. *Democracy Now!* airs across the Pacifica Radio Network as well as over hundreds of public and community media outlets across the country. Moreover, thanks to satellite distribution via Free Speech Television (FSTV), a video feed of the popular hour-long newscast, originating from Downtown Community Television (the subject of Chapter 4), is available to public access television centers nationwide, making *Democracy Now!* the largest community media collaborative in the United States.

I was among a number of community radio supporters and volunteers who wholeheartedly endorsed the acquisition of *Democracy Now!* Within a few days time, however, the station's long-time program director, Jim Manion, and the recently named news director, Chad Carrothers, unequivocally stated their refusal to air the program. Throughout the summer of 2002, a handful of programmers, management, staff, and station supporters argued the merits of *Democracy Now!* in a manner not unlike the earlier debate over news and public affairs programming. The upshot of these discussions underscores the problems associated with participatory research alluded to at the beginning of this chapter.

Eager to contribute to the station's news and public affairs initiative, I argued that *Democracy Now!*'s inclusion in the broadcast schedule achieved several important aims of the station's strategic initiative. First, as *Democracy Now!* is available on a sliding scale to community radio stations, the inclusion of this outstanding program would not take away resources from the local news department's budget.[28] By attracting listeners and underwriters, I suggested that *Democracy Now!* could in fact help to support and finance the local news department. Indeed, unlike *BBC World News Hour*, subsequently acquired by WFHB management, *Democracy Now!* does not require an expensive satellite downlink nor encumber yearly subscription fees, as does all BBC programming available to US media outlets through Public Radio International (PRI). Moreover, I suggested that as a model of independent, community-oriented journalism, *Democracy Now!* would help raise the standards of journalistic practice within the local news department.

In making my case and engaging in the online debate, I forwarded, along with my response, a message from Program Director Jim Manion to the entire list – a message he maintains was confidential and therefore not for public consumption. Mistakenly, perhaps, I understood this message to be part of the ongoing deliberations over *Democracy Now!* and of news and public affairs programming in general. Indeed, as participation in monthly meetings had dropped precipitously in recent years, the station's internal mailing list was used frequently for such policy deliberations. While Manion and Carrothers took exception to my post, numerous volunteers and supporters, some of whom I had never met before, thanked me for making what was to their minds a persuasive case for acquiring *Democracy Now!* In any event, the incident served to derail the discussion and helped seal the fate of the station's online discussion list.[29]

To my surprise, sometime later I was approached by Chad Carrothers to join the News and Public Affairs Programming Committee (NPAC), a group of volunteers and supporters charged with implementing the station's strategic initiative for improving news and public affairs. What became apparent during the course of our deliberations was the committee's lack of autonomy in identifying potential program additions and the complete lack of authority the committee had in realizing any of its recommendations. Certain programs slated for inclusion in the news and public affairs programming schedule, *BBC World News Hour* and *Free Speech Radio News*, came "pre-approved." That is, despite lively and spirited discussions surrounding the relative merits of each of these programs – equipment and subscription costs, potential to attract listeners and underwriters, accordance with the station's mission, and, of course, journalistic quality – the committee was not asked to make a determination on these two shows. Conversely, the aforementioned *Democracy Now!* was "off the table." The committee was instructed to avoid any consideration of this program, despite or, more accurately, perhaps, because of the stated objections to the show on the part of both the program director and the news director.

The committee's charge consisted primarily of constructing a "program clock" for the daily local newscast and offering suggestions on how to organize and develop a news crew. Here again, station management and staff tied the NPAC's hands. A number of committee members expressed interest in taking an unconventional approach to building a news team, one that would leverage the strategic initiative's potential for community outreach to those constituencies WFHB has yet to involve in station programming. Instead, the principal outreach efforts would be aimed at Indiana University journalism students.

While this arrangement gives student journalists invaluable broadcast experience and ensures WFHB's news department a ready pool of news workers, the station's reliance upon student journalists squanders a unique opportunity to promote community journalism – reportage of the sort produced by so-called "nonprofessionals" whose intimate stories reflect, illuminate, and celebrate the everyday lived experience of local residents – on a scale and scope previously unimagined in Bloomington.[30] That is to say, the same participatory approach WFHB takes to its music schedule – especially the station's noteworthy emphasis on providing local residents with the unique opportunity to program their own shows – has yet to be realized in the realm of news and public affairs.

Moreover, any mention of collaborative efforts with the online newsletter, *The Bloomington Alternative*, were squelched. Despite his reputation as an aggressive, yet straightforward and responsible community-minded journalist, station management and staff made a determination (without input from the NPAC) that *Bloomington Alternative* editor and publisher, Steve Higgs, practiced "advocacy journalism" of the sort that was incompatible with WFHB's operating principles.[31]

Not surprisingly, the NPAC was rather short lived. In December 2002, I attended my last NPAC meeting. Given station management's reluctance to meet with the committee to discuss concerns regarding the NPAC's autonomy and authority, coupled with the lack of transparency in station management's decision making regarding the specifics of news and public affairs initiative, I felt it was in my best interest to discontinue my involvement with the station for a time. Naturally, my frustrations have colored my relationship with station management and, to a certain extent, my sense of personal and professional investment in the station's service to the Bloomington community. This is not to say, however, that my profound respect for the station, its founding members, and its current management, staff, and volunteers has diminished.

I am, however, less sanguine over the value of participatory research than I once was. That is to say, the profound sense of engagement that participatory research affords investigators is certainly invigorating and yields considerable rewards outside of and in addition to scholarly endeavors. However, this engagement can just as easily confound one's efforts by bringing the researcher into conflict with the people and institutions under investigation. As a (returning) member of the Bloomington community, I hope one day to rejoin the ranks of committed volunteers who likewise see in WFHB the possibility of remaking local media systems and realizing their potential to foster communicative democracy. Doing so, I hope to make clear to my colleagues, neighbors, and friends that many of us who call Bloomington home share their enthusiasm for lively, engaging, and relevant community broadcasting.

Guided by a passion for radio, a group of artists, technicians, and music enthusiasts doggedly pursued a vision of eclectic and adventurous broadcasting for Bloomington, Indiana. The long history of participatory broadcasting practices in Bloomington is marked by the resilient efforts of a handful of committed individuals, faint glimmers of hope, and long periods of doubt and despair. More than this, the struggle to find a spot on the dial reveals how various technical, bureaucratic, economic, philanthropic, and socio-cultural forces articulate community broadcasting in south central Indiana.

In the next chapter, we turn our attention to another community, making use of a different communication technology, also for purposes of community communication. Whereas the architects of community radio in Bloomington, Indiana consciously avoided using the airwaves to serve the disenfranchised and underserved constituencies of the community, the founders of Downtown Community Television (DCTV) saw in the then new technology of portable video a means to empower those groups and individuals whose images, voices, perspectives, and experiences were systematically excluded from mainstream television. As we shall see, by taking up the cultural politics of the image and image-making systems, DCTV rearticulates a familiar technology and in so doing promotes progressive social change, enhances cross-cultural communication, and creates a more democratic media culture.

4 Downtown Community Television: cultural politics and technological form

> If DCTV is a reflection of Jon Alpert, some of his best work has reflected the community with which he identifies.
>
> J. Hoberman, *American Film*

On 1 March 2003, tensions were running high at United Nations headquarters in midtown Manhattan. Opposition to a US-led invasion of Iraq stiffened when, despite chief weapons inspector Hans Blix's report of "significant progress" toward achieving Iraqi compliance with UN Resolution 1441, the Bush Administration modified its demands (Barringer and Sanger 2003; Tyler 2003). Speaking at a morning press briefing, White House spokesperson Ari Fleischer announced that war could be prevented only if Iraq disarmed and Saddam Hussein stepped down from power. Prior to the announcement, regime change was never a formal US foreign policy objective. Now, all that had changed. The announcement sent shockwaves through an anxious and increasingly acrimonious diplomatic community. As members of the world body assembled in an effort to avoid rupturing already strained international relations, a group of high school and college students gathered in a cramped television studio on Manhattan's Lower East Side to take part in another historic discussion.

From the second story of a landmark firehouse that is home to Downtown Community Television (DCTV), young New Yorkers spoke via satellite with a group of Iraqi youth meeting at the Orfali Art Gallery in Baghdad. Over the course of the ninety-minute conversation, later distilled into an hour-long television program titled *Bridge to Baghdad: A Youth Dialogue*, participants discussed a host of topics relevant to their everyday lives: school, career aspirations, dating, parents, and popular culture. Foremost on the minds of both the Americans and Iraqis, however, was the outcome of ongoing deliberations at UN headquarters, and the very real possibility that within a matter of days their respective nations would be at war.

Bridge to Baghdad was produced by DCTV co-founder Jon Alpert. An award-winning independent journalist and video documentarian,

133

6. This landmark firehouse in New York City's Chinatown is home to Downtown Community Television. (Photo by the author)

Alpert's concept was simple: to provide a forum for young people in the United States and Iraq to meet one another and to share their perspectives on war and peace. Originally intended to be part of the Museum of Television and Radio's University Satellite Seminar Series, the youth dialogue was to be distributed to hundreds of colleges and universities across the United States. While Alpert and his crew were en route to Baghdad, museum officials unceremoniously withdrew their support for the project.[1] In the intervening weeks, Alpert shopped the project around to the major broadcast and cable networks and yet, despite non-stop coverage of the lead-up to war, not one of the major US media outlets saw fit to devote a single hour of programming to a discussion focused on peaceful conflict resolution.

At first blush, the project's use of hi-tech facilities and its global scope appear to be a far cry from DCTV's fledgling attempts to use the then new technology of video on the streets of lower Manhattan some thirty years earlier. As we shall see, however, *Bridge to Baghdad* is but DCTV's latest effort to use television and related technologies to facilitate intercultural communication and to promote peace and social justice. From these modest beginnings, producing and exhibiting their tapes on street corners, in union halls and community centers in and around New

York City's Lower East Side, DCTV would become one of the longest-running, most highly honored non-profit media arts centers in the United States.

This chapter charts DCTV's decades-long media activism; from its initial community service programs aimed at improving the lives of recently arrived immigrants, to its free video arts instruction for local residents, to its groundbreaking social issue documentaries and advocacy journalism for US public and commercial television. Throughout, I place special emphasis on the intersection between cultural politics and technological innovation: a common feature of community-based media organizations and one best exemplified by DCTV's work.

That is to say, through its investigative journalism, DCTV exposes social, political, and economic injustice at home and abroad: from the sweatshops of New York's Chinatown, to the struggle for affordable housing in Philadelphia, to the killing fields of Cambodia. Equally important, DCTV's community outreach and media training programs provide local residents – especially minority youth, immigrants, and low-income groups who are structurally excluded from, and systematically marginalized by, mainstream media – with the tools and resources usually associated with transnational media conglomerates. In so doing, DCTV produces television that not only illuminates but also challenges social, political, and economic inequalities, inequities that are often legitimated by and reinforced through conventional television form and content.

In many respects, then, DCTV's mission is quite similar to those of the other community media organizations profiled in these pages. Like WFHB (Chapter 3), *Street Feat* (Chapter 5), and VICNET (Chapter 6), DCTV serves as a resource for the production and dissemination of media by, for, and about local communities. Unlike these other organizations, however, DCTV is unique in terms of its longevity and its influence – an influence that has been felt throughout the community television movement, among the ranks of independent producers, as well as in the public service broadcasting and commercial television sectors. As such, DCTV serves as a model of community organizing and independent production; DCTV's long-term success and remarkable persistence of vision make it an important addition to this discussion of community-based media.

As we shall see, DCTV's longevity and continued relevance stands in stark contrast to the fate of any number of video collectives operating in New York City during the late 1960s and early 1970s. Moreover, DCTV's growth and development is intimately tied to the dynamics of the US television industry, in particular the establishment of a national public television service, as well as the vagaries of commercial network news. Most important, however, DCTV's success testifies to the socially committed, politically savvy, and aesthetically adventurous spirit of its co-founders, Jon Alpert and his wife and collaborator, Keiko Tsuno.

In Chapter 2 we noted the complex relationship between an emerging global television industry – a constellation of organizations and interests including equipment manufacturers, program producers, commercial broadcasters, public television services, independent production companies, and "new" distribution outlets such as cable, satellite, and Internet delivery systems – and the disparate efforts of local populations to make use of television for purposes of community communication. As we have seen, the community television movement draws upon a variety of traditions, including social justice and media reform movements, documentary production, avant-garde aesthetics, indigenous cultural traditions, as well as the goals and objectives of participatory and development communication. With this in mind, then, this case study of DCTV explores community video's role in facilitating, stimulating, and expanding local cultural production by, for, and about individuals and groups whose access to the tools of television production and distribution are severely limited.

Specifically, I place this discussion of DCTV in the context of likeminded video collectives and media access efforts that coalesced in New York City in the late 1960s and early 1970s. A handful of media historians have charted the development of the community video movement in New York City. In particular, I draw upon Ralph Engelman's (1990) indispensable history of the political struggle to secure public access television provisions (channels, equipment, training) from city officials and cable television representatives alike. Engelman's political history of these contentious and protracted negotiations provides a backdrop for appreciating DCTV's significance in promoting community television over the course of several decades' worth of broken promises and lost opportunities in the struggle to create a viable public access television service for the people of Manhattan.

Likewise, I make use of Deirdre Boyle's (1997) lively account of the socalled "video underground": collectives of aspiring television producers, artists, and journalists whose fervent belief in the coming cultural revolution wrought by portable television production was, in equal measures, romantic, naïve, and ultimately, short-lived. Despite auspicious beginnings, internal conflicts and external pressures undermined the success and long-term practicability of the video collectives. By the end of the 1970s, it became clear that the collectives failed to realize their own potential, let alone create a viable alternative to either commercial or public broadcast television. Whereas Boyle's analysis focuses on some of the more notorious proponents of "guerrilla television" – Videofreex and Top

Value Television (TVTV) among them – this chapter attempts to chronicle the staying power of DCTV, a contemporary of the video collectives Boyle profiles.

Following this, I turn my attention to DCTV's signature style: a style that owes as much to technological developments in small-format video as it does to DCTV's commitment to documenting the everyday lives of common people. Briefly stated, DCTV's aesthetic sensibility is distinctive for its immediacy, its intimacy, and for its unflinching, often disturbing examination of the human costs of war, economic deprivation, worker exploitation, and drug addiction. DCTV's innovations in what would come to be known as Electronic News Gathering (ENG) were at the vanguard of a revolution in television journalism that is evident in a host of contemporary televisual forms: local newscasts, the social issue documentary, and even so-called "reality television." As we shall see, it was DCTV's intimate portrait of peasants, factory workers, city dwellers, and school children in post-revolution Cuba – a documentary that is a direct outgrowth of DCTV's commitment to community-oriented television – that first brought DCTV's work to a national audience and helped usher in this new approach to television journalism and video documentary.

Crucially, DCTV's willingness and ability to negotiate the demands and constraints of public service and later commercial television allowed the organization to subsidize its community organizing efforts and video arts training. Having made significant, if somewhat ephemeral, inroads into the otherwise closed shops of network television, DCTV uses its profits to hire paid staff, upgrade equipment and facilities, and develop and expand its free and low-cost video training program. Over the course of the past thirty years, DCTV has trained tens of thousands of students in basic video production techniques. In addition, DCTV helps local artists, community groups, and independent producers create television programming of uncommon integrity, creativity, and utility. Many of these community producers have gone on to successful careers as media educators, independent producers, and video artists. A discussion of some of this material reveals the social, cultural, and political relevance of community video for local communities and wider publics alike.

Throughout, I want to underscore DCTV's significance in promoting independent production in general and community-oriented television in particular. In an era marked by media consolidation, audience fragmentation, and rapid technological innovation, DCTV continues to explore television's potential to communicate community in startling, sometimes deceptively simple, but ultimately highly effective and rewarding ways. In this way, DCTV challenges popular perceptions of television's *place* in the lives and experiences of local communities. With this in mind, let

us briefly consider the community DCTV calls home: New York City's
Chinatown and the Lower East Side.

An urban village

For visitors and natives alike, New York City's Lower East Side holds a
peculiar fascination. Born and raised in Queens, one of New York City's
five boroughs, I vividly recall my first impressions of the Lower East
Side's distinctive neighborhoods: the sense of awe and wonder when I
made my initial, rather tentative forays into the bustling street markets
along Essex and Delancey Streets; the sights and smells that greeted me
as I wandered, dreamlike, along Little Italy's Mulberry Street during the
San Gennaro Festival; or the satisfaction of a cheap yet hearty late night
(or rather early morning) meal with college friends in Chinatown after
the evening's barhopping around Manhattan. Despite having left New
York in August 1993 to pursue my doctoral studies, I consider myself a
New Yorker at heart – one whose sense of awe and wonder is rekindled
whenever I return to the city I still call home.

With that said, my knowledge of the social and cultural history of the
Lower East Side is limited – informed only by a native curiosity, pedestrian observations, and a helping of library research.[2] One explanation
for my ignorance of the rich and varied history of this remarkable section
of lower Manhattan is the absolute "otherness" of this urban geography.
Relative to my old neighborhood in Queens, certainly, and even to the
more familiar destinations and landmarks of Manhattan – Greenwich
Village, Radio City Music Hall, Times Square, Central Park, and the
Upper West Side – the Lower East Side was like another planet. Or, to
use a more down-to-earth analogy, with its unparalleled racial and ethnic
diversity, its cultural vitality, and its glaring socio-economic disparity, the
450 city blocks that make up the Lower East Side are something of a
"people's" United Nations.

Established long ago as the city's "immigrant quarter," the Lower East
Side's exotic and foreign quality renders the place mysterious, enticing,
and not a little intimidating. Yet, these very same qualities provide important clues to understanding and appreciating the distinctive character of
this 1,400-acre parcel of Manhattan real estate. In the wake of European
settlement initiated by the Dutch in the seventeenth century, the area
now known as the Lower East Side was primarily farmland and home
to the local business and political elites. Throughout the colonial period,
the landed gentry and an emerging middle class took up residence in
the area. By the early eighteenth century, however, one of the Lower
East Side's defining characteristics began to emerge: as former residents

moved out, north along Manhattan Island, to what would later become the "outer boroughs" of Brooklyn, the Bronx, and Queens, or in increasing numbers, out into the vast American interior, successive waves of newcomers would remake the area and come to call the Lower East Side home.

The first "immigrants" were freed Blacks who began to settle in the commercial and industrial district taking shape around the city's primary source of fresh drinking water, the Collect Pond. Over time, refuse and waste materials from the local breweries, slaughterhouses, and tanneries contaminated the Collect and in 1803, the decision was made to fill in the pond. Forced to relocate, freed Blacks made way for merchants and business people who would take up residence in the newly constructed neighborhood. By 1820, however, the landfill began to sink, causing the well-to-do residents to move out and leaving poor immigrants, first from Ireland and Germany, later from Italy and Eastern Europe, to take up residence in the rapidly declining neighborhood.

There, atop the doomed landfill emerged one of the city's most notorious neighborhoods, the Five Points, so-called for the five-cornered intersection of Anthony, Orange, and Cross Streets that lie at its heart.[3] The Five Points had an unflattering reputation as a rough and tumble neighborhood plagued by poverty, crime, disease, and racial and ethnic tensions: a reputation that grew as the neighborhood expanded. Upon his visit to New York City in 1842, the English writer and social critic Charles Dickens famously decried the deplorable living conditions and rampant debauchery he observed there. For their part, Manhattan's gentry did their utmost to avoid contact with the inhabitants of what was widely described as the world's most notorious slum.

In the middle of the nineteenth century, Chinese immigrants began arriving in New York in greater numbers. Fleeing the hostility of white laborers in the American West Chinese workers took up residence along Mott, Pell, and Doyer Streets, thus giving shape to New York's Chinatown – the largest Chinese community in the Western hemisphere. Overt racism, codified by the Chinese Exclusion Act (1882–1943), severely restricted Chinese immigration, effectively barring women and children from emigrating to America. As a result, the Chinese enclave turned in on itself, fostering the development of the so-called "Bachelor Society" and leaving it to the austere Chinese Consolidated Benevolent Association (CCBA) to manage almost every aspect of daily life: from employment and housing, to business deals, conflict resolution, and even funeral arrangements. In this environment, prostitution, opium addiction, and gambling flourished, further diminishing the ethnic community's standing in the growing metropolis. Bloody gang warfare between the rival On

Leong and Hip Sing tongs (fraternal orders) likewise tainted the area's reputation and instilled fear in residents and visitors alike.

Throughout the nineteenth century, then, the Lower East Side developed an unenviable reputation as the world's most infamous immigrant ghetto: people and places to be shunned, pitied perhaps, but nevertheless beyond the pale of decent, civil society. What these histories and perceptions fail to acknowledge, however, was the quarter's vibrant, multicultural working class culture. That is to say, what is missing from most of these accounts is the crucial and decisive role successive waves of immigrants played in building America's formidable industrial strength, generating its considerable wealth, forging its political history, and shaping its distinctive culture.

All of which is to suggest that as appalling and oppressive as conditions on the Lower East Side were, resistance to worker exploitation, inadequate and overcrowded housing, lack of economic opportunity, systemic racism, and political disenfranchisement manifest themselves in a host of strategies and tactics employed by immigrant communities struggling to cope with and adapt to their new surroundings. A more accurate and complete history of the Lower East Side, therefore, highlights the area's long tradition of community organizing, labor protest, and direct action campaigns, as well as its vibrant street life and prodigious cultural production.

Consider, for example, the fundamental role street gangs played in the everyday lived experience of immigrant communities. To the city's gentry, the gangs of New York were evidence of the inferiority of immigrant cultures from Europe and Asia. These gangs represented a threat to the health, safety, and well being of the city's emerging middle class and legitimated the exercise of political power and police authority in dealing with the underclass. Without underestimating the very real threat gangs posed to city residents, a more nuanced understanding of urban street culture underscores the ways in which gangs provided a refuge for immigrant populations to retain, preserve, and defend their cultural identities, and lay claim to their turf.

What's more, the militancy and solidarity expressed in gang culture would inform the more progressive tendencies of working class culture, especially in the ongoing labor struggles of the middle and late nineteenth century. Indeed, despite open hostility between immigrant communities, by the 1880s Irish, Jewish, Italian, German, and Polish workers formed strategic alliances that led to the establishment of the Knights of Labor, America's first national labor union. Thus, progressive social movements and radical labor organizations, most notably the Wobblies (Industrial Workers of the World), flourished in the working class culture of the Lower East Side.

This same dynamic was evident in the streets of Loisaida (Spanglish for the Lower East Side), the Puerto Rican enclave that grew around Tompkins Square Park in the second half of the twentieth century. Taking a page from the Black Panthers, the Young Lords Organization (YLO) operated a community service organization throughout the late 1960s and early 1970s. The YLO served young and old alike – from adult education classes to a free breakfast program for school children – at a time when the programs associated with President Lyndon Johnson's Great Society failed to materialize there.

In a similar vein, Charas Inc. (originally known as "The Real Great Society"), a community arts and empowerment organization that operates out of a repurposed school building on East 9th Street and Avenue B, grew out of two rival Puerto Rican gangs, the Chelsea-based Assassins and the Dragons of Loisaida. Since the 1970s, Charas' community activities have included stints building geodesic domes under Buckminster Fuller's supervision, rehabilitating abandoned buildings and vacant lots, and an extensive arts program that encourages young people to express themselves through street murals, photography, theater, music, and dance (Maffi 1994).

A long tradition of community activism of this sort led to the formation of mutual aid societies such as the world-renowned Henry Street Settlement. In addition to providing basic services for whole populations neglected by a largely indifferent middle class, these organizations provided a meeting ground for diverse peoples and cultures to meet, mingle, clash, and cross-pollinate. Similarly, urban spaces, such as the Chatham public library or Union Square Park, were not merely recreational destinations. These spaces were the site of popular protests – including the 1857 workers' march on Wall Street and, more recently, the 1988 Tent City riots in Tompkins Square Park. In short, the settlement houses, community centers, libraries, parks, and street corners of the Lower East Side served as a staging ground for the construction of a wholly new culture: a modern, industrialized, urban, and uniquely American culture.

Here, we can detect the role cultural production has played in informing not only the immigrant experience in American but also the whole of American culture and society. Barred from fully participating in mainstream culture by economic barriers, linguistic differences, religious customs, and traditions, immigrant communities nonetheless reveled in the music, dance, and storytelling traditions of their own making. These cultural practices and traditions not only reinforced a sense of individual and collective identity for particular immigrant communities but also served to attract other cultural minorities (and increasingly, the city's middle class) to "foreign" songs, dance, literature, theater, and writing.

Far from being a ghetto devoid of culture, then, the Lower East Side has long provided a home to, as well as served as a source of inspiration for, artists whose work reflects the lives and experience of immigrant communities or which otherwise challenges conventional tastes and sensibilities. In doing so, this work, and the cultural output of countless writers, poets, musicians, filmmakers, dancers, actors, and playwrights would eventually be embraced by and incorporated into mainstream culture.

In sum, the community activism and cultural production described above constituted an array of countervailing forces and tendencies to the oppressive conditions confronting newcomers to America. Moreover, this culture of resistance was giving shape to the modern metropolis and, in a very real sense, helped create a uniquely American identity. Cultural historian Mario Maffi puts it this way: "The Lower East Side as a whole made up of different parts thus entered into a peculiar relationship with the rest of the country – one which, while shaping and reshaping immigrant cultures, also shaped and reshaped mainstream culture" (1995: 8).

Maffi's emphasis on the dialects at work in what he calls the "sociocultural laboratory" of the Lower East Side is useful here inasmuch as this interpretation rejects the notion that immigrant cultures are submerged and purged through a one-way process of assimilation. Moreover, this approach questions the equally suspect notion that these same immigrant cultures remain intact, untouched by contact with other languages, customs, or traditions, let alone by the influence of mainstream American culture. Rather, this analysis points to the importance of community activism in helping disparate groups adapt to, and ultimately survive in a sometimes inhospitable new world. Furthermore, we see here the centrality of cultural production in articulating local cultural identities and informing the wider society and culture.

With this in mind, then, we turn our attention to DCTV. Rather than view Downtown Community Television as a curious cultural anomaly, the vestige of a bygone era of grassroots activism, this perspective encourages us to consider DCTV's community outreach, media education programs, and independent video production as part of the long tradition of cultural politics in the Lower East Side, albeit a cultural politics enacted within and through a seemingly unlikely technological form: television.

A new kind of television

When it premiered in February 1975, *Video and Television Review* (*VTR*) was the first regular series on American television produced exclusively to showcase the work of video artists and independent television producers.

Sponsored by the New York State Council on the Arts (NYSCA) and produced through WNET's innovative TV Lab,[4] *VTR* sought to keep viewers appraised of the latest aesthetic and technical developments in video, then an exciting new medium of communication. According to the series' executive producer, David Loxton, *VTR* had two main objectives: "to create a regular forum and means of presentation for the increasing number of important new works being created, and to establish in the viewing audience's consciousness, a clearer identity for the whole spectrum of independent and experimental work on TV" (WNET/Vision News 1975). To that end, *VTR* profiled the work and work habits of an assortment of video makers.

Prior to *VTR*, innovative approaches to television form and content using portable recording devices and techniques were a rarity on broadcast television. *VTR* provided an outlet for this innovative, often challenging work. From experimental art and short documentaries, to reports on video's psychological effects and its therapeutic value, *VTR* aired material quite unlike anything else found on broadcast television at that time. In his opening remarks to the 4 April 1975 broadcast, *VTR*'s host Russell Conner observed: "A lot of pious things have been said and written about community video. This is a place where it is really needed and where it is really happening: New York's Chinatown and the Lower East Side. The means by which many people are getting their hands on television, using it for information, education, and for gaining a new sense of their own identity is the Downtown Community Television Center." For the next thirty minutes, DCTV's founders Keiko Tsuno, Jon Alpert, and Yoko Maruyama displayed and discussed their work in community video; work that had taken them to health fairs in Chinatown, school board meetings in the embattled Crown Heights section of Brooklyn, and, most recently, to the farms, factories, churches, and schoolyards of Cuba.

Like other young artists of the time, interested in recording their activities, Keiko Tsuno used film as a means of documenting the kinetic sculptures she assembled in her Chinatown flat. And, like many of her peers, Tsuno found the costs involved in filmmaking prohibitive and the delays associated with film processing frustrating. In the late 1960s and early 1970s, artists began looking to the new technology of video to record and analyze their work. Video's low cost, relative ease of use, and uncanny sense of immediacy was especially appealing to an artistic sensibility, in vogue at the time, informed by the aphorism: "process, not product." Tsuno likewise took an interest in the new medium and, with the money she earned waiting tables, had her mother purchase and ship a Sony half-inch portapak system from Tokyo to New York City.

7. Jon Alpert and Keiko Tsuno describe their work on the public television series *VTR*. (Courtesy of DCTV)

At the urging of an art school instructor, Tsuno began to look beyond
video's rudimentary documentary facility to explore its creative and aesthetic potential. Tsuno recalls her mentor's advice that video would be
"the next big thing" in contemporary visual arts and he encouraged his
former student to experiment with the new medium. Taking up this suggestion, Tsuno began creating what she describes as "video poems"–
short, abstract, and strikingly beautiful visuals produced by subtle ma-
nipulation of focus, focal length, depth of field, light and shadow, and
so on. In turn, this work informed the ethnographic sketches she began recording around the neighborhood. With her gear concealed in a
shopping cart and dressed as a boy in hopes of staving off unwanted
and unwelcome attention, Tsuno clandestinely recorded daily life on the
Lower East Side.

Her neighbor, Jon Alpert, a taxi driver and fellow community activist,
took notice of these rough yet absorbing "street tapes"[5] and together they

began exploring the medium's ability to capture everyday life with a veracity and vitality unlike anything they had seen before – certainly unlike anything on broadcast television. Like Tsuno, Alpert had an interest in film. While pursing a degree in Urban Studies at the prestigious, if somewhat unlikely setting of Cornell University in rural New York State, Alpert lobbied unsuccessfully to receive course credit for his self-directed film studies. Despite a keen appreciation of cinema, however, Alpert was not interested in "art." A self-professed "jock" with something of a checkered academic background, Alpert's real passion was community organizing. Out of favor with school administrators at Cornell, Alpert headed for the big city, completing his course work at New York University in the heart of Manhattan's Greenwich Village.

Although they were both active in the anti-war movement, Alpert and Tsuno focused their energies on struggles closer to home – affordable housing, health care, unemployment, drug abuse, street crime, and education reform – problems which they and their Chinatown neighbors encountered on a daily basis. Not until Alpert hit upon the idea of using video in his efforts to organize the taxi drivers union, however, did he and Tsuno begin to understand the vital yet largely untapped role television might play in community organizing strategies.

Throughout the early 1970s, the taxi drivers union, under the contentious leadership of Harry Van Arsdale, Jr., was in complete disarray. A hero in certain accounts of modern labor history, Van Arsdale was an early practitioner of "conglomerate unionism" – a strategy that effectively consolidated the power of labor officials but which often proved disastrous for the rank and file. Under his leadership, the Taxi Drivers and Allied Workers local 3036, the union that represented New York City's yellow (so-called "medallion") cab drivers, became a divisive and dysfunctional organization that could do little to offset the fleet owners' price gouging, let alone improve working conditions. Fierce competition among drivers compounded by racial tensions within the union likewise made organizing difficult.

Efforts to address worker safety issues and improve worker relations were met with contempt, if not outright hostility, by both drivers and union management. As a result, monthly meetings were unruly and unproductive affairs. Into this environment Alpert and Tsuno brought a portapak unit and proceeded to create a very rough, but nonetheless highly effective "dialogue" tape[6] that demonstrated to a diverse, often unreceptive workforce the value of collective action and the need for new union leadership. The tape was an unprecedented success; not only did the video facilitate communication between antagonistic parties, but it also proved instrumental in mobilizing the cab drivers. Within a matter of months, Van Arsdale caved in to pressure from the rank and file and resigned as head of the union. This was the first decisive step toward improving the wages and working conditions for the city's yellow cab drivers.

Although Alpert does not recall any direct inspiration for producing a tape of this sort, it is likely several currents of the nascent community television movement influenced him. Working on the grassroots level, Ken Marsh's People's Video Theater (PVT) used live and pre-recorded video to facilitate community communication and promote progressive social change in politically disenfranchised urban neighborhoods. In this regard, PVT's commitment to using video as a means of community empowerment was something of an anomaly in New York City's alternative video scene. For the most part, groups like Videofreex and TVTV used video for artistic and cultural expression, not overtly social or political ends (Boyle 1997). Not only did Marsh and his cohort use video for purposes of conflict resolution and political mobilization, the People's Video Theater practiced the sort of community video journalism that DCTV champions to this day.

On the other end of the spectrum was the Alternative Media Center (AMC) at New York University. Unlike PVT and the other collectives, the Alternative Media Center enjoyed considerable financial support from the likes of the Markell Foundation. As noted in Chapter 2, the AMC's director, George Stoney, built his reputation as a champion of what might be described as "participatory filmmaking" – an approach that invites the subjects of documentary films to participate in the production process, from concept, through the shooting phase and on into the editing process. This approach is evident in DCTV's visual style and one that unmistakably informs its commitment to community television.

Whether by conscious design, creative inspiration, or the ruthless pragmatism that informs many community media initiatives, DCTV might well be seen as heirs to this rich tradition of participatory production. All of which is not to suggest, however, that DCTV's visual style and philosophical approach to community television emerged fully formed. As we shall see, DCTV's distinctive style developed over time based on a fortuitous combination of trial and error, technological innovation, and not a few "happy accidents." Still, in terms of the organization's overall philosophy, its educational mission, social issue documentaries, and advocacy journalism we can detect in DCTV a palpable if unconscious affinity with what was described in Chapter 2 as "the Vertov process." Having said this, I want to make clear that I am not interested in uncovering antecedents to DCTV's video style, per se. Rather, my primary concern here is to gain greater insight into the relationship between cultural politics and new technologies and to interrogate this dynamic in the context of community television.

Indeed, as noted earlier, residents of the Lower East Side actively sought out, created, and embraced any means at their disposal to help them retain their cultural heritage, cope with substandard living conditions, and organize their respective community's resistance to socio-economic deprivation and political disenfranchisement. As Jon Alpert and Keiko Tsuno began to realize video's mobilizing potential, they likewise came to appreciate the importance of sharing their insights, as well as their limited resources, with other community activists. On Thursday evenings, they offered free video production workshops to any interested parties. In addition, they provided free equipment rentals to community groups and local residents, all from the cramped but welcoming environment of their living room.

Doing so allowed the newlyweds to pursue ever more ambitious projects while encouraging others to use video for their own needs. Throughout the 1970s, local residents, recently arrived immigrants, school teachers, and community organizers came to recognize the value of a host of community video services offered by Jon, Keiko, and Yoko Maruyama, Keiko's cousin, under the collective designation Downtown Community Television. Among those early programs, *PS 23 Needs a Chinese Principal*, news reports from the Chinatown Health Care, and an exposé on voting irregularities during a local school board election were pivotal in attracting the attention of community groups and funding agencies alike. At a time when the other video collectives were losing their grant support, DCTV received funding from the NYC Department of Cultural Affairs, and soon thereafter from the New York State Council on the Arts (NYSCA): an organization Alpert credits with nurturing DCTV in those first years. According to Alpert, funding agencies were impressed by DCTV's localism, its video workshops, and the impact its arts and education programs were having on the local community.

Indeed, DCTV's tapes helped publicize the community's concerns, mobilize various constituencies, and achieve tangible results. For instance, DCTV's Chinatown Health Fair tapes – produced in Chinese and English language versions – were used in several ways. For immigrants whose access to health care services was limited by economics, language, and custom, DCTV created short tapes illustrating the benefits of routine medical check-ups and demystifying modern medical practices for an apprehensive immigrant population. To ease the anxiety of older immigrants Chinese language tapes were played back at community centers throughout Chinatown. The following week, DCTV would help arrange transportation for elderly Chinese to travel to and from health care facilities. Furthermore, local activists used the tapes to lobby city administrators for the establishment of health care facilities for Chinatown – a community plagued by unsanitary living and working conditions, illness, and the lack of treatment for otherwise curable diseases. In doing so, DCTV's community video work helped put health care in Chinatown on the city's political agenda.

In a similar vein, DCTV produced a tape for Puerto Rican union organizers. Agribusiness in New York and New Jersey routinely courted immigrant farm labor from Puerto Rico with promises of employment opportunities, good pay, and clean, modern living conditions. As the DCTV tape graphically demonstrates, these specious claims lured unsuspecting immigrant labor away from their homes and families with false and misleading promises of "the good life." Working in collaboration with union organizers, DCTV produced the tape and made kinescopes that were shown to workers in Puerto Rico. The short documentary was effective in giving workers a more candid appraisal of what they might expect upon their arrival in the United States. As such, the project played a valuable role in union organizing efforts.

Some years later, the tape's unambiguous empathy for immigrant farm laborers endeared the DCTV crew to members of the Cuban consulate at UN headquarters in New York. These UN contacts helped secure travel visas for the DCTV crew during their historic trip to Cuba in 1974. Over the course of the next few years, DCTV's reputation grew considerably due in large part to the unprecedented success of their documentary work for the Public Broadcast Service (PBS). Despite the critical acclaim and national audiences their broadcast work garnered, DCTV's commitment to the people of the Lower East Side never wavered; DCTV's work for public and commercial broadcasters, and later for cable television, is informed by and helps support its work in the local community.

Writing in 1978, about the time of Jon and Keiko's first trip to Vietnam, making them the first American TV crew to enter the country since the war's end, one observer noted, "The center's headquarters, located above a Chinese beauty salon at the corner of Canal and Centre Streets in Manhattan's Chinatown, is a hub of activity for Chinatown teenagers, community organizations and just about anyone else who wants to learn how to handle portable video equipment" (Abrams 1978). Within the year, DCTV would move to its present location, a landmark firehouse on Lafayette Street, two blocks south of Canal Street, thus enabling the media arts organization to expand its impressive array of community video services.

Significantly, DCTV provided these services at little or no cost at a time when the equipment and training promised Manhattan residents in lucrative cable franchise agreements failed to materialize. As noted earlier, providing equipment and training to individuals and community groups was never a priority for the more celebrated video collectives. That is, not until the NYSCA announced a major funding initiative to support community-based video training. As a result, the spirit of cooperation that once defined the video underground had turned to competition and insularity (Boyle). Only Stoney's Alternative Media Center (AMC) and Theadora Sklover's Open Channel provided the sort of community-based training DCTV offered, albeit in decidedly more humble surroundings.

Both DCTV and Open Channel understood the importance of community outreach to immigrants, minorities, and low-income groups for creating a more democratic media culture. However, under Sklover's direction Open Channel's strategy for achieving this was markedly different than DCTV's. Whereas Open Channel's instructors came from the ranks of the broadcast industry, DCTV's instructors were local activists and artists who came from the local community. As a result, the methods and emphases of each organization's video instruction were quite distinctive.

A long-time advocate of access television, Sklover understood the politics of cable franchising quite well and was determined to demonstrate to city and state politicians, cable industry representatives, funding agencies, as well as cable television subscribers, public access television's relevance to a diverse population. Sklover feared that programming that failed to reflect the city's diversity or that came across as amateurish, unpolished, and unfamiliar, would undermine the viability of Manhattan's public access channels. "If these channels are not used, or if they carry programming that no one cares about . . . or if they are utilized for the entertainment of the esoteric few, then we probably will have provided the necessary fuel for those who are fighting against opening up this medium" (Sklover, quoted in Engelman 1996: 248). To that end, Open Channel's outreach efforts to marginalized groups were matched by a reliance upon, and uncritical acceptance of, broadcast television standards and practices in the hopes of creating "professional looking" television that would attract large audiences.

For their part, DCTV's video pedagogy encouraged novice producers to question and critically examine the codes and conventions associated with conventional broadcast television.[7] In this way, DCTV's production workshops instilled first time producers with a more nuanced understanding of the subtle and not so subtle ways in which television reinforces racial and ethnic stereotypes, naturalizes class and gender inequities, and otherwise legitimates relations of dominance and subordination. Chief among these strategies was DCTV's emphasis on documenting the struggle of "common people" and forcefully advocating for progressive social change. To that end, DCTV production classes encouraged workshop participants to produce tapes by, for, and about their local community; communities whose cultures, problems, and perspectives were largely absent from mainstream television.

Furthermore, DCTV was less sanguine over public access television's future than either AMC or Open Channel.[8] This is not to suggest that DCTV was uninterested in reaching larger audiences, nor that it was opposed to access television in principle. Rather, given the demographic make-up and socio-economic conditions of Chinatown and the Lower East Side, DCTV realized that franchise holders were unlikely to offer cable television services to area residents any time soon. Whatever potential access television might have for democratizing television, it was unlikely to affect the people of the Lower East Side, thus rendering cable television in general and community access in particular, largely irrelevant to the community DCTV calls home. In this light, broadcast television seemed a more appropriate, if improbable, outlet for DCTV's work.

Undaunted by the lack of either a conventional broadcast outlet or a community access channel to exhibit their work, DCTV took their brand of community television directly to the people. Throughout the early 1970s, DCTV brought their cameras, playback decks, and television monitors to meeting halls, community centers, and, quite literally, out onto the streets of the Lower East Side. As we shall see, this approach not only brought community-oriented television directly to the people, but also helped refine DCTV's participatory program production techniques: techniques that continue to inform DCTV's style and approach and that would, eventually, shape public broadcasting's early institutional identity and ultimately influence commercial television form and content as well.

In sum, DCTV consciously and deliberately tailored its community programs and media arts training workshops to meet the needs of minorities and low-income groups and individuals. Today, this approach continues to yield a wealth of innovative programs that vividly capture and eloquently speak to the Lower East Side's racial, ethnic, and cultural diversity. In this way, DCTV promotes local cultural production of the sort that rarely finds its way onto broadcast television. Indeed, the tapes produced by community video makers and those created through DCTV's training programs – available to all through DCTV's impressive community tape library – constitute a veritable storehouse of information, arts, and cultural programming unrivaled by any commercial or public service broadcaster in all of New York City.

Despite dramatic changes in the neighborhood and in television technology, one constant remains: DCTV's unflinching commitment to communicative democracy. In a self-published profile, DCTV sums up its mission this way: "We are working to create a new kind of television – with artistic strength, with roots solidly based in the community – television that improves people's lives and enriches our culture" (DCTV 1978). DCTV's formative work demonstrates how the organization's commitment to a democratic media culture shaped its signature style and, in turn, how this commitment continues to inform DCTV's vision of community television.

Elements of style

The "new kind of television" championed by DCTV owes a great deal of its visual style and aesthetic sensibility to the development of portable video production equipment. When Sony introduced its half-inch open reel CV portapak in 1968, video quickly became an essential tool for artists and activists alike. For an initial investment of $1,500 (US), so-called "non-professionals" could become independent filmmakers (Stoney 1971). Unlike film, however, which involves expensive processing fees and time-consuming sound synchronization, sound and image could immediately be played back through the same camera and recording deck used to acquire the footage.

As noted in Chapter 2, these technological innovations encouraged a heretofore-unknown populism in television production. As film scholar Thomas Waugh observed:

New lightweight cameras encouraged filmmakers to go beyond their traditional observational modes toward modes of participation and even collaboration, intervention, and social catalysis . . . new accessibility of film and video hardware dramatically multiplied forms of collective and grass-roots authorship to match the democratic aspirations of the new political movements.

(1984: xxiv)

Capitalizing on portable video's inherent immediacy and the sense of intimacy engendered by unobtrusive modes of production, DCTV developed a distinctive style – an approach to television production, distribution, and exhibition that owes as much to technological innovation as it does to a commitment to progressive social change. As we shall see, DCTV's style developed over time, through an iterative process that sought to make television relevant for communities whose voices, perspectives, and concerns were more often than not distorted and trivialized by, if not altogether absent from, mainstream television.

Living and working in and around New York City's Chinatown, DCTV's founders were struck by broadcast television's ambivalence

8. A repurposed mail truck, purchased for $5, brings DCTV's commu-
nity television to the streets of the Lower East Side. (Photo courtesy of
DCTV)

toward their neighborhood. Television news crews would show up regularly to capture a few moments of Chinese New Year celebrations. After
all, the fireworks, elaborate costumes, and dramatic street performances
made for "good visuals." Throughout the rest of the year, however, those
same news crews were nowhere to be found. Apart from this yearly ritual, for broadcasters it was as if the community never existed. What
the broadcasters missed or, more accurately, refused to take notice of –
the neighborhood's vibrant artistic and cultural offerings, the deplorable
working conditions, the woefully inadequate housing, health care, and
educational system, and the community activism that sought to address
these pressing issues – was the stuff of DCTV's earliest tapes.

As noted earlier, Chinatown is a rather insular ethnic enclave. Cultural
barriers such as language and custom, coupled with an acute sensitivity to
immigration issues, made some Chinese residents, especially members of
the older generation, suspicious of DCTV's video cameras and recorders.
In an effort to overcome their neighbors' reticence, DCTV brought along
large television monitors whenever they taped in public spaces. Similarly,

DCTV fitted an old mail truck with cameras, recording decks, and large monitors to showcase their work on busy street corners in Chinatown and the Lower East Side. In doing so, DCTV demystified the new technology, demonstrating its recording and playback capabilities, exhibiting pre-recorded programs, and encouraging local residents to use this new tool to document neighborhood meetings, preserve local arts and cultural events, as well as for educational and community organizing purposes.

One of DCTV's earliest efforts, a series of English language instruction tapes titled *The Adventures of Uncle Fong*, helped the group win the trust and support of local residents. In short vignettes designed to teach non-English speakers useful words and phrases, we follow an elderly Chinese gentleman throughout the course of his daily activities: Uncle Fong's difficulty navigating the subway system; his comic visit to the dentist (played with malevolent glee by Jon Alpert); or his trip to the corner grocer. By involving local, "non-professional" actors in these projects and providing community residents with useful information presented in an appealing and relevant fashion, DCTV built a formidable reputation – one based on trust and mutual respect – within an otherwise closed society.

DCTV's populist approach to television production, distribution, and exhibition had benefits for both the local community and the fledgling production collective. For locals, DCTV opened the door to more expansive uses of video within the Chinese community. Throughout the early 1970s, DCTV was the only media organization in New York City producing Chinese language tapes. In fact, DCTV's recordings of acupuncture were the first images of this ancient medical treatment aired on American television.[9] Having "discovered" this untapped demographic, DCTV set the stage for others – non-profits as well as commercial producers – to serve this large, under-served television audience.[10]

For DCTV's founding members, this neighborhood work served as a video boot camp of sorts. Showcasing their programs on street corners was particularly helpful in refining the group's shooting skills and developing editing strategies that would capture and hold an audience as they passed by. Jon Alpert recalls, "It was a terrific school for us because the public judged whether the work was interesting to them. . . . When we showed a tape we thought was pretty terrific and noticed there wasn't anybody standing on the sidewalk, we knew we had to rethink our concepts" (St. Lawrence 1987: 77). From these public exhibitions, the DCTV crew came to understand and appreciate audience tastes and preferences. Working in this iterative fashion, DCTV developed a number of production strategies and techniques that make for compelling viewing.

For instance, DCTV learned the crucial distinction between showing and telling. That is to say, audiences respond more readily to action on the screen rather than someone relating a story. Here, then, DCTV leveraged video's immediacy, its ability to capture a slice of life and convey this experience in an economical but no less engaging fashion. The Lower East Side's cultural and linguistic diversity likewise fostered an emphasis on visuals, which effectively transcend language barriers. To that end, DCTV developed narrative strategies using imagery rather than words. When it was needed, narration was used sparingly and, depending upon the audience, voiced in English, Chinese, or Spanish. Written in a conversational tone and with an economy of style, DCTV's voice-overs complemented but rarely overwhelmed the imagery.

Furthermore, these street corner sessions gave DCTV an opportunity to develop successful interviewing techniques. With a gregarious yet unassuming manner, the DCTV staff interviewed people on the street and treated them as equals whose opinions and perspectives were just as important as those of the politicians, celebrities, and business leaders who routinely appeared on television. For example, unlike their broadcast counterparts, whose minimal coverage of local school board elections relied heavily on "official sources" – school board officers, city administrators, and the like – DCTV took the opposite tack, documenting the acrimonious board meetings from beginning to end and speaking in-depth with concerned teachers, parents, and students. In short, DCTV cultivated an interest in "common people" – an interest in their work, their pleasures, their struggles, and their everyday lived experience – and managed to convey this to audiences in a lively, informative, and entertaining fashion.

DCTV's abiding interest in the lives of common people is matched by an uncommon intimacy with the subjects of their tapes. Over the course of the past thirty years, DCTV has produced candid, intimate, often stark and unsettling portraits of people whose lives are rarely acknowledged, let alone profiled on mainstream television. For instance, the flawed yet striking *Third Avenue: Only the Strong Survive* (1980) profiles the lives of six people who work or live along New York City's Third Avenue: a sixteen-mile thoroughfare that runs from Brooklyn, through Manhattan and on into the Bronx. This Emmy Award-winning documentary gives viewers unprecedented insight into the everyday lives of a male prostitute, a welfare mother, an alcoholic living in the Bowery, a factory worker, and two small business owners struggling to keep their livelihoods, and their families, intact. Like other work in the DCTV oeuvre, especially Jon Alpert's more recent work for Home Box Office (HBO) – *High on Crack Street: Lost Lives in Lowell, Life of Crime I & II*, and *Lock Up: The Prisoners of Rikers Island* – *Third Avenue* is disturbing inasmuch as it deals with thorny socio-economic issues, explores contradictions, and eschews narrative closure in favor of stories that encourage audiences to wrestle with the imagery and evidence presented in stark and unyielding fashion.

Stylistically, *Third Avenue* represents a major breakthrough for DCTV. Unlike DCTV's earlier work, *Third Avenue* has no narration whatsoever. Using direct interview techniques, the people profiled in *Third Avenue* speak for themselves, often straight into the camera, and without comment by the filmmakers. Prior to this project – the last long-form documentary DCTV produced for US public television – Jon Alpert provided the voice over for DCTV's news reports and documentaries. Alpert's voice-over work is distinctive inasmuch as it is effusive, registering surprise, alarm, wonder, and concern all in a high-pitched, New York accent. For audiences and not a few critics, Alpert's voice over was a welcome relief from the authoritative, self-assured, and seemingly omniscient narration common to television journalism.

Others, most notably documentary filmmaker D. A. Pennebaker, were not so enthralled. For Pennebaker, the use of voice-over narration constituted failure on the part of the filmmaker. Alpert smiles as he recounts meeting Pennebaker, a pioneer of "direct cinema" at a film festival sometime in the early 1970s:

He insulted our work. And you know what? He was right. When you use voice-over you're admitting that you didn't get the shot. So despite the acclaim our work was getting, his [Pennebaker's] criticism stuck with me. It really shook me. For years, we tried really hard to eliminate narration from our tapes. It took some time, but we finally did it. And when we did it in our pieces for NBC, it was like nothing else on commercial television.

Despite the abbreviated and somewhat disjointed quality of its portraits, *Third Avenue* nonetheless marked a sea change in DCTV's approach to subject-centered news reports and long-form documentary. Praising *Third Avenue* for the intimacy of its portraits, TV critic Tom Shales wrote, "There is more drama, more life, more love and passion in this short hour than in a week's worth of prime-time pot boiling" (1980: C1). The intimacy Shales observes indicates DCTV's ease and familiarity with the subjects of their tapes.

In large measure, this intimacy, and the trust upon which it is based, stems from DCTV's use of participatory production techniques. Honing their skills on the streets of New York, DCTV crew routinely recorded and played back footage for program participants to review. In doing so, interview subjects grew more comfortable with the equipment and the entire production process, lending this process a collaborative feel. The result is a far more intimate, candid, trusting relationship between the video maker and interviewees.

Inevitably, working in this fashion dramatically alters the relationship between the video's subject and the video producer. As Deirdre Boyle observes, "Given the intimacy of the taping, it's not surprising that the DCTV staff became involved in the lives of their subjects" (1992: 25). Indeed, Ricky, the male prostitute featured in *Third Avenue*, was Jon and Keiko's houseguest for a time when the young man was particularly troubled. Likewise, Rob, the petty thief profiled in two of Jon Alpert's documentaries for HBO, *Life of Crime* and *Life of Crime 2*, remained in contact with the filmmakers during his long incarceration. More recently, when the US bombing campaign began in March 2003, Alpert and the DCTV crew attempted, sometimes in vain, to check in on the Iraqi students featured in *Bridge to Baghdad*. Maintaining relationships with people they profile in their news reports and long-form work is routine for Alpert and the DCTV crew. This intimacy, based upon a collaborative relationship that develops between the video makers and the subjects of their work, helps to explain how DCTV manages to get the stories it does.

Indeed, DCTV has built a formidable reputation on its facility for gaining access to people and places that other journalists and filmmakers cannot or dare not. This talent also has its roots in DCTV's formative work in community centers, church basements, and on the street corners of Chinatown and the Lower East Side. In large part, DCTV's ability to gain access to people's personal lives stems from a mode of production that is less intrusive and therefore less intimidating than traditional film and television production. That is to say, the portapak, and later one-piece camera units, allow video makers to work with a smaller crew and with less ancillary equipment. Consciously avoiding the use of tripods, in an effort to maximize the camera's mobility, and shooting with available light, DCTV typically works with a crew of no more than two or three people.

Throughout the 1970s, Keiko Tsuno served as the group's principal photographer. Her cousin Yoko Maruyama handled the recording deck and monitored incoming audio, while Jon Alpert recorded sound and conducted interviews. In contrast, then, to the male-dominated technical crews of the video collectives described above, DCTV's division of labor is significant in that it played to each crew member's particular strengths and abilities, regardless of gender. Keiko's artistic sensibility and considerable knowledge of the camera's technical capacities and limitations yielded striking, memorable images. Yoko, a petite young woman, nevertheless handled the heavy recording deck with great agility. Jon's innate curiosity, boyish good looks, and affable manner put interview subjects at ease.

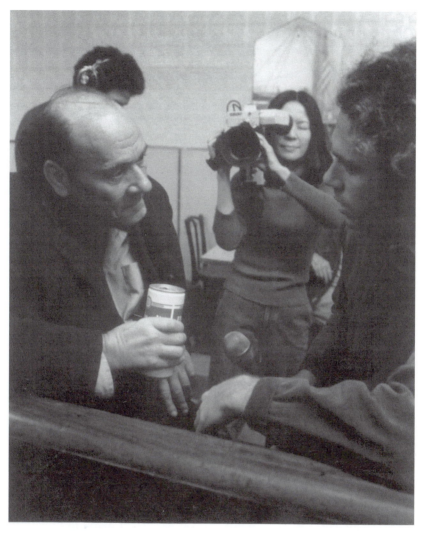

9. Keiko Tsuno, with the camera, and Jon Alpert conducting interviews for their award-winning documentary, *Third Avenue*. (Courtesy of
DCTV)

The next generation of portable video gear presented DCTV with a
number of logistical problems. Although this equipment produced high
quality color images, it was far more cumbersome than previous units
DCTV had worked with. To enhance their mobility DCTV hit upon a
rather ingenious method of equipment transport. In an interview with

Videography, one of several trade publications to emerge in tandem with the development of portable video, Alpert recalls:

We began to try to find a way to carry the camera control unit and the recorder and still be portable. Some people were experimenting with backpacks. We looked at some and we decided that it made you look like a spaceman [with] all the wires and stuff sticking out. And then we wondered how we could carry all this without being intimidating and still be portable. A shopping cart? No. A baby carriage we thought! That conveys something rather cushiony and delicate and at the same time, it is rather disarming.

(*Videography*: 60)

The baby carriage helped secure DCTV's reputation in the Lower East Side and far beyond.[11] Indeed, the sight of a television crew pushing their gear around in such a prosaic fashion caught most people off guard and suggested a certain homey quality to their video work. Refinements in portable video, including the development of 3/4$''$ U-Matic cassettes and later Beta Cam, precluded further use of the baby carriage. Still, DCTV's grassroots sensibility grew even more intimate and engaging, albeit for far less technical reasons.

In 1978, Keiko was pregnant with the couple's first and only child. When the pregnancy kept Keiko from operating the camera, while on foreign assignment, Jon picked up the camera and assumed the role of both photographer and interviewer. This "happy accident" helped further refine DCTV's visual style: from behind the camera, Alpert would ask questions. As a result, when interview subjects responded to Jon's questions, they would invariably speak directly into the camera lens. This form of "direct address," usually reserved for authoritative figures like politicians and journalists, not only heightened the intimacy of DCTV's work, it helped give interview subjects a sense of self-esteem and legitimacy that conventional television reportage rarely achieves. As one reviewer commented on Jon Alpert's *Today* show profile of a heroin addict: "It's weird stuff to write about – it sounds almost absurdist or funny – but [the report] manages to give dignity to people living with humiliation" (Morrison 1982: 2).

On occasion, Alpert also serves as his own translator, simultaneously posing questions in broken Spanish, Cantonese, or Vietnamese and then interpreting his subject's response. Given Alpert's rudimentary foreign language skills, his questions are rather blunt and somewhat simple, but deceptively so. That is to say, Alpert's interest in communicating the everyday lived experience of his interview subjects leads him to ask questions that most anyone can relate to. For instance, while shooting in a war zone in El Salvador, or in the rice fields of Vietnam, or in a run-down tenement in Newark, New Jersey, Alpert invariably asks the same sorts of questions: "How do you make a living?" "How many people live in this house?" "Are you getting enough to eat?" In doing so, Alpert rather ingeniously underscores the commonality of human experience across linguistic, geographic, and cultural differences.

As Alpert's style matured, his reports grew less conventional; and yet, they made for ever more compelling television. Veteran network television producer Steve Friedman puts it this way: "Most television reporting is done through the correspondent's eyes. Jon's is done basically through the camera's eyes. It's a different perspective. The result is Jon can get things out of people because he sort of looks like the people he covers. He's not intimidating or threatening and people let down their guard" (Kellog 1983: 32). In sum, this "folksy" approach to reportage and "I-am-the-camera" visual style would distinguish DCTV's work from other independent producers and help secure Jon Alpert and his DCTV crew a unique place in network news.

Indeed, Alpert's easygoing manner stands in stark contrast to the self-important posture assumed by most "professional" broadcasters. Unlike their counterparts in the industry, who often use television's technical apparatus to secure and defend their monopoly control of the chan-nels of public communication, DCTV seeks to demystify television, to make it accessible to local communities and to encourage minorities and low-income groups in particular to explore the communicative poten-tial of technologies generally associated with large, profit-oriented media conglomerates. This approach allows DCTV to produce starkly origi-nal and intimate portraits of "ordinary people"; and, as we shall see, it encourages these same individuals and groups to produce self-portraits within and through the previously inaccessible, yet pervasive medium of television.

Yet another distinction between DCTV's approach and that of "pro-fessional" television journalists is the time DCTV producers spend re-searching stories, cultivating contacts, and shooting in the field. Here again, we can detect the symbiotic relationship between DCTV and the surrounding community. Whereas most television reporters work on as-signment, DCTV producers choose projects that reflect local interests and concerns. Put another way, DCTV producers often have a vested interest in the people they report on and the conditions they survey. Far from being detached and disinterested observers, DCTV producers and crew invariably get involved in the stories they cover, driven by a desire to expose injustice and to affirm the humanity of those whose lives are all too often deemed unworthy of respect, dignity, or attention. Jon Alpert explains, "One of the things that drives us to pick certain stories is the belief that we can still do things to make this world a better place" (Kellog: 33). Alpert's embrace of advocacy journalism is indicative of DCTV's commitment to using video to improve the lives of local communities.

In sum, DCTV's style is informed by what film scholar Thomas Waugh (1984) describes as the "committed documentary." DCTV producers are not satisfied with "simply" recording people's stories or documenting the places where they live and work. Rather, by choosing to capture the everyday lived experience of common people, to document and call attention to their plight, and to affirm their humanity, DCTV acts in solidarity with people struggling to survive and with those who struggle to improve their lives and the life of their community. Put differently, it is an approach to television that does not seek to reflect the world as it is, but to transform it.

This critical engagement with popular struggles, at home and abroad, informs the look and feel of DCTV programs, those produced by Jon Alpert and Keiko Tsuno for public television and commercial network news, as well as the countless tapes produced by community activists, local artists, students, and others who fervently believe that "another world is possible." Waugh's definition of the committed filmmaker, as one who is actively engaged in "ongoing political struggles, by making films . . . not only about people engaged in these struggles, but also with and by them as well," succinctly summarizes DCTV's philosophy and provides important clues for interpreting the community media organization's work and appreciating its legacy.

Access at the margins

DCTV's low-budget aesthetics, its affinity for "common people," and its sympathy for popular struggles made for some remarkable community video. The question remained whether or not material of this sort would "play" on broadcast television. Eager to bring their work to wider audiences, DCTV, like the other video collectives operating in New York City at the time, set their sights on the fledgling public television service, and even more ambitiously, on commercial television. However, unlike the other collectives, whose relationships with the industry were short-lived, Jon Alpert and the DCTV crew have presented their work on broadcast and cable television for the past thirty years.

Writing in 1981, at a time when independent video makers were struggling to find outlets for their work, media critic J. Hoberman summed up Jon Alpert's enviable status as an independent journalist and documentarian this way: "Jon Alpert holds a unique position in the world of video. His tapes have been seen on the street, at alternative media centers, in institutions, on local and network public TV, and on news programs on network commercial television. As the 'independents' say, Jon Alpert has 'access'" (Hoberman 1981: 54). Significant as Alpert's independent status is vis-à-vis the industry; here I want to underscore the marginal character of Alpert's access to mainstream television outlets.

That is to say, notwithstanding twelve Emmy Awards, three Columbia-DuPont Citations, and countless other professional accolades to their credit, DCTV's relationship with the television industry has been rather tenuous and not without controversy. Indeed, despite critical acclaim, the group's first long-form documentary for public television, *Cuba: The People* (1974), engendered hostile reactions among some commentators and not a few Cuban exiles. With the group's 1977 production of *Health Care: Your Money or Your Life*, a graphic exposé on the health care industries, DCTV's days with public broadcasting were numbered. Here we can detect the increasingly uneasy relationship between the independent production community and the shifting institutional prerogatives of public broadcasting (Bullert 1997).

Conversely, the vagaries of the commercial broadcast industry, most notably the fierce competition within and between news organizations, provided independent producers with a modest, if fleeting opportunity to make inroads into the otherwise closed shops of commercial television. DCTV's unique ability to get stories from war zones and other global "hot spots" – Vietnam, El Salvador, Afghanistan, Tiananmen Square, and most recently from the rubble of the World Trade Center in Lower Manhattan – when other journalists could not, endeared the community video producers to network news producers.

For the same reason, DCTV's unconventional reportage and uncanny knack for scooping their counterparts in network news fostered professional jealousies within the press corps. The industry's response to DCTV's *Vietnam: Picking Up the Pieces* (1977) is a case in point. The first comprehensive US television report from Vietnam since the war's end, *Vietnam: Picking Up the Pieces* received an Emmy Award – the US television industry's highest honor. And yet, industry leaders belittled the documentary and DCTV's efforts. Doing his best Walter Cronkite impression, Alpert recalls the icon of American television news grumbling about non-professionals "waltzing into Vietnam" without the supervision of a network news organization. CBS News President Dick Salant was likewise unimpressed by DCTV's report: "We want seasoned journalists to do our reporting for us" (Alpert, personal conversation with the author).

Moreover, DCTV's sympathetic depiction of popular uprisings and subtle, yet forceful critiques of US foreign and domestic policy irritated conservative media watchdog groups, most notably Reed Irvine's

Accuracy in Media (AIM). Irvine famously interrupted an NBC stock-holders meeting by railing against the network's "liberal bias" and singling out Alpert, charging "He's carved out a niche of providing misinformation to the American people" (Faye 1986: 4). Throughout the 1980s and 1990s, as network news divisions yielded to economic pressures associated with the corporatization of news programming and to external pressures from the likes of conservative politicians and right-wing ideologues, the limited opportunities for independent journalists to "break into" mainstream news organizations evaporated.

Over the course of the past thirty years, Jon Alpert and DCTV have been at the vanguard of this effort to increase the presence of independently produced programming on the nation's airwaves. As we shall see, DCTV's unprecedented, if precarious access to public and commercial broadcasting has as much to do with industry dynamics of the time as it does with Alpert's persistence, his facility with the new video technologies, and his distinctive style; a style which, as noted above, owes a great deal to DCTV's commitment to community-oriented television and participatory production techniques. A detailed discussion of DCTV's first long-form documentary, *Cuba: The People*, serves to illustrate this last point.

Like much of their subsequent work for broadcast, and later, cable television, *Cuba: The People* stems from DCTV's engagement with local issues as well as the group's remarkable capacity to form lasting relationships with people from all walks of life. Alpert recalls the initial inspiration for the tape this way: "We were very involved in health care, education, and a lot of other community issues. Hispanics we met kept telling us how Cuba was trying to deal with the same problems. It really whetted our appetite to go, so we began pressing people at the Cuban mission to the United Nations" (Daviss 1985: 30). As it happened, Alpert's softball team enjoyed a friendly rivalry with members of the Cuban diplomatic corps who likewise played ball on Sunday mornings in New York City's Central Park. Heading back downtown one day, a member of the Cuban mission asked Jon about his "filmmaking." Seizing the opportunity, Alpert discussed DCTV's community video work in the Lower East Side and related the group's interest in shooting a documentary on Cuba.

Establishing a pattern that would serve him well over the course of his long career, Alpert charmed, pestered, and ultimately impressed the Cubans with his good humor and hard work.[12] Upon reviewing DCTV's vivid and sympathetic depiction of Puerto Rican farm workers, members of the Cuban mission helped arrange DCTV's visit to the island nation. The result was an hour-long broadcast for public television, the first documentary shot with $1/2''$ color portapak ever broadcast on national television. Indeed, *Cuba: The People* was a "first" in many respects.

Throughout the early 1960s, network television devoted considerable airtime to documentaries denouncing socialism and exposing the communist threat to world peace and security. Notwithstanding the fact that American television crews were barred from the country since the revolution, Cuba was a perennial subject of broadcast documentaries of the time. And yet, as television historian Michael Curtin (1995) observes, the industry abandoned long-form documentary almost as quickly as it had embraced the format. Despite the precipitous decline in network documentary, however, broadcasters still cast a wistful eye toward Cuba. Weeks before PBS aired *Cuba: The People*, CBS news broadcast a report on Cuban exiles. Around this same time, ABC scheduled *The Missiles of October*, a dramatization of the Cuban missile crisis. What makes *Cuba: The People* distinctive is that DCTV was the first American television crew permitted into the country since the revolution toppled the Batista regime in 1959. In short, the grassroots video collective achieved what network news organizations had long sought: a formal invitation from the Cuban government to visit the island nation and the ability to travel the country unescorted and to speak with the people free from government interference.

When they returned to New York City, the DCTV crew realized they had a major scoop on their hands. With forty-five hours of footage featuring intimate portraits of ordinary Cubans – school children, church goers, cigar makers, medical students, farmers, fishermen, and factory workers – and their reflections on life before and after the revolution, DCTV sought a broadcast partner to help them complete post-production and air this extraordinary material. To their surprise and consternation broadcasters were, almost without exception, uninterested. The struggle to bring *Cuba: The People* to air served as a primer on the peculiar politics of broadcast news and documentary: a lesson that was not lost on the members of DCTV.

With a 25-minute "rough cut" in hand, DCTV made the rounds of local broadcast outlets. Here, the significance of portable video for independent production cannot be overstated; the new technology represented a sea change in the relationship between independent producers and the broadcast industry. According to Alpert, small format video gave independent producers access to the once closed shops of broadcast television:

When you're working in 1/2″ videotape, you can at least go through the workprint stage financing the thing yourselves. You don't get paid for your time but you can get to that stage. In film, you couldn't do it. But in videotape, you can get to the point just before you bump it to quad and take it around. That really appears to be where it's at right now [mid 1970s] . . . who do you know that can go to a TV station with a proposal and get funded out of the blue.

(Perlman 1975: 43)

DCTV's first stop was WNET, the local public television station. WNET passed, but suggested DCTV try WGBH, the public television affiliate in Boston and a major program producer for the national public television service. Initially, WGBH expressed great interest in working with DCTV on the project. But after months of stalling, WGBH unceremoniously pulled out of the deal. Recalling the episode, Alpert equates the experience to the old gag from the *Peanuts* cartoon strip in which Lucy snatches away the football just as Charlie Brown tries to kick it.

Back in New York City, DCTV contacted the commercial network affiliates. ABC declined. So too did NBC. But not before network executives brought in their engineering staff to evaluate the technical merits of the recording. NBC engineers were stunned to learn that what they were looking at was not film or even one-inch tape, but rather $1/2''$ portable video. Within days, NBC outfitted its news department with color portapak systems. This was the first of many instances when DCTV "proved" the performance and reliability of new field acquisition equipment, tape formats, and post-production equipment, thereby endearing the media arts organization to equipment manufacturers, Sony, CMX, Avid, and Apple, among others, who continue work with DCTV for "beta testing" of their latest gear.

Surprised and a little confused by the network's ambivalence toward their footage, DCTV's next stop was CBS. Sometime earlier, CBS had purchased the raw footage of independent journalists Frank Mankiewicz and Kirby Jones' exclusive interview with Fidel Castro. When DCTV brought its footage to CBS, network executives offered a similar deal. In exchange, CBS would retain the exclusive rights to the footage. Despite the considerable financial loss DCTV was taking, the group declined CBS's offer, opting instead to retain editorial control over the project. In retrospect, Alpert suspects CBS had less altruistic motives for offering to purchase the footage. Anxious to avoid getting scooped by rival news organizations, CBS might simply "shelve" the footage in order to keep it out of the hands of its competitors. A "quick study" of Alpert's insights into the machinations of network television have helped DCTV survive where the other video collectives failed.

DCTV did not leave CBS empty handed, however. Acting on a tip from veteran CBS documentary filmmaker, Burton "Bud" Benjamin, DCTV returned to WNET, this time to meet directly with program director George Page and his colleague David Luxton. Luxton had recently established the aforementioned TV Lab, a discrete production unit within WNET dedicated to promoting independent video production. Throughout the 1970s and early 1980s, the TV Lab worked with the likes of video artists Nam June Paik, Bill Viola, and William Wegman; future film and television producers Michael Shamberg, Don Mischer, and Diane English; as well as other video collectives. For instance, both DCTV's *Cuba: The People* and TVTV's seminal agitprop tape, *Gerald Ford's America,* were produced under the auspices of the TV Lab. These two distinctive programs were the first independently produced documentaries aired on US public television.

Alpert credits Luxton and the TV Lab with "providing support and shelter for independent producers" and for creating a space for documentary work that "offered a diversity of opinion on pressing social issues." Serving as both a catalyst and a forum for innovative, experimental, and decidedly unconventional approaches to television form and content, the TV Lab enabled independent producers, like DCTV, to mount a formidable challenge to conventional broadcast television. Arguably, then, working with DCTV and other independent producers, the TV Lab helped establish public television as a viable alternative to commercial broadcasting.

Luxton further demonstrated his enthusiasm for DCTV's Cuba project by securing financial support from the Ford Foundation, a philanthropic organization that was instrumental in establishing the US public broadcasting sector (Engelman 1996). Equally important, Luxton partnered DCTV with two seasoned television professionals. For editorial guidance, he assigned veteran filmmaker Patricia Sides to supervise post-production on *Cuba: The People.* Sides's patience with the young producers, who by their own account were in way over their heads, was matched by her formidable aptitude for visual storytelling. Pat Sides became a close confidante and trusted adviser for DCTV on this and other projects. According to Keiko Tsuno, Pat Sides played a significant role in shaping the group's approach to long-form documentary.

On the technical end, the TV Lab's supervising engineer, John Godfrey, would shepherd the project through the arduous process of ensuring that DCTV's video met the technical standards required for broadcast. Throughout this process, Godfrey made extensive use of a relatively new piece of equipment, the CVS-504 Time Base Corrector (TBC). Based on his recent experience editing *Cuba: The People* and *Gerald Ford's America*, Godfrey explained the significance of the TBC to independent production in the TV Lab's newsletter (1974).

Small-format acquisition gear, Godfrey observed, such as the JVC portapak DCTV used in Cuba, enabled the young video makers to visit factories, schools, clubs, and other public places that would preclude the use of conventional "broadcast quality" equipment. Thus, DCTV treated American audiences to a rare glimpse of the everyday lives of the Cuban people. On the downside, Godfrey notes, the JVC unit is a "loose-wrap" deck that prohibits very much movement while recording. In addition, the unit has problems with color reproduction, especially in high contrast areas and under low light conditions. These problems soon became apparent to the DCTV crew when they recorded images of dark skinned Cubans under the glare of the equatorial sun or in the darkened interiors of factories and churches. The solution that presented itself was to shoot close-ups and to eliminate any but the most essential camera movement.

These on-location solutions certainly enhanced the intimacy of the footage, but only went so far in accurately reproducing color, especially skin tones. Aside from maintaining the video signal's integrity during its conversion from $1/2''$ to the quad format used for broadcast transmission, Godfrey utilized the TBC for purposes of color correction and contrast control. "Tweaking" the image in this fashion was essential for ensuring that DCTV's footage met the industry's technical standards. Thus, along with Godfrey and the TV Lab, DCTV championed the use of the TBC in video post-production and helped pioneer the process of inter-format editing that enabled independent producers working with "small-format" video to air their material on broadcast television. DCTV therefore played a decisive role in pushing the envelope and creating opportunities for independent producers to reach wider audiences.

Luxton placed one condition on his offer to assist DCTV with their Cuba documentary: Harrison Salisbury, the respected foreign affairs correspondent from *The New York Times*, would introduce the tape. Salisbury's brief comments provided the socio-political context for this exclusive look at contemporary life in Cuba. At the tape's conclusion, Salisbury would then conduct a follow-up interview with Jon Alpert. DCTV accepted Luxton's generous offer without reservation. Given the nature of the material and its presentation style – the tape has the informal feel of a travelogue, a far less didactic approach than conventional news reports and documentaries – Salisbury's presence lent the program an air of legitimacy that might not have been afforded the tape as a stand-alone piece. Equally important, the post-screening discussion gave viewers a better understanding of the motivations behind the documentary's production and insights into DCTV's participatory production techniques.

By most accounts, *Cuba: The People* was a critical and popular success. Television reviewers hailed the documentary for lending balance to US press coverage of Cuba, thereby breaking the "information blockade" that surrounded the island nation since the revolution. Despite its informality – or perhaps precisely because it eschews "authoritative" narration and a reliance upon "official sources" – the documentary reveals the Cuban people's optimism and revels in their gregariousness. Furthermore, the tape demonstrates the Cuban people's individual and collective identification with the revolution as well as the significant progress of, and considerable national pride in, the country's industrial development, agricultural productivity, and educational reform. DCTV's report stands in sharp contrast, then, to conventional news reports that focused on economic deprivation and political repression under Castro's regime. As such, *Cuba: The People* suggests that the picture of Cuba presented in US media was incomplete and in large part inaccurate.

Significantly, for both DCTV and public television, *Cuba: The People* was the highest-rated documentary aired on PBS up to that time. For the fledgling public television service, the documentary's performance demonstrated the system's viability as an alternative source of news and information for the American people: a key component of its institutional mandate. Likewise, with *Cuba: The People*, PBS signaled its ability to support independent production, thereby fulfilling public television's directive to open up the airwaves to a greater range of voices, opinions, and perspectives.

For DCTV, the broadcast signaled that community television had arrived. National recognition would help attract funding and institutional support for additional long-form documentary work. When other video collectives were falling out of favor with broadcast outlets and financial sponsors, DCTV made significant inroads into the broadcast industry and attracted sponsorship from various agencies, most notably the New York State Council on the Arts (NYSCA). As a result, between 1975 and 1980, DCTV produced a string of distinctive, innovative, and engaging documentaries for public television: *Chinatown: Immigrants in America* (1975); *Health Care: Your Money or Your Life* (1977); *Vietnam: Picking Up the Pieces* (1978); and *Third Avenue: Only the Strong Survive* (1980).

Equally important, DCTV's critical success on broadcast television would directly support the non-profit media center's work in the local community. Funneling their modest profits back into its community programs, DCTV expanded its media arts training in Chinatown and the Lower East Side and initiated one of its most successful programs: an intensive production program for "at risk" high school students. This program and others like it offered under the auspices of DCTV continue to provide young people with the tools, the skills, and the confidence to communicate within and through a familiar, but all too often inaccessible medium.

It would be a mistake, however, to view *Cuba: The People* as an unqualified success. In certain respects, the tape was a harbinger of the controversies and difficulties DCTV would face over the course of the next three decades. For instance, prior to the documentary's national broadcast, several public television affiliates refused to air the tape. Responding to political pressure from Cuban exile groups, a local PBS station in Florida did not carry the program. And in Texas, a public television affiliate removed the program from their broadcast schedule after the station received bomb threats. Some months later, DCTV's documentary was castigated during Congressional hearings on yearly appropriations for public television – an indication of public broadcasting's precarious financial status and the "chilling effect" this condition has on US public broadcasting. Alpert recalls that on the night of the national broadcast, nervous public television executives reconsidered the wisdom of airing independently produced programs of this sort. These were the first stirrings of a more precipitous falling out between DCTV and public television that surrounded the broadcast of *Health Care: Your Money or Your Life*.

Health Care is an important and widely celebrated work that remains one of Alpert's personal favorites. A comparative analysis of conditions at two Brooklyn hospitals – the privately owned Downstate Medical Center and the city-run Kings County Hospital – the tape vividly documents the disparities in health care services available to poor and working class patients at Kings County and their more affluent counterparts at Downstate. The stark and unsettling investigative report angered health care workers, patients, and reviewers who assembled for a sneak preview of the tape prior to broadcast. As one critic noted, the tape's graphic nature and explosive revelations would "alternatively sicken and infuriate" viewers (Kelly 1977: 48). The tape likewise enraged business leaders in medical insurance, health care services, and the pharmaceutical industry, albeit for very different reasons. As such, *Health Care* helped seal DCTV's fate with public television.

According to Alpert, PBS deliberately undermined the program's promotional campaign. Here was an engaging, effective, and uncompromising investigative report. And yet, publicity for the tape was both inadequate and inaccurate. Contemporary print reviews and promotional materials support Alpert's claim and indicate that publicity for *Health Care* focused almost exclusively on the policy makers and social critics involved in the post-screening discussion rather than on the tape itself: the antithesis of the approach David Luxton employed with such great effect for *Cuba: The People*. All of which supports Alpert's contention that *Health Care*'s forceful indictment of the medical establishment frightened PBS brass. As drug companies, health care providers, and insurance firms were increasingly viewed as valuable "patrons" of public broadcasting, network executives were loath to offend influential and generous underwriters.

Here we can detect a fundamental flaw in funding mechanisms for US public television and the implications this has had on independent production. That is, funding for the Corporation for Public Broadcasting (CPB), the nongovernmental organization responsible for administrative and financial oversight of the Public Broadcasting Service (PBS), is determined by congressional budget appropriations and therefore subject to the political and ideological battles within and between various branches of the federal government. Never has this dynamic been more evident than during the late 1960s and early 1970s when the Nixon Administration mounted a sustained attack on PBS' news, documentary, and public affairs programming.

According to media scholar Patricia Aufderheide, Nixon intimidated public television executives and in so doing "tamed" the emerging service by "politicizing the CPB board, eliminating endowment plans, reducing foundation funding, and siphoning more federal funds to local stations – which, as he [Nixon] had hoped, were less critical of the status quo than Eastern producers were" (2001: 109). Since that time, the CPB board, PBS staff, and independent producers alike have understood the political expediency of treading lightly on controversial subjects that might challenge, embarrass, or otherwise offend political and economic elites.

This is not to suggest that independent producers were unwilling to take on controversial subjects or to experiment with innovative approaches to the medium. Rather, public television executives no longer supported or encouraged independent work of this sort. Thus, if an independent producer wanted to reach a national audience, they would have a much better chance of securing funding and getting airtime if they played it safe. As evidenced by PBS' lukewarm response to DCTV's *Health Care*, investigative reports, social issues documentaries, and advocacy journalism of the sort practiced by an emerging independent production community was quickly falling out of favor with PBS bureaucrats.

In the absence of secure financial support and fearful of alienating politicians and economic interests, CPB began courting corporate sponsors whose image management strategies were well suited to a depoliticized public television service specializing in safe (and marketable) educational television and prestigious and inoffensive "high culture" offerings (Ledbetter 1998). As Jon Alpert once famously remarked, "Public broadcasting is basically real chicken. If they could get away with just opera and ballet, they'd put in on twenty-four hours a day" (Christensen

1986: 36). In this environment, it is not surprising that DCTV's subsequent program proposals dropped like a stone at PBS. With good reason, then, Alpert contends that he and DCTV were "blacklisted" by PBS for their unconventional, often controversial reports.

Just as their fortunes with public television were declining, the DCTV crew began exploiting new opportunities in commercial broadcasting. Specifically, the intense competition between rival network's evening newscasts coupled with DCTV's fortuitous presence in Southeast Asia at the outbreak of the Cambodian-Vietnamese border conflict helped the community video producers get their first reports on commercial network news. What's more, around this time competition between the network's morning newscasts began to intensify. This condition, coupled with the fact that these morning programs represented an enormous "news hole," helps explain commercial broadcasters' willingness to work with DCTV at the same moment when public television shunned DCTV's innovative and challenging work. In any event, the competitive nature of commercial television news coupled with changing dynamics within the industry provided DCTV with a unique opportunity to reach ever-wider audiences.

DCTV's big break came when PBS passed on the group's follow-up report on Cuba. Impressed with DCTV's long-form documentaries, Sonja Selby-Wright, an associate producer for ABC's *Good Morning America* program, purchased four six-minute segments. Like the original report, these stories feature intimate portraits of the Cuban people. This new material was all the more distinctive in that it also featured a concise report of a recently completed Communist Party Congress (perhaps the first detailed discussion of this event ever broadcast on American television). Moreover, the second segment, a report on a state visit from the Angolan president, featured the first of DCTV's many exclusive interviews with Fidel Castro. Here again, DCTV's ability to gain access to closed societies and their reputation for scooping their colleagues in the mainstream press enabled the community video producers to break into the rarified realm of commercial network news.

As Deirdre Boyle observed at the time: "Until quite recently, the networks have unofficially restricted coverage of news and public affairs events to reports from their own staffs. But since March 1979, DCTV has worked freelance for NBC-TV, which broadcast the group's reports on Cambodia and on Fidel Castro's November 1979 visit to the United Nations" (Boyle 1980: 23). Indeed, 1979 marked a watershed for DCTV. Following on from their success covering the border war in Southeast Asia and DCTV's exclusive reports of the Sandinista revolution in Nicaragua, NBC offered Alpert a staff position. An increasingly savvy industry player, Alpert turned down the network's offer, opting instead to retain his journalistic independence and support the DCTV's expanding community video services through lucrative freelance arrangements with NBC.

The precedent Alpert established with *NBC Nightly News* informed the relationship between DCTV and Steve Friedman, executive producer of the *Today* show, NBC's morning news program. Taking advantage of a loophole in union rules, Friedman hired DCTV on spec, paying only for those projects he deemed suitable for broadcast. In DCTV's subject-centered approach, Friedman found a unique sensibility that complemented the *Today* show's more traditional reportage and enhanced its emphasis on human-interest stories. For Alpert and DCTV, the arrangement gave the collective unprecedented editorial control over its news reports. Moreover, because DCTV retained the rights to all of its footage, the non-profit media center taps into additional revenue streams from foreign distribution rights and educational sales of its tapes.

Between 1980 and 1991, the DCTV crew – Jon Alpert, Keiko Tsuno, and later, Maryann De Leo and Karen Ranucci – produced a body of work unique in the annals of American broadcast television. Working primarily for NBC's *Today* show, DCTV produced hundreds of reports that vividly demonstrated the viability of advocacy journalism on a commercial television network. The award-winning *American Survivor* series, for example, covered a range of pressing domestic problems – housing, drug addiction, crime, unemployment, environmental policy, and health care – in a manner that made complex issues accessible, comprehensible, and relevant to commercial television audiences. These reports, typically broadcast over the course of several days in what might be described as a "serial documentary," not only addressed fundamental questions of social, economic, and political justice, but did so in a manner that allowed "ordinary Americans" to voice their fears, hopes, opinions, and perspectives with a native eloquence rarely seen on American television.

In a similar and equally striking fashion, DCTV's international reporting uncovered the contradictory impulses behind US foreign policy and in so doing humanized those people and popular struggles, such as the Iranian revolution, the Nicaraguan Sandinista and Mexican Zapatista movements, that conventional American press coverage tended to either ignore or demonize. For instance, DCTV's reports from El Salvador graphically demonstrated the brutality of US backed counterinsurgency forces operating illegally in neighboring Honduras.

Significantly, DCTV's advocacy journalism led directly to policy changes. For example, prior to a series of reports titled "Hard Metals

Disease," workers in the tungsten-carbide machine tool industry were systematically prohibited from seeking compensation for cobalt poisoning that was directly attributable to their working conditions. Following the report, the New York State legislature granted workers the opportunity to sue their employers for health and safety violations. In Michigan, tool works were ordered to install proper ventilation in their facilities. Thus, this series of reports not only put industry on notice but also helped pressure state regulatory bodies to address labor issues they had long ignored. Likewise, DCTV's stories from Cambodia graphically illustrated the human costs associated with the US State Department's refusal to send humanitarian relief to the war-ravaged country. As Alpert later recalled, "The US was refusing shipments of food on the grounds that it would all be appropriated by the Vietnamese or something. We were able to show that was just ridiculous, that other countries were getting food in. The US policy was changed" (Christensen 1986: 36).

Perhaps no other series of reports demonstrated the power of DCTV's approach to international reporting, nor the volatile reaction these reports engendered back home, more than their news stories from the Philippines. In 1984, when US press coverage was dominated by celebratory accounts of Corazon Aquinos's "People Power" movement, DCTV's reports underscored the "revolution's" limited impact on the Filipino underclass and highlighted the militancy of the ongoing struggle, especially in the Philippine countryside. One especially poignant report concludes with the image of a young pregnant woman, scouring a garbage heap for scraps of food. Back in the NBC studio in New York City, Jon Alpert bluntly informs a visibly shaken Jane Pauley, the *Today* show host, that the teenager's experience is not uncommon: "People are born in the dump. They live in the dump. And they die in the dump."

An equally provocative news story captured a rebel group's ambush of a Filipino government troop transport. The graphic footage, part of a report aired on *NBC Nightly News*, documents a swift and merciless attack that left fifteen soldiers dead. Outraged viewers called the network with complaints over the report's violence and its shocking and disturbing imagery. Equally troubling for the network were charges that Alpert and his crew were somehow complicit in the attack. At one point, Alpert is heard from behind the camera shouting: "Here comes the enemy!" Although producers and audiences were accustomed to Alpert's self-described "chirping" from behind the camera – this technique is an integral part of Alpert's reporting style, an approach to video journalism that avoids voice-over narration in favor of a more conversational approach to interviewing and narrative structure in television news – this incident bolstered the claims of fellow journalists and conservative critics alike, that Alpert was too involved in his stories. Some went so far as to claim that Alpert staged the event for the camera.

Following a thorough review, NBC executives stood behind Alpert and confirmed the veracity and authenticity of the report. NBC news anchor Tom Brokaw, whose personal and professional respect for Alpert is evident by his long-time participation on the DCTV board of directors, defended Alpert's approach and his journalistic integrity.

Jon becomes almost organically a part of the story he is covering. He may be less informational but he captures a mood. He goes out to reflect the flavor of the personality or the story. He has enormous curiosity and high energy. If you have to use labels, Jon is probably more a filmmaker than a journalist, but the lines are sometimes blurred. He has demonstrated he is a man who is responsible for his actions; if you look at his work over the long haul you will see all manner of opinion expressed. There's no Jon Alpert party line.

(Brokaw quoted in Kellog: 32)

Still, the Philippine ambush controversy began to color Alpert's relationship with NBC. In January 1989, when Alpert did in fact stage an event for the camera – Marines reenacted the lowering of the American flag at the US embassy in Kabul prior to their evacuation from the Afghan capital – Alpert's credibility with the network grew more precarious.

Alpert's increasingly uneasy relationship with the new corporate leadership at NBC came to a head in early 1991. Despite the fact that at the time of the Persian Gulf War, Jon Alpert and the DCTV crew had earned the network six Emmy awards, their report from inside Iraq – a story that never aired on *NBC Nightly News,* or on any major television network for that matter, but has been independently released under the title *Nowhere to Hide* – effectively ended DCTV's long and productive relationship with NBC.[13]

Steve Friedman, formerly of the *Today* show, then Executive Producer of *NBC Nightly News* had given Jon Alpert and Mary Ann De Leo the green light to report on the war from the ground. Equipped with the latest small format gear, Sony's Hi-8 camera, Alpert and De Leo would travel to Iraq in the company of former US attorney general Ramsey Clark. Clark, who had been to Libya following the US bombing campaign of Tripoli in 1986, wanted someone along for his visit to Iraq to document the air war's impact on the ground. Alpert's willingness and ability to report from war zones made him an obvious choice for this assignment, and through his contacts abroad Clark secured travel visas for the DCTV crew.

Just as the two reporters were leaving for Iraq, however, NBC News executive vice-president Donald Browne pulled the plug. According to Browne, NBC correspondent Tom Aspell could not obtain a visa from Iraq because Alpert had already obtained one from Amman, Jordan. The network did not want Alpert to be the only NBC reporter on the ground in Iraq. Besides, the network wanted to distance itself from former US attorney general Ramsey Clark, who had been and remains a vocal critic of US militarism. Rather than cancel their trip, DCTV traveled to Iraq as freelancers, unaffiliated with NBC. Upon their return, NBC would review the footage and retained the right of first refusal.

On 31 January 1991, NBC News anchor Tom Brokaw provided what would be the perfect set-up for Alpert's footage. Brokaw noted that there are only two news sources covering the air campaign in Iraq – footage taken by US aircraft and subsequently vetted by Pentagon officials and reports broadcast by state-run Iraqi TV. Implicit in Brokaw's remarks was the fact that both the Pentagon reports and those of the Iraqis were biased. What was missing was independent reporting on the ground. For Brokaw, Friedman, and others at NBC, DCTV's report would add a much needed balance to official Iraqi reports and the sanitized version of the air campaign that dominated US press coverage. Following a whirlwind tour of Iraq led by Ramsey Clark, Alpert and De Leo managed to smuggle their exclusive footage past Iraqi censors. As it turned out, getting the report past the corporate gatekeepers of American broadcasting provided an even greater challenge.

Upon viewing DCTV's raw footage, NBC producers hastily arranged to air this extraordinary material. They asked Alpert and De Leo to have their report ready for broadcast in a few days time, making certain to remove any reference to Ramsey Clark. *Nightly News* scheduled the first report for 12 February 1991; three subsequent reports would run on the *Today* show later that week. As they completed their final edit, however, NBC News executive Michael Gartner summoned Alpert and De Leo into his office. Gartner informed the independent producers that the network would not run their story. Gartner also used the occasion to terminate DCTV's eleven-year relationship with NBC, effective immediately.

Writing about the incident in the Columbia *Journalism Review*, Michael Hoyt (1991) suggests that Gartner used the Afghanistan episode as cover for Alpert's dismissal. Gartner's stated objections had nothing to do with the content of the Iraqi report, but centered on questions surrounding Alpert's journalistic integrity. Yet, as Hoyt observes, NBC had no qualms about airing Alpert's exclusive report on the Tiananmen Square massacre not long after the network reprimanded Alpert for his earlier indiscretion.

In short, while NBC eagerly accepted Alpert's reports of the brutal repression in Beijing, the network took great exception to the Iraqi report. Not surprisingly, given mainstream media's unapologetic jingoism during the Persian Gulf War, the other major networks likewise refused to run the story. All of which vividly demonstrates that, in the eyes of network executives, unpopular stories about Iraqi civilian casualties had no place on American television. Neither, so it seemed, did Jon Alpert and the DCTV crew.

Vox pop, hip hop, agit prop

Following his dismissal from NBC, Alpert's attention returned to long-form documentary of the sort DCTV produced for public television in the late 1970s. As it happened, during the late 1980s and early 1990s cable television was in much the same position that the commercial networks had been in some years earlier. That is, with rising cable penetration rates and a growing number of networks coming on line, cable television grew ever more competitive. As a result, cable programmers eagerly sought out less conventional, more risqué material in an effort to differentiate themselves from competitors and attract subscribers. With its *America Undercover* series, Home Box Office (HBO) took the lead in this regard and embraced the long-form documentary that commercial networks had long since abandoned and which public television had essentially neutralized. Throughout the 1990s, the investigative documentary made another comeback, this time on cable television, and once again, Alpert and the DCTV crew were in the vanguard of this revival.

Alpert's documentaries for HBO, including *One Year in the Life of Crime*, *Lock-Up*, *High on Crack Street*, and *Life of Crime* (Part II), are disturbing, yet insightful and thought-provoking investigations into the everyday lived experience of people living on the margins of society: petty criminals in New Jersey's inner city; prison inmates on New York City's Riker's Island; and crack addicts in the former textile town of Lowell, Massachusetts. This later work is striking inasmuch as it is less a departure from Alpert's initial approach to community video than a refinement of his political perspective and aesthetic sensibility. According to Alpert, "I think there was a time when every single tape we were making was part of an overall plan to change the world and make it a better place... this may be a reflection of my advancing years, but maybe its not always to change things now but sometimes to understand things" (Strum 1994: 32). Although his emphasis on advocacy may be tempered, in terms of form and content, Alpert's affinity for "everyday people" remains firmly intact, as does the implicit critique of contemporary journalistic routines

and practices DCTV's work represents. Observing the unequivocal populism of the HBO documentaries, one critic noted that Alpert's camera
is there "wherever there's a common-man's story to be told amid the official versions and expense account journalism" (Werts 1994: 16). Like
DCTV's first long-form documentaries for public television, then, this
later work examines the complex and contested character of community
relations in a graphic and often poignant style that echoes the empathy, as
well as the direct cinema approach DCTV first achieved in *Third Avenue*.

Throughout the 1990s, as they immersed themselves in long-form documentaries for HBO, Alpert and the DCTV crew gradually returned to
public and commercial broadcasting. Just as they had done in the past,
broadcasters grudgingly acknowledged Alpert's knack for scooping the
competition or working a unique angle on a breaking news story. For
instance, in the aftermath of the terrorist attacks of 11 September 2001,
the CBS *Early Show* aired Alpert's exclusive dispatches from the ruins of
the World Trade Center. In typical fashion, Alpert surreptitiously made
his way behind the police barricades and, with his Sony Mini-DV camcorder, captured remarkable footage of the rescue and recovery efforts.
More recently, Bill Moyers' *Now*, a weekly half-hour news program for
public television, ran excerpts from DCTV's documentary *From Ground
Zero to Ground Zero*, a forceful indictment of the civilian costs of the so-
called "war on terror" as seen through the eyes of Masuda Sultan, a
young Afghan-American woman who lost nineteen members of her family, mostly women and children, during the US air campaign of October
2001.[14]

All of which underscores the significance of DCTV's access to public
broadcasting and commercial network and cable television. As media activist and scholar Tony Downmunt observes, popular access to television
has two distinct, but related dimensions: one political, the other aesthetic.
"The process of inclusion and exclusion from media power themselves
resulted in stultified and boring programmes and televisual forms being
in some way molded and deadened by this inequality" (2001: 2). By promoting independent production and championing innovative approaches
to television form and content, DCTV revealed the aesthetic potential of
the medium when it serves the needs and interests of people and places
historically marginalized by contemporary media forms and practices.
Tenuous as this access to mainstream media has been, DCTV nonetheless vividly demonstrates the viability of "a new kind of television" – a
cultural form that is inclusive of and relevant to the lives and experiences
of local communities.

Not surprisingly, however, the television industry has hollowed out
the most progressive elements of DCTV's visual style and populist

orientation. Writing in the early 1980s, *New York Times* television critic John O'Connor observed in commercial television's mimicry of the emergent style championed by DCTV and others working with "small format" video, the beginnings of a disconcerting trend that dominates television form and content today: so-called "reality television." "The new 'people' shows, however, represent an escalation in the merchandising of the oddball and the offbeat. More often than not, under the guise of saluting supposedly ordinary folk, the producers are on the well-trod territory of blatant exploitation and easy titillation" (O'Connor 1980: 42). Here, O'Connor makes a crucial distinction between the democratizing potential of independent production and network television's disingenuous celebration of "everyday people." Indeed, with its verité affectations, its claims to authenticity and its focus on "real people" reality television demonstrates what sociologist Todd Gitlin (1994) describes as the "domestication" of progressive, subversive or potentially disruptive social, political and cultural forms and practices.

Despite the fact that "reality television" sometimes resembles DCTV's innovative visual style and narrative strategies, programs like *Cops, Survivor, Temptation Island,* and so on are the antithesis of DCTV's populist vision of television. That is to say, rather than celebrate human ingenuity, illuminate the value of collective action, and reveal unsettling contradictions, "reality television" of the sort currently in vogue wallows in voyeurism, commodity fetishism, spectacle, and humiliation; in so doing, these programs re-position viewers and participants alike as little more than "anti-political, privately accumulating individuals" (Gitlin: 518). In the end, so-called reality television appropriates and ultimately tames the progressive possibilities of technological innovation and participatory production routines that inform DCTV's philosophical orientation and televisual style. Thus, DCTV's goal to create a "new kind of television" remains a work in progress, an ongoing engagement in the cultural politics of television production, distribution, and reception.

DCTV's emphasis on youth media is especially relevant in this regard. From the outset, DCTV worked with all sorts of community groups: artists, activists, social service providers, and not a few street gangs. Not until 1975, however, when budget cuts eliminated arts programs in New York City public schools, did DCTV work with young people in a formal classroom setting. Since that time, DCTV has trained thousands of young people, primarily minority and "at risk" students, whose engagement with video has transformed their lives in ways both subtle and profound. Aside from gaining marketable skills in written and visual communication, DCTV youth producers consistently win awards for their video work. More important, students who were unlikely to earn a high school diploma have gone on to college, in some instances, through scholarships awarded on the basis of their video work.

The initial success of their ad-hoc high school training programs prompted DCTV to formalize its youth media initiatives. For instance, DCTV's Summer Youth Employment Program (SYEP), one of the city's most successful jobs programs for young people, provides students with gainful summer employment as well as technical training. DCTV's collaborative efforts with New York City Literacy Centers have been equally successful. Fusing traditional literacy skills with television production training, this program emphasizes the importance of critical thinking and analysis. The short video *Bobbyland System* is a case in point. Produced by students from the James Baldwin Literacy Center, this tape addresses issues of race, class, and law enforcement in a candid and insightful fashion. In doing so, the documentary not only underscores the lack of trust between young people of color and law enforcement, but crucially also seeks to promote dialogue between the police and minority youth. Thus, DCTV's interventions into the city's public schools have effectively leveraged social change initiatives with media arts education.

With financial support of the Rockefeller Foundation, DCTV further expanded its media education program by incorporating video arts into the curriculum at the Satellite Academy of Career Education, an "alternative" high school in Lower Manhattan. Under the guidance of DCTV instructor Steve Goodman, program participants produced a series of short documentaries that not only demonstrate students' technical prowess, but more critically, illuminate video's potential to engage students in issues that have significant implications for themselves and the wider community.[15] One such documentary, the award-winning *Between C & D,* is a surprisingly sophisticated and nuanced examination of the drug trade in Manhattan's infamous "Alphabet City." In addition to conducting an interview with Margarita Lopez, a community organizer working to rid the streets of dealers and addicts, novice producers Tyrone Mitchell and Jeffery Stella produced strikingly intimate portraits of dealers, users and, in an especially poignant sequence, Suzette, a young mother struggling to care for her children by working as a "runner" – a go between for heroin dealers and their clients.

Aside from encouraging his students to explore the world around them through the documentary form, Goodman and his colleague at the Satellite Academy, Liz Andersen, designed a program of study that integrates video and language arts instruction. Specifically, the "Living Language" program gives students the opportunity to create their own instructional tapes on English grammar. One of the most successful projects in this vein, *Double Negative Lesson* – a hybrid video featuring "vox pop"

10. A student enrolled in DCTV's Envision Television (eTV) program prepares. (Photo by the author)

style interviews, music video imagery and editing techniques, as well as comedic skits – reveals young people's rather sophisticated understanding of televisual forms and the impressive pedagogical results that come from honoring and incorporating students' knowledge, background, and experience into the learning process.

A similar dynamic is at work in the Envision Television initiative (eTV), an outgrowth of DCTV's Youth Living in Temporary Housing Program. With funding from the Soros Foundation, eTV works with homeless teenagers living in city shelters. DCTV trainers work on site with students living in shelters in New York City. During these first weeks of "basic training," novice producers learn basic camera operation and editing techniques. Following the successful completion of a public service announcement (PSA), students then "graduate" to an advanced production course in which they produce long-form videos working in DCTV's impressive firehouse facilities. Regardless of the program format or running time, these projects vividly reflect the everyday lived experience of young people living in temporary housing.

For example, one particularly moving PSA opens with a beautiful yet ominous image of a fire. As the flames grow in intensity, we hear the voice-over narration of a teenage boy as he relates the events surrounding the fire that destroyed his home, leaving his family homeless and forced to take up residence in a city shelter. In another video, a young woman describes her vision of a better future, if only she and her family can secure affordable housing. These projects, like so many of the videos created under the auspices of DCTV's educational programs, articulate the profound alienation of homeless youth, as well as their promise and potential.

The affective quality of the long-form pieces is equally striking. In their documentary *Straight from the Hood*, residents of the Amboy Neighborhood Center in Brooklyn discuss the gang culture that permeates every facet of their lives. In stark, candid, and matter of fact language, gang members, parents, siblings, and neighbors describe the banality of the violence, drug abuse, and economic deprivation that shapes their experience. For their part, students from the Crotona HELP family shelter in the Bronx produced a parody of television news coverage of the "homeless problem." By exploding stereotypes surrounding people living in poverty, the tape critiques contemporary journalistic practices and denounces public policy that does little to eradicate poverty but instead criminalizes homelessness.

Finally, DCTV's flagship youth education initiative, the Professional Television Training Program (Pro-TV), is an unusually intensive media education program. Combining media theory, history, and practice, this two-year program of study provides a handful of students with comprehensive technical training in electronic field production, non-linear editing and multi-camera production in DCTV's "Cyberstudio," a state of the art multi-media production facility that transmits directly into the homes of 500,000 cable subscribers by way of Manhattan Neighborhood Network (MNN), the borough's public access television center.

During their first year, Pro-TV participants produce individual and collective projects related directly to their everyday lived experience. These award-winning tapes range from intimate self-portraits, to investigative journalism, to breaking news reports. Thus, while Natalie Neptune's *Ocean Blues* uses video as autobiography to relate her painful experience as a Haitian immigrant, Aaron Snaggs joined hundreds of student journalists from around the country to cover the April 2000 meeting of the International Monetary Fund (IMF) in Washington, DC. During their second year of study, Pro-TV students are sent on overseas reporting assignments. Part of DCTV's "Global Exchange" program, DCTV works in tandem with community media centers around the world, such as the Tomsk Media Arts Center in Siberia and indigenous media centers in Chiapas, Mexico, to promote intercultural communication and foster cooperative efforts between young media producers.

These collaborations have likewise yielded extraordinary dividends. For instance, in April 1999, Pro-TV's *El Sueno Zapatista: Cinco Anos Despues* was screened at the Museum of Modern Art's prestigious New Documentary Program. The tape went on to win awards at various national and international meetings, including the Do It Your Damn Self Film Festival in Boston as well as the Hague Youth Video Festival in the Netherlands. All of which demonstrates DCTV's pivotal role in promoting and supporting youth media initiatives on the local, national, and, with increasing frequency, international levels.

Youth education programs are but one aspect of DCTV's broader mission to promote a democratic media culture. As noted earlier, since its inception, DCTV provided area residents with free and low-cost production workshops and equipment rentals. At a time when cable operators failed to provide city residents with adequate training, facilities, and resources for its public access channels, and long after both the Alternative Media Center and Open Channel closed their doors, DCTV expanded its operations and encouraged local residents to produce programming that reflects the city's racial, ethnic, and cultural diversity. What's more, because the community media center enjoys a congenial relationship with equipment manufacturers, DCTV has the unique ability to offer training and access to leading-edge technologies, an enviable position for any non-profit community organization. In doing so, DCTV fostered a culture of community television at a time when indifferent cable television providers managed an altogether stagnant public access sector.

Thus, despite DCTV's well-founded reservations regarding cable access, DCTV nonetheless promoted community-oriented television and independent production throughout the city. In no small way, then, DCTV played a vital role in filling the ranks of community producers who have and continue to create programming for the borough's public access channels. Today, DCTV enjoys a productive and mutually beneficial relationship with Manhattan Neighborhood Network (MNN) the largest public access television center in the United States. Aside from serving as a "satellite" production, training, and screening facility for MNN, DCTV has partnered with MNN on a number of important initiatives, including the aforementioned Cyberstudio.

The Cyberstudio is home to an innovative series called *Live from Downtown*. Part of DCTV's Project Phoenix, an effort to revitalize arts in the Lower East Side, *Live from Downtown* features the work of artists and performers whose unconventional work finds a welcome home in the firehouse. On Monday evenings, viewers of Manhattan Neighborhood Network (MNN) Channel 34, might find *Circus Amok*, a troupe of performers who mix theater, music, dance, and video art with political commentary, or the equally engaging *Roulette TV*, a showcase for the likes of Laetitia Sonami's evocative "performance novels" or the multimedia cultural critique of Frankie Mann. *Live from Downtown* also has the distinction of being the first regular series to complement its live cablecast with streaming video over the web.[16]

DCTV Presents is another program DCTV distributes over Manhattan Neighborhood Network. A bi-weekly program, *DCTV Presents* features work produced through DCTV's facilities, including one of its most ambitious community outreach programs to date, Media Instruction for the Disabled (MIFD). Moreover, *DCTV Presents* provides an opportunity for the media arts center to sponsor the work of other independent producers and video collectives, including videos by the Chiapas Media Project and the New York Independent Media Center (IMC). DCTV also enjoys a productive relationship with WNYC, an educational broadcaster that airs *IMNY*, a weekly television series featuring news reports, personal essays, mini-documentaries, and video poetry created by city high school students.

Viewed in this light, then, *IMNY* and *DCTV Presents* are logical extensions of DCTV's long tradition of promoting independent media production through public screenings. Aside from showcasing DCTV's own work, these public screenings help support the work of independent producers, production collectives, and film distributors, including Women Make Movies, Paper Tiger Television, Latin American Video Association (LAVA), the Association of Independent Video and Filmmakers (AIVF), and others. These events, free and open to the public, encourage neighbors and visitors alike to drop by the firehouse for an evening of community television as well as engaging post-screening discussions between independent video makers and the viewing public.

Supporting independent production and enlarging the range of voices, opinions, and perspectives available through electronic media likewise motivated DCTV's offer of sanctuary to *Democracy Now!*, Pacifica Radio's daily newscast, when the operation was forced into exile by WBAI management. Aside from giving the staff and crew of *Democracy Now!* a permanent home in the landmark firehouse, through DCTV's facilities, *Democracy Now!* produces a companion video feed that is available to city residents via Manhattan Neighborhood Network. Moreover, as noted in Chapter 3, the video version of *Democracy Now!* goes out nationwide through a collaboration between DCTV and Free Speech Television (FSTV), the nation's first full-time progressive satellite television channel (Dish Network 9415).

Most recently, DCTV has gone back to the future, hitting the road again and using television as an organizing tool. This time, however, rather than operating from the back of a re-purposed mail truck, as they had done in the early 1970s, DCTV's Cybercar is a state-of-the-art mobile production center, complete with post-production capabilities, multi-camera switching, and satellite connectivity. Moreover, the Cybercar is equipped with screening facilities inside and out. Funded with grant support by the National Endowment of the Arts, Free Speech Television, and others, and outfitted with in-kind contributions from a host of equipment manufacturers, the Cybercar traveled across New York State during the 2002 gubernatorial campaign to promote voter registration.

Throughout the fall of 2003, DCTV and its partners, Chat the Planet and Next Next Entertainment, two new programming services that promote intercultural communication between young people, got on board the Cybercar and embarked on the *Main Street, USA* tour. The thirty-city tour featured verité-style portraits of "ordinary" Americans and interviews representing a cross-section of the American people discussing their thoughts and concerns on the second anniversary of the September 11th terror attacks. In many respects, then, the Cybercar brings DCTV full circle, back to the days when Jon Alpert and Keiko Tsuno took television directly to the people. Then as now, DCTV seeks to create a new context for the production, distribution, and reception of television, one that challenges the hegemony of the culture industries by fundamentally rearticulating the medium's place in the lives and experience of local communities.

5   A poor people's press: *Street Feat*

> Halifax is very much a writer's city not only because it has long been
> one of Canada's major literary centres, but also because of the richness
> of its history and architecture, as well as the appeal of its strong sense
> of community and tradition.
>
> John Bell, *Halifax: A Literary Portrait*

An editorial in the 9 August 2001 edition of *The Coast*, a "free newsweekly
reporting on Halifax's cultural, artistic and political life," took exception
to a profile of the port city published in the *National Post*, one of Canada's
leading daily newspapers. *The Coast* characterized the *Post*'s portrait as a
"disgrace," protesting the paper's propagation of "the Halifax stereotype –
pub-crawling, sou'wester-wearing, drunk-on-history Halifuckwits" (*The
Coast*: 7). Yet, another piece appearing in the very same issue of the
National Post passed without comment. That article, written by a local
business owner, portrayed the city in positively glowing terms. With its
fabulous restaurants, family-friendly harbor, rich maritime heritage, and
formidable cultural attractions, the author suggests that Halifax is one of
the nation's most desirable and livable cities. The article concludes: "Our
economy is booming, it's modern, diverse and dynamic and anchored by
exciting offshore developments mixed with good old-fashioned Maritime
pride and ingenuity. Prosperity is everywhere and realistic optimism is
the order of the day" (Smith 2001). Presumably, the editors of *The Coast*
found this portrait of Halifax neither offensive nor inaccurate.

For the growing number of the city's poor and disadvantaged any suggestion that Halifax is flush with economic opportunity and awash in optimism runs counter to their everyday lived experience. Rarely, however,
are poor people's opinions – their skepticism, their frustration, and their
despair – published in national newspapers, city dailies, or free weekly
papers like *The Coast* for that matter. *Street Feat: The Voice of the Poor*
serves as a vehicle for the city's poor and disadvantaged to communicate
their experience, perspectives, and concerns to the wider Halifax community. Published since December 1997 by Hope Community Enterprises,[1]
Street Feat also provides modest, but welcome economic opportunity for

the homeless and the working poor. *Street Feat*'s mast head succinctly sums up the paper's organizing principle: "The paper is not a charity. It is a social and economic enterprise which generates income from both sales and advertising."

Like the previous case studies included in this volume, which investigate the process by which local populations rearticulate communication technologies to create media systems that better reflect the diverse needs and interests of local populations, this chapter explores the use of newspaper publication for purposes of community communication. Whereas the discussion of WFHB highlighted the enormous barriers of entry confronting community broadcasters in the United States and the previous chapter explored Downtown Community Television's role in shaping the cultural politics of community video and independent television production, here I place particular emphasis on the role community media play in creating an alternative public sphere for marginalized constituencies within a geographic community. Of particular interest here, then, is an effort to gauge street newspapers' capacity to produce and disseminate news and opinion, which challenge mainstream media's "version of reality." Throughout this chapter, I contend that *Street Feat* does just this by publishing competing, often oppositional positions to dominant discursive formations surrounding economic relations and social policy.

As noted in Chapter 2, street newspapers emerged during the 1990s as an expression of dissatisfaction with press performance, especially in terms of news media's coverage of poverty, homelessness, and the wholesale dismantling of social assistance programs. By communicating the experience of the poor to wider publics, street newspapers seek to give a voice to individuals and groups who lead an increasingly marginalized existence. What's more, street papers provide job opportunities in an era marked by widespread economic displacement and fiscal policies that depress wages and cheapen labor. As a case study of a publication by, for, and about the poor, this discussion of *Street Feat* illuminates the complex and contested relationship between communicative forms and practices and material relations of power throughout Halifax, Nova Scotia.

Specifically, this chapter explores the many and varied ways that *Street Feat* challenges stereotypical representations of the poor, the unemployed, and the working poor: representations that contribute to public indifference toward the disadvantaged and legitimate a system of socio-economic relations that benefits the few at the expense of the many. Moreover, I discuss *Street Feat*'s efforts to publicize community activism, collective action that draws attention to the social construction of poverty and critiques so-called "reform" measures – policy initiatives which contribute to and exacerbate political inequality and economic injustice. This aspect of *Street Feat*'s work is crucial inasmuch as it serves as a mechanism for community activists to promote their efforts. In doing so, *Street Feat* counteracts mainstream media coverage of progressive political action campaigns; press coverage that either demonizes these efforts through slander and innuendo or effectively silences oppositional messages by ignoring organized protests altogether.

Aside from examining *Street Feat*'s invaluable referential function in publishing news and information, which helps offset purposeful distortions of the poor and influence public policy, I also take a more interpretive approach to *Street Feat*.[2] In doing so, I argue that *Street Feat* serves a vital "sense making" function for writers and readers alike. That is to say, *Street Feat* vividly conveys the everyday lived experience of a diverse group of people – anti-poverty activists, single parents, community service providers, social assistance recipients, the working poor, and the homeless – as they negotiate the contradictions of neo-liberal economics and its attendant, often draconian, social "reforms."

In addition, I discuss *Street Feat*'s organizational culture, with particular emphasis on the relationship between the paper's financial support mechanisms, its editorial philosophy, and its modes of production and distribution. Here, we can detect and more fully explore the contradictory tendencies within the street paper movement described in Chapter 2. This discussion foregrounds *Street Feat*'s status as a socio-economic enterprise in relation to its role in promoting community communication: albeit communication within and between a diverse community of individuals and groups who are, nonetheless, systematically excluded from Halifax's public spaces, social institutions, economic opportunities, and political processes. I conclude this chapter with some thoughts on the street paper movement and its relationship to the long tradition associated with the alternative press.

Street Feat contributors speak eloquently to the forces and conditions that contribute to the social isolation, political exclusion, and economic marginalization of whole populations. By publishing this material *Street Feat* counters the "poor-bashing" rhetoric (Swanson 2001) of fiscal conservatives and economic rationalists by emphasizing that poor people find themselves living in circumstances not of their own making. That is to say, poverty is not a matter of individual shortcomings or failures – the inability to save money, lack of drive or ambition, drug or alcohol addiction – rather, poverty persists as a direct result of conscious policy decisions and, indeed, a whole way of life predicated on economic relations of domination and subordination.

Equally important, *Street Feat* publishes material that asserts the fundamental worth of people whose lives are rarely acknowledged, let alone examined, in mainstream publications. In this regard, then, *Street Feat* constitutes a site for oppressed peoples to establish their individual and collective identities and forge relations of solidarity in the face of formidable economic, institutional, and cultural barriers and constraints. As we've seen in previous chapters, community media organizations provide a staging ground for individuals and groups to construct personal and collective identities within and through communication technologies. In this light, *Street Feat* constitutes what Nancy Fraser (1992) calls a "parallel discursive arena": a space for marginalized groups to construct and distribute oppositional discourses which reflect the values, concerns, and everyday lived experience of Halifax's poor and disadvantaged.

In short, *Street Feat* offers an exceptional opportunity to investigate the role street newspapers play in communicating community. This is not simply a matter of "publicity," to use Habermas' (1989) formation, in which a community of like-minded individuals organizes and recognizes itself through language and discourse. Rather, by making public the troubled, often desperate lives of the homeless, the unemployed, and the working poor, street papers *problematize* popular perceptions of what it means to be a member of a community. To paraphrase Raymond Williams (1973) *Street Feat* creates a "knowable community" by articulating the crucial and decisive relationships between disparate social actors in an increasingly complex urban environment. That is to say, *Street Feat* not only provides a staging ground for identity formation, but also encourages readers to understand their own subject positions in relation to those whose experience may be quite foreign, yet whose lives are nonetheless intimately connected to their own.

The promise of street papers in fostering precisely this sort of critical consciousness of the interdependent character of our lives is, however, continually undermined by the amplification of ignorance and prejudice in mainstream news coverage of poverty, social policy, and economic injustice. Despite Halifax's celebrated literary tradition, the city's daily newspapers are rather notorious for their acquiescence to vested interests and political elites. Writing some thirty years ago, local author and historian Thomas Raddall noted an ominous trend in media consolidation and press performance: "It soon became apparent that the new monolith of the daily press was set on a new monotonous course, with much attention to advertising and filler, and spotty attention to hard news. This course continued. In 1970 a Senate committee's report on Canadian mass media gave the Halifax papers a low rating" (1971: 319). For anti-poverty activists, social workers, and the growing ranks of the poor in and around

Halifax, local media outlets are not simply performing poorly, they are complicit in refusing people living in poverty a voice in contemporary Canadian society. In this environment, *Street Feat* provides a voice for the poor. A brief description of Halifax, Nova Scotia provides a context to consider *Street Feat*'s efficacy in constructing an alternative public sphere for those who lack, and are often denied, the economic, material, and symbolic resources to publicize their concerns to the wider community.

SuperCity

Halifax bears empire's unmistakable imprint. From its elegant Victorian south side, to the industrial North End, to the Citadel's imposing presence above the downtown business district and the harbor below, the city's cultural heritage is intimately bound up in imperial rivalries, the Atlantic slave trade, European migration to and subsequent commercial development in the New World. Throughout the late fifteenth and early sixteenth centuries once modest fishing ports for the major European powers – Portugal, Spain, England, and France – evolved into coastal settlements to support resource extraction from the vast North American interior. The French were the first Europeans to establish permanent settlements in and around the Chebucto Peninsula: the native Mi'kmaq people's name for Halifax Harbour, one of the world's largest natural harbors.

During the seventeenth and eighteenth centuries tensions between England and France played out across what is now eastern Canada and the Atlantic Provinces. Early victories codified in the Treaty of Utrecht of 1713 secured the new colony of Nova Scotia for England. By mid-century, however, hostilities resumed and intensified as France and England vied for control of North America. When the military stronghold at Louisbourg, the eastern-most defensive position for New France, was returned to the French in 1748, New Englanders successfully lobbied the British crown to establish a military presence in the increasingly important strategic area of Acadia.

Commonly referred to as the "Warden of the North" the city of Halifax was founded in 1749 by some 2,500 colonists – including over 100 slaves – under the leadership of Edward Cornwallis. As the French had by that time killed off or enslaved thousands of Mi'kmaq, English settlers faced little resistance from native peoples. Over the course of the next two and a half centuries, the garrison town grew in size and strategic importance, and came to play a pivotal role in the development of British North America, what would eventually become Canada.

Indeed, throughout most of its modern history, Halifax's fortunes were inextricably bound up in a war economy. During the Seven Years War,

British General James Wolfe launched several military operations from Halifax that proved decisive in defeating the French and consolidating British control of the North American continent. Years later, Halifax provided a staging ground for British troop movements during the American War for Independence. Since that time, Halifax played a significant role in subsequent conflicts involving the British Empire, from the Napoleonic Wars of the early nineteenth century to World War I.

During the American Revolution, British loyalists, eager to flee hostilities in the American colonies to the south, found refuge in and around Halifax. In an effort to weaken American resistance, British authorities also encouraged free Blacks and slaves to join loyalists in Nova Scotia. Promises of freedom, security, and equal opportunity never materialized, however. Instead, Blacks were given title to small parcels of land rejected by white colonists as unfit for cultivation. In the post-revolutionary period, hundreds of Blacks left Nova Scotia for Sierra Leone. This pattern of Black migration to and from Nova Scotia would be repeated over the course of the next two hundred years.

Between 1928–1971 "Canada's front door," the affectionate name given Halifax's Pier 21, served as a point of entry for millions of immigrants, displaced persons, war brides, British evacuees, and troops entering Canada from abroad. Despite waves of immigration, however, Halifax never developed into a major metropolis on a par with other North American port cities. Several factors may account for this. First, Halifax's status as a garrison town produced long-standing tensions between military personnel and the citizenry. Two episodes in particular – the servicemen's riot of 1918 and the V-E Day Riot of 1945 – graphically illustrated the consequences of the city's low housing stock and overcrowded living conditions, especially in wartime. Indeed, Halifax suffers from a chronic housing shortage. For instance, in his analysis of the Halifax explosion of 1918 – a catastrophe that killed hundreds, injured thousands more, and left well over 10,000 people homeless – social historian Samuel Prince suggests that recovery efforts were made all the more difficult by the city's inadequate housing stock: "The question of housing," Prince noted, "is recognized as an old Halifax problem" (132). Not surprisingly, then, Halifax's military affiliations have contributed to the rise of peace movements and anti-conscription campaigns throughout the city's history.

Second, at the time of Confederation, Halifax enjoyed its status not only as a military stronghold, but also as a major center for trade and commerce. Following Confederation, however, the balance of power shifted dramatically and decisively from Nova Scotia in general and Halifax in particular, to the Canadian interior. Over the passionate, if prescient objections of some civic leaders, Halifax conceded its independence, and in large measure its economic and political power, to the federal government in Ottawa. Distraught by the prospect of federation, historians note, on Dominion Day, 1867 the people of Nova Scotia draped the streets of their province in black (Jackson and Jackson 1990). Ever since, Halifax has been less a final destination for newcomers than a way station for people heading for the Canadian mainland.

With the completion of the St. Lawrence Seaway in 1954, Halifax's importance to the nation's economy was reduced further. Periods of extreme economic volatility followed. When times were good, laborers from across Canada flocked to Halifax, further taxing the city's low housing stock. As the economy weakened, however, economic displacement swelled the ranks of the province's social service programs. Lean times for the coal and fishing industries in particular have increased Nova Scotia's dependency on federal transfers in recent years. The perception that Nova Scotians are a drain on the federal budget inflames resentment between the province and the rest of the country (Brewster 2001: 3). Even the prospect of economic benefits from offshore natural gas deposits is diminished by squabbles between the Atlantic Provinces, further undermining Canadian national unity.

Over the past decade, Halifax has sought to reassert itself as a vibrant center for trade and commerce. In June 1995, Halifax played host to the G7 Economic Summit. Local business leaders and investors enthusiastically supported the meeting in the hopes of reinvigorating the regional economy. The event also provided an occasion for the establishment of the Halifax Initiative: a coalition of fourteen NGOs – environmental, religious, human rights, and labor organizations, as well as anti-poverty activists – who challenge the emerging global economic order.[3]

In 1996, as part of an effort to consolidate resources and attract business and investment, the four municipalities of Halifax, Dartmouth, Bedford, and Halifax County merged, forming the Halifax Regional Municipality (HRM). The SuperCity, as it is now known, is home to nearly 400,000 people. Today, HRM boasts seven degree-granting universities, eleven business and industrial parks, and thousands of acres of recreational parks and beaches. In addition to a lively, but seasonal tourist trade, HRM has cultivated investment in oil and gas, information and communication technology, research and development, and the culture industries.

At a time when the SuperCity attracts investment from various sectors, the lack of affordable housing, rising college tuition rates, and unprecedented cutbacks in essential social services threaten to create a permanent underclass of unskilled, low-wage workers. As a result, various grassroots efforts, including *Street Feat*, developed in response to the growing disparities in income and economic opportunities. A persistent undercurrent

11. A handbill from the summer of 2001 echoes earlier struggles in the Africville neighborhood of Halifax, Nova Scotia. (Photo by the author)

of political unrest and organized protest parallels Halifax's better-known history as military outpost and commercial port. It is in this context, then, that we now consider *Street Feat* and its role in facilitating community communication in and around the SuperCity.

The voice of the poor

Conceived by Michael Burke and Roberto Menendez with the support of the Catholic Archdiocese of Halifax, the Bedford United Church, and the Halifax Development Agency, *Street Feat* is the outgrowth of an economic development project titled "Hope Community Enterprises: An Economic Development Alternative for Street People." In their capacity as community activists, Burke and Menendez both understood the depth of the problem confronting low-income and unemployed people living in and around Halifax. Following several failed attempts to create business opportunities for this growing population, the two hit upon an idea that was succeeding in cities across North America: the publication of a "street newspaper."

Although neither Burke nor Menendez had any previous experience with the publishing industry – Burke is a civil engineer by training, Menendez is a professional architect – they both understood the enormous potential of a street paper. Not only could the unemployed earn a modest income selling newspapers – a steady job that could serve as a "stepping stone" to more viable employment – they might also learn new skills in marketing, sales, and in an emerging industry: desktop publishing. What's more, the idea of publishing an alternative newspaper that addressed issues of economic injustice appealed to Burke and Menendez's sense of civic responsibility, community activism, and social conscience. Thus, *Street Feat*'s mission is "to provide a voice for the poor and the needy, to educate and develop a critical conscience, to develop a community based solution to poverty and to generate income for those in need."

According to their business plan, the street paper would provide economic opportunities for skilled workers who were displaced and forced out onto the streets during the recession of the 1990s. The goal was to create a viable enterprise that would return ten street people back into the labor pool each year and make wage earners of five additional skilled people within six months. In the process, *Street Feat* would call readers' attention to the plight of the needy and challenge what Roberto Menendez once described as "the near religious" faith in a market economy that perpetuates social and economic injustice.

With the help of Juan Carlos Canales-Leyton, first in his capacity as publishing consultant, and since May 1998 as the paper's managing editor, *Street Feat* would grow into a viable and self-sustaining publishing concern. Juan Carlos's formidable technical skills and publishing acumen allows *Street Feat* to make use of desktop publishing tools and Internet-related technologies to facilitate the paper's production and distribution processes. One direct result of Juan Carlos's publishing experience is the street paper's colorful and distinctive look: *Street Feat* is one of only a handful of street newspapers in North America that publish in full color. And yet, Juan Carlos's efforts are undermined by other demands on his time, most notably supervising office staff and coordinating the weekly publication of the *Royal Gazette*: one of several publishing assignments *Street Feat* uses to capitalize its operation.

In addition to his editorial, design, and layout responsibilities for both *Street Feat* and the *Royal Gazette*, Canales-Leyton is the general manager of Fenix Consultants, Inc, a local communications consulting firm providing technology, communications, and interpreting services to local business and individuals. Moreover, Juan Carlos volunteers his time and talents to various community groups, including a local Islamic cultural centre and the Centre for Diverse Visible Cultures.[4] Suffice it to say, without such a dedicated and committed individual overseeing the day-to-day operation of *Street Feat*, the paper's continued success is far from certain. Indeed, in the absence of an active editorial board, Juan Carlos single-handedly provides managerial oversight for production, distribution, advertising sales, and marketing.

Despite his managerial authority, however, Juan Carlos's management style is anything but authoritarian. To the consternation of some readers, Juan Carlos has an extremely light editorial touch; although this may be as much a product of the paper's philosophical commitment to preserving the integrity of the writer's work as it is a matter of time constraints and resource allocations. In his dealings with office staff and vendors, Juan Carlos wears many hats – office manager, employment advisor, legal counsel, technical trainer, and father confessor. In many respects, Juan Carlos provides precisely the sort of respectful, empathetic, and nurturing support that the impoverished and the working poor rarely find in their dealings with governmental social services.

The cover story of *Street Feat*'s inaugural issue of December 1997 introduced readers to the new publication. Written by the paper's co-founders, the article defines street newspapers as an "alternative press" written by, for, and about the poor. Offering a rationale for producing a paper dealing with issues of poverty and social justice in Halifax, the first-time publishers assure readers that like other street papers across the country, *Street Feat* will publish news, opinion, and analysis to counterbalance the mainstream media's habitual disregard for the poor. Burke and Menendez make two observations in this regard. On one hand, the local press fails to address the alarming disparity between rich and poor throughout Nova Scotia and across Canada. On the other hand, these same media outlets enthusiastically support economic and social policies – corporate tax breaks, welfare to work programs, and the abolition of the Canadian Assistance Program (CAP) – that exacerbate existing inequities, cheapen labor, and criminalize the poor. Under these circumstances, the two community activists promote *Street Feat* as a vehicle to publicize the concerns and perspectives of those whose voices and opinions are routinely ignored by both media outlets and elected officials.

The article continues that while dramatic reductions in federal and provincial social assistance programs are indeed well documented in the local press, the implications of these cutbacks, especially for those most vulnerable segments of the population, are rarely discussed, let alone critically evaluated. Citing studies by Statistics Canada, Burke and Menendez argue that huge government deficits are not the result of wasteful social service programs; rather, budget shortfalls come from rising unemployment, high interest rates, and lower tax revenues – all directly attributable to the implementation of neo-liberal economic policies over the past decade.

Equally troubling, the authors argue, the lack of substantive public debate over Canada's entry into multilateral trade agreements indicates a fundamental crisis of deliberative democracy in Canadian society. In this context, then, Burke and Menendez offer *Street Feat* as a mechanism for enhancing and enlarging public participation in policy deliberations. To that end, *Street Feat* seeks to educate readers on matters of public policy and, equally important, to highlight the relevance of these issues for the health and well being of all who call Halifax home.

Street Feat's first issue demonstrates the paper's editorial commitment to exploring issues of social and economic justice as they relate directly to the homeless, the unemployed, and the working poor. The paper's debut featured an interview between *Street Feat* and local law enforcement officials concerning the legal rights of panhandlers, staff reporter Chris LeRue's story about a local soup kitchen, and a personal narrative written by a social assistance recipient who equates welfare with prison. In addition, representatives from the Congress of Black Women of Canada, the Sisters of Charity, and the local branch of OXFAM/Canada address various aspects of an emerging "culture of denial" surrounding the issue of poverty in Canada. Likewise, caseworkers from Phoenix Centre for Youth and other social service agencies discuss the problems facing their constituents during the holiday season.

Throughout its first year of publication, *Street Feat* adhered to an editorial vision that sought to balance first-person accounts of living in poverty with calls to action and policy analysis from social workers, health care providers, and others who work alongside and on behalf of the poor. As we shall see, however, the depletion of grant funding and ongoing financial instability led to cutbacks in *Street Feat*'s office staff and precipitated a decline in editorial contributions from analysts and others whose perspectives were sometimes deemed "too academic" for inclusion in a poor people's press. Nevertheless, *Street Feat*'s steadfast critique of the consequences of neo-liberal economics, its forceful "native reporting" on poverty in Halifax, and its role in advancing a progressive political agenda dedicated to social and economic justice remain prominent features of Atlantic Canada's first street newspaper.

As noted above, *Street Feat* emerged at a time when federal and provincial policies regarding social assistance were undergoing dramatic changes. For the most part, local media outlets depicted these policy decisions as carefully considered and measured responses to widespread abuses of social assistance programs: abuses which inevitably led to enormous federal and provincial budget deficits. *Street Feat*'s coverage of these policy initiatives belies such claims and underscores the contradictions embodied by cutbacks in essential social services at time of rising unemployment and increasing poverty rates among Canadians.

Organizing its monthly publications thematically, *Street Feat* illuminates these contradictions in relation to wider social, political, and historical contexts.[5] For example, the January/February edition celebrates African Heritage Month. This edition routinely makes explicit connections between the historic struggle of Black Nova Scotians to achieve economic and political equality and contemporary articulations of systemic racism: most notably the commercial and financial abandonment of the once vibrant Gottingen Street neighborhood. The parallels between the failure of urban renewal programs of the 1960s that decimated the economically depressed but culturally prominent neighborhood of Africville and the economic evacuation of Gottingen Street are striking and well observed in the pages of *Street Feat*.[6] Likewise, the February/March and April/May editions focus on women's rights, environmental issues, and labor history respectively. Again, *Street Feat* makes explicit linkages between the social and political activism of the women's, environmental, and labor movements with contemporary struggles to achieve economic justice.

In addition to providing useful tips on having fun on a limited budget, *Street Feat*'s summer issues examine the tourism industry's relationship to the local economy, including the impact of tourist dollars on the livelihoods of buskers (street performers), panhandlers, and *Street Feat* vendors. In addition, these summer issues also focus on the legal system. These issues describe the economic barriers that preclude the poor, the disabled, and the unemployed from receiving justice. With the return of students to area colleges and universities in late August and early September, *Street Feat* publishes an edition dedicated to learning and education. Here, contributors note the growing inequities in higher education due to rising tuition costs and the privatization of university education across Canada. October brings a special issue, produced in

12. *Street Feat* demonstrates its solidarity with global peace and justice movements with this cover illustration commemorating International Food Day. (Courtesy of *Street Feat*)

association with members of the North American Street Newspaper Association (NASNA), in observance of International Food Day (16 October). In November, *Street Feat* acknowledges the nation's debt to its veterans and war dead. Typically, this installment highlights the economic hardships confronting Nova Scotia's elderly population. Finally, in December, *Street Feat* celebrates its anniversary with reflections on the past year and calls for continued financial, spiritual, and volunteer support during the New Year. The common thread running through these disparate theme issues is, of course, the question of economic justice.

What emerges from each issue of *Street Feat* is a far more complex understanding of what it means to be poor, to be denied a living wage, or to be forced to contend with an increasingly inhospitable community that has neither the compassion nor the political will to care for those who need assistance. Topics appearing most frequently in *Street Feat* include the lack of affordable housing and gainful employment opportunities in the city, the preferential treatment city administrators and regulatory bodies bestow upon real estate developers and landlords, the increasingly intolerable conditions at area shelters, and chronic shortages at local food banks. Troubling as these conditions are, *Street Feat* contributors are most alarmed by what they see as widespread indifference and a growing intolerance toward the poor.

No social condition exemplifies this disturbing trend better than the rising number of Canadian children living in poverty. In 1989, the House of Commons, amid great fanfare, passed a unanimous resolution calling for the elimination of child poverty by 2000. And yet, recent estimates suggest that as many as 1.5 million children experience hunger. Notwithstanding official proclamations to the contrary and recently enacted welfare "reform" measures intended to improve the lives of Canadian children, working families across Canada live in increasingly desperate circumstances. Over the years, *Street Feat* has taken both the federal and provincial government to task for their abandonment of this important goal.

For instance, the consequences of the "Child Tax Benefit" program are a major topic in the pages of *Street Feat*. Paul O'Hara, a local health care worker, deconstructs a program designed to "renew and modernize" social policy across Canada. O'Hara (1998) argues that this regressive policy is little more than administrative smoke and mirrors. On one hand, the Child Benefit increases federal allowances to low-income families. On the other hand, the provincial government deducts the increase from family benefit checks. O'Hara notes that neither New Brunswick nor Newfoundland have instituted these "adjustments" to family benefits. As a result, working families in Nova Scotia are denied what little benefit they may have realized from the federal government by the provincial government's "claw back" of these funds. As is so often the case, local media outlets failed to criticize the provincial government's scheme to balance its budget on the backs of the poor.

Perceptive critiques such as this find exceptional complement in first-person accounts written by single parents struggling to provide for their families. For instance, a local woman writing under the pseudonym of Chantal relates her feelings of frustration, despair, and self-recrimination surrounding her inability to care for her child. Although she has a GED Chantal's lack of work experience prohibits her from finding a job that pays enough to get her off welfare. Her child's health problems make stretching her modest $880 monthly budget all the more challenging. Even if she did receive financial support from the child's father, Chantal notes, the provincial welfare office would subtract that amount, dollar-for-dollar, from her assistance check.

Chantal concludes: "What is there to do but live in a small place that's cheap and dirty, no phone, no bills, no celebrating holidays, no going anywhere, no special time alone and only buying the bare essentials in groceries and make do" (1998: 3). Clearly, then, Chantal is not "living easy" on social assistance, as fiscal conservatives and media pundits might have it. As Chantal and an escalating number of working families in Halifax and across the province can attest, highly touted changes in family benefits payments have not kept up with the cost of living, let alone improved the quality of life of young children.

The contradictory nature of these so-called reform measures is all the more galling when one considers that modest increases in Family Benefits payments were paid for by reducing housing allowances for single men and women. The aptly named April Fool's Day 1996 cutbacks in housing allowances were designed to "standardize" food and shelter payments across the country. Needless to say, the cost of living varies dramatically across Canada. Therefore, while some families may indeed benefit from these adjustments, single employables and working families in Halifax are worse off now than they had been. Not surprisingly, then, an air of despondency permeates the personal narratives found in *Street Feat*.

Writing in the February/March 1999 edition, Dave Howard succinctly describes his bleak existence as "One hundred and sixty two dollars a month and a bottle of pills" (3). Howard's frustration comes from the humiliation of waiting in line at the soup kitchen, the painful social isolation associated with depression, and the self-recrimination that comes from feeling unwanted and unproductive. The government supplements its meager assistance with drugs to stave off Howard's depression. Rather than lift him out of his despair, however, this regime makes matters worse and fosters an insidious form of dependency that so-called "reform" measures claim to eliminate. The irony is not lost on Howard. "I seek help and I'm given the chemical lobotomy. My blood is tested to prove I'm taking these chemicals because if I don't it proves to someone that I'm refusing to help myself." Under the guise of promoting self-help and in the name of fiscal responsibility, government programs grow ever more intrusive while promoting insidious forms of dependency and exacerbating feelings of alienation and despair.

Astute observers of the hypocrisy of welfare reform efforts, *Street Feat* contributors bring uncommon insight to the plight of the poor and disadvantaged precisely because they speak from personal experience. This participatory brand of journalism is a hallmark of the street newspaper movement and connects this emerging practice with a long tradition of community media similarly dedicated to communicative democracy. That is to say, like other forms of community media discussed thus far, *Street Feat* provides individuals and groups who lack the economic, material, and symbolic resources associated with the media industries with access to the tools and techniques of media production and distribution. In doing so, *Street Feat* encourages the poor, the disadvantaged, and those who work on their behalf to articulate their common concerns and express feelings of fellowship and solidarity. Moreover, *Street Feat* communicates the experience of the poor to wider publics in an effort to promote a more thorough understanding of the consequences of a system of socio-economic relations that puts profits before people. A more detailed examination of *Street Feat*'s contents illuminates the crucial relationship between self-representation and individual and collective agency.

Grassroots and city streets

Over the years, *Street Feat* has published provocative, occasionally offensive, often quite moving work by writers whose experience of poverty guides their approach and informs their sensibility. For instance, in a series of articles called "From the Poverty Front" (1999) Erica Lewis voices her anger toward an increasingly indifferent society that neglects the poor and the disabled. A middle-aged woman in poor health, Lewis levels her invectives at greedy and unresponsive landlords, the city's ineffective Tenancy board, and local social service organizations, among others. Acknowledging that her pieces come off sounding shrill and abusive, Lewis nevertheless makes no apologies for her self-described "rants and raves."

In contrast to Lewis' abrasive style, Erin Wilson – a single mother and recent college graduate – writes concise analyses of racism, class structure, gender discrimination, and poverty in contemporary Canadian society.

13. Long-time *Street Feat* writer, former editor, and volunteer coordinator, Peter McGuigan. (Photo by the author)

Along with Linda Harpell, who despite a debilitating medical condition, served for a time as *Street Feat*'s features editor, Wilson produced a series of articles that speak plainly to economic injustice in all its varied forms and insidious manifestations. Writing in yet another idiom, *Street Feat*'s poet vendors, the enigmatic Dominique Rosseau and the elusive Jack MacDonald, have both published short verse lamenting public indifference toward the poor and documenting life on the streets of Halifax.

Perhaps no writer better exemplifies the power of this grassroots literary style than Peter McGuigan. *Street Feat*'s former managing editor, Peter McGuigan writes discerning, sometimes-pointed essays from the perspective of a single, able-bodied, university educated man who nonetheless finds it difficult to secure gainful employment. McGuigan receives a modest living allowance from the government and frequently avails himself of meals provided by local soup kitchens. McGuigan supplements his meager wages as a school crossing guard with occasional freelance writing assignments and the money he earns selling *Street Feat*. A lifetime resident of Halifax and an avid student of history, McGuigan writes essays that demonstrate an intimate knowledge of the city's neighborhoods and a keen awareness of the forces and conditions that have shaped modern Halifax.

Over the course of the past five years, McGuigan has written on labor issues, the economics of higher education, tenants' rights, and social and economic policy at the provincial and national levels. McGuigan also writes self-reflexive pieces detailing the growth and development of *Street Feat*. In his capacity as vendor coordinator, McGuigan is privy to the inner workings of *Street Feat*, from production and distribution, to circulation, vendor conduct, and public relations. Aside from providing readers with an "insider's" view of *Street Feat*, this knowledge informs a good deal of his writing on broader issues.

For instance, in an article titled "Why Is It So Hard To Get People To Work?" McGuigan (2001) observes parallels between the city's inability to attract and retain school crossing guards and *Street Feat*'s chronic vendor shortage. Based on his own employment history, McGuigan observes that low wages and difficult working conditions are common for street vendors and crossing guards alike. Several factors, including the provincial claw back of wages for single employables, inhospitable weather conditions, and unusual work schedules, further discourage people from taking employment as crossing guards. These same factors, McGuigan explains, coupled with the fear of rejection associated with street sales dissuade others from working as *Street Feat* vendors.

Moreover, because he spends long hours on city streets McGuigan is familiar to area merchants, local law enforcement officials, pedestrians, and the growing number of people who spend their days soliciting spare change from passersby. Occasionally, McGuigan's essays evidence an antagonism toward panhandlers. For example, a piece entitled "Portrait of a Socially Unfit Person" tells the story of the late Robert Stewart, a rather notorious panhandler who frequented downtown Halifax's trendy shopping thoroughfare, Spring Garden Road. Throughout the piece, McGuigan recalls several unpleasant encounters he had with Stewart when the panner worked, for a brief spell, as a *Street Feat* vendor. Harsh at times, the essay ends on a note of sympathy for Stewart and the other "anonymous dead" of Spring Garden Road.

Despite this ambivalence, McGuigan's essays on panhandling in downtown Halifax, and meal times at local soup kitchens are among the most arresting depictions of street culture in Halifax. For example, writing in *Street Feat*'s second annual edition commemorating International Food Day, McGuigan observes two distinctive suppertime rituals:

It's 5 PM on Halifax's once fashionable Brunswick Street. Two lines have formed in front of the irregular row of faded Victorian mansions. Fifty or more drivers who are trying to reach the MacDonald Bridge wait patiently to get home for supper with their families. Paralleling this, fifty or more people who are trying to reach the threshold of Hope Cottage wait patiently to have supper at Halifax's original soup kitchen. . . . Although the traditional older guys are prominent, there are also the young. Both young and old are largely white, but there are blacks and natives. Orientals are very rare, but two are here tonight. Others leaning against the small pre-Victorian brick cottage use braces and canes. One or two, including a pleasant looking and polite young man, are blind. Then there is the guy with a graying beard, a torn winter coat and faint smile who "directs" the stalled traffic while mumbling something.

(1999: 4)

In a few sentences, McGuigan captures the dramatic social and economic upheavals Haligonians have experienced in recent years. Underscoring the disparities between commuters making their way home and the poor lining up for a hot meal are the changing demographics of the patrons of Hope Cottage. In years past, Hope Cottage served a relatively homogeneous clientele. Over the past decade, however, economic conditions have swelled the ranks of the working poor. As a result, elderly men with disabilities or substance abuse problems are but a portion of the population served by Hope Cottage, St. Andrew's, St. George's, and other area soup kitchens. In the absence of a living wage, soup kitchens are inundated by working people eager to save on expenses any way they can.

Likewise, area food banks report that their client base has changed dramatically in recent years. Once a place where social assistance recipients, senior citizens, and the disabled might find items to supplement their diets, food banks throughout the HRM are serving greater numbers of single parents and working families. As a result, the Metro Food Bank and other local agencies face chronic shortages. Back issues of *Street Feat* indicate the severity of the problem. Several times each year, Dianne Swinemar, the executive director of the Metro Food Bank Society, writes impassioned appeals to *Street Feat* readers to donate to besieged food distribution centers (1999a, 1999b). To offset these shortages, some food banks enforce strict eligibility requirements for their patrons. These new policies exacerbate the shame and self-recrimination many people feel when they visit the food bank.

In an imaginatively rendered piece, Susan LeFort, the Atlantic Canada representative for the National Anti-Poverty Organization (NAPO), captures the antipathy patrons feel toward food bank personnel and prying administrative procedures. Taking the form of a "dialogue" between a single mother and a food bank administrator, LeFort illustrates the humiliating quality of these exchanges.

I understand you can't give me a full order.
No, I don't think I will have time to take a budgeting class.
I will try to make it last.
Why didn't I pray?
I wonder if she was so intent on praying how she noticed I wasn't, perhaps she was the prayer police, who knew??
Why did you make us pray?
To show gratitude and thanks for what we are given.
Oh. Why should I be grateful?
Yes, I want the food; I need it to feed my family.
So you believe that I should be grateful because someone is giving me food?
Do you believe in Basic Human Rights?
Yes, of course you do.
Then why should I be grateful for having my basic human need filled?

(1999: 6)

LeFort's clever take on the question/answer format suggests that what were once rather banal intake interviews have in recent years adopted the tone and tenor of a criminal interrogation. This device underscores the notion that eligibility tests are not merely demeaning, they are increasingly intrusive. What's more, this exchange reveals an underlying tension between faith-based solutions, which sometimes require spiritual acquiescence, and the moral obligation to fulfill basic human rights.

Another of *Street Feat*'s more prolific contributors, Bill Krampe, writes on much these same issues, but in a style that owes more to the literary tradition of gonzo journalism than either McGuigan's native reporting or LeFort's formalism. That is to say, Krampe's essays read as extended ruminations, rather than fully fledged arguments, critical analyses, or conventional reportage. This sometimes makes for challenging reading; Krampe's pieces are meandering, esoteric, emotionally charged, and highly personal reflections of a middle-aged man who once enjoyed a comfortable bourgeois existence.

Abiding few journalistic constraints, Krampe's essays weave the personal and the political, the spiritual and the physical, the sublime and the ridiculous. More than any other *Street Feat* contributor, Krampe's work foregrounds the writer's subjectivity regardless of the topic: from astrophysics to youth culture. As maddening as his prose often is, Krampe nevertheless demonstrates the "sense making" role street newspapers play for contributors. Krampe's candor, eclecticism, and rawness of expression are functions of his efforts to comprehend and negotiate the contradictions he finds in his personal life and in the world he inhabits.

For example, in a piece based on his comments before the provincial government's public hearing on restructuring social assistance, Krampe forcefully articulates his frustration with government jobs programs, temporary housing, and the Department of Community Services. The sense of fatigue that permeates this essay is not uncommon to social assistance recipients but is here uncommonly rendered for bureaucrats and, through *Street Feat*, for the reading public to consider. The aptly titled testimony "A Day in the Life" details Krampe's living conditions at a men's shelter in the local YMCA and his efforts to reclaim his life.

I wake up. Waking up is a bitch. Here I go. Another twelve hours on my feet, always moving, always searching, always aching feet. I start my day with hope. Meaning: I am going to Hope Cottage soup kitchen for breakie/brunch. Then I am walking over to the Halifax Shopping Centre (Human Resources Development Canada) Job Centre Office. I'll check the job bank computer while there. I go every morning after Hope. Same faces every day. They tell me the same thing every day: No jobs today.

(1999: 9)

Describing his daily rituals, Krampe captures the central paradox of his existence: he spends his days in constant motion, yet he doesn't get anywhere. Despite his best efforts, his life does not change in any perceptible fashion. With characteristic bluntness, Krampe relates the agonizing repetition he endures – the product of a tenacious desire to regain some semblance of his former life and the stark realization that to do so he must overcome formidable obstacles. Doing so, Krampe demonstrates that looking for meaningful employment is in and of itself hard work, especially in hard economic times. Far from fitting the stereotype of the idle social assistant recipient disinterested in employment and unwilling to search for a job, Krampe struggles to understand his situation and, in so doing, alter the circumstances in which he finds himself.

Krampe then relates how debilitating this condition is to both his mental and physical well being. Here, Krampe reminds readers that the poor, the unemployed, and the homeless enjoy the same pleasures and suffer the same pains that all people do. Struggling to stave off depression, Krampe turns to music for solace. But with the joy that comes from music come painful memories of what life had once been. These bittersweet memories whet his appetite for affection and physical intimacy. Then he adds:

But maybe all I want to do is lie on a bed, fully clothed, in a nice hug instead of sex? Yet this champagne – nirvana desire on my beer less budget sucks especially when the woman at the front desk does her sexy thing while asking me for another late rent payment. Meaning: this is as close as I get to a sex life.

(1999: 9)

As painful and difficult as such admissions must be, Krampe's forthright acknowledgment of his sexual longing forcefully reasserts his humanity in the face of a system that deals with "street people" as abstractions: ciphers with no personal history, no future aspirations, and no desires.

This chronicle of despair is not without its humor, however; yet another indication of Krampe's resiliency, and that of countless others whose lives of quiet desperation go unnoticed by an increasingly indifferent society. "Welfare," says a janitor buddy "spells farewell backwards." Gallows humor aside, the chronic deprivation, the insidious cyclical nature of his routine wears Krampe down. He notes the cruel irony of his job search:

You don't get a job in the late 1990s. You romance a job. Maybe I'll drop off a resume at a prospective job lead I've been courting, another 1–2 kilometers there, then another 1–2 kilometers back. Gottingen Street Employment Centre and facilities, Halifax Shopping Centre HRDC for more resources and job bank double check; then, follow-ups, leads then suppertime at Hope. I'm hungry. Rapidly burning off calories, rapidly wearing out shoes. So I need to check the clothing bank at St. Andrew's Church or back again to Brunswick Street United next time around the circuit . . . walking everywhere gets to be spiritually exhausting.

(1999: 9)

Physically and emotionally spent after an unusually raucous dinner at Hope Cottage, Krampe returns "home" to the men's shelter. But he does not seek out the company of his fellow travelers: too many "shitty welfare stories" to endure, too much petty larceny to leave his room unattended very long. There in his cramped, windowless room, he retires for the evening.

Bedtime. I'm tired as f*#k, my feet are killing me. I wish we had a bathtub. No booze, no drugs, no snuggles to go to sleep with tonight. Will I ever see my kids again? I turn out the lights; go to bed, hoping for release. I try to settle down; night encircles and embraces me. I begin to dream dreamless dreams. Darkness prevails.

(1999: 9)

Powerful and disturbing, grassroots journalism of this sort explodes the myths surrounding poverty in contemporary Canadian society and exposes the inadequacy of both private and public "solutions" to hunger, unemployment, and homelessness. Less frequently, but no less eloquently, depictions of street culture provide insight into the rationale of those who make conscious decisions to live on the streets. Significantly, this choice is not, as poor-bashing stereotypes hold, based on indolence, lethargy, addiction, or a lack of ambition. For some, life on the streets is an act of silent, public defiance to a way of life that promotes avarice and envy and diminishes any sense of solidarity and community. An essay by Stephen Stiles delineating this sensibility is worth quoting at length.

Why would some people choose to live on the streets? In hostels and under overpasses and at drop-in centres, homeless people are engaged with very serious issues about life, and where they fit into it. Usually sensitive and intelligent, the homeless often cannot see value in the rat race. Working at meaningless jobs to buy goods they do not need, living in a suburb beside neighbors they will never know, and the other good-standard-of-life definitions, can't be what is important. On the street there is time to think. From our corners the homeless observe the games we are all playing. And – something many are not aware of – there can be truer community amongst homeless people than most ever experience.

(Stiles 1999: 6)

In this very personal, yet reasoned and articulate fashion, Stiles addresses a paradox that is not easily accommodated by either conservative or liberal "solutions" to the problem of homelessness across Canada. Political conservatives have long argued that some people choose to live in poverty. From this perspective, homelessness is framed not as a social problem, but rather as a "lifestyle" choice. For their part, liberals bristle at any such suggestion. They contend that these arguments obscure the failure of social and economic policy to provide a safety net for those who "fall through the cracks."

Contemporary debates over welfare reform across Canada can be viewed in terms of this oscillation between individual rights and responsibilities on the one hand, and on the other hand, government's obligation to help those in need. Stiles takes issue with both these views by calling attention to the ineffective and increasingly intrusive policies promoted by both camps. What gets left out of these debates, Stiles argues, is any substantive critique of a system of socio-economic relations that creates poverty in the first instance. Welfare reform measures are therefore predicated on sustaining a sometimes faulty but otherwise viable system. For Stiles and many of his acquaintances, the dominant socio-economic order is not merely defective, it is untenable. Living on the street, then, is a conscious act of resistance to a whole way of life based on acquisitiveness and conspicuous consumption that neither enriches lives nor fulfills fundamental human needs and desires.

Lest his comments come off as outlandish, or worse yet indifferent, Stiles acknowledges that for many, homelessness is not a matter of choice. Rather, ever increasing numbers of people are displaced for health reasons or economic circumstances beyond their control. Stiles asserts these people deserve government assistance and community support. With that said, Stiles argues that current policies are not only ineffective but inevitably perpetuate feelings of hopelessness, inadequacy, and misery.

Make-work projects and grossly under-funded subsidized housing programs just won't do it. . . . I am not saying leave the homeless in destitution and poverty. Not at all. There are, and I emphasize this, humane, non-intrusive alternatives that work. . . . Perhaps the most exciting of these is when we see the homeless banding together to create their own forms of intentional community living. Endeavors like this, originating with the homeless themselves, should receive first priority for funding – on their own terms.

(6)

Here, Stiles makes a critical distinction between so-called "self-help" initiatives, like welfare to work and job re-training programs of the sort advocated by conservative think tanks, business leaders, and "well-meaning" bureaucrats, and local solutions that are at once relevant to and truly beneficial for the homeless and the working poor. Such an approach requires a fundamental reassessment of social priorities and the reassertion of basic human rights in the wake of neo-liberal policies that reinforce and legitimate a social-economic-political system based on relations of domination and subordination.

First person accounts like those described above attest to the unjust and inhumane treatment afforded those who find themselves living in poverty. What's more, in their ability to startle readers with tales of indifference and quiet desperation, these narratives indicate the extent to which poor bashing rhetoric has been naturalized within and through the discourse of the free market. Most important, however, the voice of the poor found in the pages of *Street Feat* reasserts and defends the dignity of those whose lives are deemed worthless in an increasingly acquisitive culture. These voices speak eloquently to the need for progressive social change that recognizes individual self-worth and promotes a caring community. With this in mind, we turn to a consideration of *Street Feat*'s capacity to improve the lives of the poor, to educate readers to the consequences of recent changes in social policy, and to mobilize political action in the struggle for economic justice.

Spare Change

The cover of *Street Feat*'s November 1999 issue features a photograph of a defiant protestor, Suzzette St. Clair, taken during a public meeting held

The reality of poverty is a wake up call for anyone. All that's needed to convey the message is a strong voice, a little participation, some leadership, good will but, above all, a desire to make change. We look at the role of governments, non-government organizations and poverty in this issue.

Suzzette St. Clair complains against the re-launching of the Spare Change program in June of this year. *(See story on page 3)*

14. *Street Feat* issue documenting a demonstration against the Spring Garden Road Business Association's "Spare Change" program. (Courtesy of *Street Feat*)

on the grounds of the Halifax Public Library. Just steps away from Spring Garden Road's upscale restaurants and trendy shops, the library's inviting front lawn is a popular gathering spot for weary tourists, local students, enterprising buskers, and a growing contingent of panhandlers. On this occasion, representatives from area businesses gathered to announce the revitalization of the Spare Change Program: a scheme first developed in 1991 by the Spring Garden Road Business Association (SGRBA) and other merchants groups to help the municipality's needy.[7] Under the Spare Change Program, shoppers are encouraged to make charitable donations at designated drop boxes throughout the city rather than give their money directly to individual panhandlers. The business association then matches this money and distributes these funds to the Metro Homeless Network, an organization that helps private charities throughout the Halifax Regional Municipality.

St. Clair's indignation reached new heights when representatives of the business association suggested that panhandling is neither appropriate nor justified behavior. According to local business leaders, panhandlers' claims that they go hungry in order to get handouts from pedestrians are overstated. After all, they point out, meals are available seven days a week at area soup kitchens. Moreover, when panhandlers become "too aggressive" they frighten off prospective customers. Not only do local merchants suffer, this conduct tarnishes the city's image, thereby compromising the tourist trade and effectively undermining the entire local economy. Besides, area merchants are quick to point out, panhandlers have a range of "alternative employment opportunities," such as busking, enlisting in job training programs, and selling *Street Feat*. Finally, by convincing shoppers to give their donations to "legitimate" charities, advocates claim that the Spare Change program reduces the number of young people who take up "recreational panhandling" during the summer months.

Like other demonstrators on hand for the announcement, St. Clair argued that the Spare Change Program is an ill-conceived and self-serving mechanism developed by the business community to eliminate "undesirables" from local thoroughfares. What's more, protestors asserted, referring to young people living on the streets as nothing more than bored suburban kids looking for a cheap thrill obscures the problem of child poverty plaguing Canadian society. Finally, opponents claim that like the deployment of private security guards to keep commercial thoroughfares free of vagrants, the Spare Change initiative is part and parcel of a broader agenda to criminalize panhandling. This, despite the Canadian Supreme Court's recent decision defending the rights of panhandlers to pursue their livelihood as they see fit. For opponents of the Spare Change Program, then, these measures fail to address the root causes of homelessness and poverty in the SuperCity: the evisceration of social assistance programs, the lack of decent and affordable housing, and the absence of viable employment opportunities. Acting as spoilers for the business association's public relations scheme, St. Clair and her fellow demonstrators demanded real change, not spare change.

For all of her forceful criticism of the Spare Change Program, St. Clair does not consider herself an anti-poverty activist. Rather, she is a working mother who happens to speak her mind when it comes to matters of social and economic justice. An occasional contributor to *Street Feat*, Suzzette St. Clair once enjoyed a comfortable middle class lifestyle. A failed marriage and bitter custody battles over her children then forced her on to the streets. In the midst of her troubles, Suzzette happened upon the offices of *Street Feat*, located in the Bloomfield Recreational Centre, a few miles north of downtown Halifax. There, *Street Feat*'s office workers, most notably, the paper's longtime publishing consultant and current managing editor, Juan Carlos Canales-Leyton, befriended her.

Since that time, Suzzette has chronicled her legal battles in the pages of *Street Feat* (1999, 2000a, 2000b). These brief yet deeply disturbing pieces underscore the complacency that comes from the insularity of middle class lifestyles, thereby confronting readers to question their class position and privilege. Indeed, on several occasions these stories prompted readers to write angry letters to city and provincial government officials demanding investigations into Suzzette's allegations that social service and legal aid workers repeatedly deny her assistance. Equally important, Suzzette began the long and difficult process of remaking her life. Whether it was chance, fate, or divine intervention that led her to *Street Feat*'s door, Suzzette credits the staff and volunteers of the street publication with opening her eyes to social injustice and sustaining her morale in the depths of her despair.

Other contributors and vendors tell similar stories – small victories and modest gains made with the support of the paper and its staff. In *Street Feat*'s second anniversary issue, staff and volunteers explain what "Street Feat Means to Me." For example, Ferne Riley and Judy Deal both acknowledge *Street Feat*'s role in introducing them to people they might otherwise not know. In her position as the paper's Sales Representative, Ferne not only developed important skills, but also has made lasting friendships. Street vendor Judy Deal draws upon her experience as a performer to sell and promote the paper. Judy's antics endear her to locals and tourists alike. Unable to find steady employment due to a debilitating health condition, Judy tells readers that street sales give her much more than a few extra dollars; they give her a sense of purpose. Likewise, office volunteer and editorial contributor Linda Harpell eloquently relates the paper's importance as a vehicle of self-expression. And with the self-knowledge that comes from writing, Harpell asserts, comes a greater understanding of her relationship to the wider community.

> I've been able to gain a great deal more to put to use in my life. I love to learn, to grow in a constructive knowledge so that I can help others in my local community. I've had the opportunity to find out about the facts in my community. *Street Feat* has shown me many of the issues and concerns affecting other people, just like me, in society.
>
> (1999: 5)

Finally, poet vendor Jack MacDonald succinctly relates the difference *Street Feat* has made in his life. First and foremost, Jack's earnings from sales of the street newspaper have immediate, tangible consequences. "*Street Feat* has a very strong impact on my life mainly because it helps to supply my basic needs for groceries and clothing." Deemed a more respectable means of making a living than panhandling, selling *Street Feat* also gives Jack the wherewithal to aspire to more viable creative and employment opportunities. Equally important, MacDonald acknowledges the paper's potential to agitate for progressive social change. In this light, Jack MacDonald views selling *Street Feat* as nothing short of "a mission" to enlighten readers to the plight of the poor. For MacDonald, then, *Street Feat* is implicated in a broader political project to eliminate poverty and end social injustice. A concise evaluation of *Street Feat*'s advocacy on behalf of the poor supports this assertion.

For instance, writing in *Street Feat*'s debut issue, Jeanne Fay, a legal aid worker affiliated with Dalhouise University's law program, describes the origins and activities of the Community Advocates Network (CAN). An alliance of individuals and member organizations, CAN was created "to resist the direction of welfare reform in Nova Scotia." Fay notes that CAN represents "persons with disabilities, single parents, Black Nova Scotians, Mi'kmaq and other people" adversely affected by changes in social assistance legislation. In addition, Fay points out, CAN members include representatives from local churches, unions, women's groups, homeless shelters, and other community and social service organizations.

This article chronicles the provincial government's stonewalling tactics on pending social policy legislation. Meant to frustrate and marginalize opposition to social assistance "reform" measures then under consideration, the government repeatedly failed to include welfare recipients and local anti-poverty activists in its decision-making process. As early as October 1996 community activists planned to meet with elected officials and representatives from the Department of Community Services at Veith House, one of Halifax's most venerable women's shelters, to discuss the government's welfare reform plan. However, the bureaucrats backed out of the meeting and postponed future deliberations indefinitely. Following a costly three month delay, the meeting was finally convened, but on conditions set by the provincial government. Although bureaucrats promised to convey anti-poverty activists' concerns to policy makers, they gave no indication when their Issues Paper would be published, nor did they make any provisions for public participation in this process, or for public comment on the paper's recommendations.

Furthermore, requests that the government consider several critical issues, including a proposal to raise shelter assistance rates for single people, were categorically denied. When anti-poverty activists reconvened in May 1997, they "identified the government's lack of genuine consultation on the reform as a common concern" (Fay 1997: 8). The following month, this disparate group of social assistance recipients and anti-poverty advocates organized the Community Advocates Network and launched a massive lobbying effort aimed at elected officials and other key decision makers requesting that they make public consultation a central component of any welfare reform process. CAN's principal demand was that the government provide anti-poverty activists 120 days to evaluate and then respond to the Issues Paper once it was finally released.

Amid rumors that the government intended to withhold the policy paper's release until just before the November by-election, CAN mobilized a "rapid response" team that could hold a press conference to evaluate the Issues Paper at any time. Meanwhile, the government hired an independent consultant to conduct focus groups regarding welfare reform. Not surprisingly, these handpicked participants rarely included people who were most directly affected by proposed reform measures: social assistance recipients, single parents, working families, minorities, students, and the disabled. Effectively barred from participating in this decision-making process – deliberations that would result in the most sweeping changes in social policy in a generation – CAN filed a Freedom of Information Act (FOIA) request to obtain a copy of the long awaited Issues Paper. Within days of filing its request, one of CAN's member organizations, the AIDS coalition of Nova Scotia, received an invitation to participate in the government's focus groups.

With the publication of Fay's report in its inaugural issue, *Street Feat* came to play a decisive role in promoting CAN's agenda and keeping the pressure on elected officials and government bureaucrats. For instance, in May 1998 Michael Burke wrote a stinging editorial of the government's reform plan when *Street Feat* published the much anticipated Issues Paper in its entirety: a public service no other publication saw fit to provide. Burke's critique notes that the government's plans were obtained at some cost, through the FOIA request. *Street Feat* publishes the government's report, Burke writes, in the hopes of generating public debate on these issues and enhancing public participation in future policy deliberations.

Periodically, *Street Feat* has published CAN's guide to provincial elections for first-time and low-income voters. Noting that the stakes are indeed high for the municipality's most vulnerable populations, CAN encourages voters to exercise their rights and, more pointedly, to mobilize against the provincial government's welfare reform measures. These efforts culminated on 24 November 1999 when hundreds of demonstrators took to the streets of Halifax to protest the provincial government's welfare reform plans. Unlike other periodicals that either trivialized or simply ignored the protests – demonstrations that coincided with actions across Canada – *Street Feat* meticulously documented mounting resistance to the government's plans to cut back on social assistance programs: policy changes that would prove disastrous to the HRM's most needy individuals and groups.

It is precisely this willingness and ability to publish the activities of local advocacy groups, to promote community service organizations, and to challenge the received wisdom of neo-liberal social and economic policy, that makes *Street Feat* distinctive. Whereas other local media outlets' coverage of welfare reform measures is informed predominantly by government press releases and the "expert" analysis of conservative think tanks and other free market enthusiasts, *Street Feat* covers news stories, such as CAN's FOIA request, that are unmistakably critical of the provincial government's fiscal policy and which challenge the government's irresponsible efforts to balance the provincial budget on the backs of the poor.

Likewise, *Street Feat*'s coverage of improvements in local social services takes a critical perspective to the government's spin on such changes. For example, *Street Feat*'s Managing Director, Michael Burke writes with some ambivalence on enhancements made to the aforementioned Hope Cottage and the Metro Turning Point, a local men's shelter. Although the relocation of Metro Turning Point from its former site, a rundown and neglected space that operated for years despite numerous health code violations, is applauded, Burke (1998) wryly notes that soup kitchens and night shelters are Halifax's growth industries. Burke writes with some authority on such matters; in his capacity as the national vice-president of the National Council of the Society of St. Vincent de Paul and director of Hope Cottage, he has seen first hand the overcrowding of homeless shelters and the increased demands at local soup kitchens.

Following years of hard-fought lobbying efforts, Hope Cottage and Metro Turning Point finally received funds from the municipal and provincial governments to expand their facilities.[8] While other media outlets dutifully covered these news events as little more than photo opportunities for elected officials and government bureaucrats, *Street Feat* takes a far more critical perspective to these stories. Burke's commentary suggests that while improvements in existing social services are desperately needed, these measures simply treat the symptom, not the causes of hunger and homelessness. Burke adds that substantive change can only be achieved if the commercial and financial abandonment of local neighborhoods, like the once vibrant Gottingen Street district, can be reversed.

Street Feat does its part to sustain grassroots efforts that seek to do precisely that. The Creighton-Gerrish Development Project is one case in point. Over the years, *Street Feat* has studiously followed the progress of ongoing efforts to rebuild this historic downtown neighborhood. Writing in the April 1999 edition of *Street Feat*, Anthony Clark describes a four-year plan to develop a two-acre parcel of land on Gottingen Street. These plans included the construction of several types of homes, including studio apartments, starter homes, and two-story houses scheduled for completion by the end of 2001.

Supervised by the Creighton-Gerrish Development Association, a non-profit partnership between the Black Community Work Group, Harbour City Homes, the Affordable Housing Association of Nova Scotia, and the Metro Non-Profit Housing Association, the project includes the construction of a multi-purpose community center (Clark 1999). In the absence of affordable options to Gottingen Street's notorious public housing blocks, the modest development project is part of a broader strategy to assist "the under-housed be a part of the community, not housed by the community" (Goodin 2001: 3). Significantly, *Street Feat*'s periodic updates on the Creighton-Gerrish development project feature the perspectives not only of local business concerns, but also those of affordable housing advocates, health care providers, and prospective residents.

In addition to publicizing political action campaigns and neighborhood redevelopment plans, *Street Feat* draws attention to community service organizations that rarely receive press attention for their important, but frequently overlooked work. In keeping with the tradition of participatory journalism, volunteers and staff representatives oftentimes write about their organization's mission and the clientele that they serve. Among those local agencies that have been profiled in *Street Feat*'s pages are the Phoenix Centre for Youth, a shelter, employment, and health care services provider for young people; Bryony House, a safe house for women and their children fleeing abusive relationships; and the Metro Resource Centre for Independent Living, an employment service for people with disabilities.

Likewise, *Street Feat* publicizes the work of local chapters of national and international organizations, such as the Elizabeth Frey Society, a legal aid organization for women; anti-poverty groups like OXFAM/Canada and Food Not Bombs; and the Raging Grannies, a collective based in British Colombia known for the performative dimension of their direct action campaigns. Here again, *Street Feat* publicizes the activities of organizations that rarely receive consistent, let alone sympathetic press attention. In the absence of this publicity, oppositional movements and political action campaigns struggle mightily to gain support for their efforts. In this regard, then, *Street Feat* operates much like other forms of community media in providing a venue for dissident opinion and resistant practices to reach wider audiences.

Finally, *Street Feat* gives readers frequent updates on its own operation. These self-reports provide yet another occasion to consider *Street Feat*'s efficacy as an agent of social change. For example, in the paper's first anniversary issue, *Street Feat* co-founder Roberto Menendez (1998) lists a number of the paper's accomplishments. According to Menendez, during its first year of publication *Street Feat* employed as many as fifty street vendors. In July 1998, vendors sold well over 4,000 copies of the paper, yielding a profit of $2,000; a considerable sum for those without a steady source of income. Equally important, Menendez notes, *Street Feat*'s offices provide a safe and welcoming place for people to talk about their lives and their experience of poverty. Prior to relocating from its downtown offices on Grafton Street, opposite the Halifax Public Library, to the Bloomfield Recreational Centre, *Street Feat* was a frequent destination for downtown panhandlers in need of a safe and comfortable place to rest and to socialize. Menendez concludes that the difficult task confronting *Street Feat* is two-fold: first, to make substantive change in the social and economic lives of Nova Scotians; and second, to continue its work as "a little stone in your shoe."

Michael Burke (1998) amplifies the difficulties Menendez alludes to in his reflections on the street paper's first year. Burke calls attention to numerous changes that have taken place at *Street Feat* over the previous twelve months. Notwithstanding modifications in the paper's format and the departure of several key personnel, Burke assures *Street Feat*'s readers that the paper's mission remains unchanged. In addition to thanking the paper's office staff and street vendors, Burke acknowledges the support *Street Feat* has received in certain quarters, especially from labor unions, church groups, and to a lesser extent, from government agencies.

Street Feat's co-founder is quick to point out, however, that the paper's long-term viability is far from certain. These concerns are underscored by an editor's note appearing in the same issue, which calls attention to the paper's upcoming subscription drive. In an effort to supplement the paper's financial support from advertising and street sales, the paper seeks to increase its subscription base from 600 to 1,000. Rather ominously, the editor's note suggests that if this modest goal goes unmet, publication of the next edition of *Street Feat* is uncertain. As it happened, *Street Feat* barely survived its second year. Declining revenues and staff reductions compromised every aspect of the paper's operation from production and distribution to advertising sales and marketing. *Street Feat*'s financial troubles were precipitated by several factors, not least of which was the depletion of a one-time federal grant that provided start-up funds for the fledgling publication.

The expenses associated with newspaper publication – computer hardware, software, and peripherals, layout, design and printing costs, office supplies, overhead, and salaries for the paper's office staff – quickly depleted grant money administered through Human Resources Canada, long before the paper achieved any measure of self-sufficiency. By September 1998, a mere nine months after *Street Feat*'s first issue appeared, the paper's three full-time staffers – staff reporter Chris LeRue, circulation manager and cartoonist Marie Koehler, and managing editor Peter McGuigan – were removed from the payroll. Of the three, only Peter McGuigan remained on, serving as acting managing editor for a time and taking on the task of vendor coordinator.

Street Feat's October 1998 issue marked the paper's format change from twelve down to eight pages and a dramatic reduction in print runs. As a result, advertising revenues and street sales in particular suffered. What's more, staff reductions caused long delays to the paper's production schedule, further undermining street sales and creating tensions between production personnel and street vendors. These tensions, coupled with *Street Feat*'s mounting financial troubles, supplanted the heady enthusiasm that marked the paper's first months with a profound sense of urgency to keep the paper afloat until it could support itself through advertising, street sales, subscriptions, and commercial publishing contracts.

As noted above, *Street Feat* does not operate as a charity. Whereas charities help alleviate hardship for those in need, street papers challenge dominant discursive formations surrounding issues of economic justice and in so doing seek to alter prevailing social, economic, and political conditions. To this end, *Street Feat* has two main objectives. First, *Street Feat* aims to provide economic opportunities for the poor and needy of Halifax; second, *Street Feat* works as an advocate alongside and on behalf of all those who seek a more egalitarian social order. *Street Feat*'s advocacy role therefore is enabled and constrained by its status as an entrepreneurial enterprise. A brief discussion of *Street Feat*'s role as a

15. Izzy White selling copies of *Street Feat* along Halifax's fashionable Spring Garden Road. (Photo by the author)

social-economic enterprise reveals the complex and contradictory relationship the paper has with its diverse supporters: local advocacy groups, community service organizations, religious institutions, the political establishment, commercial interests, and of course, the paper's readership. As we shall see, these relationships have a profound influence on the paper's day-to-day operation and its organizational culture.

"Sorry If I Asked You Twice"

Izzy White sells *Street Feat* in various locations throughout Halifax but like most vendors she finds Spring Garden Road a particularly advantageous location to ply her trade. By most accounts, Izzy is one of *Street Feat*'s more accomplished vendors. Despite her success and well-deserved reputation along the busy commercial thoroughfare, Izzy found it necessary to write a brief note of apology for her persistent entreaties to passersby. Writing in the March 2001 edition of *Street Feat*, Izzy explains that poor eyesight hinders her ability to discriminate between potential customers and those who have already purchased a copy of the street paper. In her short essay, "Sorry If I Asked You Twice," Izzy begs readers' kind indulgence if she repeatedly asks them to buy a copy of *Street Feat*.

Street Feat's vendor coordinator, Peter McGuigan, suggests with mild consternation that Izzy White's success is due in large measure to the sympathy the diminutive vendor elicits from passersby. Izzy does not dispute McGuigan's assessment of her sales record. Indeed, in my conversations with Izzy she made plain her unease with patrons who barely conceal their pity. Still, she appreciates the extra income *Street Feat* provides for herself and her new family. Given her persistent health problems, Izzy's prospects for gainful employment, apart from selling *Street Feat*, are remote. Like other vendors, then, Izzy White supplements modest social assistance and disability payments with her earnings from selling *Street Feat*. When we spoke in September 2001, Izzy was four months pregnant and planned to use her supplemental income to buy essentials for her new baby.[9]

Izzy White's success underscores one of the central paradoxes of the street paper movement. Ostensibly an economic project designed to provide viable employment opportunities for the poor in lieu of panhandling, many patrons purchase street papers for charitable reasons. Anecdotal evidence suggests that patrons frequently discard street papers without reading them (see, e.g., Green 1999). Notwithstanding claims made by street paper enthusiasts to the contrary, then, many patrons view street papers as simply another form of charity. Not only does this attitude undermine street papers' ability to communicate the experience of the poor to wider publics, this perception may account for the dismissive attitude some people have toward street vendors.

Over the years, the derision street vendors endure has been well documented in the pages of *Street Feat*. Perhaps no other vendor better captured the cruel irony of public reaction to *Street Feat* vendors than Dominique Rousseau. In a letter appearing in the September 1998 edition of *Street Feat*, Dominique discussed the rude and malicious comments she suffered while selling the paper along Spring Garden Road. Dominique's dispatch touched a nerve. Running alongside her letter were brief but eloquent notes of support from *Street Feat* staff. Fellow vendors in particular rallied around Dominique in an impressive show of solidarity for one of their own. An enigmatic figure, Dominique's past was something of a mystery to most of her acquaintances, including her *Street Feat* comrades. Nevertheless, Dominique distinguished herself among downtown Halifax's homeless community. Known for her infamous short temper, her resilient spirit, and, most notably, for the care and compassion she extended to the street kids congregating along Spring Garden Road, Dominique was affectionately referred to as *Street Feat*'s "Warrior Vendor."

Dominique's relative obscurity in life stands in stark contrast to her notoriety in death. When Dominque's body was discovered in her boarding house room on 1 July 1999, the coroner determined that she had been dead for several days. Local media outlets seized upon the story of Dominique's death with unusual vigor and brought renewed, if short-lived, attention to the plight of the municipality's elderly and infirm. In an unlikely turn of events, Dominique's death not only gave *Street Feat* sorely needed publicity but also garnered the struggling periodical a financial benefactor: Dominique's son, David Ash, whose generous and timely gifts have kept the paper from going under on several occasions.

The contradictions of Dominique's death were not lost on *Street Feat*'s writers. The August 1999 edition of *Street Feat* was dedicated to the Warrior Vendor, whose passing shocked and shamed the paper's staff. In addition to running background stories submitted by estranged family members, tales that described Dominique's life – her birth in 1933 to a Montreal prostitute, her adoptive family and the abusive relations she endured as a young girl, her marriage and family life, her career as a nurse's aide, and her bouts with mental illness – *Street Feat*'s contributors expressed their sense of frustration and guilt over Dominique's tragic death. Years later, managing editor Juan Carlos Canales-Leyton still feels the sting of Dominique's passing. Assessing *Street Feat*'s relationship with the cantankerous poet vendor, Juan Carlos laments: "We let her down." A man whose Islamic faith informs his commitment to human rights and social justice, Juan Carlos' anguish over Dominique's loss is palpable. To this day, Dominique Rousseau's memory exerts a powerful influence over Juan Carlos' relationship with street vendors, editorial contributors, and office volunteers.

In one final irony, following the publication of a tribute to the Warrior Vendor published one year after her death, an anonymous reader (2000) describes her sense of self-recrimination upon recognizing Dominique's photograph on *Street Feat*'s cover. The letter writer recalls with great shame several encounters she had with Dominique and relates her repulsion at the sickly woman. The letter concludes with an admission of the woman's indifference toward Dominique and her kind. She pleads for forgiveness and calls upon readers to reconsider their relationship with and responsibility toward so-called "street people" like Dominique. In death, Dominique continues to move readers who take the time to read her poetry, often reprinted throughout the year, along with the other exceptional writing found in the pages of *Street Feat*.

Despite the paper's increased visibility throughout the HRM, however, *Street Feat* continues to struggle against widespread public ignorance of the paper's mission. The ambivalence local politicians and area business people exhibit toward *Street Feat* is especially disturbing inasmuch as these very same community leaders fervently proclaim solidarity with

Street Feat and its goals. Elected officials and government bureaucrats in particular appear unfazed by the criticism directed at them in the pages of *Street Feat*. Rather than address these critiques in any substantive fashion, politicians rarely acknowledge the condemnation *Street Feat* contributors level toward disingenuous "reform" measures. Instead, politicians and community service representatives continue to deploy poor-bashing rhetoric that obscures the social construction of poverty and reaffirms the infallibility of the market.

Indeed, despite *Street Feat*'s frequent publication of analyses which draw attention to the inconsistencies of new social assistance regulations and the folly of back-to-work legislation, the Department of Community Services and other provincial offices continue to promote the government's "reform" plans in the street paper. Sadly, provincial government officials are not alone in their imperceptive behaviors. For instance, in a brief but nonetheless revealing interview published in the March 2001 edition of *Street Feat*, HRM Mayor Peter J. Kelly alludes to what he calls the "perceived problem" of panhandling in downtown Halifax (Canales-Leyton 2001). In a similar vein, representatives from the Spring Garden Road Business Association (SGRBA) – an organization that supports the street publication with half-page, full-color advertisements – dismiss the problem of child poverty by suggesting that street kids are merely engaging in "recreational panhandling." Notwithstanding critical assessments of the Spare Change program described above, Paul MacKinnon, Executive Director of SGRBA continues to defend the ill-considered initiative in the pages of *Street Feat*. The inability, or more accurately, the unwillingness of the local business and political elites to acknowledge the seriousness of poverty in and around Halifax undermines their oft-stated support for *Street Feat*.

Ongoing struggles between *Street Feat* vendors and local merchants further demonstrate the contradictions of the business community's support for a street paper that is often critical of local business practices. In his capacity as vendor coordinator Peter McGuigan frequently documents the abuse he and other vendors receive from local merchants, overzealous employees, and security guards who appear ignorant of an agreement *Street Feat* has with the HRM that allows vendors to sell their papers on city streets. Again, despite their avowed support for *Street Feat*, and indeed their willingness to place ads in the street paper, the local business community fails to give vendors the respect they deserve.

With that said, it is important to note that *Street Feat* vendors and contributors are likewise sensitive to the lack of respect they receive from anti-poverty activists and others who work on behalf of the poor. Several informants suggested that during its first year of publication *Street*

Feat was "too academic" for a street publication. They intimated that while discussions of free trade agreements and detailed policy analyses are certainly relevant to questions of economic injustice, these pieces were far too abstract to be of much use to the poor and fail to communicate the plight of Halifax's most needy to the wider community. *Street Feat*'s renewed commitment to publishing the material written by the homeless, the unemployed, and the working poor appears to be part of broader concerns over self-representation and participatory democracy.

Throughout 1999, *Street Feat* published a series of pieces, including news reports, op ed pieces, and letters to the editor that foreground these issues and underscore a growing resentment toward church groups, middle class activists, and other "experts" who claim to speak on behalf of the poor. For example, Erica Lewis' December 1998 column on what she described as the hypocrisy of charitable giving initiated a heated but thoughtful exchange on the topic of charity and *Street Feat*'s commitment to free expression. In her acerbic style, Lewis (1998) criticized the exorbitant amount of money then being spent on the restoration of one of the Halifax's most beloved houses of worship, St. George's Church. Lewis suggested that the money raised by St. George's parish would be better spent on providing affordable housing in the North End: a neighborhood notorious for its inadequate housing stock.

The following issue featured several responses to Lewis' condemnation. One letter, written by a Franciscan minister and sometime street vendor, recalls his decision to resign from the paper in protest to its publication of Lewis' invective (1999). Following a conversation with the paper's management and Father Thorne of St. George's, the Franciscan thought better of his decision. Such a move, it was argued, would undermine the paper's mission by censoring the poor. Peter McGuigan raises similar concerns in an article titled: "Let the Marginalized Speak." Recounting several objectionable incidents at community meetings, McGuigan (1999) suggests that anti-poverty activists are sometimes guilty of silencing the poor in much the same way the provincial government and the media do.

More recently, these criticisms have subsided as anti-poverty activists have incorporated the perspectives of "first voice" peoples – those who speak from first hand knowledge of systemic racism, homelessness, and unemployment – into their meetings. For example, in September 2001 a meeting of the Community Action on Homelessness (CAH) project featured testimonies from numerous first voice people. Aside from making their public testimony before the entire assembly, homeless and formerly homeless people also participated in the days' workshops on affordable housing and economic development initiatives. Not only did *Street Feat* provide extensive coverage prior to and following the two-day conference, but vendor and occasional contributor Judy Deal spoke eloquently on the need to improve the once vaunted Canadian health care system, especially for the homeless and the working poor. Although Judy did not represent *Street Feat* at this meeting, her affiliation with the street paper no doubt contributed to her forceful critique and, perhaps, to the audience's appreciative response to her comments.

Street Feat's relationship with other community structures and organizations is indeed complex and often contradictory. As we have seen, *Street Feat*'s efforts to alter the social, economic, and political relations of power within Halifax are largely determined by the paper's ability to successfully negotiate the needs and desires of the poor and disenfranchised with those of various supporters and contributors. In this light, the experience of *Street Feat* provides important insight into successful strategies for sustaining an alternative publication committed to participatory democracy and dedicated to progressive social change: two goals that are the hallmarks of community media organizations.

Street papers as an alternative public sphere

The study of community media, like scholarly work on the alternative press and participatory communication, is confounded by a lack of definitional precision and theoretical cohesion. As noted in the introduction, the uses and meanings of these terms and others like "small," "grassroots," and "independent" media share a number of salient features, which figure prominently in debates over the constitution, and viability, of an alternative public sphere. Central to these discussions is a commitment to the movement for communicative democracy, or popular struggles to achieve greater correspondence between the democratic principles of freedom of speech and expression, the political economy of the media industries, and the content and character of public communication (Hackett 2000). Aligning itself as it does with the alternative press, *Street Feat* embraces a long and varied tradition that embraces advocacy journalism, supports and encourages grassroots organizing, and is dedicated to the realization of a more just and equitable social order. On the other hand, by articulating an affinity with these traditions *Street Feat* must confront the many obstacles that have marked the history of the alternative press: chronic funding problems, divisive organizational disputes, worker burnout, and sporadic and uneven distribution.

Print scholar Chris Atton's (1999) analysis of alternative publications in Britain provides a basis to briefly consider *Street Feat*'s relationship to the alternative press and to evaluate the street paper's viability as a resource for community communication. Atton questions pessimistic assessments of the alternative press which suggest that the inability or unwillingness of these publications to adopt the methods of finance, production, and distribution associated with conventional publications inevitably leads to marginalization and, ultimately, irrelevance. Drawing on public sphere theory, Atton argues that the success of alternative publications ought not be measured by financial indicators like circulation figures and market penetration – indices associated with profit-oriented publications – but rather in the alternative press' capacity to support and nourish a viable alternative public sphere. Indeed, Atton asserts that the alternative press is integral to the formation of these discursive spaces.

The relationship is mutual and synergetic; the alternative public sphere provides opportunities and outlets for the production and consumption of the alternative press, at the same time as the press itself provides material that sustains the sphere's function as a place for the formulation, discussion and debate of radical and dissenting ideas.

(Atton: 71)

Street newspapers, like *Street Feat*, are contemporary manifestations of this relationship between alternative publications, oppositional discourse, and social movements. As we have seen, by facilitating participatory communication within and between Halifax's most needy and impoverished inhabitants, *Street Feat* taps into existing realms of marginalized communication, such as homeless shelters, soup kitchens, community meetings, and street corners. Moreover, *Street Feat* provides a platform for various constituencies – social assistance recipients, anti-poverty activists, religious groups, and community service providers – to articulate their resistance to neo-liberal social and economic policies. Put another way, *Street Feat* constitutes and is constitutive of an alternative public sphere for the poor, and those who work on their behalf, throughout the city of Halifax, Nova Scotia.

Atton's reassessment of the alternative press also demonstrates the fallacy behind the assumption that a commitment to democratic communication is somehow inconsistent and incompatible with managerial authority, advertising support, sophisticated production techniques and distribution methods, and other practices associated with mainstream publications. Rather than ignore the economic realities confronting resistant media, Atton suggests that alternative publications, like street papers, are successful precisely because they develop innovative ways to survive in light of the constraints facing radical, dissident, or oppositional publications in capitalist societies.

Offering job opportunities to the unemployed and the working poor as an entrepreneurial alternative to panhandling is but one example of this. Accepting advertising is another. As we have seen, *Street Feat* supports itself through a variety of mechanisms including advertising, subscription, direct sales, and charitable donations. Unencumbered by concerns for "ideological purity" which prevent some street papers from accepting advertising support, *Street Feat* accepts ads from all sorts of clients: retail merchants, charitable organizations, local churches, politicians, grocery stores, and even upscale restaurants.[10] More recently, *Street Feat* contracted with the provincial government to produce the *Royal Gazette*, an official publication of the Province of Nova Scotia. In this regard then *Street Feat* takes a pragmatic approach to financial stability by diversifying its revenue streams.

This is not to suggest, however, that *Street Feat* avoids the inevitable contradictions associated with this pragmatism, let alone that the street paper has achieved financial solvency. For instance, whilst money from the *Royal Gazette* helps finance the paper, the demands of this contract redirect the energies of staff and volunteers away from their primary objective: monthly publication of *Street Feat*. Subsequent publication delays undermine the economic incentive for street vendors and serve to heighten tensions between vendors and the office staff. And when distribution is postponed for weeks at a time, the paper's circulation falls, its readership declines, and vendors make that much less money.

Other contradictions manifest themselves in less visible, but no less troubling ways. For instance, a number of the paper's part-time employees are paid through government jobs programs, including the very same welfare-to-work schemes that are frequently criticized in the pages of *Street Feat*. On the other hand, some office volunteers and editorial contributors simply burn out after a time. As a result, exceptionally talented editorial contributors like Elizabeth McGibbon, whose promising column "The Nurse Is In" spoke plainly to the relationship between community health care and economic justice, ran for only a few months in 1998. And finally, as noted earlier, despite claims that *Street Feat* is not a charity, were it not for charitable donations, the paper would have gone under long ago.

Like the community media organizations discussed earlier, then, *Street Feat* is both enabled and constrained by various social, economic, and political forces and conditions within the local community. In this light, community media offer an exceptional site of cultural analysis inasmuch as locally oriented, participatory media organizations like *Street Feat* shape and are shaped by popular perceptions and articulations of communities. In short, street papers provide yet another opportunity to examine the symbolic construction of community. In the next chapter, we turn our attention away from one of the earliest forms of mass communication, print media, to assess the process by which the state of Victoria, Australia has appropriated the latest communication and information technologies for purposes of community communication: socio-technical systems commonly known as community computer networks.

6   Victoria's Network: (re) imagining community in the information age

> For if it is the case, as it is fashionable to assert, that media give shape
> to the imaginative boundaries of modern communities, then the
> introduction of new media is a special historical occasion when
> patterns anchored in older media that have provided stable currency of
> social exchange are reexamined, challenged, and defended.
>
> Carolyn Marvin, *When Old Technologies Were New*

Much of what I know about Australia in general, and Victoria in particular, comes from my frequent "travels" there through the global information infrastructure commonly referred to as the Internet. As noted in Chapter 2, while the Internet has focused considerable popular and academic attention on the role computer-mediated communication plays in articulating community without propinquity, the community networking movement's principal objective is to facilitate communication within place-based communities.

Thus, community computer networks manifest the central paradox of computer-mediated communication. On one hand, community networks exist to improve community relations, revitalize civic life, and support cultural production and economic development efforts on the local level. On the other hand, however, community networks are an integral part of an emerging global communication system and play a significant role in promoting and sustaining a global dialogue on a scale and scope unprecedented in human history. Viewed in this light, Victoria's Network (VICNET) provides a vehicle not only to consider this phenomenon, but also to become an active participant in this global conversation.

Put differently, my decision to investigate a community computer network is fueled by a desire to realize the time and space-collapsing capabilities of computer-mediated communication: to "visit" and in some fashion "participate" in, and perhaps even "belong" to a community regardless of my physical proximity to a particular place. Of course, I could investigate any number of community networks here in North America. Likewise, many of the community networks of Europe offer English-language mirror sites that would facilitate my research. But to fully appreciate the global dimensions of community computer networking, I chose to explore the impact of these new technologies on a region halfway around the world: Victoria, Australia. In short, to go Down Under by desktop.[1]

My ability to investigate VICNET solely through information and communication technologies presents unique opportunities and formidable challenges. Insofar as computer-mediated communication affords me an opportunity to conduct my research in an unobtrusive fashion, this form of (virtual) participant observation is superior to the more traditional modes of investigation employed in Bloomington, New York City, and Halifax. In other respects, however, making observations solely through a technological interface highlights but one dimension of these multifaceted socio-technical systems. I have yet to fully understand and appreciate the complexity of this aspect of my research design. Throughout this discussion, I briefly reflect upon this experience. However, my more pressing concerns revolve around investigating the contradictions embodied by the use of a global information infrastructure to (re) articulate local identity and promote a sense of community.

A collaborative effort between the state library of Victoria (SLV) and the Royal Melbourne Institute of Technology (RMIT), VICNET was developed as a means of "Empowering Victorians to create an electronic environment where they can publish, share and find information and form online communities both locally and globally."[2] VICNET's emphasis upon online, so-called virtual communities stands in contrast to community radio in Bloomington, community television in Manhattan, and Halifax's street paper. That is, while VICNET stresses the development of online community, WFHB, DCTV, and *Street Feat* foreground their relevance to the physical and psycho-social dimensions of place-based communities. Moreover, VICNET engenders local and extra-local interaction of a scale, scope, and intensity quite unlike the previous case studies. As we shall see, this dynamic adds an intriguing new wrinkle to the already complex relationship between communication and community.

Indeed, this condition raises several important questions: How does VICNET embody the contradictory impulses behind community media initiatives? That is to say, how does VICNET represent a bulwark against the encroachment of global communications? In what ways does VICNET embrace and extend this growing global information infrastructure? More important, how does VICNET negotiate these conflicting tendencies? To that end, what are the implications of the public library's involvement in constructing and maintaining this electronic environment? How does this association promote equitable access to these new technologies? Conversely, is popular participation in VICNET problematized by this association? Finally, what can VICNET tell us about the impact of new media on our understanding and perceptions of community? In short, this chapter examines the complex and contradictory process by which local populations articulate community within and through computer-mediated communication. Before addressing these issues, however, we should have some understanding of Victoria's relatively brief, but rich history.

Australia Fair

Australia's second largest and most densely populated state, Victoria is a land of distinctive terrain and disparate people. Roughly the size of the state of Utah, Victoria boasts rugged coastlines, plush farmland, snow-covered mountain ranges, and fertile river basins. This diverse topography was once home to the Koori, the indigenous people of southeastern Australia. European expansion and successive waves of immigration eventually transformed Victoria's population into a multicultural mélange of racial backgrounds and ethnic heritages. And while the traditions associated with British imperial rule have left an indelible stamp on the character of the region, Victoria has crafted its own modern identity. Victoria's varied social, cultural, and geographical features make it a remarkably vibrant place.

European settlement of the Australian continent did not begin in earnest until the early part of the nineteenth century. Upon their arrival, Europeans declared the territory "terra nullius": a land without people. Like earlier excursions into unknown territories, European settlers had little understanding, and even less tolerance for the indigenous peoples they encountered. In short order, Australian aboriginals, like their Native American counterparts, were quickly and ruthlessly eradicated by European indifference and the insatiable appetite for land and resources. Unlike earlier settlements on the Australian continent, however, Victoria was not established as a penal colony. Searching for pastoral runs and rich, abundant farmland, sheepherders and farmers from the colonies of New South Wales and Van Diemen's Land (Tasmania) pushed into the continental interior. In his report on the fertile lands and scenic beauty he encountered in what would one day be central and western Victoria, surveyor-general Major Thomas Mitchell dubbed the territory Australia Felix (Australia Fair). Prompted by such reports, settlers soon migrated to the region and set up sheep stations and subsistence farms.

In 1851, the southern territory was granted separation from New South Wales and the colony of Victoria was established with the port city of Melbourne as the capital. The gold rush of the 1850s promoted waves of immigration from Europe and Asia, transforming Melbourne's humble, rustic environs into a resplendent, world-class city almost overnight. The enormous wealth generated by Victoria's natural resources lured prospectors and investors from around the world. Boosted by its rich agricultural tracts, abundant mineral deposits, and a growing manufacturing and industrial base, Victoria became an important economic player in colonial and later national development. Over the years, Victoria's capital city has grown in size and stature; and the constant influx of immigration has contributed to Melbourne's reputation as Australia's cultural center. Not surprisingly, given its distinctive terrain and vast and varied human and cultural resources, Victoria is the nation's communication hub. The world-renowned Australian cinema is based in Melbourne and the state of Victoria accounts for 45 per cent of the nation's communication industry production.

As Victoria's fortunes waxed and waned in the wake of boom times and prolonged economic downturns, regional and national development became inextricably linked with population growth. So much so that following World War II, a federal program characterized by the slogan "Populate or Perish" was initiated in order to enhance the nation's defensive posture and stabilize the erratic Australian economy. Spurred on by congenial immigration policies, people from the United Kingdom and the war-ravaged European continent arrived in Australia through the port of Melbourne. More recently, immigrants from Southeast Asia and Indonesia have landed in Melbourne. Significantly, most of these immigrants remain in the state capital, lending the city a sophisticated, multicultural air. Of Victoria's 4.4 million people, 3.1 million call Melbourne their home.

Predictably, Melbourne's rapid development and enviable prosperity exacerbates long-standing tensions between city dwellers and regional Victorians. These pressures are compounded by persistent calls to return vast pastoral tracts to aboriginal peoples. The struggles of native peoples to regain ancient lands, preserve indigenous cultures, and improve their standing in contemporary Australian society, coupled with the influx of non-European immigrants, contributes to the uneasiness many Victorians feel regarding their cultural heritage, political autonomy, and economic well being.

In the early 1990s, the Australian economy all but collapsed as a result of the wide-spread, if ill-advised deregulatory policies of the 1980s. The formidable economic growth Victoria enjoyed during the previous decade has, of late, given way to a lackluster regional economy. Like many postindustrial societies, then, Australia began to explore the use of telecommunications and information technologies to improve its economic well being and maintain its enviable standard of living. The VICNET initiative is best understood as a response to the tensions associated with economic instability, cultural diversity, and the transition from an industrial-based to an information society.

Metaphors of the information age

Few community computer network initiatives are as imaginative, ambitious, or as well financed as VICNET. As envisioned by project supervisors, VICNET will provide the state of Victoria with a sophisticated information infrastructure unique to Australia and the world. The project's formidable goals suggest the enormous capital investment and considerable human and technical resources required for the creation of an electronic environment for the entire state of Victoria.

The breadth of the VICNET initiative becomes clear when one considers the range of services the project expects to provide and the diverse user population the network seeks to serve. According to an online document, "VICNET is like a shopping mall" for information, products, and services; a "Free-Net" providing free and low-cost access to computer networks; the information-rich, technologically advanced "twenty-first century face" of the public library; and a "soapbox" for Victorians to speak out and exchange information, opinion, and perspectives. Taken in turn, each of these analogies suggest the complex and paradoxical relationship between communication technologies and contemporary articulations of community.

The shopping mall metaphor is commonly employed as a means to acclimate the general public to computer-mediated communication. The mall is envisioned as a safe, friendly environment in which the whole family can "shop" for information, products and services in a visually appealing, easy to navigate and non-threatening manner. Significantly, this strategy stands in stark contrast to the approach taken by the community media initiatives described in the preceding case studies. Whereas VICNET uses commercial services to draw Victorians to the system, WFHB, DCTV, and *Street Feat* emphasize their non-profit status in an effort to attract audiences frustrated by commercially produced media form and content. VICNET's consumer-based appeals are therefore designed to lure a diverse range of users to the network while avoiding, or at least easing the anxieties associated with information technology. More important, VICNET's shopping mall analogy highlights the network's role in fostering economic development.

VICNET's emphasis on local business promotes established commercial enterprises and spurs investment and entrepreneurialism. Not surprisingly, many of the local businesses listed on VICNET are involved with information technologies, computer applications, and electronic publishing. In this way, VICNET stimulates the growth and development of emerging technologies throughout Victoria. However, the inherent danger of this strategy stems from the possibility that the consumer element might overwhelm civic and other forms of noncommercial content. A cursory examination of VICNET's homepages highlights these concerns.

Understandably VICNET provides links to its backers: the state library and RMIT, as well as corporate sponsors Sun Microsystems Australia Pty. Ltd. and Dataplex Pty. Ltd. For the most part, business and consumer-related sites are listed under specific subject headings, along with other types of information: arts, community, education, government, philosophy, science, and religion, to name a few. During its formative years, a link on VICNET's homepage invited visitors to "put your banner message on VICNET," suggesting that the volume of consumer-related information on VICNET is bound to increase. Advertising featured prominently on VICNET's front page may distract users from seeking non-market-based forms of information: in effect hollowing out the noncommercial dimension of the network.

Crucially, the wealth of consumer options available through VICNET is meant to appeal not only to a local or regional audience, but also to national, and international net surfers. For example, the wealth of tourist information is a clear indication of the importance of the tourism industry to the Victorian economy. What's more, the prominence of this information in a global communication context suggests VICNET's subtle, yet unmistakable role as Victoria's calling card to world travelers. Something of a virtual come-on, a digital inducement to visit the Land Down Under, VICNET's tourism information reaches desirable demographic groups – the majority of Internet users are upscale professionals with disposable incomes – with timely and tempting lures to travel to Victoria.

In addition to tourist dollars, VICNET provides regional Victoria with the means to attract large-scale capital investment from the Pacific Rim and around the world. The following posting in the VICNET guest book suggests that this strategy is paying off. "Great site. We are considering a corporate relocation in Victoria and needed some information on the area. This site has it all. Keep it up." In this respect, VICNET attracts investment to the region by promoting Victoria as a world leader in information technology and multimedia applications. No doubt, this aspect of the VICNET initiative explains the state government's enthusiastic support of the project.

Despite the enormous costs associated with telecommunications, and the long-term investment VICNET represents for the Victorian government, the potential benefits derived from VICNET appear to outweigh current budgetary concerns. In the face of formidable economic, technical, and logistical obstacles, the state government enthusiastically allocated funding for a pilot project. According to the project proposal the total cost for the one-year, trial run was put at $390,000 to cover expenses related to telecommunications, hardware, software licensing, and staffing.[3]

Quite unlike the other community media initiatives described above, the VICNET initiative received large-scale capital investment from the outset. The effort to bring community radio to Bloomington, Indiana was severely constrained by the lack of economic resources. Until the BCR gained the confidence of local benefactors and business people, fundraising activities were characterized by their modest, grassroots quality. Likewise, DCTV's earliest efforts to bring television to the people were self-funded until various funding agencies, most notably the Department of Parks and the New York State Council for the Arts (NYSCA) provided grant support for DCTV's community outreach efforts. Although *Street Feat* received modest financial support from the provincial government of Nova Scotia, these funds did little to ensure the project's long-term economic viability.

Of course, the Victoria state government's ardent support for the VICNET initiative was not purely altruistic; a host of economic, social, cultural, and political factors guided the government's actions. Indeed, the Community Support Fund financed a host of improvements to the state library of Victoria, including VICNET. This program was established as a means to offset the detrimental effects of the gaming industry in Victoria. Some years earlier, casino gambling was introduced to the region as a means to increase revenue. Speaking to the state legislature on 23 May 1995, PM Victor Perton observed: "The Labor Party decided to try to fix its budget deficit and debt problems by changing the fabric of Victorian and indeed Australian society by introducing the electronic gaming machine and the casino to Victoria."[4]

Appreciation for the state's largesse therefore should be tempered by the realization that key policy makers, legislators, and private investors envisioned the VICNET initiative as a means to spur economic growth in the areas of information technology and software development. In remarks to members of parliament on 23 May 1995, Victoria's Premier Jeff Kennet summed up the government's position this way: "VICNET is a very good way of positioning Victoria in terms of information not only for those who are pursuing information for educational reasons but also for those who pursue it for business reasons. . . . Importantly, it will help develop a new industry in this state in which, through post-production, Victoria already has the leading edge around Australia." Building on Victoria's national and growing international reputation as an information and entertainment content provider, VICNET represents considerable public investment in the region's communication industries. In this respect, VICNET serves a crucial role for enhancing Victoria's competitiveness in the emerging global economy. Indeed, VICNET is an essential component of the state government's multimedia policy: the Victoria 21 strategy. As one parliament member noted: "The government disseminates information on VICNET. It promotes Victoria's multimedia industries and benefits flow from it by the establishment."

VICNET's technical manager, Stuart Hall, suggests the network's strategic importance to the state's economic redevelopment plans not only provides the initiative with a stable funding source, but serves to insulate the organization from undue political pressures. "The potential is always there for the government to withdraw support from this area, but at the moment, our State Government in particular is very keen on developing the state as a multimedia industry leader and is supporting all our efforts. At the moment, in practice, VICNET operates almost independently of Government." VICNET's relative autonomy not only frees the project from direct government interference, with state sponsorship VICNET can operate at a considerable deficit.

This rather enviable situation enables VICNET to pursue one of its most ambitious aims: equitable and affordable access to information networking for all Victorians. As Stuart Hall observes, VICNET's ultimate goal is the provision of universal service for computer networking. "This is similar to making sure everyone can get access to TV or radio or telephones. The internet is an important basic facility for the future similar to the telephone. We want to make it ubiquitous in Victoria, just another utility." To that end, VICNET is based upon the successful Free-Net model developed by Tom Grundner of the National Public Telecomputing Network (NPTN) described in Chapter 2. Guided by the sensibilities of the Free-Net, VICNET allows users with business or home computers to tap into regional, national, and international electronic networks and provides public access terminals for those without personal computers.

Like many Free-Nets across North America and around the world, VICNET's terminals are located in local host organizations, most notably public libraries. However, whereas most Free-Nets are driven by community organizations, and are locally owned and operated, VICNET is based in two state-sponsored institutions: the state library and RMIT. Moreover, through its commercial arm, Informit, RMIT seeks to establish

VICNET as one of Victoria's premiere electronic publishers.[5] To that end, VICNET offers web publishing and technology consultation services to area businesses. Significantly, VICNET does not have its own dial-in infrastructure, as do many community networks. In these respects, then, VICNET operates much like a commercial information service provider (ISP).

These distinctions are neither subtle nor trivial; they tend to confound and obscure the community orientation central to the Free-Net model. VICNET's unique and somewhat contradictory character rests upon this rather curious hybridity: VICNET is at once a Free-Net, a state-sponsored public service organization, and a commercial venture. As a result, VICNET's aims are more varied and complex than the typical Free-Net. The network's opaque character is captured by the following comments elicited through an online survey of VICNET users.[6]

I was looking for a service provider and this one was cheap.

Liked their mission statement. Thought that if Telstra (phone company) decided to enter the race as an ISP, a larger, semi-government funded organizations may have a better chance of surviving.

It is a locally run network with useful information about the state and city which I live in.

I saw VICNET advertised about 18 months ago and liked the community aspect of VICNET as an ISP. I also figured they wouldn't be 'fly by night'. Plus the price was right.

I learned about VICNET while investigating possible Internet providers. I decided on VICNET because it was nonprofit and had a strong community focus.

Until this questionnaire, I wasn't aware VICNET was a community-based organization.

These remarks suggest VICNET's multifaceted appeal to Victorians. Some VICNET subscribers appreciate the local orientation; for others this dimension is irrelevant, if not imperceptible. Not surprisingly, government sponsorship goes a long way toward making VICNET a viable option to commercial ISPs. Indeed, without government subsidies, VICNET might not attract very many subscribers and surely would not be able to pursue its goals of equitable and affordable computer networking access.

Significantly, VICNET's universal service aims to serve a conspicuous, if seldom acknowledged economic function. In remarks to parliament on 28 May 1996, legislator Robert Clark argued that VICNET "will encourage Victorians to become familiar with the new technology and to increasingly gain confidence with it, which will further improve the attractiveness of Victoria as a place to conduct multimedia business." VICNET therefore serves an important skills-building function, acclimating Victorians to emerging technologies and preparing the workforce for the information-intensive work environment of the twenty-first century.

In this light, VICNET's universal service provisions have little to do with the ideals of an informed and enlightened citizenry often promoted by community networking advocates. For policy makers at any rate, VICNET's high-minded goals of equitable and affordable access to information technologies suggest a calculated response to market forces and conditions. As parliamentarian Carlo Carli observed, Victoria's racial and ethnic diversity give the region a distinct competitive advantage in the growing global information economy. "We have an enormous skills base in the languages spoken in Victoria and we need to provide information in those languages. At the moment, the Internet is predominantly in English, but it need not be. Providing other languages will develop new skills and products and meet the needs of various markets." From this perspective, VICNET not only helps build a highly skilled labor force, but also promises to create and nurture new markets. In short, classic free-market economic philosophy, not some abstract notions of participatory democracy and social justice, provides the impetus for VICNET's universal service goals.

This situation is neither surprising nor especially unique. As we have seen in preceding chapters, the term community is invoked in order to secure widespread support for local media initiatives. However, the communitarian impulses behind these projects are questionable. Occasionally, the call to community obscures far less egalitarian motives and conceals assorted agendas. Viewed in this light, VICNET is a strategic investment on the part of the Victorian government to create an information infrastructure that will support local business, and more important, enhance Victoria's viability as a global center for highly skilled information workers and cutting-edge technologies and applications. Couched in the ideological framework of public service, community development and social-political equity, the state government's enthusiastic support of VICNET is based largely upon economic considerations.

This is not to suggest that VICNET is simply a disingenuous and thinly veiled government attempt to jump start the regional economy and promote long-term investment. VICNET is clearly founded upon far more altruistic, but no less contradictory motives. Dedicated to bringing the benefits of the so-called "information age" to the greater Victorian populace, a group of concerned educators, computer scientists, information specialists, and librarians have committed enormous personal and professional resources to the growth and development of

VICNET.[7] In fact, VICNET would never have been realized without the efforts of a handful of politically savvy, technologically sophisticated, civic-minded public servants.

In late 1993, the state government of Victoria received a proposal from representatives of the state library and the Royal Melbourne Institute of Technology for the establishment of a state-wide, community-based computer networking initiative that would provide Victorian's access to the Internet and its Australian subset, the Australian Academic and Research Network (AARNet). Although some national and international databases and bulletin board systems (BBS) were available to those with network connections – and then only through cumbersome access and retrieval methods – most Victorians could not access either AARNet or the Internet.

The original proposal[8] suggests that VICNET would add value to these existing information infrastructures in a number of ways: providing a simple method to access these electronic networks; establishing a cheap and efficient means to disseminate local, regional, and federal government information; creating common access screens and information retrieval methods for a variety of public and privately held databases; and founding a user-driven facility for community groups and other organizations to disseminate information to the wider Victorian community, and the world.

As noted in Chapter 2, given its role as a community-wide resource for the collection and dissemination of information, the public library is often considered an ideal candidate to sponsor a community network. According to one community network advocate, "The library is such a wonderful location for a Free-Net because it already is an information source, has open hours and serves the public. Libraries are often computerized so the computer-literacy skills transfer, and it is non-political, serving all populations" (Featheringham, quoted in Commings 1995). The VICNET proposal suggests as much, "The traditional and historic role of the state library and public libraries has been to act as the community's gateway to its information requirements and recorded heritage. . . . The proposal envisages the state library fulfilling the same role in organizing access to databases as it currently does for printed materials." Basing VICNET in the public library system, then, embraces, extends, and reinvigorates the library's time-honored role within the local community and throughout society. Combining as it does the library's traditional role with its new mission as information technology hub, VICNET is very much the twenty-first century face of the public library. Through electronic storage and retrieval methods, VICNET permits greater access to a wealth of information, from across Victoria and around the world: in essence creating a library without walls.

What's more, basing the project in the public library distinguishes VICNET from commercial ISPs in a number of important ways, most crucially in its role as a tool for political action and social change. Customer Service Officer Adrian Bates sums up VICNET's advantages over commercial providers this way:

There is not a wealth of public service or community based online media [or] information in Victoria or Australia for that matter. VICNET is filling a much needed role both in terms of public access for those who could never afford home access, and in enabling and training groups across the state to publish their own information on the web. It is all about passing on skills and empowering the people of Victoria so they can use the emerging Net as a powerful social tool and not just as another means of receiving government information, but as a means where they can challenge and change government thinking.

These comments recall the previous discussion of community-based media. Aside from their role in promoting local economic development, community media initiatives are a vehicle to promote a dialogue between local populations and elected officials. Like the Canadian *Challenge for Change* project, and New York University's Alternative Media Center described in Chapter 2, VICNET abjures the notion that communication is simply or unproblematically a matter of transmission. Rather, these decentralized forms of media production and distribution are intended to facilitate the exchange of information, opinion, and perspectives throughout the community.

VICNET's strength therefore, rests in large measure on its willingness and ability to mount information by, for, and about regional Victoria. Through outreach efforts, VICNET collects and disseminates vast stores of information relating to a wealth of issues, concerns, and interests. What makes VICNET unique has little to do with computer hardware and network infrastructure; VICNET's distinctiveness stems from its role as the primary content provider for information about Victoria and of interest to Victorians. The provision of locally relevant information keeps VICNET from being "just another content provider." A quick perusal of VICNET's holdings supports this assertion.

Updated weekly, the What's New! section contains a wide variety of educational, recreational, commercial, and social-political information. This page lists information on music and arts festivals, job announcements, government and non-profit agency reports, local, national, and international political action campaigns, and, on occasion, calls to participate in research projects.[9] But it is the Contents page that best captures the breadth of information VICNET mounts on its server for (g)local browsing. For example, the Aboriginal and Torres Strait Islanders (TSI) page "is designed to be the starting point for links to Aboriginal and Torres Strait Islander information in Victoria and Australia."[10] A Disability page covers issues related to physical, sensory or mental disabilities. This page features links to resources with information concerning computer accessibility issues for the disabled. Several prominent organizations, including the Trace Research and Development Center at the University of Wisconsin-Madison and the Canadian-based Starling Access Services group, are listed here.

Likewise, a Labor and Trade Union page features general information on the Victorian Labor Movement, updates on job training programs for the unemployed, and calls to action that promote worker solidarity by linking local union members with labor movements around the globe. Significantly, some of these links include subscription information to LEFT-LINK, a Victorian-based electronic mailing list for "Victoria's Broad Left Community," updates on the dock workers' strike in Liverpool, England, and calls for solidarity with Indonesian sailors struggling for improved working conditions from the Dutch-owned Nedlloyd company.

Other pages include listings of Australian and Usenet news groups and mailing lists, Health, Kids, Senior Citizens, and Men's and Women's Issues pages, and of course, VICNET's Multicultural page. As with most of VICNET's pages, each subject area includes links to an array of local, regional, national, and international organizations and information resources. Moreover, VICNET allows users to make their databases available to the entire Internet audience via the World Wide Web. In addition to the Victorian Government Publications Database, VICNET currently supports the OzLit database, featuring information on Australian books and writers, regional bookstores, and resources for literary researchers. Other databases include the Islamic Community Database and a directory of Emergency Accommodations in Greater Melbourne for the homeless and victims of domestic violence.

In these ways, VICNET empowers local non-profit groups and community-based organizations with the benefits of information networking by providing these groups with an opportunity to place their information on VICNET's server at no cost.[11] Moreover, by working with local social service agencies and other non-profits, VICNET provides computer literacy training and technical skills to groups and individuals with little or no access to new technologies. Without VICNET's generous support, community-based, non-profits groups would likely be left out of Victoria's emerging electronic environment. VICNET's government sponsorship and its affiliation with the State Library of Victoria facilitates these efforts.

However, this relationship is not entirely unproblematic. Collecting, cataloguing, and preserving recorded materials are neither value-free nor unconstrained activities: the library's functions are determined by a host of social, cultural, political, and economic factors. The library, then, is not simply a receptacle of information and recorded history; rather the library constructs a given society's knowledge base. Moreover, through its holdings, the library legitimizes certain information sources and knowledge systems at the expense of different perspectives and divergent ways of knowing.

In this way, the library serves to support "official histories" and reify a particular world view. Of course, this situation is not new. Libraries have long operated under certain assumptions regarding the organization, classification, and dissemination of information. In their role as intermediaries between the community and recorded information, the library organizes and constructs knowledge in a manner that reflects and reinforces existing social structures and underlying philosophies. In short, as arbiters of the community's recorded heritage, libraries do not merely act as gateways to information, they are in effect gatekeepers as well.

Operating under the auspices of the state library, then, VICNET extends the library's mediating function into this new media environment, thereby (re)establishing the library's role as gatekeeper in the world of online information. As a result, VICNET acts to collect, structure, and ultimately legitimize online information. While there is a certain utility in all of this, there is also a danger that the dynamic, collaborative, and creative quality of online interaction is undermined by the library's organizing function.

Curiously, this condition is reminiscent of the early days of radio broadcasting. The radio amateurs reveled in the collaborative, decidedly anarchic quality of radio communication (see Douglas 1986). Amateur broadcasters embraced radio's communitarian potential by exploiting the medium's ability to collapse time and space in order to enhance social interaction within and between communities. In short order, however, powerful social, economic, and political forces and interests stifled the emerging medium's popular, democratic potential. Under these conditions, radio (d)evolved from a productive activity to a consumptive practice: the amateur radio broadcasters quickly disappeared, displaced by radio audiences. In a similar vein, through its role as information intermediary VICNET threatens more democratic forms of knowledge production and distribution by (re)establishing the public library's structuring function in the digital realm. This is to say, by institutionalizing online interaction,

VICNET may stifle the dynamic character of computer-mediated communication.

Significantly, the library's ideological function in perpetuating a specific worldview through its organizing principles and institutional biases is obscured by its public service mission. As VICNET's Stuart Hall notes, "Because of our unusual position, we are regarded as not having (much of) a vested interest and we try to live up to that as far as possible." The library staff appears to share this same perception. According to Adrian Bates VICNET has no content restrictions, "we cannot and do not impose anything, and most [local libraries] to my knowledge have no content restrictions at all." Moreover, he suggests that the library has nothing to fear from the calls of some parliamentarians to regulate online speech. "I don't think censorship will come to anything, and as for our content it has had no effect at all. We already will not allow racist, sexist stuff on our own server."

These assurances are not likely to placate some politicians, however. Indeed, in terms of "questionable content" VICNET's position appears somewhat precarious. Speaking on the floor of the Victorian parliament on 24 November 1995, K. M. Smith noted, "I can get on the screen a depiction of adults in various sexual positions. That was accessed from the internet through VICNET. We are able to do that because it is considered acceptable for adults to see other adults having sex. I have some problem with that." In short, by minimizing, and perhaps even dismissing their function as gatekeepers, VICNET staff members fail to acknowledge the inherent contradictions in their position as information intermediaries.

VICNET's criteria for determining what constitutes inappropriate content are rather nebulous: editorial guidelines are conspicuously absent from VICNET's pages. In the absence of clearly determined parameters, one must assume that content restrictions are based upon the professional judgment and personal tastes of VICNET's editorial board. These biases are perhaps less pronounced, but no less profound than those of overtly partisan organizations and institutions. Indeed, the decidedly quixotic manner with which VICNET represents the state of Victoria has not been lost on VICNET users.

As an ex cop I would say that I believe we have a very good community, but then when I was on the job I only seemed to see the worst, but that seems to have lost itself and I only seem to see the good things now.

It is a very exclusive community if one regards it this way – available only to the rich and technologically informed. I find it a very sterile environment.

It is carefully politically correct.

My main concern...is that non-indigenous people are publishing information about indigenous people without their permission.

VICNET was described to me as the public face of Victoria by a senior member of the Premier's department's computer section. That is what it is.

As these comments suggest, the state government's influence on VICNET rather paradoxically complicates and confounds VICNET's ability to represent the enormous diversity of experience in Victoria. The "public face" VICNET presents to itself and the world reflects the aspirations and embodies the biases of the state's intellectual and political elite.

In this respect, VICNET's articulation of Victoria stands in stark contrast to two of three preceding case studies. Whereas WFHB tends to gloss over differences within Bloomington, DCTV and *Street Feat*'s cultural politics highlight the often strained, highly contested nature of community relations in New York City and Halifax respectively. VICNET's ability to faithfully represent Victoria is constrained in a fashion roughly analogous to the condition discussed in Chapter 3. Dependent upon listener-support and local business underwriting to sustain its efforts, WFHB depicts Bloomington as a cooperative, harmonious socio-cultural haven free from ethnic, racial, and class-based antagonisms. The "depoliticized" view of Bloomington espoused by WFHB limits rather than enlarges the range of voices, interests, and concerns articulated through community radio.

Ironically, then, by assuming the role of intermediary between disparate information sources (i.e. the government, schools, social service organizations, political action groups) and the greater Victorian community, VICNET "imagines" Victoria in an alarmingly sectarian fashion. Furthermore, the preponderance of government, social-service and other quasi-governmental information suggests that VICNET does little to promote an open and ongoing exchange of ideas and opinions amongst the general populace. The electronic forum VICNET provides is unusually quiet. For instance, the VICNET Soapbox – a site where users are invited to speak their piece on virtually any topic – is literally devoid of comments. Moreover, VICNET's own mailing lists, *com-vic* and *vicnet-users* – forums for VICNET users to communicate with each other – are similarly silent, save for the occasional posting from a VICNET staff member. When I commented on this, Adrian Bates quipped: "Yes vicnet-users has not been the hotbed of discussion we would have liked." At first glance, then, VICNET's success as an electronic forum is questionable.

Many of the views presented on VICNET's pages reflect those of "traditional" and "official" information sources. For example, the Issues page features synopses of current events and contemporary social issues. For the most part, the opinions expressed on these pages are those of government officials or the mainstream press. Discussions and analysis of current events and contemporary social issues are predominantly government reports and electronic versions of editorials appearing in local and national periodicals like the *Daily Telegraph*, *The Weekend Australian* and the *Sydney Morning Herald*. In many respects, this situation is reminiscent of news and public affairs programming at WFHB. As noted in Chapter 3, WFHB embraces "traditional" news-gathering practices which favor official sources and are founded upon time-honored, but suspect notions of journalistic objectivity. The adventurous, innovative approach WFHB takes to its music and arts programming has failed to materialize in the area of news and public affairs.

Crucially however, VICNET does make sure other perspectives are available. Groups like the Acland Street Residents Association, Gun Control Australia, and the Mullers and Packers Union Homepage, to name but a few, appear alongside links to the Premier's Drug Advisory Council Report and press clips from the major dailies. In this respect, VICNET's approach to news and public affairs recalls that of DCTV and *Street Feat*. In Chapter 4, we observed DCTV's predilection for transmitting news, information, and opinion from marginalized and decidedly non-traditional sources. Similarly, *Street Feat* provides an outlet for the views and perspectives for economically marginalized populations throughout Halifax to speak their piece and present the general public with thoughts, views, and perspectives largely absent from other news outlets. Unlike mainstream media, then, which cater exclusively to official sources like government officials, business people, and other "opinion leaders," VICNET does provide a vehicle for citizens groups and political action committees to raise issues and voice concerns on a variety of topics that are often neglected, minimized or trivialized by the dominant media. The implications for this are best summed up by one survey respondent who observes, "there is a much wider range of views 'out there' than represented by the media [and] when given a 'space' even extremist 'loonies' can argue cogently and convincingly."

Moreover, by providing easy access to local, national, and international newsgroups and mailing lists, VICNET allows users to interact with people from across town, throughout the country and around the world. For instance, through the Melbourne newsgroup (melb.general), city residents get a sense of what their neighbors are thinking. One of my informants noted: "The themes discussed on the [local issues] newsgroup have ranged from the Grand Prix to the Gun debate over the last six months. This online discussion group is one part of VICNET that I often browse, it reflects the opinions and mood of the community and therefore helps give people a sense of community." Moreover, by mounting information from community-based organizations and other special interest groups, VICNET encourages individuals to learn more about pressing social issues that have local, national, and international relevance.

For instance, the Youth Affairs Council provides a debate page called "Spit It" where participants discuss a range of topics including education, job training for young people, and youth suicide. The InfoXchange, an online community information network that pre-dates VICNET, maintains a Victoria-based mailing list related to issues of affordable housing and homelessness. Finally, recog-l is a lively information resource and discussion list documenting the struggles associated with the reconciliation movement. Acting as monitor of the federal government's deliberations on indigenous peoples' rights, recog-l subscribers share personal narratives and insights, circulate press clips and critique mainstream media coverage, and actively promote aboriginal rights in Australia and abroad. These lists represent a venue to voice dissent and a vehicle to promote coherent, collaborative efforts within and well beyond Victoria.

For Stuart Hall, this is the most dynamic, if not the most crucial dimension of VICNET: "It is aimed at relieving the fragmentation of modern society by providing ways for people to communicate with one another." In this light, VICNET is not seen as a substitute for social intercourse, nor is online community necessarily superior to, nor more desirable than, place-based community; rather, this electronic environment serves as an adjunct to enhance social interaction throughout Victoria. For example, one anonymous subscriber recalls:

When I noticed a Filipino web page was set up on VICNET, I contacted the creator of the page to congratulate him on his efforts. Twelve months later, he and I along with other like-minded individuals have ... initiated a people-based network of professionals. It is our hope with this network of people to aid each other with our various fields of expertise.

Clearly, then, the wealth of information and opinion available through VICNET serves to articulate the significance of local, regional, national, and global relations in a dramatic and undeniably profound way. At times, these relations of significance are forged into relations of solidarity, as in the case of local/global labor and human rights struggles. This is not to suggest, however, that VICNET unproblematically and unequivocally reduces alienation and relieves social fragmentation. VICNET certainly has the potential to exacerbate existing social-political imbalances and dissolve social cohesion, especially at the local and regional level.

Even in the most advanced industrial societies access to information technologies is limited to a financially secure and well-educated minority. Victoria's online community reflects this tendency. Moreover, with the bulk of Victoria's telecommunication infrastructure centered in and around Melbourne, rural Victorians may be hard pressed to gain access to information networking. Unless initiatives like VICNET are truly successful, the gap between those with access to information technologies and those without will surely intensify societal tensions and continue to fragment Australian society.

Furthermore, as another anonymous survey respondent suggested, with national and international information simply "a hot link away" VICNET users may ignore local information, altogether, or forge relationships with people far removed from the local community. To the detriment of place-based community, then, VICNET promotes the establishment of communities of interest irrespective of physical proximity and regardless of national borders. As one subscriber notes, "I don't have a real sense of VICNET's being a community, my sense of community is with the discussion groups I access through VICNET, both of which are US based, with some participation in Britain." Like the other community media initiatives profiled in these pages, VICNET must negotiate tensions within the local community as well as those associated with the interpenetrations of encroaching regional, national, and global forces.

Human bandwidth

Despite VICNET's considerable efforts to provide free and low-cost access to computer networking, the range of "voices" on VICNET is quite narrow. The profile of VICNET users obtained through the online survey suggests a relatively homogeneous user population. Apart from some obvious drawbacks,[12] the online survey instrument nonetheless permits some insight into the demographic makeup of VICNET's user base as well as some remarkable insight into the nature of electronic data collection.

For example, I was struck by the surprising number of responses I received during the first week my survey appeared on VICNET. By the end of the second week responses began to trickle in and all but dropped off completely by week three. This suggests several things. First, the "novelty" of the survey's presence on VICNET's homepage may have worn off after a short time. Alternatively, users may bypass VICNET's homepage altogether and go directly to specific pages on VICNET's site. Of course, without corroborating evidence, I have no way of knowing if these are plausible explanations. But I note with great certainty that this sort of online interaction elicits a curious mixture of candor and reticence.

The survey's impressive rate of return stands in stark contrast to the brevity of the actual responses. Rather involved open-ended questions covering a range of topics consistently received one and two sentence responses. And yet, despite their initial reserve, the majority of respondents gave me explicit permission to contact them directly with follow up questions. Some responses were guarded: for instance, asked to share anecdotal accounts of online experience, one respondent said, "The word 'share' troubles me. Couldn't we just talk about this?" Other responses were quite cordial and suggested a surprising sense of immediacy and authentic human contact as exhibited by the following message: "I think there is a need for more advertised free entry points (libraries, community house etc.) but I'm confident they're+ working+ on it t... Soory my son has just joined the survey+."[13]

On the other hand, many respondents provided rather vivid self-portraits. One gregarious gentleman wrote: "I'm a twenty four year old male, a failed University student. I work for the government (but that's not going to be my career (I hope), I'm in a band (my career? I think not). I like TV, books, and falling down drunk." Another, making note of my Indiana University affiliation, informed me that he was an alumnus. "I attended Indiana University in the mid 60s and played basketball as a freshman student. I lived in Foster Quadrangle which was the 'jock' dorm at the time.... if you contact me Kevin, let me know what happened to the IU basketball team last year."

Most significantly, however, the picture that emerges from survey responses suggests that an overwhelming majority of VICNET users have considerable computer-related skills and formidable information networking experience. The following comments are indicative of VICNET's highly educated, technologically sophisticated user population.

I began writing computer programs in 1972.

20+ years on mainframes, minis, LANS, WANS.

14 years experience with PCs and minis running networks of up to 20 machines.

As a specialist reference librarian I am an experienced online user.

I completed a first year computing subject at La Trobe University, and a Graduate Diploma in Information Services in 1987. Since then I have worked constantly with computers, as Information Services and IT Support person in an organisation with 40 staff.

This evidence suggests that VICNET simply provides an alternative means for the "information rich" to access computer networks, rather than a viable option for the vast majority of Victoria's population with little or no computer skills to access online information.

This condition is not unique to VICNET. Indeed, it reflects the glaring contradictions of many community media initiatives, especially those in industrial societies or within well-to-do communities. While these organizations are nominally inclusive of the entire community, philosophically committed to egalitarian principles, and wholly dedicated to participatory forms of media production, distribution, and management, community-based media are oftentimes dominated by individuals and groups with a substantial measure of economic, symbolic, and cultural capital (i.e., education and skills level, prestige, and aesthetic sensibilities). For those segments of the overall population without these "prerequisites," community media are rather obscure, inconsequential, and largely irrelevant institutions. In this respect, community-based media sometimes marginalize those very same underserved constituencies they purport to serve.

VICNET staff members are neither unaware of, nor unconcerned by this situation. As Editorial Manager Gary Hardy notes, VICNET personnel are cognizant of the rather formidable task that confronts them. "I think the real challenge is to get access to as many people as possible – especially the fringes – which is about 60 per cent of our society – women, non-English speakers, rural, young, old, disabled . . . increase the human bandwidth." To this end, VICNET employs a number of strategies designed to enhance and promote equitable and affordable access to Victoria's emerging electronic environment. As we shall see, however, these efforts are constrained by various economic, technical, social, and political factors.

In order to fulfill its mission VICNET provides public access terminals in libraries, community centers, and neighborhood houses across Victoria. In large measure, these terminals are VICNET's most visible, and certainly most tangible feature. This is profoundly ironic, however, considering the dearth of public terminals throughout the state. For instance, VICNET's headquarters in the historic state library building in downtown Melbourne houses a scant eight terminals. Due to the overwhelming demand for these machines, patrons are advised to book their requests in advance via telephone. What's more, these sessions are limited to thirty minutes. Public libraries throughout the state likewise restrict online time. With few exceptions, the majority of libraries across Victoria have but one or two terminals each. Increased demand for network access, coupled with a lack of hardware and on-site support staff seriously compromises VICNET's accessibility.

Indeed, considering the enormity of VICNET's task, and the tremendous fanfare associated with the project's ambitious and high-minded aims, it is unsettling to note that in late 1996 there were fewer than 100 public terminals throughout the entire state. Moreover, these terminals were, according to Adrian Bates, "situated about two-thirds in the city and one-third in rural Victoria." Thus, the scarcity of public access terminals throughout Victoria is exacerbated by their wildly uneven distribution around the region. In sum, the disproportionate diffusion of information technology is evident not only throughout Victoria's social strata, but across the state's geographic landscape as well. This situation aggravates the library's burdensome task of promoting computer literacy throughout Victorian society.

That said, VICNET has embarked on a number of initiatives designed to bring computer technology and training to wider publics across the state. For instance, working with Informit, RMIT's commercial arm, VICNET has developed training courses and materials to acclimate new users to VICNET and the Web. A two and a half hour training program provides a brief social history of the Internet followed by an intensive hands-on training session. Patrons learn how to use Netscape, surf the web, access Internet Rely Channels (IRC, commonly referred to as chat channels), read and post messages on electronic bulletin boards, and use electronic file transfer and remote log-in procedures (telnet). Hard pressed to meet the challenge of teaching computer novices to make effective use of CIT and productively navigate an electronic environment, VICNET has forged relationships with a number of training organizations. While most participating organizations are VICNET accredited, many of these services are fee based. As a result, individuals and groups interested in computer training but short on cash are once again left out of the information loop. Moreover, these training centers are concentrated in and around Melbourne, further isolating regional Victorians.

In an effort to offset the burden this condition places upon library facilities and staff, VICNET provides public terminals in community centers across the state. For instance, the Duke Street Community House in Melbourne's Sunshine neighborhood is not unlike other neighborhood houses throughout Victoria. In many of Victoria's economically depressed and racially mixed communities, neighborhood houses provide essential services for low-income groups and individuals. Duke Street serves recently arrived immigrants from such disparate regions as Vietnam and Greece with ESL classes, job training, and employment referral services and for working families, low-cost childcare.

With VICNET's assistance, Duke Street has a unique opportunity to promote computer literacy for constituencies largely absent from the on-line population. Duke Street's adult literacy classes integrate computers into the curriculum, providing students with valuable reading, writing, and computer-based skills. In a supportive and non-threatening environment, first-time users become acclimated to a variety of software applications and computer networking procedures. More important, perhaps, local residents, students, volunteers, and house participants gain a greater sense of belonging and solidarity through their electronic publishing endeavors.

Working collaboratively on the house's web pages, Duke Street members have constructed what they lovingly refer to as a "higgledy-piggledy site." Struck by the glaring inconsistency of their web presence, staff and residents had considered coming up with a standard Duke Street look. Upon some reflection, however, this approach was abandoned. Instead, the patchwork quilt look was embraced. Duke Street's pages are "inconsistent" by design. According to Duke Street's online newsletter, "The site reflects the work of a severely under-resourced community grappling to come to terms with this technology. It is a diverse site and it will stay that way. We have realized that we should be proud that it represents diversity and that it encourages a broad spectrum of people to participate."[14] This candid self-appraisal reflects a truly collaborative approach to learning, self-determination, and self-expression. In the midst of slick, high-concept pages, Duke Street's web presence is refreshing for its candor, playful abandon, and respect for difference.

In this respect, VICNET's efforts are reminiscent of the outreach programs described in Chapter 4. Like DCTV, VICNET provides technical and logistical support to local non-profit organizations in order to promote the use of communication technologies by disenfranchised individuals and groups. Alarmingly, however, the low-cost network connections VICNET provides to neighborhood houses – ostensibly for increased public access in local neighborhoods – are rarely used for such purposes. According to Adrian Bates, "VICNET has supported a lot of these centres and some offer access but normally [computer time is] charged as they need to make money." As such, the provision of computer terminals in community houses might be seen as a rather cynical effort on the part of the state government to make up for the economic austerity measures which in recent years have dramatically reduced state and federal social service spending.

Indeed, placing public access terminals in neighborhood houses appears to be a rather hypocritical way for the state government to make localities more self sufficient. For some observers, then, VICNET's access provisions are not merely inadequate, they are somewhat disingenuous. As one anonymous social services worker notes, "VICNET seems a good place to hang stagnant pages but it costs an hourly Internet rate to access. This is therefore a barrier for most low income earners or agencies funded (usually poorly resourced) to work with those people."

Despite the enormous constraints on VICNET's ability to provide equitable and affordable access to information technologies, there is evidence to suggest that VICNET has engendered greater participation in Victoria's emerging online environment. As the following comments suggest, VICNET represents the extraordinary possibilities of computer-mediated communication for enhancing local social interaction and, rather remarkably promoting a larger, global conversation which acknowledges and often celebrates difference while paradoxically, and rather profoundly proclaiming commonality.

I repeatedly come across people who have been down the road for many years but only through discussion groups have we found each other.

I feel part of the community because I am aware of the changes and developments made in the community. I may not take an active role in these changes but the mere awareness of these developments gives me a sense of belonging.

A few weeks ago VICNET was promoting a new page for the Victorian Hungarian community. As I am of Hungarian background, but not involved with the community, I would never have found out about the site otherwise.

I'm now in contact with 2 guys I knew in London 20 years ago.

An IT firm in a small town in the north of Finland contacted me to ask if they could use our web page in a seminar for woodworkers in their town to explore uses of information technology. . . . A woodworker in Sacramento, California used our page to answer a question on Australian timber for a woodworker living in Tasmania!

I've experienced the "global village" effect of websites and email – e.g. completing this survey.

These comments suggest VICNET's enormous potential for increasing an awareness of one's own community as well as facilitating greater understanding of those people and places far beyond Victoria's borders. VICNET encourages Victorians to (re)discover the distinctive qualities of their neighborhood, region, and state, to renew old friendships and affiliations, and to forge new relationships with people down the street and around the planet. Moreover, VICNET engenders a collaborative spirit and a search for common ground despite enormous cultural differences and regardless of vast geographic distances.

Undeniably, then, VICNET promotes a level and intensity of social intercourse unique to most forms of electronic media. Surely increased access to computer-mediated communication will reinvigorate civic involvement throughout greater Victoria, revitalize local communities across the region, and engender widespread interaction between distant and distinctive individuals and groups. Or will it?

Participation, policy, and pragmatism

The phrase "If you build it, they will come" is a rather naive, if not specious prescription, especially when ascribed to community computer

in the design and implementation of the system have a sense of ownership. They are no longer merely recipients of technology; rather they are stakeholders in the system, committed to building, maintaining, and enhancing the system's integrity and its viability.

VICNET's top-down approach to community networking inhibits localized forms of participation in Victoria's emerging online environment. In large measure, VICNET's public service orientation denies the importance of local collaboration in the design and development of the network. Leaving VICNET's decision-making process to information specialists, technicians, librarians, and other "experts" fails to realize community networking's full potential as a participatory medium (Schuler 1994).

Clearly, Victorians are participating in some fashion. Electronic forums encourage Victoria's growing online community to participate in any number of discussions and debates. Web page development and other forms of electronic publishing likewise inspire individual and collective self-expression. What's more, by promoting local and regional events (e.g., music and arts festivals, volunteer opportunities, public demonstrations, and political actions) Victorians get a better sense of who they are, how they can get involved, and how they might make a difference. However, without greater public involvement in VICNET's policy making, management, and design decisions, a crucial element of community networking is lost: participatory democracy.

As noted earlier, VICNET operates under the auspices of the directors of the state library and the RMIT library. Furthermore, VICNET's advisory board is drawn from the ranks of public library administration, local government, and the computing and telecommunications industries. Conspicuously absent from VICNET's board are individuals without government affiliations or technical expertise. Community organizers, political activists, social services personnel, and others have no say in VICNET management. Rather, groups and individuals make suggestions, address concerns, and "inform" policy in an ad hoc fashion. As one VICNET staff member puts it, "There is no direct individual/community involvement in VICNET management, but there is a lot of interaction. Informality has worked so far." In short, only those with some measure of "expertise" have direct influence over organizational policy. Undoubtedly, this arrangement "streamlines" VICNET's decision-making process by avoiding lengthy and sometimes contentious deliberation. Crucially, it also serves to insulate VICNET from the sort of public involvement that makes a community-based organization more accountable to local constituencies and more flexible in meeting the community's needs.

The Community Networking and Skills Development (Skillsnet) program appears to address some of these concerns.[16] An integral component of the state government's Victoria 21 initiative – a statewide effort to "ensure that all Victorians – regardless of age, income, education, gender, race or place of residence – have access to the new Information Superhighway and other online resources, backed up by the necessary training and education to enable them to use it effectively" – the project seeks to enroll community organizations, social service agencies, and local businesses in the development of community information resource centers. By 2000, VICNET helped establish over one hundred community computer centers across Victoria through this competitive grant program.

The Skillsnet initiative works this way. Community organizations interested in establishing a community computer center are invited to apply for either Level 1 or Level 2 funding: $100,000 and $10,000 respectively. Grant recipients may use the funds for equipment installation, telecommunication costs, hardware and software, training, promotional efforts and outreach programs, and consultation services. The Skillsnet initiative hopes to integrate information technologies into local communities across Victoria by promoting the use of new media, providing a range of online services, and establishing extensive training programs. The project's ultimate goal is to establish a network of community-based information resource centers throughout regional Victoria. In this regard, then, the Skillsnet program seeks to empower local communities with improved and enhanced access to information technologies. Moreover, by encouraging local participation in the development of this new community-wide resource, there is a measure of local autonomy in determining the shape and character of the local center.

Significantly, projects receiving the top dollar amount must meet a rather curious condition. In order to receive Level 1 funding, submissions "must show a significant component which is internationally competitive or capable of gaining international recognition." The Skillsnet (http://www.vicnet.net.au/~skillsnet/) project is therefore yet another illustration of the contradictory impulses behind community computer networking initiatives. Ostensibly designed to promote local and regional information capabilities and competencies, the Community Networking and Skills Development project has a decidedly global orientation.

VICNET's attempts to create an electronic environment that is relevant, accessible, and participatory are certainly paradoxical. These efforts highlight the dynamic and conflicting forces which shape the character of place-based and virtual communities alike. Equally important, the VICNET initiative suggests the manner in which local communities are being reoriented away from regional and national allegiances toward global interactions and relationships. These competing local, national, and transnational forces influence VICNET's character and determine the role it plays in Victorian society. Nowhere are these tensions more evident than in the realm of Australian telecommunications policy.

VICNET's most formidable obstacle comes from an unlikely source: the government-owned telephone company, Telstra. Ironically, Telstra's market dominance confounds VICNET's ability to serve its constituencies. VICNET's editorial manager, Gary Hardy, notes:

Basically one of the largest hurdles in our way is the telecommunications over-charging and charging structure in Australia – idiot things like timed calls for people living within a few miles of population centres, and massive overcharging on ISDN [Integrated Services Digital Network] (not to speak of rotten service, slow installation etc. . . .) it seemed that the Federal Government did show some signs of tackling these – but they have adopted a narrow economic rational-ist line now, and seem interested only in propping up Telstra so that they can sell it.

As noted in Chapter 2, regulatory regimes once predicated on public service moved to deregulate media industries throughout the 1980s and 1990s. And indeed, since 1989 the Australian federal government has embarked on an ambitious course to liberalize (i.e. privatize) Australian telecommunications. For example, AUSSAT, the Australian national satellite service, was sold outright to Optus Communications, a consortium of US and UK telecommunications firms who each hold 24.5 per cent ownership. Majority ownership is in the hands of domestic investment companies.[17] Despite vehement objections from the Australian research community, the federal government granted Telstra de facto ownership of the Australian backbone (AARNet). Initially a university run research network, the AARNet's nodes are no longer housed at Australian universities, but in Telstra's facilities. These so-called "reform" efforts were designed to increase domestic competition in order to drive the development of the nation's telecommunications infrastructure. Needless to say, the efficacy of the government's efforts are debatable; Telstra has consolidated its holdings and continues to dominate the Australian telecommunications industry.

As a result, VICNET has found it necessary to forge strategic alliances with commercial ISPs throughout Victoria in order work around Telstra's inadequate and costly regional service. In this regard, the commercial service provider Access One has proven to be a valuable ally for Victoria's network. Despite VICNET's pragmatism in dealing with conditions which threaten to undermine its goals, new developments, again stemming from the deregulations described above, may seriously endanger VICNET's universal service aims. On 24 March 1997, the Australian parliament passed legislation that allowed Telstra to charge for timed data calls.

While residential customers were not affected, as of 1 July 1997, businesses were billed accordingly. Specifically, with the Australian Senate's approval of Telstra's timed call request, the only recourse left to Australian Internet users was to protest through online campaigns. These efforts were all that stood in the way of Telstra's goals.[18] This strategy threatens to cripple Australia's burgeoning ISP industry, and may well compromise VICNET's future as well. Faced with exorbitant charges from Telstra, ISPs will inevitably pass those charges on to their customers. These increased rates will likely widen the gap between those who can and those who cannot afford Internet access. Like other ISPs VICNET lost a significant number of subscribers.

According to some observers, Telstra's motivations are twofold. First, Telstra's timed data calls will in all likelihood force smaller ISPs out of business, effectively removing competition to Telstra's recently inaugurated Big Pond Internet service. Second, Telstra's increased profits from timed data calls and its so-called "Big Pond" venture will enhance Telstra's attractiveness to private investors, many of whom are foreign-owned telecommunications corporations. Incredulously, the Australian federal government appears willing to decimate one of its major growth industries, the ISP and computer-related service sector, in order to attract foreign investment in the government-owned telephone company. Here, then, the Victorian state government and the Australian federal government appear to be working at cross purposes. With the state government's support, VICNET has sparked the development of computer-related services across Victoria. However, the federal government's legislative support of Telstra's efforts threatens domestic entrepreneurialism and is specifically and unambiguously designed to attract foreign investment in Australia's national information infrastructure.

This condition suggests a radically different orientation for Australia's telecommunications industries. For years, Australian public service media have operated on the assumption that these services would foster a sense of national unity by promoting and preserving Australian cultural sovereignty. In an era of global markets and multinational corporations, government initiatives like VICNET on one hand, and the sale of Telstra on the other suggest an entirely new trajectory for public service organizations. Rather than promote a unified Australian identity, these institutions are subtly and not so subtly redirecting local populations toward international markets and global identities.

Telecommunications have played a vital role in Australia's social, cultural, and economic development. A sparsely populated, culturally diverse, and geographically isolated island-nation, Australia has made effective use of electronic media to engender social integration across the continent, throughout the Pacific Rim, and around the world. Equally important, these industries have facilitated the development of an autonomous Australian national identity and helped forge a distinctive Australian culture. As Australia's communications center, the state of Victoria acts as a bellwether for the nation.

Therefore, Victoria's Network (VICNET) provides a glimpse into recent developments in Australia's media industries and insight into future trends in Australian telecommunications policy. More important for our purposes, VICNET represents a dynamic site to interrogate the paradoxical relationship between community and communication in an increasingly global media environment. As noted throughout this discussion, the advent of computer-mediated communication holds enormous opportunity to further integrate Victorian society on a local, national, and global level. (Not surprisingly, given the continent's geography, Australians are among the heaviest users of the Internet.) However, these developments might also exacerbate social-political inequities within Victorian society and undermine local, regional, and national autonomy. These tensions are evident in the growth and development of VICNET.

VICNET seeks to create an online environment which reinvigorates civic participation, reflects and celebrates Victoria's multicultural heritage, and facilitates local cultural production and economic development. VICNET promises to alleviate the fragmentation of contemporary Australian society by providing all Victorians with equitable and affordable access to computer networking. In this way VICNET encourages "ordinary people" to voice their opinions, share their ideas, challenge official policy, mobilize public opinion, and debate contentious, often divisive, social-political issues.

In addition, VICNET has embarked on an ambitious program to collect and disseminate a wealth of information by, for, and about the state of Victoria. In so doing, VICNET hopes to preserve and enhance Victoria's cultural autonomy. Moreover, through its affiliation with the state library and the RMIT, VICNET allows constituencies who have been marginalized by recent technological developments to take part in the construction and maintenance of this virtual encyclopedia of Victorian information. Furthermore, by promoting electronic publishing across the state, VICNET stimulates economic development in computer-related industries. In the wake of high unemployment and economic stagnation throughout Victoria, VICNET has been a catalyst for entrepreneurism in this profitable and increasingly competitive growth industry.

Still, large segments of the Victorian populace are being left behind in the rush to create online communities through VICNET. As a result, the disparities between information haves and have nots threatens to further polarize Victorian society. Moreover, the unprecedented ease with which Victorians can access people and places far beyond Victoria's borders may diminish the level and quality of social interaction throughout greater Victoria. Perhaps most alarmingly, VICNET's global presence attracts a level of foreign investment which serves to reduce, rather than strengthen Victorian economic autonomy. In essence, VICNET's appeal to community spirit, social cohesion, and a common identity obscures the network's role in confounding communal relations, obfuscating local identities, and problematizing local sovereignty.

Conclusion

> A community will evolve only when a people control their own communications.
>
> Frantz Fanon

Across the globe, in post-industrial and so-called "developing" societies, in large urban centers and small rural villages, through grassroots organizing efforts and in collaboration with NGOs and international aid agencies, communities are working to remake media systems that serve local interests, address local concerns, and otherwise shape, reflect, and inform local experience. In some cases, communities turn to radio – arguably the most affordable, easiest to use, and by far the most ubiquitous form of electronic media around the world – as a means of enhancing community communication. For other communities, the advent of small-format and, more recently, digital video cameras provides an occasion for local populations to more fully participate in contemporary media culture: a built environment increasingly dominated by the image-making regimes of multinational corporations. Still other groups and individuals, dissatisfied with conventional press reports on poverty, homelessness, and economic justice, construct alternative discursive spaces through the printed word and in so doing create community among those who, quite literally, live on the margins of society. Conversely, computer-mediated communication represents an opportunity to re-create local community, paradoxically enough, within and through an emerging global information infrastructure.

Despite the disparate peoples involved, the distinctive communities to which they belong, and the particular motives behind their appropriation of communication technologies, the impulse to "communicate community" appears irresistible. Community media, therefore, provide an exceptional site of cultural analysis to consider the fundamental, yet enigmatic relationship between communication and community: a relationship that stirs the popular imagination and stimulates academic debate. Moreover, when we consider these locally oriented, participatory

258

media organizations in the context of likeminded efforts to reform existing media institutions and practices or otherwise construct more responsive, responsible, and egalitarian media systems, community media are deeply implicated in an emerging global struggle for communicative democracy.

With this in mind, this final chapter brings together the preceding case studies in an effort to illustrate commonalities and differences between what I have characterized as popular and strategic interventions into media culture. Doing so, I want to revisit some of the theoretical perspectives and analytical insights discussed in the introductory chapters and to foreground community media's relevance to contemporary social and cultural theory. I begin with a few observations regarding the role communication technologies play in articulating community in each of the four settings described above. Here, I note the decisive role communication and information technologies play in coordinating cooperative efforts between community media organizations across the globe, and for that matter, how these technologies helped to realize this study. I conclude with some thoughts, inspired by the lasting influence of communication and literary theorist Raymond Williams, on the cultural significance and local currency of community media in an increasingly global communication context.

Articulating community media

In the introduction, I observed the centrality of communicative forms and practices to community building and maintenance. Whilst my analysis foregrounds the symbolic construction of community, I do not dismiss the importance of place nor neglect material relations of power, which likewise shape, inform, and define community. Rather, by drawing on the concept of articulation outlined by Stuart Hall and other cultural studies practitioners we have seen how community media organizations challenge essentialist notions of community by underscoring the constructed, contested, and contingent character of these social formations. Throughout, I have suggested that by using this theoretical framework, we can better appreciate the central role communication plays in distinguishing communities by containing difference within unity while simultaneously forging a shared collective identity. Furthermore, each of the case studies demonstrates how locally oriented, participatory media systems are fashioned out of strategic social alliances operating under particular historical and cultural conditions.

For instance, in Chapter 3 we noted how local musicians, sound technicians, and audiophiles conceived a vision of community radio in Bloomington, Indiana. Long associated with adventurous musical

expression, the city of Bloomington nevertheless had few broadcast outlets that would support, encourage, and nurture the local music scene.
This vision of vibrant, lively, and locally oriented radio went unfulfilled
for nearly two decades as a group of dedicated media activists – Jeffrey
Morris, Jim Manion, and Brian Kearney, among others – struggled to
overcome the formidable economic, political, and bureaucratic obstacles
to community broadcasting. However, were it not for the support of local
business leaders, a generous patron of the arts, and one enlightened and
well-connected university administrator, the struggle to establish community radio in Bloomington, Indiana might have been lost. Thus, a series
of strategic alliances was born between media activists, local business interests, university officials, and countless numbers of listener supporters
who helped the people of Bloomington find a spot on the dial.

Just as community radio in Bloomington, Indiana was inspired by
broader socio-cultural trends and tendencies – most notably the tradition of community broadcasting associated with Pacifica Radio and
the student and counterculture movements of the late 1960s and early
1970s – the inspiration for New York City's Downtown Community Television was "in the air" as artists and activists began to explore the expressive and communicative potential of a new technology: the video
portapak. For Jon Alpert and Keiko Tsuno, portable video represented
a powerful tool to support their community organizing efforts. What's
more, by leveraging the intimacy and immediacy afforded by the portapak, DCTV empowered local communities with access to television
technology and in so doing, helped cultivate cross-cultural communication within and between the racial and ethnic enclaves of Manhattan's
Lower East Side.

Taking television directly to the people, Downtown Community Television encouraged local residents, gang members, community activists, and
recent immigrants to remake television in their own image. Through public demonstrations, media education, and community outreach, DCTV
made television relevant to the everyday lived experience of local populations. And, as noted in Chapter 4, these outreach efforts were critical to
DCTV's success and longevity. Formally, DCTV's emphasis on participatory production techniques helped shape the organization's signature
"video verité" style – an innovative approach to television form and content that helped redefine televisual aesthetics and to carve out a space for
independently produced, community-oriented journalism on US public
and commercial network television. Equally important, DCTV's self-
financed outreach projects soon found enthusiastic supporters among local and state arts organizations, the city's educational and social services
sector, as well as equipment manufacturers who appreciated DCTV's

rigorous "field testing" of their latest production gear. Viewed in this light, DCTV's cultural politics are realized not simply through a new technological apparatus, but by a constellation of players, institutions, and socio-political and cultural practices.

Working in the service of marginalized individuals and groups, *Street Feat* likewise promotes community communication within and between disparate socio-economic groups who call Halifax, Nova Scotia home. By confronting readers, in print as well as in person, with material written by, for, and about the poor and needy, *Street Feat* enhances the public's awareness of the interdependent character of community relations. The brainchild of homeless advocates Michael Burke and Roberto Menendez, *Street Feat* is supported by donations from charitable organizations, including the Catholic Archdiocese of Halifax and Hope Cottage Community Enterprise, as well as sporadic grants from the provincial government of Nova Scotia.

Through its monthly publication of news, information, and critical commentary, *Street Feat* creates a discursive space for the homeless, the poor, and the working poor. In this way, *Street Feat* challenges common sense assumptions, legitimated through and propagated by local news outlets, about poverty and the poor. Equally important, *Street Feat* provides some, albeit limited economic opportunity for those living in poverty. As such, *Street Feat*'s modest, but nonetheless forceful intervention into the "politics of exclusion" is realized within and through alliances between social service organizations, homeless advocates, antipoverty activists, and of course, the economically impoverished writers, contributors, and vendors who produce and distribute the publication.

Whilst the provincial government of Nova Scotia's support for *Street Feat* has been intermittent at best, the state government of Victoria, Australia enthusiastically pursued an ambitious economic redevelopment plan with VICNET, a community computer network, as its centerpiece. Here we can detect the varied, sometimes competing motives of disparate players involved in creating a formidable community information infrastructure. For legislators and equipment manufacturers, VICNET leverages the state's cultural and linguistic diversity in an attempt to attract foreign investment and "jumpstart" the regional economy. Others, most notably librarians and information technology specialists, including Adrian Bates, Gary Hardy, and Stuart Hall, envisioned VICNET as a tool to enhance communication within and between disparate peoples and cultures and to promote a shared sense of identity among Victorians.

Each in its own way, then, *Street Feat* and VICNET seek to create capacity and economic opportunity, albeit on a dramatically different scale and scope. Equally important, however, by putting communication technologies at their disposal, *Street Feat* and VICNET provide local populations, especially those with limited access to the tools and techniques of media production, with an opportunity to express their opinions, perspectives, and experiences to wider publics, thereby asserting their claim to community.

Looking across each of the case studies, we can detect a correspondence between the particular and distinctive articulations of people, places, and communication technologies and the novel, but no less exceptional manner in which each organization communicates community. Consider, for example, WFHB's status as a community broadcasting service. Media scholars have long observed broadcasting's ability to summon dispersed individuals into a listening or viewing public, or national community of sorts (Scannell 1996). Addressing the medium's community-building capacity, Roger Silverstone notes that radio's "transmission for that audience of a range of schedules, narratives and highly charged events that together provided, for those who were willing to listen, the symbolic framework for participating in the community" (1999: 100). Following a tightly structured and rigidly timed program schedule, WFHB broadcasts music and arts programs, poetry modules and newscasts, nationally syndicated and locally produced public affairs programming with a regularity and consistency that provides listeners with the "symbolic raw materials" communities use to express, define, and sustain collective identity (100).

In contrast to WFHB's principal focus on music and cultural offerings, DCTV's formidable reputation has been made in the realm of news and long-form documentary. Indeed, DCTV's emphasis on documenting the everyday lived experience of so-called "ordinary people" represents a dramatic reversal of television's *place* in contemporary American society. Through its commitment to participatory production routines and techniques, DCTV decenters television, turning media consumers into media makers, and transforming the atomistic and isolating experience of television viewing into a communal event. In doing so, DCTV encourages local populations to use the medium for purposes of creative self-expression, critical reflection and analysis, and community organizing. Not content to simply record events or transmit the news, DCTV's affinity for the "committed documentary" vividly demonstrates people's capacity to make a difference in their own lives and the lives of their communities.

For its part, *Street Feat* replicates the form and content of the tabloid newspaper, complete with feature reports, community calendars, advice columns, exposés, and, of course, letters to the editor. In addition, *Street*

Feat occasionally publishes creative non-fiction, poetry, and prose. By adapting a familiar form and using it to publicize, that is to make knowable and comprehensible, the human cost of economic injustice, *Street Feat* explodes myths, stereotypes, and other forms of media bias – what anti-poverty activist Jean Swanson (2001) refers to as "poornography" – that help legitimate social, economic, and political relations of domination and subordination. Like other street papers, then, *Street Feat* at once creates a parallel or alternative discursive space for the poor while working to reintegrate the homeless and the impoverished into the wider community.

This desire for connection, for communion, and for a shared sense of fellowship and belonging is less visible perhaps, but every bit as evident in the so-called virtual communities of cyberspace. Ostensibly designed to facilitate and enhance community communication locally, VICNET allows users to enter into social relations with people a world a way. Tellingly, however, this will to "go global" within and through community-based media is not unique to VICNET or community networking in general, for that matter. What makes VICNET distinctive, insofar as the other cases are concerned, is the sheer scale, scope, and intensity of local/global interaction. That is to say, although VICNET users have unprecedented access to far-flung people, events, and cultural forms and artifacts this same impulse is obvious in WFHB's enthusiastic support for world music, DCTV's commitment to intercultural communication, and *Street Feat*'s solidarity with international anti-poverty campaigns and global peace and justice movements.

Before moving on to a final consideration of community media's global appeal and cultural significance, I call attention to the vital role communication and information technologies play in facilitating cooperative efforts within and between community media initiatives. As I completed the preparation of this manuscript, I learned that WFHB planned to broadcast the National Homeless Marathon on 12 February 2004. Now in its sixth year, the fourteen-hour marathon to "voice the silent struggle of the homeless" is distributed to public and community radio stations via satellite and broadcast quality webcasting technologies. Although this marks the first year WFHB has aired the event, community stations across North America have coordinated their efforts to "simulcast" the live broadcast.

Similarly, community radio stations across the globe are using computer and information technologies to coordinate a 21 March 2004 broadcast in commemoration of the International Day for the Elimination of Racial Discrimination. Sponsored by Radio Voix San Frontieres (Voices Without Frontiers) and AMARC, community radio stations from

North America, Latin America, Asia, Africa, and Europe are participating in this worldwide campaign for social justice and civil rights. These complex collaborative efforts are thus made far easier to coordinate and have become increasingly commonplace, thanks in large part to computer-mediated communication. Likewise, this study could never have achieved its global dimension without the cooperation of distant community media workers made "present" through electronic mail, listserves, search engines, and websites. All of which serves to underscore the notion discussed at length in Chapter 2 that community media provide a fruitful site to explore the complex social, economic, political, and cultural dynamics of globalization from the perspective of local communities.

Knowable communities: articulating the local and the global

I close with a reference to the late Raymond Williams: a presence that, in his words, persists and connects with the arguments I have been advancing. Throughout much of his writing, either as a central theme or a more general subtext, Williams illuminates a structure of feeling that permeates modern society – a profound sense of loss of and an equally profound yearning for community – and links this condition directly to a problem of communication. Using Williams' conceptual frameworks and analytical insights I want to underscore the theoretical and practical importance of the cultural analysis of community media I advocate. Equally important, by invoking Williams' passionate commitment to mutual recognition and common understanding, I hope to emphasize the political urgency of this line of inquiry.

In an essay on the nineteenth-century English country novel Williams coins the phrase "knowable communities" to describe the distinctive approach of the novel, as a cultural form, in dramatically and forcefully revealing the character and quality of people and their relationships. Tracing the historical development of the novel, Williams observes the increasing difficulty of this task – a challenge confronting not only the novelist but also the whole of society – in the wake of the profound social, economic, and political transformations associated with the Industrial Revolution. Williams notes:

identity and community became more problematic, as a matter of perception and as a matter of valuation, as the scale and complexity of the characteristic social organization increased. . . . The growth of towns and especially cities and a metropolis: the increasing division and complexity of labour; the altered and critical relations between and within social classes: in changes like these any assumption of a knowable community – a whole community, wholly knowable – became harder and harder to sustain.

(1973: 165)

At the dawn of the twenty-first century, the scale and complexity of social organization grows ever more unwieldy. Indeed, the developments in transportation and communication technologies that once engendered the formation of the "imagined communities" (Anderson 1991) of modern nationalism challenge the nation-state's ability to contain and control the movement of people, goods, and services, thereby fundamentally altering social relations within and between nations and making the possibility of realizing a knowable community ever more remote. Not surprisingly, then, the crisis of community and identity that Williams observes in English literature of the eighteenth and nineteenth centuries is apparent in a number of contemporary social movements and cultural formations: religious fundamentalism, ethnic nationalism, and, I would argue, a growing global interest in community communication.

Then as now, the solution to this crisis of community and identity in an increasingly complex and interdependent world is not simply a matter of transmitting information; rather, the significance of relations between people and their shared environment must, according to Williams, "be forced into consciousness" (165). Here then, in a discussion of the English novel, Williams develops a theoretical perspective that views modern communication as an important and necessary cultural response to the increased complexity of social organization and the attendant problems of individual and collective identity. And yet, in his analysis of mass communication systems proper, Williams finds the content of modern communications a poor substitute for direct observation and interaction.

Significantly, this inadequacy is not simply nostalgia for some lost ideal of face-to-face community, nor is it merely a problem of technology or technique; rather, it stems from a mode of production: the minority ownership of communication systems. For Williams, this mode of production is a perversion of communicative practices in that it encourages exclusive access to the instruments of mass communication and the one-way transmission of information: information that promotes a shared, though limited and uneven consciousness in the support of systems of domination (1983). Williams concludes that by serving the narrow and particular interests of a relative few, this prevailing – but by no means inevitable or unalterable – condition ultimately corrupts a necessary and vital resource for a vibrant culture and a democratic society.

Throughout this book, I have argued that community media represent an important, if imperfect, corrective to this condition. Furthermore, drawing on Williams' formulation, I suggest that community media serve to create knowable communities in much the same way as the novel. Like the fiction of Charles Dickens, whom Williams singles out for his genius in revealing the "unknown and unacknowledged relationships, [and] profound and decisive connections" (1973: 155) between people of the city, community media articulate the significant and decisive relationships within and between community members. That is to say, by providing a venue for individual and collective self-expression, community media make knowable not only the enormous variation of people, interests, and relationships within a locality, but also, critically, the commonalty and interrelatedness of these individuals, groups, and concerns. In this way, community media engender a two-fold recognition of difference and significance: a new awareness of belonging to and responsibility toward the community.

Equally important to Williams' notion of the knowable community are the varied and multifaceted subjective impressions of community life. "For what is knowable is not only a function of objects – of what is there to be known. It is also the function of subjects, of observers – of what is desired and what needs to be known. . . . it is the observer's position in and towards it; a position which is part of the community being known" (Williams: 165). Here, I would argue, community media are superior to the knowable community of the novel in one important and decisive way. For while the novelist may take great pains to capture and convey the attitudes and perspectives of disparate community members, the writer can never faithfully inhabit a subject position other than his or her own. Despite the considerable talents of the novelist, then, as a cultural form, the novel has serious shortcomings in this respect. On the other hand, by giving voice to individuals of different social classes, racial and ethnic affiliations, lifestyles, and generations, community media make available the unique interpretations and subjective impressions of community life from a multiplicity of alternative perspectives. Community media therefore create a shared consciousness within and among community members who voice their concerns, express their hopes, communicate their needs, and share their experiences.

With this in mind, I maintain that community media recover an ancient but enduring quality of communication that has been historically, but not irrevocably displaced by market-oriented approaches to communicative forms and practices. Community media do this by embracing a perspective that vehemently rejects minority ownership of communication systems and adopts a different attitude to transmission, one which will ensure that its origins are genuinely multiple, that all the sources have access to common channels. This is not possible until it is realized that a transmission is always an offering, and that this fact must determine its mood: it is not an attempt to dominate, but to communicate, to achieve reception and response.

(1983: 316)

Not only is this approach vital for creating and sustaining knowable communities on a local level, it suggests new configurations for appreciating the cultural dynamics of globalization. Indeed, community media rather forcefully undermine the binary opposition of the categories of "local" and "global" in two discrete, but interrelated ways. First, by historicizing and particularizing the penetration of global forces into local contexts, community media undermine normative or nostalgic ideals of local communities as insular or discrete formations that until recently were uninfluenced by extra-local factors and conditions. Rather, by preserving popular memories, celebrating local cultural traditions, and tracing the movement of various groups into local neighborhoods, community media vividly demonstrate the influence extra-local forces have had, and continue to exert, on the formation of local identities and cultures. Moreover, by appropriating and indigenizing disparate cultural forms and practices, community media deflect fears of an emerging, homogeneous global culture. In this way, community media are an important aspect of the process of local adaptation to foreign cultural traditions, practices, and artifacts.

Second, by embracing the notion that communication is an offering, an effort to share and celebrate, rather than an attempt to command and dominate, community media contribute local cultural forms and expressions to the matrix of translocal interactions that characterize the present era. In other words, community media make a substantial, but often overlooked contribution to the endless stream of variation and diversity of cultural forms and practices around the world.

All of which suggests that community media represent an important site to illuminate the interpenetrations of local, regional, and national cultures within and through communication technologies. Hence, a sustained, multiperspectival analysis (e.g. Kellner 1997) of community media of the sort I advocate here engenders a more nuanced understanding of the dialectical relationship between the local and the global. Indeed, in light of the universalizing discourses of globalization and the perceived threat of cultural homogenization, community media dramatically demonstrate the particular and multidimensional nature of collective identity in the modern world. In this respect, then, the study of community media can make significant contributions to social and cultural theory.

Furthermore, by treating community members as citizens, not as consumers, community media foster a greater awareness of the interdependent nature of social relations and shared environments both locally and globally. For instance, community media provide a resource for a host of social, political, and environmental movements to increase local awareness of these pressing issues and, significantly, a vehicle to link these local issues with global concerns (Downing 1991). In this way, community media engender a global consciousness of sorts. Clearly, this is not the monolithic or totalizing consciousness popularized by Marshall McLuhan – an attitude embraced by transnational corporations in their desire to conflate consumer ideology with the principles of social justice and political democracy. Rather, it is an emerging, critical awareness of the profound and decisive connections between peoples and localities in an increasingly interconnected and interdependent world: what Doreen Massey (1993) has described as "a global sense of the local." In this light, community media can be understood as contributing to the creation of global villages: communities of significance and solidarity that recognize difference and acknowledge mutual responsibility on a local, national, regional, and global level.

Lest these remarks be taken as so much wishful thinking, I would suggest that they are no more romantic than the plethora of studies that suggest the emancipatory potential of resistant readings of popular television texts or the liberating possibilities of a trip to the shopping mall. Rather, I have argued that community media initiatives around the world are making a modest, but vitally important difference in the lives of local populations by enthusiastically affirming our individual and collective agency as cultural producers and political subjects. Similarly, by acknowledging the value of diverse cultural expression, encouraging local forms of cultural production, and rejecting the rather staid and sterile form and content of mainstream media, community media contribute to a vibrant and challenging local cultural environment. Moreover, in confirming the ability of local populations to effectively utilize the instruments of mass communication, community media belie the notion that use of communication and information technologies is best left to a handful of economic and technical elites. Most important, however, by recognizing and affirming local populations as citizens first and foremost, community media encourage political participation and civic engagement in the life of local communities.

And yet, as noted throughout this discussion, community media initiatives are imperfect; these institutions and practices are replete with contradictory impulses and tendencies. For the cultural analyst, then, community media represent a host of theoretical problems concerning democratic processes and cultural politics. But community media invite much more than critical investigation. As one of the few remaining vestiges of participatory democracy, community media demand the active engagement of media intellectuals whose expertise can inform and enhance the vital work of these organizations and help maintain and secure a dynamic resource for cultural production and democratic processes (Rosen 1994).

In this way, community media represent both a unique opportunity and a formidable challenge. On the one hand, community media permit analysts to interrogate the dynamics of global media culture in a local context. On the other hand, community media require cultural analysts to reconsider their celebratory tone and commit themselves, as intellectuals and as community members, to creating viable alternatives to the culture industries and promoting a more democratic media culture. If cultural studies is to recapture its social and political relevancy, scholars must resist the temptation to equate semiotic democracy with political democracy and temper theoretical excess with practical interventionism. Community media initiatives invite cultural scholars not only to test their theoretical propositions in particular and distinctive contexts but also to contribute their analytical insights to the everyday lived experience of their local communities.

Notes

Introduction

1 For a discussion of qualitative methods appropriate to the study of community media, see Jankowski, N. (1991) 'Qualitative Research and Community Media', in N. Jankowski and K. B. Jensen (eds) A *Handbook of Qualitative Methodologies for Mass Communication Research*, London: Routledge, pp. 163–174.

Chapter 1

1 Culled from footage recorded by hundreds of media activists, two videotapes produced by the Seattle Independent Media Center (IMC) "Showdown in Seattle" and "This is What Democracy Looks Like" vividly demonstrate the dynamic relationship between community media organizations, independent journalists, and the emerging "indy media" movement.
2 Like the 1996 Telecommunications Act, this legislation was crafted by private concerns, most notably by representatives of the software and electronic publishing industry, over strenuous objections from public interest groups like the Digital Future Coalition (DFC) and representatives from a host of library associations, including the American Library Association, the American Association of Law Libraries, as well as the Association of Research Libraries (Reply Comments of the Library Associations, 5 September 2000).
3 Although Sony's first attempt to realize the benefits of synergy with the 1993 release of Last Action Hero was a financial disaster brought on by a culture clash between "hardware" experts from Japan, marketing executives from New York, and "software" producers in Los Angeles, Sony has, rather profitably, refined its project development strategy.
4 Adorno and Horkheimer's Frankfurt School colleague, Paul Lazarsfeld, went to work as administrative researcher for radio industry. This work focused on areas of prediction and control and quantitative audience studies.
5 Nick Couldry makes a related argument for alternative media. See his 'Mediation and Alternative Media: Or Reimagining the Centre of Media and Communication Studies,' Paper presented to the ICA preconference 'Our Media, Not Theirs,' 24 May 2001.
6 A rather telling exception to this condition came during the 1991 Persian Gulf War. Unable to compete with their counterparts in broadcast and cable

television, US public television actively sought out the work of community producers for timely and topical programming related to the conflict. This short-lived, but nonetheless significant occasion indicates that the work of community producers is not only relevant to local populations but that such programming can in fact attract a national audience.

Chapter 2

1 Although industry and congressional opposition eventually gutted the FCC's measure, among policy makers former FCC Chairman Kennard was a vocal proponent of LPFM.
2 For a comprehensive historical account of the British governments' response to the demand for local radio, see Lewis and Booth, 1990, pp. 89–114.
3 For a detailed, first-hand account of these efforts, see the Irish Era website developed by Jack Russell http://dxarchive.blackpool.ac.uk/eire.html
4 For complete information regarding AMARC's guidelines, see http://amarc .org/amarc/ang/
5 From the outset, then, cable access television operated under greater scrutiny and with more thorough restrictions than either the BBC or IBA.
6 Over the years, *Street News* has changed ownership several times. And on more than one occasion, it looked as if the paper might fold altogether. For instance, in 1995, just when the paper appeared to be making a comeback, the Metropolitan Transit Authority (MTA) passed a regulation prohibiting vendors from selling *Street News* on the city's subways. As a result, *Street News* lost up to 70 percent of its readership (Leone 1995; McAllister 1995).
7 In all but one illustration of the synergies and close relationships that have developed between community media organizations and the independent media movement of the late 1990s, the San Francisco Independent Media Center (IMC) published ongoing accounts of NASNA's direct action campaign.
8 Presently, there are regional editions of *The Depths* published in Siberia and Ukraine.
9 Here, I am referring to the so-called "cyber-fiction" associated with William Gibson's *Neuromancer*.
10 Active in research and policy analysis, the Benton Foundation also helps support technology initiatives that seek to enable "communities and nonprofits to produce diverse and locally responsive media content" (Benton Mission Statement). For more information, see www.benton.org.

Chapter 3

1 The phrase "sound alternative" was used in promotional literature published by Bloomington Community Radio (BCR) and used for fundraising purposes throughout the late 1980s.
2 The media watchdog group FAIR produces "*CounterSpin*." The thirty-minute weekly show features news, interviews, and media analysis. *Making Contact* is a weekly radio program aired across the United States and around the world.

Produced by the National Radio Project, *Making Contact* provides an outlet for independently produced investigative radio reports.

3 Michael White is Director of Bloomington Community Access Television Services (CATS). For a short time, White also served on the WFHB board of directors.

4 In 1816, the Indiana State Constitution established a general system of education and made provisions for the establishment of state-sponsored colleges and universities.

5 In 1828, an act of the Indiana State Legislature formally changed the name of the State Seminar to Indiana College. Ten years later, the legislature again changed the institution's name to Indiana University.

6 Bedford and Bloomington are part of the "stone belt" – a rich deposit of limestone – that runs throughout southern Indiana. In addition to connecting these two stone-producing locations, the Monon's stops included some of Indiana's finest colleges and universities, including Indiana University (Bloomington), DePauw University (Greencastle), Wabash College (Crawfordsville), and Purdue University (Lafayette).

7 Wells' middle name is "B" and not an abbreviation or initial; hence the unusual punctuation.

8 In 1951, television interference problems of the sort that would confound the establishment of a noncommercial, community radio station in Bloomington led WFIU to move its broadcast frequency from 90.7 FM to a portion of the commercial broadcasting band, 103.7. WFIU's call letters stand for "From Indiana University."

9 Writing in his memoirs, Herman B Wells recalled the Book Nook as "a remarkably fertile cultural and political breeding place in the manner of the famous English coffee houses."

10 Indeed, south central Indiana has long been a refuge for writers and artists. In the early nineteenth century, the town of Nashville, Indiana, some twenty miles southwest of Bloomington, was established as an artists' colony.

11 In one particularly moving sequence, rare in American film for its candid depiction of class disparities, the young protagonist's father relates his feelings of inadequacy and resentment over the recently completed IU Library. In his mind, he and his fellow workers who removed the stone from the earth and gave it shape are somehow deficient and unwelcome to make use of the impressive structure they helped to create.

12 NARK was the predecessor of the National Federation of Community Broadcasters (NFCB), an organization dedicated to promoting and supporting community radio throughout the United States. According to the NFCB, "Nearly 20 years ago on a hot, muggy day in Madison, Wisconsin, in the basement meeting room of the YMCA, a small group of visionaries and counter culture types gathered to ponder the future of community radio." NFCB – Yesterday and Today. [online resource] http://soundprint.org/~nfcb/mission.html

13 In homage to the roots of Bloomington's community radio movement, Morris played selections from Bar-B-Q records during test broadcasts over WFHB's frequency 91.3FM. Morris recalls, "When we had the construction permit, but we weren't on yet, I rigged an antenna in a garage and put 91.3 on the air for a couple of hours. [Laughs] with the 250 watt transmitter and played some old Bar-B-Q records. [Laughter] Called up Jim and blew his mind."

14 According to Manion, one of the more esoteric factors leading to the name change was an attempt to disassociate the initial project, CRP, with the infamous Committee to Re-elect the President (CRP) associated with the Nixon Administration and the Watergate scandal.

15 Since joining the station, I had heard this seemingly apocryphal story many times. Not until the station's tenth anniversary celebration at the Buskirk-Chumley Theater, hosted by longtime WFHB programmers "Tall Steve" Volan and D. James, did I hear the recording of this historic event.

16 As noted earlier, WFHB's broadcast tower is located some eleven miles southwest of downtown Bloomington. As a result, reception in the heart of the city over 91.3FM is problematic. The translator alleviates this problem. However, in order to continue to accommodate the austere conditions imposed on WFHB's signal strength due to the aforementioned Channel 6 interference issues, the main transmission signal at 91.3 has been reduced from 2500 watts to 1600. Although the station welcomed improved reception downtown, the reduction in signal strength outside of town reduces listenership and therefore denies the station potential revenue from listener supporters living on the outskirts of town.

17 In response to copyright concerns surrounding enactment and reinforcement of the Digital Millennium Copyright Act, WFHB, along with hundreds of community, college, and noncommercial stations, pulled the plug on their web streaming in 2001.

18 For a lively discussion of free form radio, see Steve Post's account of his work at WBAI, the Pacifica Radio affiliate in New York City. Post, S. (1974) *Playing in the FM Band: A Personal Account of Free Radio*, New York: Viking Press.

19 In the station's internal music programmer guidelines as well as its promotional materials, including the station's website, WFHB program philosophy is summed up this way: "Welcome to the world of free-form community radio, WFHB, from deep in the heart of downtown Bloomington, Indiana. You'll hear a different sound on WFHB, a broad mix of eclectic musical styles, music chosen by our volunteer music programmers. The key to our lively and unique air sound is having volunteer music programmers with a passion for many musical styles and giving them the freedom to explore their own segued path through it."

20 WFMU-FM from Jersey City, New Jersey is one of the more "tradition bound" free form stations still in operation.

21 One notable exception to this is the Old Time Train program, produced by long-time WFHB host "Colonel" Mike Kelsey. Ostensibly a "specialty" program highlighting bluegrass, mountain, and "old time" music, "Old Time Train" frequently features in-studio guests, skits commercial parodies, and the exceptional story telling of occasional co-host Arbitus Cunningham.

22 An outspoken proponent of locally oriented, participatory radio, Milam is sometimes referred to as the "Johnny Appleseed" of community radio in the United States. For more on Milam's anarchist-flavored approach to community radio see his rambling, yet remarkably lucid tome *Sex in Broadcasting*.

23 Gaal, an attorney and Bloomington City Council member, is a long-time supporter of community radio. He currently serves on the station's Board of Directors.

24 A recent addition to WFHB's public affairs schedule is a case in point. BloomingOUT is a first of its kind radio broadcast specifically for members of the gay, lesbian, bisexual, and transgender community of south central Indiana. The program was launched not long after the city of Bloomington announced its "gay-friendly" tourism initiative, known around these parts by the motto: Come Out and Play.

25 Neher is one of several WFHB volunteers who have taken on paid positions in local media outlets. Neher is the co-host of *The Afternoon Edition*, a local call-in show, on AM1370 WGCL.

26 This perspective appears to have evolved over time. In its early promotional literature, BCR promised listeners much more than music. As the station sought community support, various "mock programming schedules" included significant amounts of news and public affairs programs as well as locally produced educational, children's, and spoken word offerings. While these different forms have some, albeit quite limited space on WFHB's program schedule, music is unmistakably the station's principal focus.

27 In addition to its acquisition of syndicated news and public affairs programming, WFHB broadcasts a number of nationally syndicated music, culture, and arts programs, including *E-Town*, *Putumayo World Music Hour*, *Euroquest*, and *On Your Health*. Undoubtedly, these programs are popular with local listeners. Likewise, they take away resources from locally produced programs.

28 At the time of these deliberations, *Democracy Now!* was available at no cost for a six month trial. DN! is delivered via C-band satellite or, via broadcast quality MP3 computer files.

29 It is Manion's stated position that he will no longer respond to messages posted online. Moreover, the spot_online now operates as a "moderated list," which means that messages must be approved by the list administrator, General Manager Ryan Bruce, before being posted to all subscribers. Only station management can use spot_online for broadcast messages. The station's other, less populated list, The Kennel remains an "open forum."

30 Over the past ten years or so, Bloomington's independent press has suffered several major setbacks. The *Bloomington Voice*, later known as the *Bloomington Independent*, went under in late 2001. Since that time several new start-ups, including *The Pinup* and most recently *The Bloomington Free Press*, have come and gone. Independent journalism with a genuine community focus has but one outlet in Bloomington these days, *The Bloomington Alternative*, available electronically, and therefore out of reach of many residents who do not have Internet or computer access.

31 Higgs has been a guest on *Interchange* to discuss local and national news events. However, he has not yet been invited to contribute his talents and expertise to the local newscast.

Chapter 4

1 Ironically, at the time the museum was holding an exhibition on controversial programming in US broadcasting. Divided into six discrete topics – ethics, censorship, violence, politics, race, and social issues – the series

"offers historic and contemporary instances of censorship and contentious programs."

2 In this last instance, much of the historical detail included here draws on Mario Maffi's *Gateway to Paradise* (1995), an encyclopedic yet eminently readable analysis of the cultural dynamics of Lower East Side.

3 The contemporary names of these streets are, respectively, Worth, Baxter, and Mosco.

4 The brainchild of David Luxton, the TV Lab sought to provide an institutional base for less conventional television producers and work within the flagship station of the emerging US public broadcasting sector.

5 Video historian Dierdre Boyle describes street tapes this way: "Many tapes made by the early portapakers frequently fell under the heading of 'street tapes,' although not all street tapes were made on the street, living rooms and bedrooms being popular locations. But the intense social, political, and cultural flux of the late 60s provided comedy and drama right on the corner. Hangin out on New York's Lower East Side and rapping with young people – drug tripping hippies, sexually liberated young women, erstwhile revolutionaries, cross-country wanderers, bums, winos, and other characters – provided great spontaneous material found literally on one's doorstep" (1997: 8).

6 Here, I am using the phrase "dialogue tape" in the same fashion employed by the members of the National Film Board of Canada (NFBC) who championed the Fogo Process briefly described in Chapter 2.

7 For an exceptional discussion of the politics of video arts instruction, see two essays by media activist and scholar John Higgins: "Night of the Broadcast Clones" and "Critical Video Pedagogy" in the *Journal of Film and Video*.

8 George Stoney observes that a large portion of the financial support his Alternative Media Center (AMC) received from the Markle Foundation directed the AMC's efforts toward lobbying and legislative efforts aimed at creating public access television in Manhattan.

9 Rather than "roll in" this footage shot with a video portapak, the black and white images were shot off a studio monitor for a local afternoon magazine program over Channel 5 in New York, then a Metromedia television outlet.

10 Within a few years, video became integral to artists and community groups living and working in Chinatown, and in other Chinese neighborhoods throughout the city. By 1975, New York City was home to dozens of groups producing video exclusively for Chinese audiences.

11 Keiko Tsuno recounts the following story of the baby carriage: "Fidel Castro noticed us at the end of an entourage of reporters. He must have thought, 'Who are those strange looking people with the baby carriage?' So he came over to us and asked, 'What is that?' and Jon said, 'A baby carriage.' Fidel gave us a look like 'Duh! I can see that.' Jon was too scared to ask any questions and Fidel just smiled and walked away. Jon couldn't sleep that night because he had let us down. We said we wouldn't work with him again if he didn't show some courage. The next day, Jon almost tackled Fidel to get an interview" (History of DCTV 1999). This seemingly apocryphal story turns out to be quite accurate, as evidenced by the videotape record of the first of many encounters between DCTV and Fidel Castro. The interview is striking inasmuch as Castro's comments are unedited and seemingly unscripted.

The Cuban leader's candor – noteworthy as much for the warm and generous greetings he extends to American viewers as it is for his incisive criticism of US foreign policy – is testament to Alpert's willingness to approach Castro as he would a neighbor, a worker, or a homeless person. "We interviewed him [Castro] the same way we used to talk to people on street corners. When you're talking to someone in the neighborhood you don't treat him like an important person, but just as an interesting guy" (Daviss: 32).

12 For instance, Alpert and Tsuno pestered Vietnamese officials for months before they were allowed to visit the war-torn country. According to Alpert, the Vietnamese were particularly impressed with DCTV''s earlier work, most notably, *Chinatown* (1975).

DCTV's entrepreneurialism and unwillingness to take no for an answer have helped opened doors for the independent producers in China, Iran, Nicaragua, and other "hot spots" around the world.

13 The tape is a stunning indictment of US military tactics in the Persian Gulf War. Particularly disturbing are images that document the fallacy of Pentagon claims that so-called "smart bombs" lead to a significant reduction in civilian casualties. Indeed, the tape demonstrates the toll the US air war had on local populations and civilian infrastructure. Equally important, the tape is a powerful condemnation of US journalism's failure in reporting this important story (see Project Censored 1991).

14 Thanks in large measure to the unique relationship between DCTV and CBS *Early Show* producer Steve Friedman, formerly of NBC's *Today* show and *NBC Nightly News*, portions of this documentary have since run on the *Early Show*. The tape was aired in its entirety on the Canadian national broadcasting service, CBC and Japan's NHK.

15 In 1984, Goodman struck out on his own and established the Educational Video Center (EVC). Like DCTV, EVC is a non-profit media arts organization that provides high school students with the tools and techniques of video documentary. For more on Goodman's work and his approach to video literacy, see "Teaching Young People Video."

16 DCTV is currently exploring the interactive potential of streaming technologies in the Cyberstudio through a service called *ConnecTV*, a program geared toward providing media access to people with disabilities.

Chapter 5

1 Hope Community Enterprises is a non-profit community development enterprise operating under the auspices of the Catholic Archdiocese of Halifax as part of its "social action mandate."

2 Here, I am drawing on John Dewey's distinction between referential and interpretive communication. See Daniel Czitrom's *Media and the American Mind* (1989) Chapel Hill, NC: University of North Carolina Press.

3 Like other political action groups around the world, The Halifax Initiative calls for more transparency and accountability from national governments and from inter-governmental organizations such as the International Monetary Fund (IMF), the World Bank, and the World Trade Organization (WTO).

4 As I was preparing my first draft of this chapter, I learned that Juan Carlos was being recognized for his important community work with an award from the Centre.

5 *Street Feat*'s production and distribution schedule is haphazard. *Street Feat*'s intermittent publication record stems from a variety of factors, not least of which are the shortage of production personnel and Juan Carlos Canales-Leyton's formidable task of pulling together each issue with little to no editorial assistance.

6 Located on the outskirts of Halifax, Africville suffered long-term neglect before the neighborhood was razed by urban development in the 1960s. Despite the community's lack of economic and physical infrastructure, Africville was a much-loved neighborhood.

7 According to published reports in *Street Feat*, the previous incarnation of the Spare Change Program failed on several counts. To begin with, donations fell flat shortly after the program was introduced. This failure was due in part to inadequate marketing efforts. Indeed, many people found this public relations campaign offensive. Promotional materials featured a panner's entreaty to prospective donors "Spare a quarter (for a can of Lysol)? plainly suggesting that panhandlers were little more than hard-up substance abusers. See Peter McGuigan, "Spare Change for Real Change," *Street Feat* 2(5) (May/June 1995).

8 Renovations at Hope Cottage were delayed several times. The first came from administrative delays due to the amalgamation of Halifax into the HRM. The second delay came when the newly formed municipality conducted an archeological study of Hope Cottage and the surrounding property as required for all renovation projects in and around historic properties.

   The case of the Metro Turning Point was quite different. Following pressure to go after local slumlords, the city government was embarrassed into keeping its own house in order. The city-run Metro Turning Point was cited numerous times for health code violations. Plans to relocate the shelter were then stalled by the predictable NIMBY (Not In My Back Yard) response by local homeowners. Despite the fact that the new Metro Turning Point would help eliminate "The Jungle," a parcel of land that was a haven for prostitution and drug abuse, residents balked at the idea of putting a homeless shelter in their neighborhood.

9 I first met Izzy on the morning of Wednesday, 12 September 2001. During our long conversation on Spring Garden Road, Izzy's empathy and compassion for me, a visiting American reeling from the previous day's terrorist attacks, moved me greatly.

10 During the course of my eight-week participant observation at *Street Feat*, I helped out with general office work, ran errands, learned basic newspaper production and layout design, wrote copy, and answered the phones. One afternoon, I answered a phone call from a concerned reader, who took exception to a small, box ad for one of the city's most elegant and expensive restaurants. As best I could, I assured the caller that the restaurant owner was well-known throughout Halifax's philanthropic community as a sincere and compassionate man whose personal and professional integrity is beyond reproach.

Chapter 6

1 VICNET's home page is *http://www.vicnet.au*.
2 VICNET's mission statement listed on "Welcome and About VICNET" page. Available at: *http://www.vicnet.net.au/vicnet/vicn.htm* (15 May 1997).
3 See VICNET Project proposal. Available at: *http://www.vicnet.au/vicnet/abtvic.htm* (15 May 1997).
4 Significantly, this comment and all those made by parliamentarians were accessed through VICNET's link to the Victoria's Hansard database. Thus, in keeping with the civic networking model described in Chapter 2, VICNET provides users with unprecedented access to government records and databases, thereby providing the potential for greater civic engagement in local and state government.
5 Informit publishes electronic databases on CD-ROM and over the Internet. One of the largest electronic publishers of educational materials in Australia, Informit works with the world-renowned Silverplatter publishing corporation.
6 An integral part of my research design, the survey featured open-ended questions regarding user's attitudes toward and perceptions of VICNET. Survey respondents names are withheld to ensure anonymity. Correspondence with VICNET staff took place on an ongoing basis and all VICNET personnel are identified by name and title. Unless noted otherwise, responses are edited for spelling and grammar. Finally, I appreciate the assistance of VICNET's technical staff in the design, construction and maintenance of this survey instrument.
7 This is not to suggest librarians do not have vested interests in the new technologies. As more and more information is stored, processed, and disseminated electronically, libraries must adapt from print culture to the new digital environment in order to remain economically viable and socially relevant. Therefore, librarians have considerable personal and professional incentives to position themselves favorably in an emerging information economy.
8 Questions of originality and temporality are highly problematic in online historical research. Of particular concern for the historian in the case of digitalization of extant print materials is the loss of primary sources in an electronic environment. For a comprehensive discussion of these issues, see Kevin Schurer, "Information Technology and the Implications for the Study of History in the Future," in Rose and E. Higges, eds., *Electronic Information Resources and Historians: European Perspectives* (St. Katherine: Scripta Mercuturae Verlage, 1993).
9 For instance, an announcement of my research project was featured in the "What's New" section. The link included information regarding the nature of my project, a call for participation in my study, electronic research consent forms, and the online survey instrument. Other research projects have likewise been posted in this fashion.
10 "Introduction to the Aboriginal and Torres Strait Islander Page." [electronic resource] *http://www.vicnet.net.au/vicnet/koorie/intro.htm*
11 VICNET users who pay subscription fees for VICNET dial-in access receive 1 MB of storage space for their own homepage. Commercial websites are

fee-based. For more information on VICNET's Web Publishing Service and Guidelines see the VICNET Web Sites Page. *http://www.vicnet.net.au/websites/*

12 The survey is flawed on several counts. Certainly, individuals with limited access to computer networks are less likely to complete an online survey than users with home or workplace access. Likewise, users with significant skills are more likely to participate than novices struggling to achieve some measure of computer proficiency.

13 To capture the immediacy I mention, this response is unedited. Anonymous, personal communication 27 June 1996.

14 The Duke Street home page is *http://yarra.vicnet.net.au/~dukest/*

15 An interdisciplinary field of study, human-computer interaction concerns itself with the "design, evaluation and implementation of interactive computing systems for human use and with the study of major phenomena surrounding them." *ACM SIGGHI Curricula for Human-Computer Interaction* (New York: ACM Special Interest Group on Computer-Human Interaction Curriculum Development Group, 1992), 6.

16 Community Skills and Networking Project [electronic resource] *http://www.vicnet.net.au/~skillsnet/*

17 For a comprehensive discussion of recent changes in Australian telecommunications industries see Marina C van der Vlies, "The Transition from Monopoly to Competition in Australian Telecommunications," *Telecommunications Policy* 20.5 (1996): 311–323.

18 This information comes from a link on the Australian Internet Alliance homepage. This document provides useful information (especially for overseas users) to gain some insight into the Australian telecommunications environment.

References

Abernathy, J. (1995) 'Creating the PBS of the Internet', *PC World*, (Feb.), pp. 62, 64.

Abrams, J. (1978) 'Vietnam: A First Look', *TV World*, (5 May), p. 7.

Abu-Leghold, J. L. (1992) 'Communication and the Metropolis: Spatial Drift and the Reconstitution of Control', *Asian Journal of Communication*, 2(3): 13–30.

Achille, Y. and Miege, B. (1994) 'The Limits to the Adaptation Strategies of European Public Service Television', *Media, Culture and Society*, 16: 31–46.

Ackerman, S. (2000) 'Prattle in Seattle', *Extra!* Fair, [Online] Available at: http://www.fair.org/extra/0001/wto-prattle.html (3 March 2000).

Adorno, T. and Horkheimer, M. (1993) 'The Culture Industry: Enlightenment as Mass Deception', in S. During (ed.) *The Cultural Studies Reader*, London: Routledge, pp. 29–43.

Adrian, L. (1998) "The World We Shall Win for Labor": Early Twentieth-Century Hobo Self-Publication', in J. Danky and W. Wigand (eds.) *Print Culture in a Diverse America*, Urbana, IL: University of Illinois Press, pp. 101–128.

AMARC/IFEX (2000a) 'World Bank/IMF Deny Journalists Access to DC Meetings', (11 April), [Online] Available at: http://www.freeworldalliance.com/newsflash/pre_2002/newsflash174.htm

(2000b) 'Twenty-five IFEX Members Condemn IMF Press Policy on Community Media', (23 May) [Online] Available at: http://www.ifex.org/en/content/view/full/10516/

Anderson, B. (1991) *Imagined Communities: Reflections on the Origin and Spread of Nationalism*, London: Verso.

Ang, I. (1990) 'Culture and Communication: Towards an Ethnographic Critique of Media Consumption in the Transnational Media System', *European Journal of Communication*, 5(2–3): 239–260.

Appadurai, A. (1993) 'Disjuncture and Difference in the Global Cultural Economy', in B. Robbins (ed.) *The Phantom Public Sphere*, Minneapolis: University of Minnesota Press, pp. 269–295.

Atkinson, D. and Raboy, M. (2003) *Public Service Broadcasting: The Challenge of the Twenty-first Century*, Paris: UNESCO.

Atton, C. (1999) 'A Reassessment of the Alternative Press', *Media, Culture and Society*, 21(1): 51–76.

(2002) *Alternative Media*, London: Sage.

Aufderheide, P. (2000a) 'Grassroots Video in Latin America', in *The Daily Planet: A Critic on the Capitalist Culture Beat*, Minneapolis: University of Minnesota Press, pp. 257–273.

(2000b) 'Public Television and the Public Sphere', in *The Daily Planet: A Critic on the Capitalist Culture Beat*," Minneapolis: University of Minnesota Press, pp. 99–120.

Axtman, R. (1997) 'Collective Identity and the Democratic Nation-state in the Age of Globalization,' in A. Cvetkovich, and D. Kellner, (eds.) *Articulating the Global and the Local: Globalization and Cultural Studies*, Boulder, CO: Westview Press, pp. 33–54.

Bagdikian, B. (1996) 'Brave New World Minus 400', in G. Gerbner, H. Mowlana, and H. Schiller (eds.) *Invisible Crisis: What Conglomerate Control of Media Means for America and the World*, Boulder, CO: Westview Press, pp. 7–14.

(1997) *The Media Monopoly*, 5th edition, Boston: Beacon Press.

Bambarger, B. (1996) 'Breaking Away: Mysteries of Life, Vida, El Nino, Salaam blossom in Bloomington', *Billboard* (4 May), pp. 88–90.

Barber, B. (1995) *Jihad vs. McWorld: How Globalization and Tribalism Are Reshaping the World*, New York: Ballantine Books.

Barlow, W. (1988) 'Community Radio in the US: The Struggle for a Democratic Medium', *Media, Culture and Society*, 10(1): 81–105.

Barringer, F. and Sanger, D. (2003) 'Diplomacy: US Says Hussein Must Cede Power to Head Off War', *New York Times*, (1 March), p. A1.

Beamish, A. (1995) *Communities On-Line: Community-Based Computer Networks* http;//loohooloo.mit.edu/anneb/cn-thesis/html (28 January 2004).

Behl, N. (1988) 'Equalizing Status: Television and Tradition in an Indian Village', in J. Lull (ed.) *World Families Watch Television*, Newbury Park: Sage, pp. 136–157.

Bekken, J. (1998) 'Community Radio at the Crossroads: Federal Policy and the Professionalization of a Grassroots Medium,' in R. Sakolsky and S. Dunifer (eds.) *Seizing the Airwaves: A Free Radio Handbook*, San Francisco: A.K. Press, pp. 29–46.

Bell, J. (1990) *Halifax: A Literary Portrait*, Lawrencetown Beach, NS: Pottersfield Press.

Bibby, A., Denford, C. and Cross, J. (1979) *Local Television: Piped Dreams?*, Milton Keynes: Redwing Press.

Blanchard, C. (ed.) (1993) *Counties of Morgan, Monroe and Brown, Indiana: Historical and Biographical*, [Chicago: F. A. Battey] Reprinted Mt. Vernon, IN: Windmill Productions.

Boukhari, S. (1999) 'The Press Takes to the Street', *UNESCO Courier*, 52(2): 43–44.

Bourdieu, P. (1984) *Distinction: A Social Critique of the Judgment of Taste*, Cambridge, MA: Harvard University Press.

Bowen, W. (1996) 'Community Networks at the Crossroads', Mountain Area Information Network Available from: http://mainsrv.main.nc.us/about/cmtynet.html (22 December 2001).

Boyle, D. (1980) 'Who's Who in Video: Jon Alpert', *Sightlines*, (Spring), pp. 23–25.

(1992) 'From Portapak to Camcorder: A Brief History of Guerrilla Television', *Journal of Film and Video*, 44(1–2): 67–79.

(1997) *Subject to Change: Guerrilla Television Revisited*, New York: Oxford University Press.

(1999) 'O Lucky Man! George Stoney's Lasting Legacy', *Wide Angle*, 21(2): 31–40.

Brech, P. (2000) 'BBC's Frost Defends Branding Strategy', *Marketing*, (6 July), p. 9.

Brewster, M. (2001) 'N.S. Tops Fed Dependency List', *The Daily News*, (28 May), p. 3.

Browne, D. (1990) 'Aboriginal Radio in Australia: From Dreamtime to Prime Time?', *Journal of Communication*, 40(1): 111–120.

Buchanan, I. (2002) 'What Is Antiglobalization? I Prefer Not to Say', *The Review of Education, Pedagogy, and Cultural Studies*, 24: 153–155.

Bullert, B. J. (1997) *Public Television: Politics and the Battle over Documentary Film*, New Brunswick, NJ: Rutgers University Press.

Burke, M. and Menendez, R. (1997) 'The Launching of Street Feat', *Street Feat*, 1(1) (December), pp. 1, 3.

Burke, M. (1998) 'Welfare Reform: Should Nova Scotians Know Better?' *Street Feat*, 1(6) (May/June), pp. 6–7.

(1998) 'Soup Kitchens and Night Shelters: Halifax's Growth Industries', *Street Feat*, 1(8) (July/August) p. 3.

(1998) 'Street Feat Is One Year Old and It's Christmas Time', *Street Feat*, 1(12) (December), p. 3.

Calhoun, C. (1998) 'Revolution and Repression in Tiananmen Square', *Society*, 26(6): 21–38.

Canales-Leyton, J. C. (2001) 'The Mayor of HRM on Panhandling', *Street Feat*, 4(2) (March/April), p. 3.

Capshew, J. (n.d.) *Alma Pater: Herman B Wells and the Rise of Indiana University*, Available http://www.indiana.edu/~libarch/Wells/wellsbio.html (30 December 2003).

Carey, J. (1975) 'A Cultural Approach to Communication,' *Communication*, 2: 1–22.

Carpentier, N., Lie, R. and Servaes, J. (2003) 'Community Media: Muting Media Discourse?' *Continuum: Journal of Media and Cultural Studies*, 17(1): 51–68.

Carrothers, C. (2002) *WFHB News and Public Affairs Strategic Outline*, Bloomington, IN: Bloomington Community Radio.

Carvin, A. (2000) 'Mind the Gap: The Digital Divide as the Civil Rights Issue of the New Millennium', in E. Bucy (ed.) *Living in the Information Age: A New Media Reader*, Belmont, CA: Wadsworth/Thomson, pp. 251–254.

"Chantal." (1998) 'Living in Poverty: A Single Mother's View,' *Street Feat*, 1(6), (May/June) p. 3.

Charlton, J. (1998) 'Word on the Street: Are Newspapers for the Homeless Headed Towards the Mainstream?', *The Front*, [Online] Available at: http://www.montrealmirror.com/ARCHIVES/1998/081398/news7.html (27 August 1999).

Chomsky, N. (1989) *Necessary Illusions: Thought Control in Democratic Societies*, Boston: South End Press.

Chomsky, N. and Herman, E. (1988) *Manufacturing Consent: The Political Economy of the Mass Media*, New York: Pantheon Books.

Christensen, M. (1986) 'His Aim is True', *Rolling Stone*, (April), pp. 33, 36.

Cisler, S. (1994a) 'Community Networks on the Internet', *Library Journal*, 119(11): 22–24.

(1994b) 'Community Computer Networks: Past and Present Thoughts', *Ties That Bind: Building Community Networks*, Cupertino, CA: Apple Computer Corp. Library.

Civille, R. (1993) 'A National Strategy for Civic Networking: A Vision of Change', *Internet Research*, 3(4): 2–22.

Clark, A. (1999) 'Re-facing Gottingen: Creighton-Gerrish Development', *Street Feat* 2(3) (March/April), p. 8.

Coalition on Homelessness (n.d.) *Street Sheet*, [Online] Available at: http://www.sf-homeless-coalition.org/streetsheet.html (14 January 2004).

Cohen, A. (1985) *The Symbolic Construction of Community*, Cambridge: Tavistock.

Cohen, A. and Wolfsfeld, G. (eds.) (1993) *Framing the Intifada: People and Media*, Norwood, NJ: Ablex Publishing Corporation.

Cohill, A. and Kavanaugh, A. (eds.) (2000) *Community Networks: Lessons from Blacksburg Virginia*, 2nd edn., Norwood, MA: Artech House.

Collins, R., Finn, A., McFadyen, S., and Hoskins, C. (2001) 'Public Service Broadcasting Beyond 2000: Is There a Future for Public Service Broadcasting?', *Canadian Journal of Communication*, 26(1): 3–15.

(1980) 'Conversation with Jon Alpert and Keiko Tsuno', *Videography*, (September), pp. 54–69.

Conversations (radio broadcast) (1996) Bloomington, IN: WFHB (25 January).

Crabtree, R. (1996) 'Community Radio in Sandinista Nicaragua, 1979–1992: Participatory Communication and the Revolutionary Process', *Historical Journal of Film, Radio and Television*, 16(2): 221–241.

Croteau, D. (1994) *By Invitation Only: How the Media Limit Political Debate*, Monroe: Common Courage Press.

Curry, R. (1988) *Freedom at Risk: Secrecy, Censorship and Repression in the 1980s*, Philadelphia: Temple University Press.

Curtin, M. (1995) *Redeeming the Wasteland: Television Documentary and Cold War Politics*, New Brunswick, NJ: Rutgers University Press.

Cvetkovich, A. and Kellner, D. (1997) *Articulating the Global and the Local: Globalization and Cultural Studies*, Boulder, CO: Westview Press.

Das, M. (1996) *Free-Nets*. National Library of Canada, [Online] Available at: http://www.nlc-bnc.ca/9/1/p1-228-e.html (14 January 2004).

Davey, J. (2001) 'Guaranteed Free Access: A Look at Australian Community Television and Its Place in the Changing Media Landscape,' *Metro Magazine*, (133): 126–133.

Daviss, B. (1985) 'Window on the World', *Skylines*, (September) pp. 29–33.

Davitt, J. (1995) 'It'll Be All Right on the Net', *Times Educational Supplement*, (21 July 1995), pp. 27–30.

Devine, R. (2000) 'Access and Community Building', Presentation given at the Alliance for Community Media National Conference, Tucson, Arizona, (10 July 2000). Available at: Listserv Alliance Forum (24 November 2003).

Dizard, W. (2002) *Old Media, New Media: Mass Communications in the Information Age*, New York: Longman.

Douglas, S. (1987) *Inventing American Broadcasting: 1899–1922*, Baltimore: Johns Hopkins University Press.

Dovey, J. (1995) 'Old Dogs and New Tricks: Access Television in the UK', in T. Dowmunt (ed.) *Channels of Resistance: Global Television and Local Empowerment*, London: BFI, pp. 163–175.

Dowmunt, T. (2001) 'Dear Camera: Video Diaries, Subjectivity and Media Power', Paper presented at the 'Our Media Not Theirs' ICA Preconference in Washington, DC: (24 May). [Online] Available at: http://www.ourmedianet .org/eng/om2001/Tony%20Dowmunt.pdf (2 September 2003).

Downing, J. (1984) *Radical Media: The Political Experience of Alternative Communication*, Boston: South End Press.

(1991) 'Community Access Television: Past, Present and Future', *Community Television Review*, 14(3): 6–8.

Drobis, D. (1992) 'The Increasing Use of VNRs Reflects a Growing Interdependency Between Television News and Public Relations', *Broadcasting*, (24 August): 17.

Eason, K. (1988) *Information Technology and Organizational Change*, London: Taylor and Francis.

Engelman, R. (1990) 'The Origins of Public Access Cable Television, 1966–1972', *Journalism Monographs*, (123) Columbia, SC: Association of Educators of Journalism and Mass Communication.

(1996) *Public Radio and Television in America: A Political History*, Thousand Oaks, CA: Sage.

Entman, R. (1993), 'Framing: Towards Clarification of a Fractured Paradigm,' *Journal of Communication*, 43(4): 51–58.

Ewen, S. (1976) *Captains of Consciousness: Advertising and the Social Roots of Consumer Culture*, New York: McGraw Hill.

Fairchild, C. (1998). 'The Canadian Alternative: A Brief History of Unlicensed and Low Power Radio,' in R. Sakolsky and S. Dunifer (eds.) *Seizing the Airwaves: A Free Radio Handbook*, San Francisco: AK Press, pp. 47–57.

Fay, J. (1997). 'Community Advocates Mobilize: Will Use Freedom of Information Act to Get Long Promised Welfare Reform Plan', *Street Feat*, 1(1) (December), p. 8.

Faye, L. (1986) 'A Controversial Reporter', *Suburban People*, (15 June), p. 4.

Fiske, J. (1989) *Understanding Popular Culture*, London: Unwin Hyman.

Forest, Trees and People (1999/2000) *FTP Newsletter*, [Special Issue on Participatory Communication], (40/41) [Online] Available at: http://www-trees.slu.se/newsl/40/40front.htm

Fraser, N. (1992) 'Rethinking the Public Sphere: A Contribution to the Critique of Actually Existing Democracy', in C. J. Calhoun (ed.) *Habermas and the Public Sphere*, Cambridge, MA: MIT Press, pp. 109–142.

Friedman, T. (1999) *The Lexus and the Olive Tree: Understanding Globalization*, New York: Farrar, Strauss and Giroux.

Fukuyama, F. (1992) *The End of History and the Last Man*, Middlesex: Penguin.

Gall, C. (1996) 'Free Speech and WFHB', *Bloomington Voice*, (11 January), p. 6.

Ganzert, C. F. (1994) 'Pirates, Outlaws, and Rebels: An Examination of Illegal Radio Broadcast Practices', Paper presented to the Radio Studies meeting of Popular Culture Association, Chicago, IL, 6–9 April.

Garafola, N. (2000) 'The Word from the Curb: Street Papers Give Voice to People Locked Out of the Major Media', *Utne Reader*, [Online] Available at; http://www.utne.com/pub/2000_101/view/1408-1.html (22 December 2003).

Garnham, N. (1993) 'The Media and the Public Sphere', in C. Calhoun (ed.) *Habermas and the Public Sphere*. Cambridge: MIT Press, pp. 359–376.

Garofalo, R. (1993) 'Whose World, What Beat: The Transnational Music Industry, Identity and Cultural Imperialism', *The World of Music*, 35(2): 16–32.

Giddens, A. (1991) *Modernity and Self-identity: Self and Society in the Late Modern Age*, Cambridge: Polity Press.

Gillespie, G. (1975) *Public Access Television in the United States and Canada*, New York: Praeger.

Gillespie, M. (1989) 'Technology and Tradition: Audio-Visual Culture among South Asian Families in West London', *Cultural Studies* 3(2): 226–239.

Gitlin, T. (1994) 'Primetime Ideology: The Hegemonic Process in Television Entertainment', in H. Newcomb (ed.) *Television: The Critical View*, 5th edn., New York: Oxford University Press, pp. 516–536.

Godfrey, J. (1974) 'Getting Technical: Living Color', *Vision News* (December), pp. 3–5.

Goldberg, K. (1990) *The Barefoot Channel: Community Television as a Tool for Social Change*, Vancouver: New Star Books.

(2001) 'Reclaiming the Airwaves', *Canadian Dimension*, 33(5): 9.

Golding, P. (1977) 'Media Professionalism in the Third World: The Transfer of an Ideology', in J. Curran, M. Gurevitch, and J. Woollacott (eds.) *Mass Communication and Society*, London: Edward Arnold, pp. 291–308.

Golding, P. and Harris, R. (1997) *Beyond Cultural Imperialism: Globalization, Communication and the New International Order*, London: Sage.

Goodin, R. (2001) 'New Housing Another Step Closer', *Street Feat*, 4(2) (March/April 2001), p. 3.

Graham, S. (1996) 'Re: New Talk Shows', [Online] E-mail: spot_online (13 April).

Green, N. F. (1998) 'Chicago StreetWise at the Crossroads: A Case Study of a Newspaper to Empower the Homeless in the 1990s', J. Danky and W. Wigand (eds.) *Print Culture in a Diverse America*, Urbana, IL: University of Illinois Press, pp. 34–55.

Griff, H. (1988) *Academic Memories: Retired Faculty Members Recall the Past at Indiana University*, Bloomington, IN: Indiana University.

Habermas, J. (1993) *The Structural Transformation of the Bourgeois Public Sphere*, trans. T. Burger and F. Lawrence, Cambridge: MIT Press.

Hackett, R. (2000) 'Taking Back the Media: Notes on the Potential for a Communicative Democracy Movement', *Studies in Political Economy*, 63: 61–86.

Hagen, U. (1992) 'Democratic Communication: Media and Social Participation', in J. Wasko and V. Mosco (eds.) *Democratic Communication in the Information Age*, Norwood, NJ: Ablex, pp. 16–27.

Haider, D. (1992) 'Place Wars: New Realities of the 1990s', *Economic Development Quarterly*, 6(2): 127–134.

Hall, S. *et al.* (1978) *Policing the Crisis: Mugging, the State, and Law and Order*, London: MacMillan.

Hall, S. (1986) 'On Postmodernism and Articulation: An Interview with Stuart Hall', *Journal of Communication Inquiry*, 10(2): 45–60.

Hamelink, C. J. (1983) *Cultural Autonomy in Global Communication*, New York: Longman.

   (1994) *Trends in World Communication: On Disempowerment and Self-Empowerment*, Penang: Southbound/Third World Network.

   (1997) 'MacBride with Hindsight', in P. Golding and R. Harris (eds.) *Beyond Cultural Imperialism: Globalization, Communication and the New International Order*, London: Sage, pp. 69–93.

Hansell, J. (2000) 'France's Telebocal: The Debate Over Community Media Models Goes On', *Community Media Review*, (Summer): 12.

Hansen, L. (2000) 'Conversations in the Public Space: Preserving and Promoting a Culture of Democratic Communication', *Community Media Review*, (Summer): 13.

Hardt, H. (1975) 'Communication as Theory and Method of Community,' *Communication*, 2(1): 81–92.

Harmon, M. (1991) 'Hate Groups and Cable Public Access', *Journal of Mass Media Ethics*, 6(3): 146–155.

Harpell, L. (1999) 'What *Street Feat* Means to Me', *Street Feat* 2(12), (December), p. 5.

Harris, T. (1999) 'An Idea Gone Global: Streetpaper Movement Builds Internationally', *Real Change News*, [Online] Available at: www.realchangenews. org/pastarticles/ features/articles/fea_janinsp.html (27 April 2001).

Hazen, D. (1999) 'Independent media makes its mark at Seattle's WTO Confrontation', *AlterNet*, [Online], Available at: http://www.alternet.org/story. html?StoryID=741 (13 January 2000).

Hemphill, C. (1990) 'Probes Put Street News in Spotlight', *Newsday*, (16 March), p. 5.

Herz, J. C. (1997) *Joystick Nation*, Boston: Little, Brown.

Higgins, J. (1991) 'Night of the Broadcast Clones: The Politics of Video Training', *Community Television Review*, 14(3): 9–12.

Hill, L. (1958) *Voluntary Listener-Sponsorship*, Berkeley, CA: Pacifica Foundation.

   (1966) 'The Theory of Listener-Sponsored Radio,' in E. McKinney (ed.) *The Exacting Ear: The Story of Listener-Sponsored Radio, and an Anthology of Programs from KPFA, KPFK, and WBAI*, New York: Pantheon.

Hoberman, J. (1981) 'Jon Alpert's Video Journalism: Talking to the People', *American Film* (June), pp. 54–59.

Hochheimer, J. (1993) 'Organizing Democratic Radio: Issues in Praxis', *Media, Culture and Society*, 15(3): 473–486.

Howard, D. (1999) 'A Voice From the "Pit" of Despair', *Street Feat* 2(2) (February/March) p. 3.

Hoynes, W. (1994) *Public Television for Sale: Media, the Market, and the Public Sphere*, Boulder, CO: Westview Press.

Hoyt, Michael (1991) 'Jon Alpert: NBC's Odd Man Out', *Columbia Journalism Review*, (September/October), p. 44–47.

Hunt, N. (n.d.) 'Fragmentation in the Global Corporate Take-Over', *Videazimut Clips* (6) [Online] Available at: http://www.videazimut.org/e/clips/6-2.html (12 Feb. 2001).

Ibrahim, Z. (2000) 'Tarzan Doesn't Live Here Anymore,' *International Journal of Cultural Studies*, 3(2): 199–205.

Jackson, L. (1999) 'A Commitment to Social Values and Racial Justice', *Wide Angle* 21(2): 31–40.

Jackson, R. J. and Jackson, D. (1990) *Politics in Canada: Culture, Institutions, Behavior and Public Policy*, Scarborough: Prentice-Hall.

Jacobs, S. (1990) 'News Is Uplifting for Homeless in NY', *Boston Globe*, (7 May), p. 1.

Jallov, B. (1992). 'Women on the Air-Community Radio as a Tool for Feminist Messages,' in N. Jankowski, O. Prehn. and J. Stappers (eds.) *The People's Voice: Local Radio and TV in Europe*, London: John Libbey, pp. 215–224.

James, S. (1990a) 'Educational Media and "Agit Prop": I. The Legacy of Vertov', *Journal of Educational Media*, 22(2): 111–123.

    (1990b) 'Educational Media and "Agit Prop": II. The Vertov Process Repatriated,' *Journal of Educational Media*, 22(3): 161–173.

Jankowski, N. W. (2003) 'Community Media Research: A Quest for Theoretically-Grounded Models', *Javnost: The Public* 10(1): 5–14.

Jenkins, H. (1992) *Textual Poachers: Television Fans and Participatory Culture*, New York: Routledge.

Kearney, B. (1996) *The Flaw in Community Radio: Captive Agent of the Left*, Masters Thesis, School of Business Administration, Indiana University.

Kellner, D. (1991) *Public Access Television: Alternative Views*, http://www.gseis.ucla.edu/courses/ed253a/MCkellner/ACCESS.html (23 October 2001).

    (1997) 'Overcoming the Divide: Cultural Studies and Political Economy', in M. Ferguson and P. Golding (eds.) *Cultural Studies in Question*, London: Sage, pp. 102–120.

Kellog, M. (1983) 'Video Verite', *The Quill*, (December), pp. 29–33.

Kelly, K. (1977) 'Hospitals Are Dying', *New York Post*, (22 November 1977), p. 48.

Kelly, A. and Gibson, J. (2000) 'Become the Media', *Arena Magazine*, [Online] Available at: http://www.nettime.org/Lists-Archives/nettime-l-0010/msg00304.html (3 March 2001).

Kennedy, J. F. (1961) *Address to Congress*, (25 May 1961).

Kennedy, M. (2003) 'Radio Ujjas', *The Nation*, [Online] Available at: http://www.thenation.com/doc.mhtml%3Fi=20030224&s=kennedy (15 July 2003).

Kidd, D. (1999) 'The Value of Alternative Media', *Peace Review*, 11(1): 113–119.

King, R. and Wood, N. (2001) *Media and Migration: Constructions of Mobility and Difference*, London: Routledge.

Klee, K. (1999) 'The Siege of Seattle', *Newsweek*, (13 December), p. 30.

Kogawa, T. (1993) 'Toward Polymorphous Radio', http://anarchy.k2.tku.ac.jp/radio/micro/radiorethink.html (15 July 2003).

Krampe, B. (1999) 'A Day in the Life', *Street Feat*, 2(9) (October) p. 9.

Kuklinski, J. *et al.* (2000) 'Misinformation and the Currency of Democratic Citizenship', *Journal of Politics*, 62(3): 790–816.

Labaton, S. (2000) 'Deregulation Called Blow to Minorities', *New York Times*, (12 December), p. C1.

Land, J. (1999) *Active Radio: Pacifica's Brash Experiment*, Minneapolis: University of Minnesota Press.

Lasar, M. (2000) *Pacifica Radio: The Rise of an Alternative Network*, Philadelphia: Temple University Press.

Ledbetter, J. (1997) *Made Possible By: The Death of Public Broadcasting*, New York: Verso.

Lee, M. and Heup Cho, C. (1995) 'Women Watching Together: An Ethnographic Study of Korean Soap Opera Fans in the United States', in G. Dines and J. Humez (eds.) *Gender, Race and Class in Media*, Thousand Oaks, CA: Sage, pp. 482–487.

LeFort, S. (1999) 'Right or Privilege', *Street Feat* 2(4) (April/May) p. 6.

—— (1999) 'Letter to the Editor', *Street Feat* 2(1) (January/February), p. 2.

Lewis, C. (2000) 'Media Money', *Columbia Journalism Review*, 39(3): 20–27.

Lewis, E. (1998) 'Christmas: Material and Other Excesses', *Street Feat* 1(12) (December), p. 6.

—— (1999) 'Helpless in Halifax', *Street Feat*, 2(4) (April/May), p. 3.

Lewis, P. (1984). 'Community Radio: The Montreal Conference and After', *Media, Culture and Society* 6: 135–150.

Lewis, P. and Booth, P. (1990) *The Invisible Medium: Public, Commercial and Community Radio*, Washington, DC: Howard University Press.

Lloyd, C. (1998) 'Extra! Extra! Homeless Papers Duel for Street Supremacy', *Salon Media Circus*. [Online] Available at: http://www.salon.com/media/1998/04/13media.html (3 June 2000).

Lull, J. (1991) *China Turned On: Television, Reform, and Resistance*, London: Routledge.

Maffi, M. (1995) *Gateway to the Promised Land: Ethnic Cultures in New York City's Lower East Side*, New York: New York University Press.

Martin-Barbero, J. (1993) *Communication, Culture and Hegemony: From Media to Mediations*, London: Sage.

Massey, D. (1993) 'Power Geometry and a Progressive Sense of Place', in J. Bird, B. Curtis, T. Putnam, G. Robertson, and L. Tickner (eds.) *Mapping the Futures: Local Cultures, Global Change*, London: Routledge, pp. 59–69.

Mattelart, A. (1979) *Multinational Corporations and the Control of Culture*, Brighton: Harvester Press.

—— (1980) *Mass Media, Ideologies and the Revolutionary Moment*, Brighton: Harvester Press.

McAuley, C. (1990) 'Liza Minnelli Sells Well, Particularly in Subway Trains', *Wall Street Journal*, (27 Feb.), p. A1.

McChesney, R. (1997) *Corporate Media and the Threat to Democracy*, New York: Seven Stories Press.

—— (1999) *Rich Media, Poor Democracy: Communication Politics in Dubious Times*, Champaign, IL: University of Illinois Press.

—— (2000) 'The New Global Media', *The Nation*, (29 November): 11–15.

McChesney, R. W., Wood, E. M., and Foster, J. B. (eds.) (1998) *Capitalism and the Information Age: The Political Economy of the Global Communication Revolution*, New York: Monthly Review Press.

McDowell, S. (1997) Globalization and Policy Choice: Television and Audiovisual Services Policies in India', *Media, Culture and Society*, 19(2): 151–171.

McGregor, K. (2000) 'Magabe Spin Doctor Quizzed over Leave', *Times Higher Education Supplement*, (7 July): 11.

McGuigan, P. (1999) 'Let the Marginalized Speak', *Street Feat*, 2(6) (June/July), p. 3.

   (1999) 'The Old Hope Cottage: A Snapshot', *Street Feat*, 2(9) (October), p. 4.

   (2000) 'Portrait of a Socially Unfit Person', *Street Feat* 3(7) (September), p. 5.

   (2001) 'Why Is It So Hard to Get the Poor to Work?', *Street Feat*, 4(1) (January/February) p. 3.

McLuhan, M. (1964) *Understanding Media: The Extensions of Man*, London: Routledge.

Menendez, R. (1998) 'Street Feat Newspaper: A Sign of Hope for the Poor', *Street Feat* 1(12) (December), p. 3.

Messman, P. (1999) 'Dissenting Voices of the Street', *Media Alliance*, [Online] Available at: http://www.media-alliance.org/voices/index.html (3 June 2000).

Milam, L. (1988) *The Original Sex in Broadcasting: A Handbook on Starting a Radio Station for the Community*, San Diego: MHO & MHO Works.

Miller, J. (1992) 'From Radio Libres to Radio Privées: The Rapid Triumph of Commercial Networks in French Local Radio', *Media, Culture and Society* 14: 261–279.

Mills, K. (1995) 'Wells Donates to WFHB Improvements', *Herald-Times*, (17 December), p. C1.

Mitchell, C. (1998) 'Women's (Community) Radio as a Feminist Public Sphere', *The Public* 5(2): 73–85.

Molnar, H. and M. Meadows (eds.) (2002) *Songlines to Satellites, Indigenous Communication in Australia, the South Pacific and Canada*, Annandale: Pluto Press.

Morino, M. (1994) 'Assessment and Evolution of Community Networking', in S. Cisler (ed.) *Ties That Bind Conference: Collected Papers*, Cupertino: Apple Computer.

Morley, D. (1980) *The 'Nationwide' Audience: Structure and Decoding*, London: BFI.

   (1991) 'Where the Global Meets the Local: Notes From the Sitting Room', *Screen*, 32(1): 1–15.

   (2000) *Home Territories: Media, Mobility and Identity*, London: Routledge.

Morrison, B. (1982) 'Jon Alpert: The Renegade Reporter of NBC's Today Show', *Times Picayune* (27 Feb.), p. 2.

Moss, C. (2000) 'Radical Export', *New Internationalist*, (December), pp. 6–7.

Murdock, G. and Golding, P. (1989) 'Information Poverty and Political Inequality: Citizenship in the Age of Privatised Communications', in M. Siefert, G. Gerbner, and J. Fisher (eds.) *The Information Gap: How Computers and Other New Communication Technologies Affect The Social Distribution of Power*, New York: Oxford University Press, pp. 180–195.

NASNA (2000) *NASNA History*, http://www.openskypress.org/nasna_information.htm (3 Nov. 2000).

—— (2001) 'A *National* Disgrace', *The Coast* (9 August 2001), p. 7.

Negus, K. (1992) *Producing Pop*, London: Edward Arnold.

Newcomb, H. and Hirsch, P. (1994) 'Television as Cultural Forum', in H. Newcomb (ed.) *Television: The Critical View*, 5th edn., New York: Oxford University Press, pp. 503–515.

Noronha, F. (1999) 'Shouting with a Gagged Mouth: India's Reluctant March Towards Democratizing Its Airwaves', http://www.radiorobinhood.fi/communityradios/articles.htm (15 July 2003).

O'Connor, A. (1990) 'The Miners' Radio in Bolivia: A Culture of Resistance', *Journal of Communication*, 40(1): 102–110.

O'Connor, J. (1980) 'A Noble Failure, Looser Language and Local "Stars",' *New York Times*, p. 42.

O'Hara, P. (1998) 'Dear Friends of Low-income Nova Scotians,' *Street Feat*, 1(8) (July/August), p. 3.

Ong, L. (1992) 'Let's Get Together Now', *The Strait Times*, (14 July), pp. L2 1.

Pacifica Foundation (1946) 'Articles of Incorporation'.

Pager, G. (1949) 'The Hobo News', *New York Folklore Quarterly*, 5(3): 228–230.

Park, H. J. (2000) 'Tomsk, Russia: An Interview with Tomsk TV2's Leonid Prokof'ev', *Community Media Review*, (Summer): 20–21.

Parrella, A. (1994) 'Community Networking in Italy.' On-line. E-mail: berny@well.sf.ca.us (4 June 1994).

Paton, D. (1999) 'War of the Words: Virtual Media Versus Mainstream Press', *Christian Science Monitor*, (3 December), p. 3.

Perlman, P. (1975) 'Video Revue', *Millimeter*, (March), pp. 41–43.

Petras, J. (1993) 'Cultural Imperialism in the Late 20th Century', *Journal of Contemporary Asia*, 23(2): 139–148.

Pigg, K. (1999) 'Community Networks and Community Development', Presentation prepared for the Conference of the International Association for Community Development, Edinburgh, Scotland (April). [Online] Available at: http://www.ssu.missouri.edu/faculty/kpigg/IACD99.html (26 August 2003).

Pool, I. (1983) *Technologies of Freedom*, Cambridge: Harvard University Press.

Prince, S. (1968) *Catastrophe and Social Change. Based upon a Sociological Study of the Halifax Disaster (Columbia University Studies in the Social Sciences, No. 212)*, New York: AMS Press.

Protz, M. (1991) 'Distinguishing Between "Alternative" and "Participatory" Models of Video Production', in N. Thede and A. Ambrosi (eds.) *Video the Changing World*, Montreal: Black Rose, pp. 31–39.

Raddall, T. (1971) *Halifax: Warden of the North*, 2nd edn. Toronto: McClelland and Stewart.

Radio St. Paula (n.d.) 'Who's radio st. paula?' http://www.ratcreature.f2s.com/paula/english/eng-sebst.html (27 April 2001).

Rheingold, H. (1993) *The Virtual Community: Homesteading on the Electronic Frontier*, Reading: Addison Wesley.

Rieder, R. (1996) 'Why the Trill Makes a Difference', *American Journalism Review*, 18(1): 6.

Roach, C. (1997) 'The Western World and NWICO: United They Stand?',
in P. Golding and R. Harris (eds.) *Beyond Cultural Imperialism: Globalization, Communication and the New International Order*, London: Sage, pp. 94–
116.

Robbins, K. (1995) 'The New Spaces of Global Media', in R. Johnston, P. Taylor,
and M. Watts (eds.) *Geographies of Global Change: Remapping the World in the
late Twentieth Century*, Oxford: Blackwell.

Roberts, A. (2000) 'Less Government, More Secrecy: Reinvention and the Weak-
ening of Freedom of Information Law,' *Public Administration Review*, 60(4):
298–310.

Rodriguez, C. (2001) *Fissures in the Mediascape: International Case Studies of Citizens' Media*, Creeskill, NJ: Hampton Press.

Roncagliolo, R. (1999). 'Latin America's Endangered Frequencies,' *UNESCO
Courier*, [Online] Available at: http://www.unesco.org/courier/1999_04/uk/
connex/txt1.htm (15 July 2003).

Rosen, J. (1994) 'Making Things More Public: On the Political Responsibility
of the Media Intellectual', *Critical Studies in Mass Communication*, 11(4):
363–388.

Rowse, A. (1991) 'Flaking for the Emir', *The Progressive*, 55(5): 20–22.

Russian Communities Online (n.d.) *CN in Russia – Through NGOs Networks to Community Networks*, Available at: http://www.communities.org.ru/
indexen.html

Sakolsky, R. and Dunifer, S. (eds.) (1998) *Seizing the Airwaves: A Free Radio
Handbook*, San Francisco: AK Press.

Sakr, N. (2002) *Satellite Realms: Transnational Television, Globalization and the
Middle East*, London: I. B. Tauris.

Salter, L. (1981) 'Community Radio in Canada', Canadian Broadcasting Corporation, Office of Community Radio.

Sanders, S. (1985) *Stone Country*, Bloomington, IN: Indiana University Press.

Savage, V. (1988) *A Brief History of Monroe County, Indiana*, Bloomington, IN:
Monroe County Historical Society Museum.

Scannell, P. (1996) *Radio, Television and Modern Life*, Oxford: Blackwell.

Schiller, H. (1976) *Communication and Cultural Domination*, New York: International Arts and Sciences Press.

(1996) *Information Inequality: The Deepening Social Crisis in America*, New York:
Routledge.

Schneider, K. (1996) 'Community Networks: New Frontiers, Old Values,'
American Libraries, (January 1996), p. 96.

Schudson, M. (1986) *Advertising, The Uneasy Persuasion: Its Dubious Impact on
American Society*, New York: Basic Books.

(2003) *The Sociology of News*, New York: W. W. Norton, pp. 117–133.

Schuler, D. (1994) 'Community Networks: Building a New Participatory
Medium', *Communications of the ACM*, 37(1): 39–51.

(1995) 'Creating Public Space in Cyberspace: The Rise of the New Community Networks', *Internet World*, [Online] Available at: http;//www.scn.org/
ip/commnet/iwdec.html (28 July 1996).

(1999) 'Second Birthday Issue', *Street Feat*, 2(12) (December/January).

Semetko, H. and Valkenburg, P. (2000) 'Framing European Politics: A Content Analysis of Press and Television News', *Journal of Communication*, 50(2): 93–109.

Senevirante, K. (2003) 'Media-Indonesia: Revolution Underway in People's Radio', *Inter Press Service News Agency*, [Online] Available at: www.internews. org/openmedia/open_media.htm (15 July 2003).

Shales, T. (1980) 'Six Stories from the Naked City', *Washington Post*, (11 April), p. C1.

Silverstone, R. (1999) *Why Study the Media?*, Thousand Oaks, CA: Sage.

Slack, J. D. (1996) 'The Theory and Method of Articulation in Cultural Studies', in D. Morley and K. H. Chen (eds.) *Stuart Hall: Critical Dialogues in Cultural Studies*, New York: Routledge, pp. 112–127.

Smedberg, P. 'WFHB Defended', *Herald-Times*, (16 February), p. X.

Smith, A. D. (1991) *National Identity*, Reno: University of Nevada Press.

Smith, M. (2001) 'Halifax: Recipe for a Lively Downtown', *National Post*, (31 July). [Online] Available at: http://www.reachcanada.com/about/ NewsItemsDetail.asp?PressReleaseID=1206 (18 September 2001).

Smits, N. and Marroquin, R. (2000) 'Technological Experiments on Amsterdam Local Television', http://www.desk.nl/~hksteen/wired.html (6 February 2001).

Solomon, W. (2000) 'More Form than Substance: Press Coverage of the WTO Protests in Seattle', *Monthly Review* (May), pp. 12–20.

Splichal, S. (1994) *Media Beyond Socialism: Theory and Practice in East-Central Europe*, Boulder, CO: Westview Press.

Sreberny-Mohammadi, A. (1997) 'The Many Faces of Cultural Imperialism', in P. Golding and R. Harris (eds.) *Beyond Cultural Imperialism: Globalization, Communication and the New International Order*, London: Sage, pp. 49–68.

St. Clair, S. (1999) 'Suzzette's Story', *Street Feat*, 2(6) (June/July), pp. 2, 6.

——— (2000a) 'Where Did I Go Wrong? Or Did I?', *Street Feat* 3(1) (February), p. 2.

——— (2000b) 'The Pain and Compassion of Homelessness', *Street Feat* 3(3) (April) p. 3.

St. Lawrence, J. (1987) 'Making Documentaries', *Videography*, (November), pp. 76–77.

Stauber, J. and Rampton, S. (1995) *Toxic Sludge Is Good for You: Lies, Damn Lies and the Public Relations Industry*, Monroe: Common Courage Press.

Stebbins, G. (1969) *Listener-Sponsored Radio: The Pacifica Stations*, PhD. dissertation, Ohio State University.

Stiles, S. (1999) 'Help the Poor Help Themselves', *Street Feat* 2(7) (August), p. 6.

Stoney, G. (1971) 'The Mirror Machine', *Sight & Sound*, 41(1): 9–11.

——— (2001) 'The Essential George Stoney', *Community Media Review*, (Summer): 29–31.

Strum, C. (1994) 'On Rikers Island, Armed with Only a Camera', *New York Times*, (5 June), p. 32.

Sussman, W. (1997) 'Culture and Communication', in *Culture as History: The Transformation of American Society in the Twentieth Century*, New York: Pantheon, pp. 252–270.

Swanson, J. (2001) *Poor-bashing: The Politics of Exclusion*, Toronto: Between the Lines.

Swinemar, D. (1999a) 'Donors, Assert Your Rights', *Street Feat*, 2(9) (October), p. 3.

(1999b) 'Safety Net Wearing Out', *Street Feat* 2(10) (October/November), p. 2.

(2000) 'Time Will Tell! What Do You Think?, *Street Feat*, 3(2) (March), p. 2.

Tacchi, J. and Davies, E. P. (2001) *Community Radio in a Global Context: A Comparative Analysis in Six Countries*, CMA, [Online], Available at: www.commedia.org.uk/reports.htm (15 July 2003).

Tarleton, J. (2000) 'Protesters Develop Their Own Global Internet News Service', *Nieman Reports*, (Winter), p. 53.

Teltsch, K. (1990) 'Editor of Street News Steps Down', *New York Times*, (10 June), p. 36.

Thrasher, S. (1996) 'WFHB Not Corporate', *Bloomington Voice*, (15 February), p. 4.

Tomlinson, J. (1997) 'Cultural Globalization and Cultural Imperialism', in A. Mohammadi (ed.) *International Communication and Globalization*, London: Sage, pp. 170–190.

Tracey, M. (1998) *The Decline and Fall of Public Broadcasting*, New York: Oxford University Press.

Traquina, N. (1998) 'Western European Broadcasting, Deregulation, and Public Television: The Portuguese Experience', *Journalism and Mass Communication Monographs*, (167) Columbia, SC: Association of Educators of Journalism and Mass Communication.

Travis, G. (2003) 'CIVITAS: Galloping Greenways,' *Bloomington Free Press* (31 July–14 August), pp. 6–7.

Tunstall, J. (1977) *The Media Are American: Anglo-American Media in the World*, London: Constable.

Tyler, P. (2003) 'New Element in Iraq's Mix', *New York Times*, (1 March 2003), p. A1.

Tyson, J. L. (1999) 'Self-Sufficiency Is Measure of Chicago Newspaper's Success', *Christian Science Monitor*, (11 April), p. 3.

UNESCO (1980) *Many Voices, One World*, Paris, International Commission for the Study of Communication Problems: UNESCO.

(1982) *Culture Industries: A Challenge for the Future of Culture*, Paris: UNESCO.

(2003) 'UNESCO Supports Creation of Free Community Telecentre in Brazil', ListServe Digital Divide (4 December 2003).

United Kingdom (2000) *Communication White Paper*.

United Nations (1948) *Universal Declaration of Human Rights*, San Francisco.

Van Lier, P. (1999) 'Selling the Street Beat', *The Quill* (November), p. 16.

WAAC (1994) 'Radio Station for Indigenous People in Bolivia', *Action*, (March), p. 3.

Waugh, T. (1984) *Show Us Life: Toward a History and Aesthetics of the Committed Documentary*, Metuchen, NJ: Scarecrow Press.

Werts, D. (1994) 'Jailhouse Confidential', *New York Newsday*, (5 June), p. 16.

Weston, J. (1997) 'Old Freedoms and New Technologies: The Evolution of Community Networking', *The Information Society*, 13: 195–201.

Williams, R. (1973) 'Knowable Communities', in *The City and the Country*, New York: Oxford University Press, pp. 165–181.

(1983) *Culture and Society: 1780–1950*, New York: Oxford University Press.

(1992) *Television: Technology and Cultural Form*, Hanover: Wesleyan University Press.

Williams, R. H. (1992) *Dream Worlds: Mass Consumption in Late Nineteenth-Century France*, Berkeley, CA: California University Press.

Williamson, A. H. (1991) 'The Fogo Process: Development Support Communications in Canada and the Developing World', in F. Casmir (ed.) *Communication in Development*, Norwood, NJ: Ablex Publishing.

Willis, P. (1990) *Common Culture: Symbolic Work at Play in the Everyday Cultures of the Young*, Boulder, CO: Westview Press.

WORT (2000) 'Community Radio Journalists Denied Access', (11 April), [Online], e-mail normstoc@olywa.net.

Zaffiro, J. (1993) 'Mass Media, Politics and Society in Botswana: The 1990s and Beyond', *Africa Today*, 40(1): 7–25.

Zhang, J. and Cameron, G. (2003) 'China's Agenda Building and Image Polishing in the US: Assessing an International Public Relations Campaign', *Public Relations Review*, 29(1): 13–28.

Zoglin, R. (1993) 'All You Need Is Hate', *Time* (21 June), pp. 63–66.

(1980) 'Conversation with Jon Alpert and Keiko Tsuno', *Videography* (September), pp. 54–69.

Index